INTERNATIONAL ECONOMIC LAW SERIES

General Editor: JOHN H. JACKSON

International Trade in Services and Domestic Regulations

Necessity, Transparency, and Regulatory Diversity

International Trade in Services and Domestic Regulations

Necessity, Transparency, and Regulatory Diversity

PANAGIOTIS DELIMATSIS

OXFORD
UNIVERSITY PRESS

OXFORD
UNIVERSITY PRESS

Great Clarendon Street, Oxford, OX2 6DP,
United Kingdom

Oxford University Press is a department of the University of Oxford.
It furthers the University's objective of excellence in research, scholarship,
and education by publishing worldwide. Oxford is a registered trade mark of
Oxford University Press in the UK and in certain other countries

First published 2007

Published in the United States of America by Oxford University Press
198 Madison Avenue, New York, NY 10016, United States of America

British Library Cataloguing in Publication Data
Data available

Library of Congress Cataloging in Publication Data
Data available

ISBN 978–0–19–953315–2

To Despina, Melina, and Lydia
—the best companions I could ever
imagine for this amazing journey

και στον Αργύρη και την Ελευθερία
—για τόσο πολλούς λόγους...

Foreword

This is a very welcome addition to the legal literature dedicated to the study of GATS. Delimatsis provides the first comprehensive account of Article VI GATS, the provision dealing with domestic regulation. Services markets are segmented largely through domestic instruments, trade instruments being often inappropriate for such use. Trade-liberalization is thus, largely a question of managing the divergent regulatory interface across national sovereignties: this book discusses both the current parameters, as well as the direction that future discussions on this score should, in the author's view, take.

The task of the author should not be under-estimated: trade economists have only recently started paying attention to trade in services, and, consequently, there is little theory on which he could rely. The law is a largely incomplete contract (GATS) which, contrary to what is the GATT-case, has to a very little, if not totally uninteresting manner, been completed through case-law. The secondary law, to which the author extensively refers in the latter part of his work, is sector-specific, and, more importantly, of uncertain legal value, WTO adjudicating bodies having provided only scattered and transaction-specific clarifications in this respect so far. Borrowing from the GATT-literature is not highly recommendable either, since, for a number of reasons that the author mentions, 'lock, stock, and barrel' solutions can do more harm than good. GATT case-law, for example, has not, as yet, provided meaningful interpretations of basic concepts such as *likeness*, for products with an important regulatory component: this is very much the case for services-products; the current interpretations concern cases where the goods concerned have little, or no, regulatory component, that is, cases uninteresting for many of the services-products. The author has had to create his own framework within which the disciplines on domestic regulation should be discussed and evaluated, and this is what he presents us with.

Previous literature has made the point that even the maximum promise (national treatment) does not necessarily mean much, since distinctions can always be drawn across two suppliers. National treatment is, of course, the maximum promise (in case no mutual recognition arrangement has been concluded, a rather infrequently used instrument), so, from a trade-liberalization perspective, the situation could be substantially worse. It comes thus as no surprise to read in many accounts that the GATS has provided a framework for trade-liberalization, but has not generated trade-liberalization itself. The author is motivated by this latter part, that is, how can we turn the GATS into a liberalization-generating instrument? This is what brought him to the study of Article VI GATS.

This provision functions as break on the private industry-driven administration of domestic legislation. Although, the experience so far—that the author masterfully explains—does not lend much to optimism, there are good reasons to believe that a different use of this instrument can change the current picture. To achieve this result, the author suggests that we need to re-visit some key concepts (such as necessity, which, loosely speaking, requires WTO Members to enact legislation no more stringent that what is required to achieve its unilaterally defined preferences). Necessity does not question regulatory diversity; it tames, nonetheless, its excesses. The multilateral surveillance of this *regulatory* principle will prove the make-or-break of the approach: courts will need to develop case-law in linear manner, for case-law to acquire legitimacy and complete the law.

It would be harsh, if not totally unfair, to equate the line taken in this work with a plea for judicial activism. The author makes a good case in favour of his approach, reminding us, whenever appropriate, that it would be unrealistic to expect a more promising (from a trade-liberalization perspective) outcome through renewed negotiations. It is, rather, management of the negotiated portfolio in between rounds that holds more of a promise, and management of Article VI GATS will be an important part in this equation.

The author honoured the task he assigned to himself. This book is, in my view, a great addition to the existing literature, a necessary companion to students and practitioners of the WTO alike. It is highly recommendable not only to those interested in trade in services, but to all those interested in trade in general, since the author's analysis is food for thought for the increasingly mainstream case where trade-liberalization occurs across regulated sectors. On a personal level, through his first book, the author has set for himself very high standards that he will have to emulate in his future scholarship.

Petros C. Mavroidis

Edwin B. Parker professor of law at Columbia Law School, New York,
Professor of Law at the University of Neuchâtel, & Research Fellow at CEPR

General Editor's Preface

It is recognized that services (compared to goods production and other parts of economies) have been steadily increasing in importance, as represented partly by the percentage of major developed country economies which are devoted to services. This percentage now exceeds other portions of those economies, for example reaching 80 per cent for the United States, 68 per cent for Japan, 70 per cent for Germany. Services are also a comparably growing part of world commerce, so trade in services can be an exceedingly important portion of trade liberalization which could in some circumstances assist in large increases in citizen welfare and reductions in poverty.

For these and other reasons, therefore, it was probably inevitable in the 1980s that interest turned to the GATT (General Agreement on Tariffs and Trade) for an institutional model that might yield for service economies the benefits achieved by goods trade liberalization. In the last GATT trade round, the Uruguay Round of 1986–1994, the negotiators opened a new chapter in the world trading system, by adding services to the portfolio of major subjects to be supervised by the UR newly created WTO (World Trade Organization). This new chapter is embodied in a text part of the UR result, titled the GATS (General Agreement on Trade in Services), and some consider this text of rules and negotiating procedures to be potentially the most exciting part of the new WTO.

Yet for reasons which the author of this very welcome book addition to the Oxford University Press series regarding 'International Economic Law', authoritatively explains, the services agreement text has not yet developed into the force for benefiting the world that should be its promise.

The author's Introduction, along with an important foreword by the author's thesis supervisor, significantly establish the framework for the reader's appreciation of this remarkable book, about a very complex and puzzling subject. The author states his motivation—to explore ways that can lead finally to the GATS becoming a liberalization-generating instrument. Clearly this is no easy task, but the author succeeds admirably in setting forth the history and current status of the GATS, while suggesting the importance of the 'regulatory' features of the GATS (especially in Article VI), and noting the major importance of regulatory goals for transparency, and a 'necessity' test.

So far, after more than 11 years of the WTO (and therefore GATS) existence, there remain huge ambiguities in the GATS text. Thus there are important needs for further elaboration, through dispute case interpretations or negotiated text and interpretations. Nevertheless, the dispute settlement history is sparse still, with only five cases (out of a total for WTO case complaints of over 360) which address services issues, and only one case that is distinctly and centrally a complete services case (namely the very curious case on internet gambling activity).

This book arrives at an important time for the world economy. It will clearly become necessary reading for those whose endeavours are interwoven with international legal and regulatory subjects.

John H Jackson

Acknowledgements

The completion of this work is attributable to a great number of people. Petros Mavroidis supervised my work in a very efficient and reliable manner from the very beginning. No words can express my gratitude for his encouraging words, the intuitive comments, the inspiring discussions, and his inconceivable amount of patience. I am also indebted to Juan Marchetti and Professor Jean-Marie Grether who read this work and provided thoughtful insights.

My initial interest in the WTO and the GATS is due to Professor Ioannis Tzionas at the Democritus University of Thrace, Greece. He taught me the mechanics and the basic principles of the WTO legal order. At the Europa-Institut in Saarbrücken, Germany, I deepened my knowledge of the WTO law thanks to Professor Werner Meng and his guidance throughout my postgraduate studies. Michael J Hahn graciously answered my numerous questions. Thomas Cottier advised me in several stages of my research. I am also obliged to him because he acted as a liaison so that I could start my PhD in Switzerland. Several discussions with Professor Armin von Bogdandy and the academic staff of the Max Planck Institute for Comparative Public Law and International Law in Heidelberg improved my understanding of the WTO mechanics. In Geneva, my experience with the Appellate Body was unique and full of intense educational moments. For their help and the willingness to share their vast knowledge on WTO issues with me I would like to thank notably Victoria Donaldson and Arun Venkataraman. In Neuchâtel, Pauline Lièvre and Laurent Sigismondi have been supportive from my very first day there. Thanks to stimulating discussions with them I became more mature and open-minded. I owe a great deal to Professor Denis Oswald because he offered me a position at the Centre for Sport Studies in Neuchâtel and thereby allowed me to promptly complete my PhD. In Berne, Pierre Sauve, Marion Panizzon, Martin Molinuevo, Susan Kaplan, and Jane Müller tirelessly contributed to the improvement of the final product.

This work would have never been completed without the help, support, and enthusiasm of my wife, Despina, and my daughters, Melina and Lydia. The inspiration that I draw from them has been enormous. I only hope that they also receive something in return for their generosity to me. The least I can do is to wholeheartedly dedicate this book to them.

Berne, May 2007

Contents Summary

Detailed Contents

Table of Cases

WTO PANEL AND APPELLATE BODY REPORTS

GATT PANEL REPORTS

ECJ AND CFI CASES

UNITED STATES' SUPREME COURT CASE LAW

ICJ

Abbreviations

ACP	African, Caribbean, Pacific
AER	American Economic Review
AJIL	American Journal of International Law
ANZCERTA	Australia–New Zealand Closer Economic Relations Trade Agreement
APEC	Asia-Pacific Economic Cooperation
Art, Arts	Article, Articles
ATC	Agreement on Textiles and Clothing
CFI	Court of First Instance
CML Rev	Common Market Law Review
CTS	Council for Trade in Services
DSB	Dispute Settlement Body
DSU	Dispute Settlement Understanding
EC	European Community
ECJ	European Court of Justice
ECR	European Court Reports
ECT	European Community Treaty
EJIL	European Journal of International Law
ENT	Economic Needs Test
EU	European Union
EUT	European Union Treaty
FDI	Foreign Direct Investment
FTA	Free Trade Agreement
G10	Group of Ten
GATS	General Agreement on Trade in Services
GATT	General Agreement on Tariffs and Trade
GDP	Gross Domestic Product
GPA	Agreement on Government Procurement
IAIS	International Association of Insurance Supervisors
IASC	International Accounting Standards Committee
ICAO	International Civil Aviation Organization
ICJ	International Court of Justice
IFAC	International Federation of Accountants
IGBA	Illegal Gambling Business Act
IIE	Institute for International Economics
ILC	International Law Commission

IMF	International Monetary Fund
IOSCO	International Organization of Securities Commissions
ITO	International Trade Organization
JIEL	Journal of International Economic Law
JWT	Journal of World Trade
LDCs	Least-Developed Countries
MFA	Multifibre Agreement
MFN	Most-Favoured Nation
NAFTA	North American Free Trade Agreement
NBER	National Bureau of Economic Research
NGOs	Non-Governmental Organizations
NTBs	Non-Tariff Barriers
OECD	Organization for Economic Co-operation and Development
OJ	Official Journal of the European Communities
QRs	Quantitative Restrictions
PRWP	Policy Research Working Paper (World Bank)
RIA	Regional Integration Agreement
SCM	Agreement on Subsidies and Countervailing Measures
SMEs	Small and Medium Enterprises
SPS	Agreement on the Application of Sanitary and Phytosanitary Measures
TARIC	Integrated Tariff of the European Communities
TBT	Agreement on Technical Barriers to Trade
TPRM	Trade Policy Review Mechanism
TRIMs	Agreement on Trade-Related Investment Measures
TRIPs	Agreement on Trade-Related Aspects of Intellectual Property Rights
UN	United Nations
UNCTAD	United Nations Conference of Trade and Development
USTR	United States Trade Representative
VERs	Voluntary Export Restraints
WHO	World Health Organization
WPDR	Working Party on Domestic Regulation
WPPS	Working Party on Professional Services
WTO	World Trade Organization

Introduction

This study attempts to come to grips with regulatory diversity in services trade.[1] Diversity is a significant idiosyncrasy of the service sector. It stems from the abundance of services sectors, as the General Agreement on Trade in Services (GATS) covers 12 broad sectors and more than 150 sub-sectors. This sectoral diversity leads to a wide array of regulatory responses, as a country may be obliged to adopt specific types of regulatory intervention, depending on the services sector at issue. The state's interference with the market may be similar from one country to another, but this is not usually the case because of differences in preferences, legal culture, domestic priorities, and so on. Therefore, a given regulatory intervention can be not only *sector*-specific, but also *country*-specific. In other words, each country usually has its own perception regarding the way that a specific market failure should be remedied and, consequently, regulatory diversity in the services realm is justified. The GATS does not gainsay this. On the contrary, it recognizes each country's prerogative to regulate trade in services in its own jurisdiction as part of the exclusive competences that WTO Members (hereinafter 'Members') have. Consequently, the GATS condones regulatory diversity. Nevertheless, the GATS and the multilateral trading system in general exist to promote the expansion of trade through progressive liberalization of trade-restrictive domestic policies. Then, how much regulatory diversity can WTO stand? And, conversely, what are the limits of Members' regulatory sovereignty?

This study argues that necessity and transparency are the two crucial tools that allow walking the tightrope between Members' right to regulate and further services trade liberalization, because, by using them, the fine line between GATS-consistent regulatory intervention and protectionism can be drawn. In fact, the GATS hints at the crucial role that these two tools can play. Necessity and transparency are embedded in Article VI GATS which requires that non-discriminatory domestic regulations be no more trade-inhibitory than necessary and, in addition, abide by the principle of transparency. Indeed, it is here, more than in any other GATS provision, that the delicate balance between the expansion of services trade liberalization and the preservation of the regulatory flexibility that each Member has in its own jurisdiction becomes obvious.

Before dealing with necessity and transparency, the intricacy and ubiquity of the remaining barriers to trade in services is reviewed. In fact, it is demonstrated

[1] The present study takes into consideration the developments and scholarly writing associated with the WTO case law and the ongoing negotiations on services as of May 2007.

that, as regards this specific trade area, domestic regulations constitute the most onerous trade barriers, in the absence of any significant impediments to trade in services at the borders. The very feasibility of trade in services may depend on domestic regulations. Although several arguments that validate the existence of such barriers are put forward, the regulatory intensity that characterizes many services sectors is not always justifiable. Hence, this study provides support for the argument that effective legal tools are necessary to avoid protectionism entrenched in domestic regulations that are regarded as legitimate at first blush and identifies the potential welfare gains from the removal of such barriers.

On the basis of the information in the first two chapters, Chapter III goes on to untangle the issue of regulatory diversity in services trade. After a review of the rationales behind governmental intervention in services and a comprehensive analysis of Article VI on 'Domestic Regulation' that reveals the mechanics of this provision, one of the thorniest systemic issues in the GATS today is examined, namely the interplay between Article VI and Articles XVI on Market Access, XVII on National Treatment, and XVIII on Additional Commitments. An examination of relevant case-law follows and a conciliatory approach is put forward. Additionally, this study identifies the rationale behind extensive regulatory intervention in the services domain. In this respect, useful tools such as cost–benefit analysis and regulatory impact assessment are discussed.

Chapters IV and V address the principles of necessity and transparency, respectively, and their impact on domestic services regulations. With respect to necessity, a comparative study is undertaken to identify the essential elements that make a domestic regulation 'necessary'. To this end, lessons are drawn from both the WTO case-law and the jurisprudence generated by the European Court of Justice (ECJ). Regional experience is also scrutinized. At the heart of Chapter IV lies the potential adoption of a necessity test that would apply across services sectors, ie horizontally. In fact, Article VI:4 GATS includes a legal mandate that requires Members to develop, inter alia, a necessity test that would ensure that domestic regulations relating to qualifications, licensing, or technical standards do not create unnecessary barriers to trade. This study examines in an exhaustive manner the complex issues which are germane to the Article VI:4 legal mandate. It also advances notions that should form part of an effective necessity test and which negotiators should take into account when discussing the development of a horizontally applicable necessity test. In this respect, proposals submitted by several Members are critically assessed.

With regard to transparency, the study reviews the transparency obligations already present in the GATS and addresses the potential creation of horizontally applicable multilateral transparency disciplines on licensing, qualifications, and technical standards in services with a view to fulfilling the Article VI:4 legal mandate. The study identifies the advantages and the drawbacks of developing transparency disciplines applicable to all services sectors and makes a realistic assessment of the current proposals relating to transparency.

The current negotiations on services were formally initiated in January 2000, five years after the conclusion of the first negotiating round on services as foreseen under Article XIX GATS. Nevertheless, actual negotiations started after the adoption of the *2001 Scheduling Guidelines* in March 2001.[2] The ongoing negotiations on domestic regulation demonstrate that the adoption of meaningful and practicable horizontal necessity and transparency disciplines can be reasonably expected in the near future. If Members succeed in this, they would be taking a crucial step towards positive integration with respect to the objectivity, necessity, and transparency of measures relating to licensing, qualifications, and standards, which can otherwise hamper the supply of services in a given market. They would also facilitate the work of regulatory authorities to a considerable extent because the work of these authorities is increasingly influenced by the existence of multilateral disciplines and they are exposed to the risk of WTO litigation if domestic regulatory measures infringe the obligations established at the multilateral level. The adoption of clear rules on necessity and transparency would also guide the WTO judiciary to interpret domestic regulation in a manner that reflects negotiators' intentions. Members demonstrate their confidence in the WTO judiciary, as they have already entrusted them with disputes that touch upon very sensitive areas of domestic regulation. In the absence of any guidance on this score, the WTO judiciary may advance interpretations that most negotiators would not necessarily support.

[2] WTO, 'Guidelines for the Scheduling of Specific Commitments under the General Agreement on Trade in Services (GATS)' (hereinafter '*2001 Scheduling Guidelines*'), S/L/92, 2001, p 8 at para 24.

I

The Multilateral Legal Framework Governing Trade in Services

A. The Uruguay Round: A rules-based system for world trade

The GATS,[1] which was created at the inception of the WTO in 1994, marked a watershed by being the first multilateral, legally enforceable agreement covering trade and investment in services that was generated by the Marrakesh 'historical deal'.[2] With the successful incorporation within the embryonic WTO structure of disciplines on goods (GATT), services (GATS) and intellectual property (TRIPs), all of which are now subject to an integrated (and much enhanced) dispute settlement mechanism (DSU), the scope of the multilateral trading system has never been broader, nor its reach more pervasive. Thus, the importance of the Uruguay Round (1986–1994) outcome lay not just with a major package of trade-liberalizing measures; after all, that had already occurred in the seven previous rounds of multilateral trade negotiations. The Uruguay Round successful negotiations reinforced the architecture of the trading system and extended its coverage through intense bargaining and a series of trade-offs.[3]

With the advent of the WTO,[4] the rule of law was enshrined in international economic and trade relations.[5] Its establishment can be considered as an answer

[1] Generally, B Hoekman and P Sauvé, 'Liberalizing Trade in Services', World Bank Discussion Paper No 243, 1994, 30; also P Sauvé, 'Assessing the General Agreement on Trade in Services—Half-Full or Half-Empty?' in R Howse (ed), *The World Trading System—Critical Perspectives on the World Economy*, Vol IV, 1998, 79; also A Sapir, 'The General Agreement on Trade in Services: From 1994 to the Year 2000' (1999) 33(1) JWT 51; G Dunkley, *The Free Trade Adventure: The Uruguay Round and Globalism—A Critique*, 1997, 176; see also WTO, 'An Introduction to the GATS', 1999.

[2] Panel Report, *US—Section 301 Trade Act*, para 4.26. For the background that allowed the Clinton Administration to obtain the congressional approval of the Uruguay Round agreements, see RE Hudec, 'International Economic Law: The Political Theatre Dimension' (1996) 17(9) University of Pennsylvania Journal of International Economic Law 12.

[3] J Whalley, 'Developing Countries and System Strengthening in the Uruguay Round' in W Martin and LA Winters (eds), *The Uruguay Round and the Developing Economies*, World Bank Discussion Paper No 307, 1995, 317.

[4] For a study on the antecedents of the WTO (ITO, GATT), see JH Jackson, *The World Trade Organization: Constitution and Jurisprudence*, 1998, 12.

[5] A Watts, 'The International Rule of Law' (1995) 36 German Yearbook of International Law 14; also E-U Petersmann, 'How to Promote the International Rule of Law? Contributions by the World Trade Organization Appellate Review System' (1998) 1 JIEL 31.

to the widespread question of whether the existing international institutions would be able to cope with the problems arising in a globally integrated world, given the increasingly accelerated pace of change in global economic relations, the faster flow of economic influences across national borders and the increasing intricacy, and thus difficulty, of appreciating the various facets of economic interdependence.

At this juncture, Members chose to participate in a package of multilateral agreements in recognition of the overall net economic and social benefits that accrue from a multilateral trading system that increasingly rests on rules rather than power and of the demanding nature of the incremental international economic interdependence. Such economic interdependence, together with the reality and the potential gains of increased trade and foreign investment in the international economy, released pro-trade forces and discouraged protectionist politics.

On a unique occasion for the world trading system, the over 140 Members decided to set universal rules and disciplines against the temptations of unilateralism. Prominently, the introduction of a new mechanism for settling disputes that has a more legalistic and automatic character and creates a level playing field on which the smaller countries can enforce their rights against the larger ones aimed to reduce the widespread cynicism about the value and the efficacy of international law rules.[6] Indeed, the inauguration of the WTO represents a further enhancement in the direction of rule orientation, and that is particularly demonstrated by the new dispute settlement procedures.[7] These procedures arguably constitute the strongest dispute settlement mechanism in the history of international law.[8] Of course, Article 36 of the ICJ Statute also foresees a compulsory third party adjudication system, but on the stipulation that Member States have expressed their consent to have all disputes adjudicated before the ICJ. Hence, this provision is far weaker than Article 23 DSU which requires that Members have recourse to, and abide by, the WTO dispute settlement system.

[6] Nevertheless, the GATT system was also fairly efficient. WF Schwartz and A Sykes, 'The Economic Structure of Renegotiation and Dispute Resolution in the WTO/GATT System', 2002, 18; also D Palmeter, 'National Sovereignty and the World Trade Organization' in K Anderson and B Hoekman (eds), *The Global Trading System*, Vol 4: *'New' Issues for the WTO*, 2002, 304.

[7] JH Jackson, 'Global Economics and International Economic Law' (1998) 1 JIEL 17; also JH Jackson, 'Reflections on Restructuring the GATT' in T Oppermann and J Molsberger (eds), *A New GATT for the Nineties and Europe' 92,* 1991, 149.

[8] Already in the mid-1950s, the GATT dispute settlement system underwent its first dramatic shift to juridification. JH Jackson, *The World Trading System: Law and Policy of International Economic Relations*, 1999, 115; also RE Hudec, *Enforcing International Trade Law: The Evolution of the Modern GATT Legal System*, 1993, 29. For the differences between the old (GATT 1947) and the new (WTO) dispute settlement procedures, see B Speyer, 'The WTO Dispute Settlement Mechanism—A New Era for the World Economy?' (1998) 53(1) Aussenwirtschaft 130.

The WTO new judicial system aspires to increase the rigorous and careful reasoning of Panel and Appellate Body reports[9] that are grappling with very sophisticated 'governing questions' of the international trading system. In this struggle, a process of reconciling two needs emerges: the need for allowing Members a 'margin of appreciation or deference'[10] so that they can attain welfare and social goals (eg environmental protection, human health) and the need for rule integrity in the multilateral trading system.[11]

The WTO Agreement brought about a historically unique 'legalization' and 'judicialization' of international relations by providing, *inter alia*:

- Compulsory jurisdiction of the WTO Dispute Settlement Body (DSB) for the establishment of independent panels for the settlement of disputes at the request of any Member (Art 6 DSU);
- Court-like procedures and strict time-limits for the conclusion of the panel and appellate procedures (Arts 9, 12, 17 DSU);
- Precise recognition of the 'right to a panel' (Art 6 DSU) and of subsequent access to the standing Appellate Body[12] composed of independent judges;
- Automatic, expeditious adoption of Panel and Appellate Body reports[13] by the DSB, except in the—unlikely—event of 'negative consensus' not to adopt the report (Arts 16, 17 DSU);
- Prompt arbitration within the WTO as an alternative means of dispute settlement (Art 25 DSU);[14]
- Multilateral surveillance procedures to ensure rapid compliance with rulings and recommendations made by the WTO adjudicating bodies (Art 21 DSU);
- Procedures for agreed compensation or authorized retaliation as temporary measures pending the withdrawal of illegal measures and the implementation of dispute settlement rulings (Art 22 DSU);[15]

[9] The emphasis by the Appellate Body on applying the Vienna Convention on the Law of Treaties (hereinafter the '*Vienna Convention*') when it comes to interpreting GATT/WTO rules is also suggestive of this. Negotiating history is now only employed as a supplementary means of interpretation (Art 32 of the *Vienna Convention*) thereby underscoring a shift to a more legalistic thinking. See also M Lennard, 'Navigating by the Stars: Interpreting the WTO Agreements' (2002) 5 JIEL 17.

[10] Appellate Body Report, *EC—Hormones*, para 117. Also Y Shany, 'Toward a General Margin of Appreciation Doctrine in International Law?' (2005) 16(5) EJIL 909.

[11] JH Jackson, 'International Economic Law in Times that Are Interesting' (2000) 1 JIEL 7.

[12] R Howse, 'The Most Dangerous Branch? WTO Appellate Body Jurisprudence on the Nature and Limits of the Judicial Power' in T Cottier and PC Mavroidis (eds), *The Role of the Judge in International Trade Regulation: Experience and Lessons for the WTO*, 2003, 15.

[13] The Appellate Body confirmed early that 'adopted Panel reports are an important part of the GATT *acquis*'. Appellate Body Report, *Japan—Alcoholic Beverages II*, p 14.

[14] E-U Petersmann, 'Dispute Settlement in International Economic Law—Lessons for Strengthening International Dispute Settlement in Non-Economic Areas' (1999) 2 JIEL 209.

[15] For Schwartz and Sykes this provision contains the major innovation of the WTO dispute resolution system. Any sanctions against the violator cannot be imposed unless they are first reviewed by a binding arbitral panel to ensure that the price for non-compliance will be set by an objective assessment of the harm to the affected party/ies. In their view, this sanctioning

- Obligations to have recourse to, and abide by, the DSU when Members seek the redress of a nullification or impairment of WTO obligations (compulsory jurisdiction), and to refrain from any legal remedies inconsistent with the DSU, such as unilateral retaliation (Art 23 DSU);[16]
- A significant amount of requirements to grant access to judicial, arbitral or administrative tribunals and independent review procedures at the domestic level, eg in the field of the GATT (Art X), the Anti-dumping Agreement (Art 13), the Agreement on Subsidies and Countervailing Measures (Art 23), the GATS (Art VI), the TRIPs (Arts 41–50, 59) and the GPA (Art XX).

All these provisions have contributed to a more rule-oriented system regarding international trade relations[17] compared with other international law areas where, in the absence of obligatory jurisdiction and judicial review (eg ICJ, compliance with UN Charter, UN resolutions, etc), deviations from international rules often remain without sanctions.[18] Traditionally, States regarded international rules as a diplomatic/political framework which could provide a basis for negotiations to attain a balance between benefits and obligations. However, the Uruguay Round confirmed a growing demand for the regulation of trade relations through the use of norms and enforcement procedures that are legal in character.[19] Thus, a shift towards juridification, pursued by the introduction of norms and practices

mechanism aims at *decreasing* the penalty for violations rather than increasing it. With the new system the violating country can continue deviating from its obligations, as long as it is prepared to pay the price of its behaviour, without worrying about any unilateral excessive sanctions against it. If the objective was to induce compliance, Members would have imposed some greater penalty for non-compliance. For this interesting viewpoint that is greatly influenced by the theory of incomplete contracts, see Schwartz and Sykes (n 6 above) 12. This interpretation appears to be the one followed by the Arbitrator in *US—Offset Act (Byrd Amendment) (Brazil) (Article 22.6—US)*, para 3.74. See, however, the interpretation in the Decision by the Arbitrators, *EC—Bananas III (US) (Article 22.6—EC)*, para 6.3; also JH Jackson, 'The WTO Dispute Settlement Understanding—Misunderstandings on the Nature of Legal Obligation' (1997) 91(1) AJIL 60, who argues that the suspension of concessions aims to induce compliance of the defending party with the DSB recommendations.

[16] Panel Report, *US—Section 301 Trade Act*, para 7.43; also C Schede, 'The Strengthening of the Multilateral System—Article 23 of the WTO Dispute Settlement Understanding: Dismantling Unilateral Retaliation under Section 301 of the 1974 Trade Act?' (1996) 20(1) World Competition 112. A Member cannot invoke Art 60 of the *Vienna Convention* in order to justify a unilateral retaliatory action. Panel Report, *US—Certain EC Products*, para 6.133 and fn 170.

[17] *But* B Hoekman and P Mavroidis, 'WTO Dispute Settlement, Transparency and Surveillance', World Bank, 1999, 4.

[18] For a proposal on 'GATTing the UN', see E-U Petersmann, 'How to reform the United Nations? Lessons from the "International Economic Law Revolution"' (1998) 53(2) Aussenwirtschaft 206.

[19] See, for instance, the Appellate Body's zeal for respecting due process requirements in Appellate Body Report, *US—Offset Act (Byrd Amendment)*, paras 193–208. For a different view, see GP Sampson, 'The World Trade Organization after Seattle' (2000) 23(9) The World Economy 1112.

of legal culture, occurred in the world trading system, which is at odds with the ethos of diplomacy.[20]

B. The position of services in world trade

The perception of services changed dramatically in the last two decades.[21] Until the beginning of the 1980s, services were regarded as ancillary activities that are not per se productive and have no independent value. Nowadays, services are ubiquitous. They are multidimensional and play a pivotal role in economic development. Trade in services encompasses a disparate array of economic activities, and amasses a similarly wide scope of issues, institutions, and interests. The increasing importance of trade in services after the early post-war years has ultimately led to intensive multilateral efforts with a view to a progressive abolition of barriers to market access and trade discrimination. Just as with the liberalization of merchandise trade under the GATT, there is a strong case for liberalizing trade in services.[22] Indeed, the economic rationale that has always inspired the GATT is equally compelling in the services milieu.[23]

To appreciate the significance of the role that services play in the multilateral trading system, it is first necessary to comprehend the increasingly crucial place that the service sector occupies in the global economy and the main technological and regulatory changes that impel this shift. Services are essential inputs in the production of goods and other services.[24] In fact, international business would not be possible without extensive international services trade. The service industries are those that provide the transportation, the communications, the financing, the insurance, the know-how, and all the other support systems that are essential to world trade. Thus, services are a determinant of overall welfare and productivity.[25]

The service sector is at the heart of an economic revolution which is very influential. In the emerging economy the creation, processing, and distribution of information are dislodging manufacturing as the primary economic activity.

[20] JHH Weiler, 'The Rule of Lawyers and the Ethos of Diplomats: Reflections on the Internal and External Legitimacy of WTO Dispute Settlement' (2001) 35(2) JWT 197. However, GATT language is still present, for instance, in Art 3:4 DSU. JH Jackson, 'Dispute Settlement in the WTO: Policy and Jurisprudential Considerations', Research Seminar in International Economics, Discussion Paper No. 419, 1998, 22.

[21] G Feketekuty, 'Trade in Services—Bringing Services into the Multilateral Trading System' in J Bhagwati and M Hirsch (eds), *The Uruguay Round and Beyond—Essays in Honor of Arthur Dunkel*, 1998, 80.

[22] Also Chapter II.F below.

[23] Inter alia, B Hindley and A Smith, 'Comparative Advantage and Trade in Services' (1984) 7(1) The World Economy 369.

[24] AV Deardorff, 'International Provision of Trade Services, Trade and Fragmentation', Research Seminar in International Economics, Discussion Paper No 463, 2000, 2.

[25] B Hoekman, 'Liberalizing Trade in Services: A Survey', PRWP No 4030, 2006, 3.

These activities seem to be so vital nowadays that it may well become known as the information revolution.[26] Since the service sector creates, processes, and distributes information, its importance grows apace. This growth has a positive impact on the overall performance of an economy.[27] In turn, the richer a country becomes, the higher the share of services in output and employment will be.[28]

Services production is a dominant economic activity in virtually all countries of the world, regardless of their level of development. Services bring about more than 60 per cent of production and employment in developed countries,[29] while several studies demonstrate that the developing world's emerging economies progressively verge upon these figures.[30] These are considerable amounts, particularly for a sector that was long conceptualized as non-tradable because of its 'ephemeral' nature and its liberalization was thought to be an oxymoron. The magnitude of these figures makes it clear that the potential gains from international cooperation and multilateral rulemaking in services are large and have scarcely begun to be tapped.

In addition, FDI in services now exceeds FDI in manufacturing.[31] Remarkably, this tendency concerns both developed and developing countries.[32] During the past 15 years, services have become more significant in international production also because of the recent liberalization efforts in this sector. Over 2001–2002, services accounted for about two-thirds of total FDI inflows (and 70 per cent of outflows), or an estimated $500 billion ($450 billion for outflows) per year. In the same period, developing countries accounted for 25 per cent of the inward FDI stock in services and 10 per cent (compared to one per cent in 1990) of the global outward stock.[33] OECD countries continue to be the major net exporters of direct investment capital with the net outward FDI reaching an all-time high of $261 billion in 2004.[34] In the OECD area, services represent more

[26] G Feketekuty, *International Trade in Services: An Overview and Blueprint for Negotiations*, 1988, 42.

[27] *Inter alia*, J Francois, 'Producer Services, Scale and the Division of Labor' (1990) 42 Oxford Economic Papers 715.

[28] Hoekman (n 25 above) 3.

[29] OECD, 'Open Services Markets Matter', Policy brief, 2001, 2. In the United States, services provide more jobs than all other sectors of the US economy combined. Only in 2001, 81.1% of total US private-sector employment was in service industries. See USTR, *2004 Annual Report of the President of the United States on the Trade Agreements Program*, 2005, 10.

[30] WTO, CTS (Special Session), 'An Assessment of Services Trade and Liberalization in the United States and Developing Economies', Communication from the United States, TN/S/W/12, 31 March 2003, p 2. Whereas trade in services has grown, on average, faster in developing economies, more than 40% of world trade in services is still carried on between the EU, United States, and Japan. A Maurer and P Chauvet, 'The Magnitude of Flows of Global Trade in Services' in B Hoekman, A Mattoo, and P English (eds), *Development, Trade, and the WTO: A Handbook*, 2002, 239.

[31] OECD, *International Investment Perspectives*, 2005, 60.

[32] The World Bank, *Global Economic Prospects and the Developing Countries 2003—Investing to Unlock Global Opportunities*, 2003, 52.

[33] UNCTAD, *World Investment Report 2004: The Shift Towards Services*, 2004, 97–101.

[34] OECD (n 31 above) 14.

than 75 per cent of the FDI inflows, while three-quarters of all net outflows from 1990–2002 were due to FDI in services.[35] Business services, transport, and communications have become the largest FDI recipients in the OECD area.[36]

Even though these aggregate figures conceal differences from country to country and sector to sector, the FDI shift towards services is obvious and fairly remarkable. These figures are valuable reminders of the economic and commercial importance of the service sector. They also demonstrate the potential benefits from prospective successful negotiations intended progressively to roll back impediments to trade and investment in this sector.

Apparently, the lack of a multilateral legal framework for international trade in services was anomalous and dangerous; anomalous because the potential benefits of services liberalization are at least as great as in the goods sector, and dangerous because there was no legal basis on which to resolve conflicting national interests. All the empirical studies explicitly indicate that for the past two decades trade in services has grown faster than, or at least as fast as, merchandise trade.[37] Therefore, continuing equation of services with non-traded goods would appear to be a travesty.

The GATS rules govern one of the most dynamic sectors of the world economy, generating a tentative level of transparency and fairness for the global trade in services the value of which is roughly estimated at \$2.2 trillion on an annual basis, which equals to 7.6 per cent of world GDP.[38] An important recent development is that the 'traditional', cross-border trade in services is today larger in absolute size than establishment-related trade in services.[39] Undeniably, technological advances and outsourcing contribute to this trend.[40]

C. Creating the GATS

The GATS was a major step in an unchartered terrain and an innovative endeavour to establish a pragmatic framework for liberalization of trade in services. The abortive Havana Charter—which was, in certain aspects, a source of inspiration

[35] F Fortanier and M Maher, 'Foreign Direct Investment and Sustainable Development', Financial Market Trends No 79, June 2001, p 109; The World Bank, *Global Economic Prospects and the Developing Countries 2002*, 2002, 72.

[36] OECD, 'Trends and Recent Developments in Foreign Direct Investment', 2004, 11.

[37] In absolute terms, total exports of services more than quadrupled in the last two decades (from \$337bn in 1980 to \$1.4 trillion in 2000). See UNCTAD, 'Exports of Services and Economic Growth in Developing Countries', UNCTAD/DITC/TNCD/MISC/2003/6, 2004, 5; also B Hoekman (n 25 above) 5.

[38] G Karsenty, 'Assessing Trade in Services by Mode of Supply' in P Sauvé and RM Stern (eds), *GATS 2000: New Directions in Services Trade Liberalization*, 2000, 52; WTO, 'A Review of Statistics on Trade Flows in Services', S/C/W/27/Add.1, 30 October 2000.

[39] Karsenty (n 38 above) 54.

[40] J Bhagwati, A Panagariya, and TN Srinivasan, 'The Muddles Over Outsourcing' (2004) 18(4) Journal of Economic Perspectives 95–96.

during the Uruguay Round negotiations—recognized services as part of international commerce only obliquely,[41] since services were not amidst the dominant economic activities at the time, not even in advanced economies.

The GATS resulted from the policymakers' appreciation that trade in services had come to play an important role in the modern global economy, while being hitherto largely omitted by the existing trade-policy architecture. Whilst the trade diplomats and the economists procrastinated, manifold policy groups and interested enterprises had foreseen the need for some kind of international rule discipline for trade in services in order to eschew the disequilibrium that seemingly existed in the international trading system without any multilateral canons regulating trade in services.[42] In the aggregate, services were beginning to overcome the production of goods in terms of GDP portion in many developed countries. Some service suppliers were exploring the possibility of exporting their activities and had begun to encounter foreign barriers that restricted their activities to preserve businesses for domestic service suppliers. Therefore, various groups began to insist on the establishment of an international cooperative mechanism that would develop rules against such protectionist actions before those actions became deep-rooted and multiplied.[43]

When the Uruguay Round agenda was being negotiated in the mid-1980s, the US government was the primary advocate for including services in the agenda with a view to making domestic laws, regulations and administrative practices subject to international rules.[44] That was partly in response to an initiative by

[41] Article 53:1 of the Final Act; also RJ Krommenacker, *World-Traded Services: The Challenge for the Eighties*, 1984, 141.

[42] WJ Drake and K Nicolaidis, 'Ideas, Interests, and Institutionalization: "Trade in Services" and the Uruguay Round' (1992) 46(1) International Organization 41; J Croome, *Reshaping the World Trading System: A History of the Uruguay Round*, 1999, 102, 207, 310; M Marconini, 'The Uruguay Round Negotiations on Services: An Overview' in PA Messerlin and KP Sauvant (eds), *The Uruguay Round: Services in the World Economy*, 1990, 19; RB Woodrow, 'Sectoral Coverage and Implementation within a Uruguay Round Services Trade Agreement: Paradox and Prognosis' in T Oppermann and J Molsberger (eds), *A New GATT for the Nineties and Europe '92*, 1991, 222; also B Hindley, 'Services' in JJ Schott (ed), *Completing the Uruguay Round: A Results-Oriented Approach to the GATT Trade Negotiations*, 1990, 136; H-D Smeets, G Hofner, and A Knorr, 'A Multilateral Framework of Principles and Rules for Trade in Services' in T Oppermann and J Molsberger (eds), *A New GATT for the Nineties and Europe '92*, 1991, 197.

[43] Jackson (n 8 above) 306.

[44] Also J Bhagwati, 'International Trade in Services and its Relevance for Economic Development' in O Garini (ed), *The Emerging Service Economy*, 1987, 26. For details on the American plan on services, see USTR, *US National Study on Trade in Services*, 25 January 1984; also WE Brock, 'A Simple Plan for Negotiating on Trade in Services' (1982) 5(3) The World Economy 229; also HB Malmgren, 'Negotiating International Rules for Trade in Services' (1985) 8(1) The World Economy 18. Essentially, the American proposal tended to focus the negotiations on the sectors that were of export interest to the United States and other developed countries (namely FDI), while excluding liberalization of labour movements, where developing countries might often have a comparative advantage. See USTR, *US National Study*, p 77; also TG Berg, 'Trade in Services: Toward a "Development Round" of the GATT Negotiations Benefiting Both Developing and Industrialized States' (1987) 28(1) Harvard International Law Journal 10. As the

the US financial services and 'high-tech' communication industries,[45] which did not want to see services relegated to the periphery of the multilateral trade negotiations. Indeed, several empirical studies[46] in that period demonstrated the quantitative and qualitative significance of services in international trade and, thus, confirmed that this trade issue was mooted as mature for inclusion in the trade negotiating agenda. After prolonged negotiations culminating in the Punta del Este Ministerial Meeting in September 1986, services became part of the agenda in a convoluted series of trade-offs that shaped the Uruguay Round.

At the threshold, the US proposal entailed an expansion of the GATT in order to include services with the contemplation that the new round of multilateral trade negotiations encompasses the negotiation of the services compact. On the other side, the Group of Ten (G10), led by Brazil and India, preferred such negotiations to be outside the GATT conceptual and institutional structure, undertaken by governments rather than GATT contracting parties.[47] At the end of the day, the Punta del Este Declaration portrayed a compromise,[48] ie two distinct tracks for negotiations on goods and services, but the Uruguay Round as a whole was considered a 'single undertaking'[49] to be conducted at the same time and under the aegis of the Trade Negotiating Committee. Hence, the developing countries did not succeed in dissociating the GATT from a potential services agreement. They did, however, succeed in the adoption of a soft framework agreement with few strong obligations.[50] In any event, the final inclusion of services in the agenda was against all odds, as an influential group of developing countries in the GATT adamantly argued that services were primarily a matter of domestic regulatory conduct and therefore did not belong to the trading system's purview.[51]

To all intents and purposes, the Uruguay Round merits a unique place in the history of international trade relations mainly due to the 'North–South grand

negotiations evolved, the United States forsook its 'open borders' rhetoric, as major US service suppliers realized that they would possibly have to compete with foreigners in their own market. MJ Trebilcock and R Howse, *The Regulation of International Trade*, 3rd edition, 2005, 358.

[45] J Bhagwati, 'Splintering and Disembodiment of Services and Developing Nations' (1984) 7(2) The World Economy 140; also JV Reyna, 'Services' in TP Stewart (ed), *The GATT Uruguay Round: A Negotiating History (1986–1992)*, Vol II: Commentary, 1993, 2343.

[46] TP Hill, 'On Goods and Services' (1977) 23(4) The Review of Income and Wealth 315; also R Krommenacker, 'Trade Related Services and GATT' (1979) 13(6) JWT 510.

[47] GATT, 'Communication from Brazil', MTN.GNS/W/3, 11 March 1987.

[48] Reyna (n 45 above) 2361.

[49] And this in order to avoid the 'fragmentation' of the GATT.

[50] B Hoekman, 'Developing Countries and the Uruguay Round: Negotiations on Services', PRWP No 1220, 1993, 14.

[51] Apart from the sovereignty concerns, the developing countries' reluctance was also due to: (a) the desire to protect 'infant industries', (b) their balance-of-payments difficulties, and (c) the crucial role of structure services. A Sapir, 'North–South issues in Trade in Services' (1985) 8(1) The World Economy 40.

bargain' that occurred.[52] Developed countries agreed to expand the GATT by including agriculture and textiles and clothing and, in return, the inclusion of services, trade-related intellectual property rights (TRIPs), and trade-related investment measures (TRIMs) commended itself to developing countries. This 'concession' from the developed countries' side was a *conditio sine qua non* in order to overcome the developing countries' concerns that the advent of a multilateral framework of rules and disciplines for services was largely inimical to their development prospects and fledgling services sectors.[53] Thus, the GATS was not an adventitious occurrence, but rather the result of a long-drawn-out process brimful of returns and concessions exchange.

D. The position of the GATS in the GATT/WTO structure—The boundaries between the GATT and the GATS

As part of the Uruguay Round, contracting parties to the GATT signed the GATS. The successful conclusion of the Uruguay Round as a 'single undertaking' marked the creation of the GATS. This round saw the WTO turn into a tripod, its three legs being the old GATT, the GATS and the TRIPs.[54] Apart from the agreement on maintaining the GATS as separate from the GATT, but placing it within the overarching framework of the WTO, negotiators did not pay particular attention to the relationship between GATT and GATS, since the two agreements were not negotiated and concluded at the same time. In fact, when the decision was taken to create a 'single package' by assembling all legal texts as Annexes to the WTO Agreement, this had the unintended consequence of creating repetitions, omissions, and possible conflicts.[55] In the aftermath of the Uruguay Round, the WTO judiciary was confronted with interpretative difficulties. There was a need to clarify the legal relationship between WTO provisions which are not explicitly addressed in the WTO (incomplete) contract[56] and to articulate the appropriate justifications for the solutions chosen.

Depending on the interpretation of the GATS/GATT relationship, the treatment of a given governmental measure by the WTO adjudicating bodies can be different. Indeed, because of the differences between GATT and GATS, any

[52] S Ostry, 'The Uruguay Round North–South Grand Bargain: Implications for Future Negotiations', 2000.

[53] Malmgren (n 44 above) 12; also UNCTAD/World Bank, *Liberalizing International Transactions in Services: A Handbook,* 1994, 20.

[54] WJ Davey and W Zdouc, 'The Triangle of TRIPs, GATT and GATS' in T Cottier and PC Mavroidis (eds), *Intellectual Property: Trade, Competition, and Sustainable Development*, 2003, 53.

[55] Ibid 81, fn 27.

[56] JP Trachtman, 'The Theory of the Firm and the Theory of the International Economic Organization: Toward Comparative Institutional Analysis' (1996–1997) 17(2/3) Northwestern Journal of International Law & Business 527ff.

measure could be found consistent with the one agreement, while it could transgress the other. This especially concerns measures that could fall under the GATS, since in the GATS context governments enjoy much more room for discretion than in the GATT context and therefore governmental measures can be outlawed less easily in the former case. In principle, this may lead to a higher degree of arbitrariness in the services milieu at the national level. In the next paragraphs, an attempt will be made to examine typical approaches regarding the position of services vis-à-vis goods, as they are reflected in the European Community Treaty (ECT) and the WTO legal order.

1. The EC approach

According to Article 50 ECT, 'services shall be considered to be "services" within the meaning of this Treaty where they are normally provided for remuneration, *insofar* as they are not governed by the provisions relating to freedom of movement of goods, capital and persons'. This indicates that this freedom has an ancillary—or residual—character, when compared with the freedoms relating to goods, capital, or persons. More generally, services are negatively defined in the alternative by reference to the other three fundamental freedoms.[57] Hence, rules on the free movement of services and those on the free movement of goods are mutually exclusive, as they cannot apply to the same aspect of a given measure.[58] However, the rules concerning the other three fundamental freedoms should also be taken into consideration when dealing with issues associated with trade in services, because they also form the framework for the principles and norms applicable to trade in services.[59] In practice, the decision of whether a given measure falls under the freedom to provide services or the free movement of goods is not always so straightforward and case law demonstrates that the ECJ will decide on a case-by-case basis.[60]

2. The WTO case law—GATT and GATS as two irreconcilable agreements?

WTO law is a convoluted unity and becomes all the more complex, as the relationship among its various components has not necessarily been the subject

[57] Case C-275/92 *Schindler* [1994] ECR I-1039, paras 16–30; also C-D Ehlermann and G Campogrande, 'Rules on Services in the EEC: A Model for Negotiating World-Wide Rules' in E-U Petersmann and M Hilf (eds), *The New GATT Round of Multilateral Trade Negotiations: Legal and Economic Problems,* 1988, 484; also J Snell, *Goods and Services in EC Law*, 2002.

[58] Case C-55/94 *Reinhard Gebhard v Consiglio dell'Ordine degli Avvocati e Procuratori di Milano* [1995] ECR I-4165, para 20.

[59] cf the ECJ's argumentation in the Case 205/84 *Commission v Germany* [1986] ECR 3755.

[60] cf the Case C-390/99 *Canal Satélite Digital* [2002] ECR I-607, paras 31ff, as compared with the Case C-71/02 *Karner* [2004] ECR I-3025, paras 46–47.

of specific provisions. By virtue of the General Interpretative Note to Annex 1A of the WTO Charter, GATT provisions should be set aside in the case of conflict between them and a provision of another Agreement in Annex 1A to the WTO Agreement 'to the extent of the conflict'.[61] Thus, all Agreements listed in Annex 1A (inter alia, the TBT and SPS)[62] are regarded as *lex specialis* and consequently take precedence over the GATT. This means in practice that, in the case of a complaint that covers both the GATT and another Agreement of Annex 1A, the WTO adjudicating bodies will first examine the claims under the latter Agreement.[63]

The Interpretative Note, however, remains silent on the exact nature of the relationship between GATT and the Annex 1B Agreement, namely GATS. Thus, unlike the EC Treaty, there is no provision in the WTO Agreement regulating the relationship between GATT and GATS. The question of whether and how the scope of the GATT and the GATS overlap was left to be resolved in dispute settlement. The WTO adjudicating bodies addressed this question of fundamental importance twice at both panel and appellate level,[64] yet without giving a definitive answer.[65] In the absence of any guidance in the WTO Agreement, panels and the Appellate Body have inevitably addressed the issues of overlaps and conflicts between the GATT and the GATS by reference to the structure of the WTO Agreement and the Annexes thereto.

a) The Canada—Periodicals *case*

In this case the Panel examined the position of whether Canada—assuming that it had intended to carve out the measure in question from the coverage of its GATT commitments—was exonerated from the Panel's scrutiny regarding the alleged GATT violation. The Panel ruled that '[t]he ordinary meaning of the texts of the GATT 1994 and GATS as well as Article II:2 of the WTO Agreement, taken together, indicates that obligations under GATT 1994 and GATS can co-exist and that one does not override the other'.[66] Hence, the Panel ruled that there is no hierarchy between GATT and GATS. If Members' intention was to eschew any overlap as to the scope of the two agreements, a provision similar

[61] E Montaguti and M Lugard, 'The GATT 1994 and Other Annex 1A Agreements: Four Different Relationships?' (2000) 3 JIEL 473; also Panel Report, *EC—Sardines*, paras 7.15–7.16.

[62] In turn, Art 1.5 TBT implies that, in case of conflict, SPS should take precedence over TBT.

[63] Panel Report, *EC—Sardines*, paras 7.15–7.16.

[64] Panel Report, *Canada—Periodicals*, and Appellate Body Report, *Canada—Periodicals*; Panel Report, *EC—Bananas III (Guatemala and Honduras)*, Panel Report, *EC—Bananas III (Mexico)*, Panel Report, *EC—Bananas III (US)*, Panel Report, *EC—Bananas III (Ecuador)*, and Appellate Body Report, *EC—Bananas III*.

[65] W Zdouc, 'WTO Dispute Settlement Practice Relating to the GATS' (1999) 2 JIEL 296, 322; also JP Gaffney, 'The GATT and the GATS: Should They Be Mutually Exclusive Agreements?' (1999) 12 Leiden Journal of International Law 136.

[66] Panel Report, *Canada—Periodicals*, para 5.17.

to Article XVI:3 of the WTO Agreement or the General Interpretative Note to Annex 1A would be included in the final text of the WTO Charter.[67]

Rather, the Panel acknowledged that overlaps between GATT and GATS were inevitable and would amplify in the future due to the progress of technology and the incremental globalization of economic activities. The Panel ultimately found that both GATT and GATS can apply to the measure at issue, since Canada also acknowledges that no conflict exists between its obligations under the two agreements.[68]

On appeal, the Appellate Body did show an implicit preference in applying GATT over GATS. For instance, while the Appellate Body acknowledged that a periodical is a good that comprises of components having services attributes, it contended that the GATT is to be applied because these components form a *physical* product, that is, the periodical.[69] Nonetheless, in the end, the Appellate Body upheld the Panel's finding that there is no hierarchical order between the two agreements. The Appellate Body did not tackle further the issue of potential overlaps, since, contrary to the *EC—Bananas III* case, the complainant, *in casu* the United States, did not raise any claims under the GATS. Thus, the Appellate Body's ruling resolved the issues on that appeal, and at the same time it was wisely crafted rather narrowly in order not to prejudge the issues that would have to be dealt with in the ensuing *EC—Bananas III* case.

b) The EC—Bananas III *case*[70]

In *EC—Bananas III* case, the issues of potential overlaps and conflicts cropped up again. The issue in this case was whether or not measures regulating the importation of goods could actually or potentially adversely affect services or service suppliers of foreign origin, ie non-EC and non-Lomé member-country banana distributor/importers ('operators'), with respect to the allocation of import licences. The EC claimed that its common market organization for bananas regulated the importation, sale, and distribution of bananas, namely goods, and not the provision of services, and therefore could not constitute a measure affecting trade in services within the meaning of Article I:1 GATS.[71] According to the EC,

[67] Ibid.

[68] Ibid, para 5.19.

[69] Appellate Body Report, *Canada—Periodicals*, p 17; also J Pauwelyn, *Conflict of Norms in Public International Law—How WTO Law Relates to Other Rules of International Law*, 2003, 404.

[70] This case can be conceptualized as 'the trade case of the last decade' due to the sovereignty lessons that can be drawn from it. See JH Jackson, 'The Evolution of the WTO Dispute Settlement Mechanism and the Prospects for the Millennium Round' in P Ruttley, I MacVay, and A Masa'deh (eds), *Liberalization and Protectionism in the World Trading System*, World Trade Law Association, 1999, 265.

[71] The EC also claimed that the application of the GATS in this case would be contrary to Art 28 of the *Vienna Convention* (non-retroactivity principle). Since the EC's import licensing

GATT and GATS should be considered to be mutually exclusive agreements, because if not, exceptions or waivers under one agreement would be rendered ineffective.[72]

The Panel took issue with the EC's approach. In the Panel's view, if the scope of the two agreements was mutually exclusive, the value of the Members' commitments and obligations would be undermined, because it could lead to the circumvention of obligations under one or both agreements by the adoption of measures under one agreement having an indirect effect on trade covered by the other without the possibility of any legal recourse for the Member prejudiced by such measures.[73] As a result, the Panel dismissed the EC argument that the scope of the two agreements was mutually exclusive by relying on reasoning similar to the *Canada—Periodicals* Panel's textual and contextual argumentation. Summing up its findings the Panel stated that no measures were to be excluded *a priori* from the GATS scope as defined by its provisions; this scope encompasses any measure of a Member to the extent that it affects trade in services regardless of whether such a measure directly governs the supply of a service or whether it regulates other matters but nevertheless affects trade in services.[74]

The Appellate Body defined the questions at issue as twofold: first, which is the scope of the GATS and second, on a more general level, whether the two agreements are mutually exclusive.[75] Regarding the former issue, the Appellate Body upheld the Panel's findings.[76] As far as the latter issue is concerned, the Appellate Body had explicitly refused to rule on it in the *Canada—Periodicals* case. The Appellate Body noted that, given the respective scope of application of the two agreements, they might or might not overlap, depending on the nature of the measures at issue. The Appellate Body identified three categories of measures:[77]

- Those measures falling exclusively within the scope of the GATT;
- Those measures falling exclusively within the scope of the GATS; and

regime predated the entry into force of the GATS, it could not be subject to review by the Panel. The Panel, however, found that the provisions at issue entail *continuing* measures and therefore it limited the scope of its ruling to the effects generated after January 1995. Panel Report, *EC—Bananas III (US)*, para 7.308. While the Appellate Body could not express its views on the Panel's *factual* finding (paras 235–237), it made clear in other disputes that the non-retroactivity principle is relevant for the interpretation of the WTO Agreements. Appellate Body Report, *EC—Sardines*, para 200 and fn 117 for the relevant jurisprudence.

72 Panel Report, *EC—Bananas III (US)*, para 7.278.
73 Ibid para 7.283.
74 Ibid para 7.285.
75 Appellate Body Report, *EC—Bananas III*, para 217.
76 Ibid para 220.
77 Ibid para 221.

- Those measures which fall within the scope of both agreements, ie measures that involve a service relating to a particular good or a service supplied in conjunction with a particular good.

The Appellate Body backed the Panel's view that such a measure could be scrutinized under both the GATT and the GATS,[78] but it stopped short of proposing a general test to determine to which category a measure may belong, stating instead that the question of 'whether a certain measure affecting the supply of a service relating to a particular good is scrutinized under the GATT or the GATS, or both, is a matter that can only be determined on a case-by-case basis'.[79] This logic of 'case-by-case scrutiny' is indeed very prudent, since the third category of measures that the Appellate Body identified can indeed cover a vast array of measures, given that services are in many cases intrinsically linked to, and often inseparable from, or incorporated into, goods. In *Canada—Autos*, the Appellate Body made it clear that when a measure needs to be examined under both GATT and GATS, 'the focus of the enquiry, and the specific aspects of the measure to be scrutinized, under each agreement, will be different because the subjects of the two agreements are different'.[80]

Thus, in *EC—Bananas III*, the Appellate Body settled the issue of overlapping between GATT and GATS and paved the way for the WTO adjudicating bodies to follow the same reasoning in any case of overlap between the three agreements-pillars of the WTO edifice. In addition, it is worth noting that the WTO judiciary seems to end up acknowledging that the GATT and other WTO Agreements can operate concurrently, and several agreements can be relevant for a single dispute, as long as the measure falls within the ambit of two or more agreements.[81]

In more generalized terms, in any similar case of overlap, the adjudicating bodies would be guided by the principle that, in a single treaty such as the WTO Agreement, all rights and obligations are cumulative and Members must comply with all of them simultaneously. In light of the principle of effective treaty interpretation (*ut res magis valeat quam pereat*), it is the duty of any treaty interpreter to read all applicable provisions, sections or parts of a treaty in a manner that does not deprive them of their *effet utile*, but, instead, gives meaning to all of them, harmoniously ensuring that all provisions have an effective meaning without any other provision being made a 'nullity'.[82] It is this principle that will be useful in

[78] Then it would be possible for a measure that falls within the scope of both GATT and GATS to be inconsistent with the GATS even if it is allowed under GATT and vice versa. M Matsushita, 'Governance of International Trade Under World Trade Organization Agreements—Relationships between World Trade Organization Agreements and Other Trade Agreements' (2004) 38(2) JWT 207.

[79] Appellate Body Report, *EC—Bananas III*, para 221; also Appellate Body Report, *Canada—Periodicals*, p 19.

[80] Appellate Body Report, *Canada—Autos*, para 160.

[81] cf Appellate Body Report, *EC—Asbestos*, para 80.

[82] Appellate Body Report, *Korea—Dairy*, para 81; also Appellate Body Report, *Argentina—Footwear (EC)*, para 81.

avoiding inevitable incompatibilities between obligations provided for in GATT and GATS.

E. The GATS at a glance

1. Measures falling within the ambit of the GATS

Much as the GATS did not entirely live up to some of the aspirations expressed at the beginning of the negotiations,[83] it constitutes a considerable, positive achievement for the world trading system. The GATS is justifiably credited with having created a more secure environment for trade in services, insofar as potential dissonances should no longer be sorted out through unilateral pressure, but are addressed by the impartial WTO dispute settlement mechanism. This is so because the DSU provisions apply horizontally, extending to all dimensions of the covered agreements, including the GATS.[84] This fact becomes more important given that the service sector in general is extraordinarily complex, consisting of approximately 150 specific, mutually exclusive sectors.[85] Moreover, this element comes to reassure the emerging economies that the new multilateral environment created a mechanism that discourages recourse to unilateral trade sanctions and reciprocity measures with respect to trade in services.

At the outset, the GATS generally refers to 'measures by Members affecting trade in services'.[86] A 'measure' is defined very broadly in the GATS to embrace any action by a Member in any form.[87] Examples of measures would include legislation of a Member or by-laws of municipal authority. For instance, in the *US—Gambling* case, three federal *criminal* laws applicable to internet gambling and other forms of remote gambling were scrutinized for their GATS consistency.[88] Rules adopted

[83] Feketekuty (n 21 above) 87.

[84] Appendix 1 DSU. To the extent that there is a difference among provisions of the covered agreements, the special and additional rules and procedures on dispute settlement contained in the covered agreements as identified in Appendix 2 should prevail over the general DSU provisions. See Art 1:2 DSU. Regarding trade in services, Appendix 2 mentions Arts XXII:3 and XXIII:3 GATS, as well as special procedural rules under the Annex on Financial Services (para 4), the Annex on Air Transport Services (para 4), and the Decision On Certain Dispute Settlement Procedures for the GATS (paras 1–5). Also PK Morrison, 'WTO Dispute Settlement in Services: Procedural and Substantive Aspects' in E-U Petersmann (ed), *International Trade Law and the GATT/WTO Dispute Settlement System*, 1997, 380.

[85] GATT, 'Services Sectoral Classification List', MTN.GNS/W/120, 10 July 1991; and Appellate Body Report, *US—Gambling*, para 180; also J Kearney, 'Benefits to Service Industries of The General Agreement on Trade in Services', US Department of Commerce, 1994; B Hoekman, 'Tentative First Steps: An Assessment of the Uruguay Round Agreement on Services', PRWP No. 1455, 1995, 14.

[86] Art I:1 GATS. cf Panel Report, *Mexico—Telecoms*, para 7.41.

[87] Art XXVIII(a) GATS.

[88] Appellate Body Report, *US—Gambling*, para 362. In the newly adopted EU Services Directive, rules of criminal law fall out of the scope of the Directive. Nevertheless, the EU Member States should not restrict the freedom to provide services 'by applying criminal law provisions

by professional bodies relative to professional qualifications and licensing would also come under this definition.

A frequently arising issue in GATT/WTO dispute resolution system on this score is whether and under which stipulations actions taken by *non*-governmental actors are attributable to a Member's government.[89] If they are, then the GATT/WTO jurisdiction is established; on the contrary, any purely private conduct remains outside the WTO competence.[90]

In public international law, private conduct can be imputed to a state if the person or entity at hand is legally empowered to exercise governmental authority.[91] Otherwise, in the absence of 'empowerment by law', there needs to be some form of instruction, direction or control by state organs for actions by non-governmental entities to be attributed to the state.[92] The interpretations developed in the GATT/WTO dispute settlement practice that are examined below would suggest that some form of *ex post* authorization or endorsement by a government could be sufficient to establish that an action was carried out on the instructions of, or under the direction or control of, a Member. This could constitute 'conduct acknowledged and adopted by a state as its own' within the meaning of Article 11 of the ILC Articles on Responsibility of States.[93] In any event, WTO law will prevail over the general rules on state responsibility according to the *lex specialis* rule of the ILC Articles on Responsibility of States (Art 55).

GATT and WTO panels have refined the meaning of the term 'measure' by referring in particular to the degree of obligation provided for in a governmental norm. Thus, deemed as a 'measure' were, inter alia:

- A law authorizing, but not requiring, a government to take certain actions;[94]
- Non-mandatory guidance by a government which recommended a certain course of action by private actors (provided that this action was accompanied by incentives or disincentives largely dependent upon governmental action for private parties to conform);[95]

which specifically regulate or affect access to or exercise of a service activity in circumvention of the rules laid down in this Directive'. See Art 1:5 of the Directive (EC) 2006/123 on services in the internal market [2006] OJ L376/36.

[89] RJ Zedalis, 'When Do the Activities of Private Parties Trigger WTO Rules?' (2007) 2 JIEL 335.

[90] cf Appellate Body Report, *Korea—Beef*, para 149.

[91] See Art 5 of the Draft Articles on Responsibility of States for internationally wrongful acts and the Commentary thereto in the United Nations, *Report of the International Law Commission—Fifty-third session (23 April–1 June and 2 July–10 August 2001)*, official Records of the General Assembly, Fifty-sixth Session, Supplement No. 10 (A/56/10), 2001, 92ff.

[92] Ibid Art 8 and the Commentary thereto, 103ff.

[93] Acknowledgement and adoption of such a conduct may be explicit (eg see the ICJ decision on the case *United States Diplomatic and Consular Staff in Tehran*, ICJ Reports 1980, 3), but it can also be inferred from the conduct of the state at hand.

[94] GATT Panel Report, *US—Superfund.*

[95] GATT Panel Report, *Japan—Semi-Conductors.*

- Informal administrative guidance that had worked as a traditional tool of government policy based on consensus and peer pressure which made the guidance effective in the context of a particular society;[96]
- Requirements which an enterprise voluntarily accepted in order to obtain an advantage from the government;[97]
- A 'hybrid' import regime which combined elements of public and private responsibility;[98]
- An action which was taken by private parties or agencies, but there was sufficient government involvement with it.[99]

According to Article 3:3 DSU, a crucial purpose of the WTO dispute settlement system is the 'prompt settlement' of situations where Members believe that their benefits under the covered agreements 'are being impaired by measures taken by another Member'. The Appellate Body ruled that 'any act or omission attributable to a WTO Member can be a measure of that Member for purposes of dispute settlement proceedings'[100] and that measures subject to WTO dispute settlement can be instruments of a Member 'consisting not only of particular acts applied only to a specific situation, but also of acts setting forth rules or norms that are intended to have general and prospective application'.[101] While an act could be a particular legislative provision, an administrative decision, a judicial decision,[102] a system of administration as a whole or overall,[103] or even an obligation to refrain from imposing particular trade restrictions, an omission can be the failure of a Member to take the required action, when a WTO law provision mandates certain action by this Member.[104] In addition, complaining Members enjoy certain discretion in the identification of the specific measure at issue pursuant to Article 6:2 DSU.[105]

Essentially, the dividing line in WTO law is between private restrictive conduct encouraged or espoused by a government as opposed to private restrictive conduct merely tolerated by the government. The former is likely to be considered as imputable to a Member's government and thus a 'measure' under WTO law, while in the latter case a government's failure to act against the private restrictive

[96] GATT Panel Report, *Japan—Agricultural Products I.*

[97] GATT Panel Report, *EEC—Parts and Components.*

[98] GATT Panel Report, *EEC—Dessert Apples.*

[99] Panel Report, *Japan—Film*, para 10.56; also Panel Report, *Canada—Dairy*, para 7.78; and Appellate Body Report, *Canada—Dairy*, paras 97, 101. Cf also Art 1.1(a)(1)(iv) SCM Agreement.

[100] Appellate Body Report, *US—Corrosion-Resistant Steel Sunset Review*, para 81; also Appellate Body Report, *US—Gambling*, para 121.

[101] Appellate Body Report, *US—Corrosion-Resistant Steel Sunset Review*, para 82; also Appellate Body Report, *US—Oil Country Tubular Goods Sunset Reviews*, para 187.

[102] cf Appellate Body Report, *US—Shrimp*, para 173.

[103] Appellate Body Report, *EC—Selected Customs Matters*, para 169.

[104] cf Appellate Body Report, *India—Patents (US)*, para 84; see also Panel Report, *Canada—Wheat Exports and Grain Imports*, para 6.16; and Appellate Body Report, *Canada—Dairy (Article 21.5—New Zealand and US II)*, para 127.

[105] Appellate Body Report, *EC—Selected Customs Matters*, para 149.

conduct would most likely escape the WTO reach. High regulatory intensity, intertwined governmental and private market-access barriers, anticompetitive market structures created or maintained in interaction between market incumbents and entities vested with regulatory powers are typical features of many services markets. Consequently, the GATT/WTO jurisprudence on what constitutes a measure in WTO law is highly pertinent to the GATS milieu for the delimitation of governmental measures from purely private conduct non-attributable to a Member's government.

In the GATS context, a 'measure' by a Member 'affecting trade in services' includes, but is not limited to,[106] measures with regard to: (a) the purchase, payment or use of a service; (b) the access to and use of, in connection with the supply of a service, services which are required by those Members to be offered to the public generally, eg essential facilities regulation;[107] and (c) the presence, including commercial presence, of persons of a Member for the supply of a service in the territory of another Member.[108] A threshold issue for the applicability of the GATS is whether the measure in question is one 'affecting trade in services' within the meaning of Article I:1 GATS.[109]

In *EC—Bananas III*, the Panel pointed out that the term 'affecting' under Article I:1 GATS has a broad scope of application and that accordingly no measures are *a priori* excluded from the scope of application of the GATS. By using such a broad term the GATS founding fathers sought to ensure that the disciplines included in the GATS would cover all measures 'bearing upon conditions of competition in supply of a service, regardless of whether the measure directly governs or indirectly affects the supply of the service'.[110] By the same token, the Appellate Body emphasized that:

> [t]he ordinary meaning of the word 'affecting' implies a measure that has 'an effect on', which indicates a *broad* scope of application. This interpretation is further reinforced by the conclusions of previous panels that the term 'affecting' in the context of Article III of the GATT is *wider* in scope than such terms as 'regulating' or 'governing'.[111] (emphasis added)

In *Canada—Autos* litigation, the Appellate Body underscored that, for a measure to be regarded as one 'affecting trade in services', the threshold issue is

[106] Thus, the list contained in this Article is illustrative and it does not intend to limit the scope of the GATS in any way. cf Panel Report, *EC—Bananas III (US)*, para 7.280; and Appellate Body Report, *EC—Bananas III*, para 220.

[107] Essential facilities regulation encompasses an array of legislative instruments that provide access to an essential input into the production process (eg telecom, gas, electricity, water, transport), owned and operated by another firm that exhibits natural monopoly characteristics.

[108] Art XXVIII(c) GATS.

[109] cf Appellate Body Report, *Canada—Autos*, paras 151–152.

[110] Panel Report, *EC—Bananas III (US)*, paras 7.281, 7.285; also Panel Report, *Canada—Autos*, para 10.231.

[111] Appellate Body Report, *EC—Bananas*, para 220; also Appellate Body Report, *US—FSC (Article 21.5—EC)*, para 209.

whether: (a) there is trade in services in the sense of Article I:2 GATS; and (b) the measure at issue 'affects' such trade in services within the meaning of Article I:1 GATS.[112] The first prong of this legal test established by the Appellate Body is satisfied if there is trade in services in one of the four modes of supply.[113] Regarding the second prong of the test the WTO adjudicating bodies should operate a market analysis. In *Canada—Autos*, the Appellate Body castigated the Panel because it based its findings on speculation as regards the situation in the Canadian market without trying to substantiate these findings.[114] It should be noted that this test should be made only in cases where the measure at issue falls within the ambit of *both* the GATT and the GATS. In *US—Gambling*, for instance, where the measures at issue clearly came exclusively under the GATS, the application of the abovementioned test would be superfluous.

In the *US—Gambling* case, the WTO adjudicating bodies pronounced on the issue of whether a 'total prohibition' of services supply (*in casu*, the cross-border supply of gambling and betting services) can constitute a 'measure' affecting trade in services for the purposes of dispute settlement. The Panel ruled, and the Appellate Body agreed, that, in the absence of a demonstration of the *source* of the prohibition, a total prohibition of services supply is rather the *collective effect* of the operation of imprecisely defined legislative provisions and other instruments and, therefore, it cannot be viewed, per se, as a single and autonomous measure affecting trade in services under Article I:1 GATS.[115] The WTO adjudicating bodies thus clarified that invoking a total prohibition is not enough for a complaining party to succeed in its complaint if that party fails to identify the specific measure that is the source of the alleged prohibition at hand, alias the source of the alleged impairment.

Hence, the concept of the effect of a measure, by covering not only measures that affect trade in services as such but also measures taken in other areas with repercussions on services—such as measures in respect of the purchase of goods—covers the potential trade as well. Consequently, this concept is given a broad interpretation under GATS keeping up that way the jurisprudence that had already been developed in the framework of the GATT 1947.

The broad reach of the GATS is only limited when it comes to the exercise of governmental authority, ie public services which are provided on a non-commercial (thus, non-profit) and non-competitive basis.[116] For a service to benefit from

[112] Appellate Body Report, *Canada—Autos*, paras 155ff. For a critical opinion regarding this two-step test, see W Zdouc, *Legal Problems Arising under the General Agreement on Trade in Services—Comparative Analysis of the GATS and GATT*, 2002, 119.

[113] Appellate Body Report, *Canada—Autos*, paras 156–157. For the four modes of supply, see Section E.2 below.

[114] Appellate Body Report, *Canada—Autos*, paras 164ff.

[115] Panel Report, *US—Gambling*, paras 6.167–6.175; and Appellate Body Report, *US—Gambling*, paras 120–126.

[116] Article I:3(b) and (c) GATS. Also EH Leroux, 'What is a "Service Supplied in the Exercise of Governmental Authority" Under Article I:3(b) and (c) of the General Agreement on Trade in

this exception both conditions have to be fulfilled, ie concurrently. Therefore, commercial supply in the absence of competitors or non-commercial supply along with other competing suppliers alone would not qualify for the exception. On the other hand, services that could come within the ambit of the exception include activities of central banks and monetary authorities and social security or public retirement systems.[117] In practice, however, the distinction between services that come within the ambit of the GATS and services that fulfil the requirements of Article I:3(c) GATS and consequently are excluded from the scope of the Agreement can be a daunting task, all the more so because nowadays any public good can be turned into a tradable commodity.[118] Notably the requirement of a non-competitive relationship makes it hard to *a priori* exclude any services sector. Having said this, it is likely that the conditions of supply the GATS calls for in order to exclude a service from its sectoral coverage will be interpreted narrowly.[119]

The GATS includes not only three levels of government (described as 'central', 'regional', and 'local'), but also non-governmental bodies in the exercise of powers delegated by these three levels of government.[120] The latter element takes cognizance of the fact that, in the service sector, it is very common that private entities, notably professional associations, are vested with the right to exercise functions of a public character in particular instances.[121] In addition, the GATS deviates from the GATT practice that sought to bind governmental entities, either directly, in the case of Members' governments, or indirectly, in the case of sub-national governments.[122]

Services?' (2006) 40(3) JWT 348. It is important to emphasize here that the coexistence of governmental and private services in the same industry (eg health services) does not mean that they are in competition in the sense of Art I:3(c). See WTO, 'Market Access: Unfinished Business—Post-Uruguay Round Inventory and Issues', Special Studies No 6, 2001, 124.

[117] Indeed, there are sectoral exclusions concerning financial services (Art 1(b) (i)–(iii) of the Financial Services Annex) and air transport services (para 2(a) and (b) of the Air Transport Services Annex). The exclusion of social security or public retirement systems concerns only financial services. D Luff, 'Regulation of Health Services and International Trade Law' in A Mattoo and P Sauvé (eds), *Domestic Regulation and Service Trade Liberalization*, 2003, 196.

[118] M Krajewski, 'Public Services and Trade Liberalization: Mapping the Legal Framework' (2003) 2 JIEL 344, 354; also R Howse and E Türk, 'The WTO Negotiations on Services: The Regulatory State Up for Grabs' (2002) 9(1–2) Canada Watch 3.

[119] WTO, CTS, 'Report of the Meeting Held on 14 October 1998', S/C/M/30, 12 November 1998, 5. The same narrow interpretation is to be found in the ECJ case-law. See, for instance, Case 147/86 *Commission v Greece* [1988] ECR 1637, para 7; Case C-114/97 *Commission v Spain* [1998] ECR I-6717, para 34; and Case 2/74 *Reyners* [1974] ECR 631, paras 51ff.

[120] Article I:3(a) GATS.

[121] cf Art 5 of the Draft Articles on Responsibility of States (n 91 above); also Trebilcock and Howse (n 44 above) 360.

[122] cf Art XXIV:12 GATT; also W Goode, 'Services' in K Anderson (ed), *Strengthening the Global Trading System: From GATT to WTO*, 1996, 87.

The sectoral classification generally used to schedule commitments under the GATS[123] contains 11 broad services sectors (each divided into several sub-sectors) and one residual category of 'other services'. It concerns international transactions involving such diverse fields as businesses, communication, construction, distribution, educational, environmental, financial, health-related and social, tourism and travel-related, recreational, cultural and sporting, and transport services. These sectors are further divided into sub-sectors and in some cases, sub-sub-sectors.

Interestingly enough, while the GATS defines the term 'service' to include any service in any sector, it does not entail a direct, straightforward definition of the term 'service'. This reflects Members' failure to agree on a generally accepted definition during the Uruguay Round negotiations. It bears mention nonetheless that the GATT does not define the analogous terms of 'product' or 'goods' either.

2. The structure of the GATS

The ambit of the GATS *rationae materiae* hinges on the concept of 'trade in services'. The GATS does not include a definition of what a 'service' exactly is. Rather, inspired by theoretical work done in the 1980s,[124] it defines trade in services by identifying four modes through which a 'service' can be delivered. The four modes of supply are the following:[125]

(i) 'Cross-border supply', which—like in trade in goods—occurs when a service crosses a physical frontier.[126] For example, a domestic consumer takes

[123] GATT (n 85 above). This list refers to the more detailed UN Central Product Classification (CPC) system. It deviates from the CPC classification primarily in telecommunications and financial services and to a lesser extent in transport services. Provisional CPC, Statistical Papers, Series M No. 77, United Nations (1991), 7; also Appellate Body Report, *US—Gambling*, para 172.

[124] *Inter alia*, Bhagwati (n 45 above) 139; G Sampson and R Snape, 'Identifying the Issues on Trade in Services' (1985) 8(2) The World Economy 172; also P Chang, G Karsenty, A Mattoo, and J Richtering, 'GATS, the Modes of Supply and Statistics on Trade in Services' (1999) 33(3) JWT 94; C Arup, *The New World Trade Organization Agreements: Globalizing Law through Services and Intellectual Property*, 2000, 121.

[125] Article I:2 GATS and XXVIII(b) GATS. During the GATS negotiations the original word 'delivery' was replaced by the word 'supply' because the latter was understood as covering those measures directly governing as well as those indirectly affecting the supply of services. See also Panel Report, *EC—Bananas III (US)*, para 7.281 and fn 455. In *US—Gambling*, however, 'supply' and 'delivery' were used interchangeably. See, for example, Panel Report, *US—Gambling*, paras 6.280ff.

[126] The scope of the four modes may not be so clear in practice. In *Mexico—Telecoms*, for instance, the Panel erroneously considered the measure at issue as falling under mode 1, since the delivery of the service was taking place by a United States' operator to a United States' customer *within* the United States' territory, regardless of the fact that the termination of the service was taking place *within* Mexico. Panel Report, *Mexico—Telecoms*, paras 7.25–7.45. Furthermore, the *1993 Scheduling Guidelines* clarify that in the case of a service supply through mode 1 '...the service supplier is *not* present *within* the territory of the Member where the service is *delivered*'. GATT, 'Scheduling of Initial Commitments in Trade in Services: Explanatory Note' (hereinafter '*1993*

a loan or purchases an insurance cover from a financial institution located abroad;

(ii) 'Consumption abroad', whereby consumers buy services abroad, sometimes by physically moving to the location of the suppliers, as in the case of tourism services, or by sending their property abroad, as in the case of ship repair services;

(iii) 'Commercial presence', whereby, for instance, a foreign bank or transport company establishes a branch or subsidiary in another Member's territory to deliver services;[127] and

(iv) 'Temporary movement of natural persons', whereby, for example, natural persons supply construction services in the territory of another Member.[128] This mode relates both to independent service suppliers and to employees of juridical persons supplying services, covering potentially the presence, for instance, of independent financial consultants as well as intra-corporate transferees.

It follows that the scope of the GATS is wider than that of the GATT 1994, since the latter covers only measures impinging on products, while the former explicitly encompasses not only measures affecting services per se, but also measures affecting service suppliers. It bears noting here that service suppliers can be *both* juridical and natural persons pursuant to Article XXVIII(g) and (j) GATS. Thus, unlike in disputes addressing trade in goods, panels dealing with disputes regarding trade in services may, depending on the circumstances of the case, be called to pronounce on the treatment of a given Member vis-à-vis another Member's services *and/or* service suppliers.

In *EC—Bananas*, for instance, the Panel found, and the Appellate Body agreed, that vertically integrated companies, ie juridical persons, whose main functions relate to trade in goods, can still be regarded as service suppliers within the scope of the GATS if they are *also* engaged in providing services and are therefore affected *in their capacity as service suppliers* by a particular measure of a Member in their supply of such services.[129] Furthermore, a dispute dealing with trade in services could even relate exclusively to the treatment accorded to natural persons in their capacity as service suppliers (eg qualification requirements for professionals).

Scheduling Guidelines'), MTN.GNS/W/164, 3 September 1993, para 19(a). Ironically, while the Panel identified this in para 7.43 of its Report, it was still led to the false conclusion. In the Panel's view, the *completion* of the customer's communications was taking place in *another* country. Hence the Panel opined that the delivery of the service occurred in Mexico, which was not the case at all. Panel Report, *Mexico—Telecoms*, para 7.42; also D Neven and PC Mavroidis, 'Mexico—Measures Affecting Telecommunications Services (WT/DS204/R) A Comment on "El Mess in TELMEX"' in H Horn and PC Mavroidis (eds), *The WTO Case Law of 2003*, 2006, 188.

[127] Also Art XXVIII(d) GATS.

[128] Annex on Movement of Natural Persons, para 2.

[129] Panel Report, *EC—Bananas III (US)*, para 7.320; and Appellate Body Report, *EC—Bananas III* (US), para 227.

The architecture of the GATS hinges on a three-tier structure:

(i) A framework Agreement, which defines the obligations accepted by the Members of the Agreement;
(ii) Eight Annexes,[130] which address horizontal (eg movement of natural persons) and sector-specific (eg financial services, telecommunications) matters; and
(iii) Schedules of Specific Commitments (hereinafter 'Schedules') that Members have chosen to undertake and which apply to services sectors, sub-sectors or activities listed therein, subject to terms, qualifications, or conditions.[131]

The most important GATS general obligations are the Most-Favoured-Nation (MFN) treatment under Article II,[132] that is, the obligation to refrain from discriminating among trading partners ('favour one, favour all'), and Transparency under Article III.[133] They apply across the board to all services sectors,[134] although MFN exemptions (the so-called 'once-off temporary exemptions') to the GATS Article II:1 obligation are permitted in specific services sectors. This is on the stipulation that the exemptions are identified in each Member's list of MFN exemptions. This list is a *negative* one in that Members are not allowed to maintain or adopt derogations from the MFN obligation other than those itemized therein. Such exemptions should not, *in principle*, extend beyond 10 years (namely, one-shot basis, subject to a ten-year sunset provision).[135] In addition, no new exemptions are allowed, unless a Member asks for a waiver under Article IX:3 of the WTO Agreement.[136] The reviews of MFN exemptions that occurred in recent years reveal Members'

130 JJ Schott, *The Uruguay Round: An Assessment*, 1994, 104.

131 The Schedules are an integral part of the GATS pursuant to Art XX:3 GATS. This indicates that, while each Schedule reflects the commitments made by *one* Member, the Schedules represent a *common* agreement among *all* Members. Appellate Body Report, *US—Gambling*, paras 159–160; also Appellate Body Report, *EC—Computer Equipment*, para 109. Commitments in Members' Schedules are part of the terms of the GATS and thus are to be interpreted in accordance with the rules of treaty interpretation as set out in the *Vienna Convention* (Arts 31–33). cf Panel Report, *Mexico—Telecoms*, para 7.15; and Panel Report, *US—Gambling*, paras 6.44–6.45. See also, generally, I Van Damme, 'The Interpretation of Schedules of Commitments' (2007) 41(1) Journal of World Trade 1.

132 A Mattoo, 'MFN and the GATS' in T Cottier and P Mavroidis (eds), *Regulatory Barriers and the Principle of Non-Discrimination in World Trade Law*, 2000, 51.

133 For a thorough analysis of this provision, see P Delimatsis, 'Article III GATS' in R Wolfrum, P-T Stoll, and C Feinäugle (eds), *Max-Planck Commentaries on World Trade Law, Volume 6: WTO-Trade in Services*, 2008.

134 cf WTO, Working Group on the Interaction between Trade and Competition Policy, 'The Fundamental WTO Principles of National Treatment, Most-Favoured-Nation Treatment and Transparency', WT/WGTCP/W/114, 14 April 1999, p 11.

135 GATS Annex on Art II Exemptions, para 6; also Sauvé (n 1 above) 81; and OECD, 'Trade in Services: A Roadmap to GATS MFN Exemptions', TD/TC/WP(2001)/25/FINAL, 2001, 4.

136 GATS Annex on Art II Exemptions, para 2.

unwillingness to terminate these derogations from the MFN obligation.[137] This does not seem to be compatible with the GATS overall objective to build a framework that entails predictable and transparent conditions, and thus a rules-based system for international trade in services.

3. The mechanics of liberalization commitments under GATS

The GATS aims to establish a legally binding set of commitments to enhancing predictability and transparency under the tenet of progressive liberalization.[138] It mandates that WTO countries liberalize their service industries and gradually phase out barriers to trade in services. Under the current scheduling approach, nothing in the GATS compels Members to bind or liberalize any specific sector, and a country could indefinitely choose to keep a sector outside the scope of its commitments. This is so because the GATS is a 'bottom-up' treaty in the sense that it is for each Member to decide where and when to undertake liberalization commitments for different services sectors and modes of supply.

Several scholars suggested that the GATS should have followed the approach adopted, *inter alia*, by NAFTA or ANZCERTA, which is based on a 'negative (or top-down) list'.[139] According to the latter, all sectors and modes of supply are automatically liberalized unless there are limitations to the contrary. Arguably, this approach enhances transparency, since potential suppliers can be reassured that, except for the scheduled limitations, they enjoy full market access and national treatment in all services sectors. Nonetheless, under the WTO, Members have always shown a strong resolve to maintain the 'bottom-up' approach to scheduling. A possible drawback of the negative list approach is that it requires a higher level of capacity in negotiating countries,[140] while it imposes full liberalization for services that may become technically feasible *after* the preparation of the Schedules. Regardless of the value that each of the two liberalization methods has, in the end, liberalization will occur as a result of domestic policymaking rather than of scheduling techniques.[141]

[137] Also R Adlung, 'Services Negotiations in the Doha Round: Lost in Flexibility?' (2006) 4 JIEL 869–870.

[138] See GATS Preamble, second recital. The *US—Gambling* Panel noted that '[p]rogressive liberalization entails including more sectors in Members' schedules and reduction or elimination of limitations, terms, conditions and qualifications on market access and national treatment through successive rounds of negotiations'. Panel Report, *US—Gambling*, para 6.313.

[139] *Inter alia*, B Hoekman, 'Assessing the General Agreement on Trade in Services' in W Martin and LA Winters (eds), *The Uruguay Round and the Developing Economies*, 1995, 328, 347; G Feketekuty, 'Assessing and Improving the Architecture of the GATS' in P Sauvé and RM Stern (eds), *GATS 2000: New Directions in Services Trade Liberalisation*, 2000, 97.

[140] UNCTAD, 'Report of the Commission on Trade in Goods and Services, and Commodities on its Eleventh Session', TD/B/COM.1/88, 2007, 27.

[141] WTO (n 116 above) 119.

The main liberalizing tools of the GATS, ie the provisions relating to market access (Art XVI GATS) and national treatment (Art XVII GATS),[142] are to be found in Part III of the Agreement. They only apply to services that are inscribed in the Members' Schedules where specific commitments on market access and national treatment are listed, typically in the form of limitations or conditions. Such limitations and conditions may be either horizontal (cross-sectoral) or sector-specific, and are listed for each of the four modes of supply.

Specific commitments with respect to services sectors or sub-sectors are categorized according to the *Services Sectoral Classification List*.[143] Although the use of this List was not compulsory and Members could theoretically use their own sub-sectoral classifications or definitions, most Members adopted this List as a basis for scheduling their commitments. As noted earlier, this List is based on the UN CPC system. Therefore, if a Member undertakes commitments based on this List (and, *a fortiori*, the CPC), the CPC becomes the document that the WTO judiciary will rely on in order to identify the scope of a Member's commitments.[144] In *US—Gambling*, the Appellate Body pronounced on the relationship between the CPC and the *Services Sectoral Classification List* and went a step further by endorsing the rather broad view first expressed by the Panel that in the absence of any indication to the contrary, 'Members were assumed to have relied on W/120 [ie the Services Sectoral Classification List] and the corresponding CPC references.'[145]

The GATS approach concerning the listing of commitments can be regarded as a hybrid one,[146] combining a *positive* list approach to sectoral coverage (bottom-up listing of sectors and/or sub-sectors) with a *negative* list approach to measures entered into a Member's Schedule that violate the market access and/or national treatment provisions (top-down identification of conditions and limitations with respect to market access and national treatment).[147] Members first choose which sectors to list *positively* in their Schedules. Afterwards, within the sectors they have inscribed, they must make up their mind as regards the limitations or conditions, if any, that they wish to maintain on market access and national treatment with respect to the sectors that they scheduled.[148] If a

[142] F Weiss, 'The General Agreement on Trade in Services 1994' (1995) 32 CML Rev 1207, 1209; also A Mattoo, 'National Treatment in the GATS: Corner Stone or Pandora's Box?' (1997) 31(1) JWT 107; C Arup (n 124 above) 113. See also Chapter III.D below.

[143] GATT (n 85 above).

[144] Panel Report, *EC—Bananas III (US)*, para 7.289.

[145] Appellate Body Report, *US—Gambling*, para 204; and Panel Report, *US—Gambling*, para 6.106.

[146] Hoekman and Sauvé (n 1 above) 34; B Hoekman (n 139 above) 337.

[147] GATT, 'Note of the Meeting of 17–27 September 1991', MTN.GNS/45, 18 October 1991, para 16.

[148] When scheduling limitations, each Member is free to impose its conditions and qualifications. For instance, a Member could allow full market access in a given services sector, but only for a certain mode of supply. For instance, in the *US—Gambling* case, the Panel appeared to suggest that it would have been GATS-consistent if the United States had exempted mode 1, ie the

Member does not enter limitations, qualifications and conditions in the sectors or sub-sectors that it scheduled (that is, 'None' in the respective column),[149] there should be no barrier for the foreign service suppliers with respect to the access to, and operation in, the respective markets. In this case, a Member commits itself not to maintain measures that prohibit the use of one, several or all means of supply of that service. It also commits itself to allow full market access and/or provide national treatment with respect to all services falling within the relevant sector or sub-sector.[150]

Again, once a Member lists in its Schedule a limitation in one of the market access or national treatment columns for one of the four modes of supply, it is presumed that, other than this limitation, that Member is open for that mode in the sector at issue. In that case, this Member does not have the freedom to make a particular limitation more onerous nor is it free to introduce an entirely new restrictive measure in its regime or its Schedule that contravenes its previous commitment. In other words, it is fixed at the existing level of openness. Hence, once made, liberalization commitments cannot be withdrawn unless the Member at hand compensates its trading partners according to Article XXI GATS.[151] Yet this is not necessary when a Member inscribes an 'Unbound' for the services sector at stake. In such case, a Member retains its flexibility as regards the imposition of restrictions on market access and national treatment.[152]

It follows that the level of liberalization for each Member is reflected in the number of restrictions that are included in its Schedule in conjunction with the number of services sectors that are listed therein. Under the hybrid approach, 'free' trade in any particular mode of supply refers to the services sector inscribed without any qualification in a Member's Schedule. Unless noted otherwise, commitments made in Schedules are binding. In addition, Article XVIII GATS offers

delivery through electronic means, from their full market access commitment in gambling and betting services. Panel Report, *US—Gambling*, paras 6.285–6.286.

[149] cf Panel Report, *US—Gambling*, para 6.278.

[150] Panel Report, *US—Gambling*, paras 6.287, 6.290. The Panel added that, in accordance with the principle of technological neutrality that is inherent in the GATS (as there is no distinction as to the different technological means through which a service may be supplied), 'a [full] market access commitment for mode 1 [ie cross-border supply] implies the right for other Members' suppliers to supply a service through all means of delivery, whether by mail, telephone, Internet etc., unless otherwise specified in a Member's Schedule.' Ibid para 6.285–6.287. Fairly surprisingly, the complainant, *in casu* the United States, did not appeal these findings with regard to restrictions on the supply of *part* of a sector, or with respect to restrictions on a *part* of a mode of supply. See Appellate Body Report, *US—Gambling*, para 220.

[151] See, however, Art XII GATS. Members adopted procedures concerning the modification of Schedules. WTO, *Procedures for the Implementation of Article XXI of the General Agreement on Trade in Services (GATS) (Modification of Schedules)*, S/L/80, 29 October 1999. They equally adopted procedures for the rectifications or improvements of existing Schedules. WTO, CTS, *Procedures for the Certification of Rectifications or Improvements to Schedules of Specific Commitments*, S/L/84, 18 April 2000.

[152] WTO, *2001 Scheduling Guidelines*, S/L/92, para 46.

the possibility for countries to inscribe additional positive commitments not dealt with under Articles XVI or XVII GATS.

As one can infer, the Agreement is at its most voluntary at the initial point of deciding whether to open a specific services sector and thus list it positively in the Schedule. According to the 'bottom-up' approach, there is no automatic inclusion of sectors. Through this system, the onus is cast on Members to delineate restrictions on the scope of the sectors they wish to reserve. Restrictions to trade in services will be dismantled through subsequent rounds of negotiations by virtue of Article XIX GATS.[153]

4. GATS versus GATT: So similar, so different

In the absence of any other guidance as to the manner in which a multilateral legal framework governing trade in services should be drafted, the GATS essentially borrowed the central concepts of the GATT system (MFN, national treatment, transparency, list of general exceptions, all these enjoy a GATT pedigree) and applied them to the GATS.[154] Nonetheless, some refinements and alterations to the relatively simple GATT structure were necessary because of the practical differences between trade in services and trade in goods.[155]

In spite of its nature as one of the three rather unequal pillars on which the juridical system of the WTO rests, the GATS enjoys considerable latitude in at least three different ways.[156] The first relates to the definition of trade in services, as four modes of supply have been identified under the GATS. The second leeway concerns the opening of services sectors. Under the GATS, the positive list approach enables a Member to pick and choose those services for which it is willing to provide market access and national treatment to other Members. Another flexibility indicator is noticeable in terms of measures and restrictions. A Member, according to a negative list approach, can specify restrictions, qualifications, and conditions on both market access and national treatment, and deviations from the MFN principle, or even may leave entire services sectors out of its Schedule.[157]

[153] P Delimatsis, 'Article XIX GATS' in R Wolfrum, P-T Stoll, and C Feinäugle (eds), *Max-Planck Commentaries on World Trade Law, Volume 6: WTO-Trade in Services*, 2008.

[154] Nevertheless, several GATS provisions such as Arts IX or VI:3 do not have any GATT counterpart.

[155] D Barth, 'Liberalizing International Trade in Services: The European Perspective' in K Deutsch and B Speyer (eds), *The WTO Millennium Round—Free Trade in the 21st century*, 2001, 86; also A Mattoo, R Rathindran, and A Subramanian, 'Measuring Services Trade Liberalization and its Impact on Economic Growth: An Illustration' (2006) 21 Journal of Economic Integration 64.

[156] N Mukherjee, 'GATS and the Millennium Round of Multilateral Negotiations: Selected Issues from the Perspective of the Developing Countries' (1999) 33(4) JWT 87–88.

[157] However, all Members were required to schedule at least one sector. B Hoekman, (n 85 above) 11; also European Commission, *GATS: The General Agreement on Trade in Services—A Guide for Business*, 1995, 42.

Admittedly, then, the GATS displays many development-friendly features that cannot readily be found in other WTO Agreements.[158] In that regard, some countries feel that it could even constitute a model for other multilateral agreements. The 'development dimension' is mainly reflected in:

- The flexibility of the bottom-up approach, ie not only in the choice of sectors to be opened up, but also in the timing by which liberalization measures are undertaken, thereby ensuring that Members can liberalize at their own pace;
- The principle of progressive liberalization and the notion of successive rounds;
- The recognized right of Members to regulate;
- The GATS provisions on appropriate flexibility for developing countries;[159]
- The right to technical assistance to be provided by the Secretariat pursuant to Article XXV:2 GATS;
- The inducement to liberalize unilaterally, mainly addressed to developing countries and LDCs, by giving credits to Members that liberalized their markets since previous negotiations without undertaking commitments under GATS;[160] and
- Of course, the recognition of the movement of natural persons as the fourth mode of delivering services.

Nevertheless, the GATS has deficiencies similar to the GATT when it comes to special and differential treatment. More specifically, it lacks a specific mechanism that would allow operationalizing Article IV GATS.[161] Of course, such provisions have always been problematic as regards their enforcement, because they are either drafted too broadly or due to the fact that they use hortatory, 'best-efforts' language.[162] At the Doha Ministerial Conference, Members confirmed

[158] cf OECD, *GATS: The Case for Open Services Markets*, 2002, 70; JM Finger and JJ Nogués, 'The Unbalanced Uruguay Round Outcome: The New Areas in Future WTO Negotiations', PRWP No 2732, 2001, 16.

[159] *Inter alia*, Art XIX:2 GATS. In May 2003, the LDC Group presented a draft text on the modalities for their special treatment, taking into account the development-friendly provisions of Arts IV and XIX GATS. WTO, CTS (Special Session), 'Draft Modalities for the Special Treatment for Least-Developed Country Members in the Negotiations on Trade in Services', Communication from the LDC Group, TN/S/W/13, 7 May 2003. The CTS ultimately adopted a less ambitious text. WTO, CTS (Special Session), 'Modalities for the Special Treatment for Least-Developed Country Members in the Negotiations on Trade in Services', TN/S/13, 5 September 2003.

[160] Article XIX:3 GATS; also WTO, 'Guidelines and Procedures for the Negotiations on Trade in Services', S/L/93, 29 March 2001, para 13. Members agreed on the way that these autonomously taken liberalization measures should be treated in 2003. WTO, CTS (Special Session), 'Modalities for the Treatment of Autonomous Liberalization', T/N/S/6, 10 March 2003.

[161] WTO, 'Developing Countries and the Multilateral Trading System: Past and Present', Background Note by the Secretariat, 26 March 1999, 26.

[162] C Michalopoulos, 'The Role of Special and Differential Treatment for Developing Countries in GATT and the World Trade Organization', PRWP No 2388, 2000, 17; also B Hoekman, C Michalopoulos, and LA Winters, 'More Favorable and Differential Treatment of Developing Countries: Toward a New Approach in the World Trade Organization', PRWP No 3107, 2003; also OECD, 'The Role of "Special and Differential Treatment" at the Trade, Competition and Development Interface', COM/TD/DAFFEE/CLP(2001)21/FINAL, 2001, 15.

the significance of special and differential treatment and called for a review of the WTO special and differential treatment provisions with the objective of 'strengthening them and making them more precise, effective and operational'.[163]

Even so, when compared to other WTO Agreements, the GATS structure can be considered as the most responsive to development concerns already due to the fact that it allows countries to open up services sectors according to their development needs. Recall that the use of quantitative restrictions is legitimate under GATS when no commitments are undertaken, whereas national treatment is a negotiable commitment, rather than a general obligation.

F. Dancing in the dark? The GATS' tentative steps towards liberalization of trade in services

The GATS heralded a new age in terms of creating multilateral disciplines in a new—for the negotiators and trade-policymakers—territory. The fact that this Agreement was only a first reconnoitring, somewhat tentative and imperfect step in the direction of trade and investment liberalization in services elucidates the fairly high degree of latitude that the GATS exhibits. Negotiators were clueless as to how to deal with policies affecting international transactions in services. Thus, the negotiating process was inevitably characterized by an extensive degree of 'learning-by-doing'.

The breadth of the GATS coverage, the novelty of the issues at stake, the sectoral diversity, the specificities associated with services where the state used to be the monopoly supplier or was actively involved in their supply, the regulatory intensity of several services sectors, and the inherent complexity of the GATS due to the multiple modes of supply are only few of the justifications for the deficiencies of the GATS. Not surprisingly, then, the GATS, more than a decade after its creation, can be regarded as work in progress. For instance, several GATS provisions represent unfinished business. These provisions, full of ambiguities and loopholes, constitute evidence of the complexity and the novelty of the issues associated with trade in services that Members had to tackle during the Uruguay Round, but they are also a reminder that the services negotiations in the Uruguay Round were completed under extreme time pressure. The negotiations fell short of the high expectations notably in four rulemaking areas; that is, domestic regulation (Art VI), emergency safeguard measures (Art X), government procurement (Art XIII) and subsidies (Art XV).[164] These areas

[163] WTO, *Doha Ministerial Declaration*, adopted on 14 November 2001, WT/MIN(01)/DEC/W/1, para 44.

[164] Also P Sauvé, 'Completing the GATS Framework: Safeguards, Subsidies, and Government Procurement' in B Hoekman, A Mattoo, and P English (eds), *Development, Trade, and the WTO: A Handbook*, 2002, 326.

constitute the so-called 'built-in' agenda for the current services negotiations that have started in early 2000. Members agreed to put in an effort to complete the negotiations on Articles VI:4, XIII, and XV prior to the conclusion of the negotiations on specific commitments.[165] After several missed deadlines, Members were urged at the Hong Kong Ministerial Conference to conclude their respective mandates under the four abovementioned provisions until the end of the Doha Round.[166]

In any event, the fact that the world of multilateral commercial diplomacy now contains a body of legally binding disciplines aimed at the liberalization of trade and investment in services accompanied by a powerful dispute settlement and enforcement mechanism hardly surprises.[167] What the processes of economic growth and development seem to be all, or increasingly, about is the promotion of greater efficiency in services industries, including first and foremost a strong services infrastructure. Services account on average for close to three-quarters of production and employment in most OECD countries and, in many emerging markets, for shares that are rapidly converging towards the levels of developed economies.[168]

Indeed, the need for the multilateral trading system to catch up with the times appears all the more justified when viewed against the growing importance of services in world trade.[169] Sweeping advances in information technology, escalating specialization and product diversification, as well as government policies of deregulation, privatization and unilateral liberalization in investment and trade regimes, have all given rise to services becoming more tradable; in other words, they have brought about a 'tradability revolution' in the services milieu.[170] They have further facilitated the provision of services at much lower cost and allowed competition to emerge in markets that were traditionally regarded as natural monopolies and, consequently, ushered in the rapid growth of trade in services

[165] WTO (n 160 above) para 7. Regarding Art X, Members missed the deadline of 15 March 2002 and accordingly decided that, subject to the outcome of the mandate, the results of the negotiations shall enter into force not later than the date of entry into force of the results of the current services negotiations. WTO, CTS, 'Fifth Decision on Negotiations on Emergency Safeguard Measures', S/L/159, 17 March 2004; also M Marconini, 'Emergency Safeguard Measures in the GATS: Beyond Feasible and Desirable', UNCTAD/DITC/TNCD/2005/4, 2005; also R Adlung, 'Negotiations on Safeguards and Subsidies in Services: A Never-Ending Story?' (2007) 2 JIEL 235.

[166] Annex C to the *Hong Kong Ministerial Declaration*, adopted on 18 December 2005, WT/MIN(05)/DEC, paras 4, 5.

[167] Whereas services are much more regulation-intensive than goods, nullification or impairment will be more difficult to prove due to the inherent weakness of the GATS commitment mechanism. B Hoekman and PA Messerlin, 'Liberalizing Trade in Services: Reciprocal Negotiations and Regulatory Reform' in P Sauvé and RM Stern (eds), *GATS 2000: New Directions in Services Trade Liberalization*, 2000, 487.

[168] See above Section I.B.

[169] WTO, 'Economic Effects on Services Liberalization', S/C/W/26, Background Note by the Secretariat, 7 October 1997.

[170] UNCTAD (n 33 above) 148.

throughout the last years in comparison to merchandise trade. Undeniably, many service suppliers sighed with pleasure when this new framework for trade in services emerged from the Uruguay Round.

The GATS leaves plenty of room for liberalization in the future. A country's participation in the GATS does not necessarily mean that it has made meaningful commitments towards market openness. The numbers demonstrate that the coverage of the services sectors and the modes of supply is limited; the Agreement covers only 47 per cent of sectors (including the key telecommunications and financial sectors) in industrial countries and 16 per cent in developing countries, with numerous limitations.[171] An instructive measurement of trade restrictions under this Agreement is the percentage of services sectors that has experienced *full* international competition in the aftermath of the Uruguay Round: 28 per cent in industrial countries and a paltry seven per cent in developing countries.[172]

Despite the antithetical interpretations regarding the novelties that the GATS brought with it and the ambitious expectations that have been belied to a certain extent, the scholars concur in the ascertainment that reducing barriers to trade in services is in its infancy. Little actual liberalization—understood as implying a rolling back of existing discriminatory measures or measures impeding market access—was locked in (ie made legally binding) in the first round of services negotiations. In many cases, Members scheduled commitments that reflect a less liberal regime than the one actually applied, thereby implying a negative signalling effect.[173] It follows that the development and welfare prospects abound in services.

The lack of meaningful liberalization to date can also be attributed to the fact that Members approached these negotiations based on reciprocity. Nonetheless, in the case of services there was no clear understanding of the economic impact or the costs of restricted market access and the potential welfare gains from liberalization. Thus, in the absence of any reliable data[174] regarding gains from liberalization or 'concessions' made, reciprocity did not work as well as it did in the case of goods and thus any reluctance in undertaking liberalizing commitments in services can be justified.[175] A form of sectoral reciprocity appeared during the Uruguay Round negotiations, but, again, with limited results.

[171] Over one-quarter of developing countries (ie 22 out of 78 countries) scheduled less than 3% of all services. B Hoekman and CAP Braga, 'Protection and Trade in Services: A Survey', PRWP No 1747, 1997, 26.

[172] B Hoekman (n 85 above) 18; also R Adlung and M Roy, 'Turning Hills into Mountains? Current Commitments under the GATS and Prospects for Change' (2005) 39(6) JWT 1168ff.

[173] B Hoekman, 'Towards a More Balanced and Comprehensive Services Agreement' in J Schott (ed), *The WTO After Seattle*, 2000. This practice is well known from the GATT. P Sauvé, 'Services' in OECD, *Regionalism and the Multilateral Trading System*, 2003, 33.

[174] *But* see European Commission, IMF, OECD, UN, UNCTAD, and WTO, *Manual on Statistics of International Trade in Services*, 2002; also WTO, CTS, *A Review of Statistics on Trade Flows in Services*, S/C/W/27/Add. 2, 11 July 2006.

[175] SM Stephenson, 'Approaches to Liberalizing Services', PRWP No 2107, 1999, 27.

Looking forward, there is a substantial potential for the further liberalization of numerous services sectors in both developing and developed economies. Given that the competitiveness of these sectors varies across countries, negotiations that involve a wide range of sectors and all the modes of supply offer the most room for trade-offs and mutually advantageous agreements.[176] That is not the case when negotiations cover a few sectors in which one Member (or group of Members) has a comparative advantage (eg the construction services sector for developing countries, or financial services for developed ones).[177] As Mattoo pointed out, '... [t]here is considerable scope for the WTO to play its traditional role of facilitating reciprocal liberalization, not only by exploiting trade-offs across goods and services but also *within* services' (emphasis added).[178]

Many of the indigenous shortcomings of the GATS can be ascribed to the 'learning-by-doing' characteristic of the Uruguay Round negotiations. Negotiating in unexplored, rather impalpable waters, especially among a large and noticeably heterogeneous group of countries, across an equally broad spectrum of sectoral eccentricities and on behalf of ever-shifting coalitions of industry supporters and opponents, could scarcely have been expected to generate perfection *ab initio*.[179] As a result, negotiators may take solace in the fact that many of the rulemaking inadequacies described above can be rectified.

[176] A Krueger, 'The Developing Countries and the Next Round of Multilateral Trade Negotiations', PRWP No 2118, 1999, 22. A trade-off in services can be a mode 3-mode 4 exchange between developed and developing countries. B Hoekman and M Kostecki, *The Political Economy of the World Trading System: The WTO and Beyond*, 2001, 272.

[177] The World Bank, *Entering the 21st Century: World Development Report 1999/2000*, 1999, 65.

[178] A Mattoo, 'Services in a Development Round', Trade Note 11, World Bank, 2003, 4. See, however, P Harms, A Mattoo, and L Schuknecht, *Explaining Liberalization Commitments in Financial Services Trade*, PRWP No 2999, 2003, 24.

[179] B Hoekman (n 139 above) 329.

II

Barriers to Trade in Services[1]

A. Introductory remarks

Large in domestic economic terms and increasingly important in trade terms, the service sector remains heavily regulated for a variety of reasons in many countries, both developed and developing, often in ways that generate substantial benefits as well as costs, at both domestic and international level. Heavy regulation is also an inevitable by-product of the nature of services. Usually, services can neither be sent from one place to another, nor be monitored, measured and taxed due to their intangible nature.[2]

Thus, services transactions frequently require that the supplier and the receiver of the service be in proximity to one another.[3] Consequently, international transactions in services commonly entail cross-border movement of the means of producing the service, or local establishment of the service supplier, but not movement of the service itself. Put differently, services are inextricably connected with international factor mobility (ie capital, labour). In fact, most services transactions involve factor mobility as one of their integral aspects. The direct consequence of this observation is that, if a government seeks to exclude or impede services transactions, any restrictions on factor inflow can suffice.[4]

According to the GATT experience, border measures—tariffs and quotas—have been prominent barriers when the aim was the protection of domestic industries producing goods from foreign competition. Nonetheless, such measures are ineffective means of protecting domestic service suppliers.[5] Border measures in general and *ad valorem* tariffs in particular are often difficult, and usually

[1] For an early definition of such barriers, see G Feketekuty, *International Trade in Services: An Overview and Blueprint for Negotiations*, 1988, 131.

[2] For the special nature of services, see B Hoekman and M Kostecki, *The Political Economy of the World Trading System: The WTO and Beyond*, 2001, 239. Messerlin puts into question this theory that considers services as totally different from goods. For instance, intangibility and non-storability are also traits that characterize several goods. P Messerlin, *La Nouvelle Organization Mondiale du Commerce*, 1995, 224.

[3] RH Snape, 'Reaching Effective Agreements Covering Services' in AO Krueger (ed), *The WTO as an International Organization*, 1998, 280.

[4] J Bhagwati, 'Trade in Services and the Multilateral Trade Negotiations' in VN Balasubramanyam (ed), *Writings on International Economics*, 1997, 453.

[5] Hoekman and Kostecki (n 2 above) 242.

expensive, to apply in order to control the entry of services or service suppliers at the border due to the invisible nature of most services transactions.[6] Take the case of a cross-border financial services delivery. This delivery is indeed invisible and instantaneous and therefore no customs official can stop its cross-border movement. What is more, when an individual is stopped at the border upon her return to her country, she will rarely (if ever) be asked what services she bought and consumed. Even if she is asked, how could a customs official ever prove that she had her hair cut or received legal advice abroad, if not by setting up an extremely costly control mechanism that would probably violate basic human rights?

This intangibility and invisibility characterize the overwhelming majority of services transactions. If anything, the value (or volume) of any services transactions that occur cannot be known until after they have been produced/consumed, and are therefore not known to customs and immigration authorities. Consequently, as the act of producing/consuming a service is more visible than the flow of the service across borders, governments have shown a disposition to rule over sales of services through the domestic regulatory process, rather than through overt controls on cross-border flows of services. Therefore, barriers to trade in services are more complicated and less transparent than the barriers to trade in goods.

Thus, governments that are willing to protect domestic service suppliers tend to use domestic regulations to achieve this objective. Therefore, services are a heterogeneous group of products, with the common thread that most of them are subject to government intervention. Protectionist measures in services trade typically have their origin in domestic regulatory regimes and, thus, protectionism in the realm of services may have peculiar characteristics which are difficult to identify. From a WTO perspective, this fact jeopardizes any negotiation, as it is easier to negotiate tariffs than regulations. Consequently any liberalization efforts can prove to be much more complex in services than in goods.

Since impediments to trade in services are present in national economies in the form of 'within-the-border' legislation and administrative practices that control entry, impose limitations on foreign equity holdings, or nationality constraints, or even require professionals to re-certify as a condition for contesting a market, their identification and the measurement of their restrictive impact is harder than is the case with tariffs and quotas. In addition, a consensus has not yet been reached where to draw the line between measures that serve legitimate national policy objectives and therefore are GATS-consistent and measures that are not. While it is clear that regulatory measures that apply to foreign service suppliers in a discriminatory manner constitute barriers to trade in services,[7] there are also domestic regulation measures that apply in a non-discriminatory manner, but still constitute barriers to the supply of a service. Barriers to trade in services are

[6] Feketekuty (n 1 above) 27; also B Hoekman and CAP Braga, 'Protection and Trade in Services: A Survey', PRWP No 1747, 1997, 5.

[7] RH Snape, 'Principles in Trade in Services' in PA Messerlin and KP Sauvant (eds), *The Uruguay Round: Services in the World Economy*, 1990, 7.

thus intermingled with, and often difficult to distinguish from, domestic regulations. Trade policy objectives and other legitimate regulatory objectives are usually completely intertwined, and this inexorably leads to a considerable bewilderment as to the objectives of domestic regulations. Domestic regulations very often encroach on socially sensitive issues and, therefore, barriers to trade in services tend to be indiscernible to the average person; just as trade in services itself.

To sum up, trade liberalization in services is substantially a negotiation on the basis of often-conflicting domestic regulations. Disciplining domestic regulations is in essence the task before negotiators. The GATS resembles to all intents and purposes the GATT story after the importance of border protection had been significantly mitigated: if the decision to liberalize domestic markets was to first dismantle border protection and then proceed to negotiate regulatory barriers, GATS did not miss much by coming into force 40 years after the GATT. For the GATT has only recently, and in a very national sovereignty-friendly manner, started discussing domestic regulatory barriers. The negotiations, however, in the services context might be much more complex than in the GATT. The fact that in the GATS, Members make commitments about sectors (while in the GATT they make concessions about products) has as a result that negotiations are usually conducted not only by trade officials (as in the GATT practice), but also by officials involved in regulating particular sectors. In that case, the danger of protectionist capture by special interests is far greater than in the trade in goods negotiations.[8]

This Chapter offers an analysis of the rationales behind protectionism. Arguments in support of protectionism from the area of trade in goods are examined and assist in better understanding of protectionism in the case of trade in services. A typology of barriers to trade in services is also advanced and reference is made to studies that have measured the positive impact of further liberalization of trade in services. The aim of this Chapter is to underscore the need to deal with domestic regulations which, while being non-discriminatory, may be trade-restrictive.

B. Usual barriers to trade

1. Few words on trade policy

Trade policy decisions affect foreign interests; this is why trade policy is an arm of diplomacy[9] and may embrace international negotiations and rulemaking.[10]

[8] A Sapir, 'The General Agreement on Trade in Services: From 1994 to the Year 2000' (1999) 33(1) JWT 56.

[9] J Goldstein, 'The Political Economy of Trade: Institutions of Protection' (1986) 80(1) The American Political Science Review 162.

[10] Indeed, the GATT/WTO is an intergovernmental organization the legislative angle of which is essentially 'institutionalized diplomacy'. E Stein, 'International Integration and Democracy: No Love at First Sight' (2001) 95(3) AJIL 502.

Likewise, the rudimentary concepts in diplomacy and rulemaking are straightforward. Negotiations entail mutually satisfactory bargaining by finding ways and means to satisfy often-conflicting objectives,[11] while rulemaking copes with the establishment of specific standards that will govern future decisions, thus promoting stability, security and predictability.

Trade policy has two components, one foreign and one domestic. The former is concerned with access to foreign markets and the successful exploitation of trade opportunities, while the latter is concerned with import competition on the domestic market. Ideally, trade policy and international trade negotiations should seek to achieve a balance between foreign and domestic priorities; a balance that ensures gradual movement towards more open and more secure trading conditions in order to increase domestic and global economic welfare.[12] In practice, however, these ideals are often tempered by political and other realities.[13]

The GATT and the WTO Agreement refer in their respective Preambles to 'entering into reciprocal and mutually advantageous arrangements directed to the substantial reduction of tariffs and other barriers to trade and to the elimination of discriminatory treatment' in international trade. Indeed, multilateral trade negotiations seek to increase economic welfare by reducing discrimination, removing trade barriers, and providing greater scope for the operation of market choices, unencumbered by artificial barriers imposed by governments.[14] They assume that the order, security and stability flowing from clear rules and equitable dispute settlement provisions are preferable to the rule of power.[15]

Under the new WTO dispute settlement mechanism, there have been relatively few cases of blatant and repeated violations of key WTO rules,[16] even by big countries against vulnerable trading partners, and strong countries have been dissuaded from abusing weaker partners.[17] Hence, the question that naturally arises is what the motives of a large country are to behave as if it was small. Why

[11] cf Appellate Body Report, *Japan—Alcoholic Beverages II*, p 15:

The WTO Agreement is a treaty—the international equivalent of a contract. It is self-evident that in an exercise of their sovereignty, and in pursuit of their own respective national interests, the Members of the WTO have made a bargain. In exchange for the benefits they expected to derive as Members of the WTO, they have agreed to exercise their sovereignty according to the commitments they have made in the WTO Agreement.

[12] *But* see P Krugman, 'What Should Trade Negotiators Negotiate About?' (1997) 35(1) Journal of Economic Literature 114–115.

[13] G Grossman and E Helpman, 'Trade Wars and Trade Talks' (1995) 103(4) The Journal of Political Economy 676.

[14] K Bagwell, P Mavroidis, and R Staiger, 'It's a Question of Market Access' (2002) 96(1) AJIL 59.

[15] JH Jackson, 'The Crumbling Institutions of the Liberal Trade System' (1979) 12(2) JWT 99.

[16] B Wilson, 'Compliance by WTO Members with Adverse WTO Dispute Settlement Rulings: The Record to Date' (2007) 2 JIEL 397.

[17] Ibid p 400. It is noteworthy, however, that the use of the DSU by developing countries is still in its infancy, as the developed countries are the ones that filed the majority of the cases. K Leitner and S Lester, 'WTO Dispute Settlement 1995–2002: A Statistical Analysis' (2003) 1 JIEL 253. For an explanation regarding the minimal use of the WTO settlement procedures by developing countries,

does a large country decide not to use its potential power and abstain from any action that might hurt its purported national interests?

Notwithstanding the implicit threat of multilateral retaliation, countries are worried by the drift and deterioration in trade relations, and by the clear risk that the GATT—the rule of law in international trade—could be so undermined and bypassed that it could lose all credibility and effectiveness.[18] It is what Arthur Dunkel, the former Director General of the GATT, once described as 'a kind of balance of terror', ie even if a government identifies the short-run benefits from a unilateral tariff increase, it does not succumb to the temptation of employing such beggar-thy-neighbour policies. This is not just because of the possibility of retaliation, but also because of the fear that, as a consequence, the whole trading system may unravel. Indeed, no Member, regardless of its size, has an interest in a multilateral breakdown of cooperation.[19] Then, even if each government has an immediate, short-term incentive to plot a stratagem and deviate from an agreed-upon trade policy in order to enjoy the terms-of-trade benefits, it simply does not do it bearing in mind the long-term costs of a consequent future loss of cooperation.[20]

More generally, the GATT/WTO system essentially performs four functions:[21] it facilitates the negotiation and conclusion of commercial agreements due to their institutional and normative setting (the 'facilitative' function); it spurs compliance and policies of restraint by Members with an evolving code of trade conduct (the 'constraint' function); it offers to smaller Members a first-rate opportunity to influence, depending on their bargaining power, the international trade regulation, since bigger countries usually are less vulnerable in the absence of international rules (the 'diffusion of influence' function); and it promotes trade growth, as the expansion of trade flows is deemed beneficial for all, diminishing at the same time the inherent systemic uncertainty through the development of a system for resolving and avoiding trade disputes (the 'promotion of interaction' function).

In a nutshell, maxims stemming from law, economics, and political economy concur that international trade agreements are mutually beneficial. Essentially, the fact that the parties continue to view adherence to their agreement as being in their mutual interest is the best guarantee that a commitment of any kind will be kept.[22] This is exact, 'particularly in an international setting where

see A Guzman and BA Simmons, 'To Settle or Empanel? An Empirical Analysis of Litigation and Settlement at the World Trade Organization' (2002) 31 Journal of Legal Studies 205.

[18] J Bacchus, 'The Bicycle Club: Affirming the American Interest in the Future of the WTO' (2003) 37(3) Journal of World Trade 439.

[19] K Bagwell and RW Staiger, 'A Theory of Managed Trade' (1990) 80(4) AER 784; also K Bagwell and RW Staiger, 'GATT-Think', NBER Working Paper No. 8005, November 2000, 27.

[20] Ibid p 62.

[21] JA Finlayson and MW Zacher, 'The GATT and the Regulation of Trade Barriers: Regime Dynamics and Functions' (1981) 35(4) International Organization 598.

[22] Also J Goldstein, 'International Institutions and Domestic Politics: GATT, WTO, and the Liberalization of International Trade' in AO Krueger (ed), *The WTO as an International Organization*, 1998, 137–144.

courts are of limited importance and, even more important, marshals and jails are nonexistent'.[23] It is this recognition of common interests that provides legitimacy to any international political authority. As a result, the legitimacy of an international organization such as the WTO derives from Member's willingness to 'internationalize' their respective political authorities. This willingness also explains the transformation of international organizations into deeper/wider cooperation and integration schemes.[24]

It is notable that 'free trade' is not mentioned as one of the GATT objectives. This is because countries have been committed to 'embedded liberalism', ie a form of multilateralism that is compatible with the requirements of domestic stability and allows for domestic interventionism, rather than for *laissez-faire*.[25] Besides, owing to embedded liberalism, the GATT complex system has proved operable. In this context, the removal of barriers has basically been a matter of goodwill and strongly associated with reciprocity.[26] The latter concept changed the political dynamics domestically, which surrounded trade protectionism, and adapted them to the economics of trade liberalization through a political constituency, ie the exporters, which have been in favour of trade liberalization.

Whatever the potential gains from free trade,[27] almost all countries in the world avail themselves of any opportunity to maintain barriers to trade;[28] only the degree and the coverage of protectionism vary. While the vast majority of the economists preach the virtues of free trade,[29] extant domestic measures that protect domestic industries against competition from imports are considerable. The fact that trade promotes competition and in turn, competition, destroys rents justifies the tendency of politics towards too little competition.[30]

[23] K Dam, *The GATT: Law and International Economic Organization*, 1970, 80. In the case of GATT, for example, as no external enforcement mechanism exists to punish violations, meaningful commitments should be self-enforcing, with violations deterred by the threat of subsequent retaliation. For the ideal level in deterring cheating, see AK Dixit and BJ Nalebuff, *Thinking Strategically—The Competitive Edge in Business, Politics, and Everyday Life*, 1993, 105.

[24] JG Ruggie, 'International Regimes, Transactions, and Change: Embedded Liberalism in the Postwar Economic Order' (1982) 36(2) International Organization 380.

[25] Ibid p 393. For the sustainability of the 'embedded liberalism' bargain nowadays, see R Howse, 'From Politics to Technocracy—and Back Again: The Fate of the Multilateral Trading Regime' (2002) 96(1) AJIL 96.

[26] E Colombatto, 'An Explanation of the Dynamics of Protectionism' (2000) 11 Open Economies Review 289; Bagwell and Staiger, 'GATT-Think' (n 19 above) 30.

[27] *Inter alia*, H Siebert, *The World Economy*, 1999, 236.

[28] RE Baldwin, 'The Political Economy of Trade Policy' (1989) 3(4) The Journal of Economic Perspectives 119.

[29] Economic theory makes it clear that unilateral reduction of barriers can produce the greatest and quickest gains. World Bank, *Global Economic Prospects and the Developing Countries 2002*, 2002, 58; also J Bhagwati, 'Introduction: The Unilateral Freeing of Trade versus Reciprocity' in J Bhagwati (ed), *Going Alone: The Case for Relaxed Reciprocity in Freeing Trade*, 2002, 4; also J Bhagwati, *Protectionism*, 1988, 24.

[30] RA Cass and JR Haring, 'Domestic Regulation and International Trade: Where's the Race? Lessons from Telecommunications and Export Controls' in DLM Kennedy and JD Southwick (eds), *The Political Economy of International Trade Law: Essays in Honor of Robert E. Hudec*, 2002, 112.

In sum, trade policy involves the pursuit of some well-established principles of law and economics tempered by the realities of domestic and international politics. In fact, four major participants whose interaction determines future trade policy decisions could be identified: citizens, common interest groups, the domestic government, and foreign governments along with various other foreign groups, such as international organizations and foreign private interest organizations.[31] While the domestic government is the key participant in the process, as it makes the final policy decisions and implements the policies, the other three actors are important as well, insofar as they influence the nature of these decisions by exerting different forms of political pressure on the domestic government.[32] But what specifically nourishes a tilt towards protectionism, particularly when the scholars emphasize that it is never a Pareto first-best policy response to a market distortion?[33]

2. The determinants of protectionism—The role of special interest groups

The state—the machinery and power of the state—is a potential resource or threat to every industry in the society. With its power to prohibit or compel, to take or give money, the state can and does selectively help or hurt a vast number of industries.

George J Stigler (1971)[34]

Ever since Adam Smith and David Ricardo challenged the intellectual foundations of mercantilism, theories of trade policy have debated the merits of free trade vis-à-vis protectionism.[35] Even though free trade would in most circumstances be a Pareto-optimal policy[36] (ie no alternative allocation of resources could make anybody better off without hurting someone else), political markets and institutions are such that the outcome is economically inefficient. Since free trade was shown to be superior in terms of economic (or Kaldor-Hicks)[37]

[31] RE Baldwin, 'The Political Economy of Trade Policy: Integrating the Perspectives of Economists and Political Scientists' in RC Feenstra, GM Grossman, and DA Irwin (eds), *The Political Economy of Trade Policy—Papers in Honor of Jagdish Bhagwati*, 1996, 163.

[32] For instance, in the US politics the so-called 'iron triangle' (ie the ties between elected politicians, bureaucrats, and the politicians' constituencies) seems to be very influential. AO Krueger, 'Government, Trade, and Economic Integration' (1992) 82(2) AER 110.

[33] Bhagwati, *Protectionism*, 1988, 32.

[34] GJ Stigler, 'The Theory of Economic Regulation' (1971) 2(1) The Bell Journal of Economics and Management Science 3.

[35] J Bhagwati, 'The Pure Theory of International Trade: A Survey' (1964) 74(293) The Economic Journal 18.

[36] Or the best solution that is simple to negotiate and enforce. P Krugman, 'Free Trade: A Loss of (Theoretical) Nerve?—The Narrow and Broad Arguments for Free Trade' (1993) 83(2) AER 365.

[37] A Ogus, *Regulation: Legal Form and Economic Theory*, 1994, 25; also FH Stephen, *The Economics of the Law*, 1988, 59.

efficiency—with side payments from the winners to compensate the losers, eg by using adequate methods of redistributing income[38]—scholars have long puzzled over why governments would ever choose to interfere with free trade flows.

Even though arguments in favour of protectionism have been refuted for centuries, protectionism has survived. This is because special interests (eg steel companies, textile industry,[39] agriculture lobbies,[40] etc) have much to gain by enlisting the aid of governments to protect them from foreign competition. In fact, the groups who seek special privileges or protection from the government, or attempt to get others to pay for their benefits (rent-seeking behaviour) will probably hire full-time lobbyists to push their agenda through the legislature. Theoretically, lobbying can be conducive to the elimination of the informational deficiencies that governments confront with. It offers a process through which information can be transmitted from those directly involved in production and consumption activities to the policymakers. This information, however, is typically biased, as it underestimates or totally ignores the impact of each lobby's preferred policy on other sectors or the overall economy. In addition, the lack of transparency in the dealings between lobbyists and public officials is also a factor that favours the final success of inefficient lobbying pressures.

On the other hand, consumers will usually not act in the same manner. The big majority of population consisting of unorganized consumers has little to lose by any particular legislation that has a protectionist effect, because the individual loss is slight.[41] Consumers may even not grasp that such measures are costing them money in the form of higher prices. Since those who gain are not usually

[38] Trade policy is known to be a particularly inefficient way to redistribute income. D Rodrik, 'What Does the Political Economy Literature on Trade Policy (Not) Tell Us What We Ought to Know?', NBER Working Paper No 4870, 1994, 17.

[39] For instance, Francois, Glissman, and Spinanger found that a full implementation of the ATC by the end of 1997 instead of 2005 would bring to EU economies over €25 billion per year, ie the discounted net income gains from a full implementation in 1997 would have amounted to over €160 billion. Moreover, they calculated that the annual cost per job saved in these industries by delayed liberalization of the EU textiles and clothing markets is on average €28,000 for textiles and €41,000 for clothing. J Francois, H Glissman, and D Spinanger, 'The Cost of EU Trade Protection in Textiles and Clothing', Kiel Institute of World Economics, Working Paper No 997, 2000, 66.

[40] Based on static effects alone, the global income loss from agricultural distortions worldwide may be equal to over $120 billion. IMF/World Bank, 'Market Access for Developing Country Exports—Selected Issues', 2002, 32. Especially in developed countries, support to agriculture is estimated to be roughly $1 billion per day. MD Ingco (ed), *Agriculture, Trade, and the WTO: Creating a Trading Environment for Development*, 2002; also OECD, *Agricultural Policies in OECD Countries: Monitoring and Evaluation 2002—Highlights*, 2002, p 31. What is more, allowing full access to developed markets can generate gains for developing countries of as much as $100 billion. The World Bank (n 29 above) 171.

[41] V Pareto, *Manual of Political Economy*, 1906, p 329; also A Downs, 'An Economic Theory of Political Action in a Democracy' (1957) 65(2) The Journal of Political Economy 149; also A Downs, *An Economic Theory of Democracy*, 1957, chapters 11–13.

willing to adequately compensate those who lose,[42] the latter have an incentive to strive for protection through influencing the trade policymaking.

As economists and consumers lack political influence on trade policy, protectionist governments tend to intervene in a sub-optimal manner[43] in order to protect economic and other parochial interests of particular groups, thereby submitting to lobbying pressures.[44] Such pressures are, as a rule, more potent than pressures for free trade given that typically the benefits of protectionism accrue to a few (producers), whilst the costs are spread over many (consumers). The few tend as a result to be much more vocal about their interests than the potential losers (the consumers), because the latter cannot acknowledge the overall value of the gains that are spread out thinly across the whole population.[45] This is mainly due to asymmetries of information (or even lack thereof),[46] or because any coercion or individually appropriate inducement is absent. Therefore, while consumers are the beneficiaries of trade liberalization, they nonetheless are reluctant to take any action because of the minimal individual gain.

Consequently, protectionism can be explained by the existence of this problem, the so-called 'free-rider' behaviour of individuals that is associated with public goods. Trade policy can be considered as a public good given that a beneficiary of a policy cannot be excluded from its benefits, although the beneficiary does not contribute to the costs of obtaining this policy. Given that consumers' lobbies are few, the consumers will prefer to free ride when the interests are shared, that is, to let others pay the costs of goods that will benefit everyone. By contrast, the winners from protection are more concentrated and well organized in groups. Therefore, they are adept at overcoming the free-rider problem and vie (even with one another) for the insulation of their vested interests[47] by trying to influence the incumbent officeholders pending the determination or enforcement of trade policy.[48]

[42] P Samuelson, 'The Gains from International Trade Once Again' (1962) 72(4) The Economic Journal 820.

[43] In this regard, A Downs, *An Economic Theory of Democracy*, 1957, 21.

[44] Paradoxically, free trade may still result from lobbying pressures. D Mitra, 'Endogenous Lobby Formation and Endogenous Protection: A Long-Run Model of Trade Policy Determination' (1999) 89(5) AER 1116.

[45] M Hart, *A Trading Nation: Canadian Trade Policy from Colonialism to Globalization*, 2002, 10; also RE Baldwin (n 31 above) 162.

[46] GJ Stigler, 'The Economics of Information' (1961) 69(3) The Journal of Political Economy 213; also GM Grossman and E Helpman, *Special Interest Politics*, 2001, 103.

[47] M Olson, *The Logic of Collective Action: Public Goods and the Theory of Groups*, 1965. Under these circumstances, political action and hence lobbying for special legislation becomes a cost-effective by-product of being organized. RD Tollison, 'Public Choice and Legislation' (1988) 74(2) Virginia Law Review 342.

[48] Grossman and Helpman argue that these groups do not aim to influence the election outcome, but rather they contribute with a view to influencing the political announcements *before* the elections. They bid for protection and the politicians, on the other hand, 'sale' their protection taking account of the available offers. Accordingly, the structure of protection reveals the outcome of a competition among these groups for political favours that is similar to an auction. GM Grossman and E Helpman, 'Protection for Sale' (1994) 84(4) AER 834.

That is, if particular groups in a society know that their income will be higher under protection than under free trade, they will be willing to spend part of that expected increase in income to keep in power those who favour protection in order to wield influence over the followed public policy.[49] In the economics and political science literature these groups are called 'special interest groups'. The main characteristic of these groups of citizens is that they share identifiable characteristics and similar concerns on some set of issues and might covet policies that would not be considered desirable by the average citizen.[50] The activities of these groups lead to the unproductive use of resources to seek future rents.[51] Interest groups spend resources in demanding legislation especially in cases where the durability of favourable laws can be ensured, and after having conducted a rigorous cost–benefit analysis, that is, after having found that these laws have a present value of benefits that exceeds the costs of obtaining them. Governments, on the other hand, formulate policies (including trade policies) and serve special interest groups in order to maximize the number of votes and thus gain, or keep, office. Their social function is essentially a by-product of their private motive.[52] In this setting, it was posited that an independent judiciary, acting as an agent of the politicians (principals), will enforce the long-term deals between legislators and interest groups in accordance with the original intent of the enacting legislature.[53]

As a result, any decision to restrain trade must be viewed in the light of, first, the pressures that domestic special interest groups bring to bear on the trade-regulating authorities, and, second, the voting behaviour of individuals whose incomes differ according to their ownership of labour and shares in profits. The latter element, ie that the voter cares about her individual well-being and, consequently, conditions her voting behaviour on the implementation of the policies preferred to her, requires a perfectly informed voter–consumer, which is not always, if at all, the case.[54] Additionally, voter's preferences can be manipulated through limited or misleading information disseminated by interested pressure groups, which 'play' with voter preferences and consequently influence political

[49] For an instructive study over special interest groups' conduct, see G Grossman and E Helpman, 'Electoral Competition and Special Interest Politics' (1996) 63(2) The Review of Economic Studies 265. It was these pressure groups that hijacked the US Congress in 1929–1930 and produced one of the highest tariffs in US history, the Smoot-Hawley tariff. See also R Hudec, '"Circumventing Democracy": The Political Morality of Trade Negotiations' in R Hudec (ed), *Essays on the Nature of International Trade Law*, 1999, 217.

[50] Grossman and Helpman (n 46 above) 75.

[51] Again, the imposition of a distortionary tariff, though unproductive from an economic point of view, '... may possess a political legitimacy and value as constituting an element of a vigorous, pluralistic democracy'. J Bhagwati, 'Directly Unproductive, Profit-Seeking (DUP) Activities' (1982) 90(5) The Journal of Political Economy 989.

[52] A Downs, 'An Economic Theory of Political Action in a Democracy', 1957 65(2) Journal of Political Economy 137.

[53] WM Landes and RA Posner, 'The Independent Judiciary in an Interest-Group Perspective' (1975) 18(3) Journal of Law and Economics 875.

[54] A Downs (n 52 above) 139.

decisions. As Becker pointed out, '...voting and majorities are not fundamental determinants of political influence even in democracies...'.[55]

Thus, most trade policy determinations essentially boil down to similar decisions to discriminate for the few against the many. In trade policy, decisions to favour a domestic group[56] often involve discrimination against foreign producers by imposing a tariff, a quota, a procurement preference, a higher product standard, or some similar measure. Many of these decisions are not predicated upon economic concepts and analysis[57] but on non-economic instincts and biases.[58] An ample range of detailed economic and social concerns, ranging from employment in ailing industries to protection of underprivileged social groups is frequently given precedence over the aggregate economic interest of the entire society.

The following paragraphs cope with arguments that 'justify' protectionist governmental regulatory intervention anchored in *economic* objectives. Of course, one should not lose sight of the fact that a government, when intervening, may pursue *non-economic* objectives,[59] like those associated with public goods such as universal provision of education, health-care services, national defence and security, or all manner of law and regulation, including trade regulation.[60]

Due to the non-rival and non-excludable characteristics of public goods, ie that the public good can be used simultaneously by many people and that once produced it is extremely costly to exclude non-paying consumers from using it, the social marginal benefit is much larger than the private marginal benefit. Potential producers, therefore, cannot fully internalize the benefits with which these goods endow. As a result, in many cases the government, instead of subsidizing the producers, does the production itself.[61] Such a decision might not be the most efficient one, but so long as the government is the only *demandeur* of the

[55] GS Becker, 'A Theory of Competition Among Pressures Groups for Political Influence' (1983) 98(3) The Quarterly Journal of Economics 385.

[56] Ibid 376, as to the determinants that lead a government to favour a pressure group over another.

[57] *But* see JM Finger and A Olechowski, 'Trade Barriers: Who Does What to Whom', in H Giersch (ed), *Free Trade in the World Economy: Towards an Opening of Markets*, 1987, 51.

[58] The US post-war trade policy, for example, has been greatly influenced by 'electoral politics'. Protectionism has also been part of the bargaining so that governments are allowed to launch or implement major trade negotiations. FC Bergsten, 'A Renaissance for United States Trade Policy?' (2002) Foreign Affairs 92–95. For the impact of domestic elections on international trade negotiations, see HV Milner and BP Rosendorff, 'Democratic Politics and International Trade Negotiations: Elections and Divided Government as Constraints on Trade Liberalization' (1997) 41(1) The Journal of Conflict Resolution 120.

[59] AV Deardorff, 'The Economics of Government Market Intervention, and Its International Dimension' in M Bronckers and R Quick (eds), *New Directions in International Economic Law: Essays in Honour of J. H. Jackson*, 2000, 77.

[60] According to G Hardin, 'freedom in a commons brings ruin to all'. To avoid this, a government should use its coercive powers to prevent excessive exploitation of a common. G Hardin, 'The Tragedy of the Commons' (1968) 162 Science 1243.

[61] Coase, however, has showed that the divide between ordinary goods and pure public goods may be fictive, as goods with public goods features may be produced by the private sector. RH Coase, 'The Lighthouse in Economics' (1974) 17(2) Journal of Law and Economics 357.

public good on the market, gains generated by perfect competition are unlikely to emerge. Another non-economic objective can be the promotion of cultural identity, or the protection of the productive capacity of an industry that could be essential in time of war. No matter which kind of intervention a government might choose it should avoid generating additional distortions while trying to redress the initial distortion.[62]

In this respect, although there is in principle a plethora of arguments when it comes to a government's motives to interfere with free trade, in practice one could simplify things by identifying two broad categories of arguments.[63]

a) *Protection of domestic production*

This broad category encompasses any electoral influences (general electorate, various special interest groups, lobbies etc) which plead their case for protection. Domestic pressure groups typically advocate a policy congruent with their interests, that is, a policy that will protect established industries in order to provide a shelter for domestic employment[64] and earnings.[65] Such a social concern intervention may arise directly as a consequence of the policymakers' preferences for the welfare of themselves and the others,[66] but it may also arise indirectly from the exigencies of maintaining the power and the desire to be re-appointed or re-elected,[67] or avoid a *coup d'état*, as the average voter seems to endorse these

[62] J Bhagwati, 'The Generalized Theory of Domestic Distortions and Welfare' in J Bhagwati, RA Mundell, RW Jones, and J Vanek (eds), *Trade, Balance of Payments and Growth: Essays in Honor of Charles P. Kindleberger*, 1971, 71. For a ranking of alternative policies with respect to non-economic objectives, see J Bhagwati and TN Srinivasan, 'Optimal Intervention to Achieve Non-Economic Objectives' (1969) 36(1) The Review of Economic Studies 27.

[63] For a historical analysis of some of these arguments, see D Irwin, *Against the Tide: An Intellectual History of Free Trade*, 1996, 102 (Chapters 7–14); For the counterarguments in favour of free trade, see, among others, D Irwin, *Free Trade Under Fire*, 2002, 21.

[64] Ibid 70; also M Wallerstein, 'Unemployment, Collective Bargaining, and the Demand for Protection' (1987) 31(4) American Journal of Political Science 742.

[65] Stolper and Samuelson, for example, showed that it is possible that trade liberalization harms a factor of production, namely the scarcest one, and lowers its real wage. According to the authors, a change from free trade to protection will raise the income of factors that are relatively scarce in a country and lower the income of relatively abundant factors. It follows that in specific cases, labour could be harmed by a shift to freer trade. However, the authors conclude that the harm for the scarce factor of production by free trade is less than the gain of the other; hence, both factors could end up better off in the existence of appropriate redistributive mechanisms. WF Stolper and PA Samuelson, 'Protection and Real Wages' (1941) 9(1) The Review of Economic Studies 65; also DA Irwin, 'Ohlin versus Stolper-Samuelson?' NBER Working Paper No 7641, 2000.

[66] As Corden contended, a government pays more attention to avoiding a reduction in welfare of any class of its citizenry than it does to maximizing the general welfare. This is the 'conservative social welfare function'. M Corden, *Trade Policy and Economic Welfare*, 1974, 107. For the quotation, see JH Jackson, 'Regulating International Economic Behavior—The WTO and the Challenge of Constructing Institutions to Manage Global Interdependence' in U Immenga, W Möschel, and D Reuter (eds), *Festschrift für Ernst-Joachim Mestmäcker*, 1996, 615.

[67] A Downs, *An Economic Theory of Democracy*, 1957, 21; also HG Johnson, 'The Economic Approach to Social Questions' (1968) 35(137) Economica 11; also GJ Stigler (n 34 above) 11.

objectives and, consequently, any re-election possibilities of the government (ie their own political welfare) are dependent on the extent to which these goals are implemented.

But for communistic or totalitarian regimes, it is impossible to give net trade protection to the national economy as a whole. Specific sectors can be protected only at the expense of other sectors (and at considerable cost to the economy at large). In this case, economists posit that trade restrictions may be an instrument of income distribution among domestic groups by means of taxing and restraining domestic consumers, taxpayers, processing industries and export industries in order to enable import-competing industries to artificially increase their prices and output. However, redistributing income is not a simple task, since changes in policy are as a rule anticipated by those whom they affect. The negatively affected sections of the populace proceed accordingly and in advance to avoid the deterioration of their income.[68]

The protection may also aim to provide adjustment assistance; then, the governmental objective will be to smooth the inter-industry shift of factors of production induced by import penetration. Similar types of concern may preponderate where the levels of protection are explained by the government's objective of ensuring that low-income workers are not hurt by imports. In this case, the solution of import protection probably prevails because it is politically more expedient to 'make the foreigners pay' rather than use direct subsidies or domestic tax receipts in order to assist the import-threatened industries and offset the distortion, although the latter would be the first-best policy.[69] By the same token, economic theory would praise the efficiency of safeguards when compared to tariffs. Based on welfare-maximizing grounds, the imposition of a safeguard appears to be an attractive solution, as it would allow for a temporary reduction of the pace of adjustment and *a fortiori* a reduction of adjustment costs.[70] The adverse effects to consumers/voters would be barely visible in this case.[71]

There are cases, however, where trade policy decisions that favour protectionism are motivated by a desire to minimize, or even delay, adjustment costs, especially to low-skilled workers. It is a truism that trade liberalization will induce adjustment that corresponds to reallocation of resources to more productive uses. In the short run, however, domestic economic activities that have been protected by successive governmental interventions may not be able to sustain output,

[68] AV Deardorff (n 59 above) 77.

[69] J Bhagwati and VK Ramaswami, 'Domestic Distortions, Tariffs and the Theory of Optimum Subsidy' (1963) 71(1) The Journal of Political Economy 45. *But* see RW Staiger and G Tabellini, 'Discretionary Trade Policy and Excessive Protection' (1987) 77(5) AER 834.

[70] H Horn and P Mavroidis, 'US—Lamb: United States—Safeguard Measures on Imports of Fresh, Chilled or Frozen Lamb Meat from New Zealand and Australia: What Should be Required of a Safeguard Investigation?' in H Horn and P Mavroidis (eds), *The WTO Case Law of 2001*, 2003, 78.

[71] P Krugman, 'Domestic Distortions and the Deindustrialization Hypothesis' in RC Feenstra, GM Grossman, and DA Irwin (eds) (n 31 above) 33.

capacity utilization, and employment once trade is liberalized.[72] This can happen to industries that face structural changes. In such cases, a hospitalization (thus protection) of the industry under regeneration may be necessary in order to become efficient again.

In other instances, the industry seeking protection is not senescent but rather senile, that is, any long-term recovery does not appear to be very likely and any protection would merely serve to perpetuate inefficiency. Even worse, it can be expected that those producers have no incentive to undertake the difficult process of adjustment needed if they know they can expect continued protection if they do not adjust.[73]

Governmental protection can also aim at giving an advantage to an industry which is in its initial stages of development and therefore cannot achieve equal footing with its foreign rivals for a variety of reasons, eg imperfect information.[74] This is the well-known 'infant-industry' argument,[75] even though Adam Smith and many of the classical economists would not accept this argument as a legitimate exception to free trade. This argument suggests that temporary, entry-promoting protection[76] can be justified on social welfare grounds. Arguably, when the industry reaches a sufficiently strong position in the world markets, ie it is sufficiently mature to exploit economies of scale and minimize unit costs, restrictions can be dismantled and the industry can face the competition on equal terms even though it may be difficult from a political viewpoint to remove protection once maturity is attained. The infant-industry argument was popular in the late nineteenth century in Europe and the United States and in recent years it has been deployed by developing countries (eg it was very popular in Latin America during the twentieth century) as part of their industrialization process. This argument (as well as the balance-of-payments foreign-exchange-scarcity argument) was given international approval in GATT Article XVIII Sections B, C, and D.

b) Market failures (distortions) and political trade interventions

In its idealized form of perfect competition (no externalities, indivisibilities, monopolies, dynamic uncertainties, learning processes, etc), a market

[72] The World Bank, *Global Economic Prospects and the Developing Countries 1997*, 1997, 58; also M Bacchetta and M Jansen, 'Adjusting to Trade Liberalization: The Role of Policy, Institutions, and WTO Policies', WTO Special studies No 7, 2003, 15.

[73] That is the case of the US steel industries. GC Hufbauer and B Goodrich, 'Steel Policy: The Good, the Bad, and the Ugly' (2003) International Economics Policy Briefs, IIE, No PB03–1, 11; also CE Barfield, *High-Tech Protectionism—The Irrationality of Antidumping Laws*, 2003, 39ff.

[74] *But* see GM Grossman and H Horn, 'Infant-Industry Protection Reconsidered: The Case of Informational Barriers to Entry' (1988) 103(4) The Quarterly Journal of Economics 770.

[75] JS Mill, *Principles of Political Economy*, [1848], 1909, 922.

[76] HG Johnson, 'Optimal Trade Intervention in the Presence of Domestic Distortions' in R Caves, HG Johnson, and PB Kenen (eds), *Trade, Growth, and the Balance of Payments: Essays in Honor of Gottfried Haberler*, 1965, 27.

economy achieves a kind of social optimum (all costs and benefits are reflected in market prices)[77] without any government intervention (Pareto optimality, or *maximum ophelimity*, according to the words of Vilfredo Pareto).[78] Then, any intervention can be justified only due to distributional objectives, as mentioned above.

Nevertheless, under certain circumstances, the production and distribution of a commodity through a competitive market in which all the relevant agents are pursuing their own self-interests[79] may bring about an allocation of that commodity that is socially inefficient. Thus, Adam Smith's 'invisible hand' will not always work;[80] competitive markets with self-interested agents can fail as an apparatus of efficiency. Distortions are closely associated with market mechanisms.[81] What is rather needed in that case is an appropriate governmental policy that tackles directly this market imperfection and redirects the economy towards the preferred result.[82] In this setting, any other policy would not restore the first-best, but it would introduce a new distortion and preclude the first-best.[83] Thus, in the presence of distortions (or market failures) the free-trade outcome would not be optimal. Rather, a surgical domestic policy aimed directly at the source of the market failure is needed.[84]

(1) Domestic distortions

To begin with, a deviation of the Paretian Optimal may be of domestic origin, ie a domestic distortion. The classic example of a domestic distortion is an externality. Externalities usually arise when a third party, who is otherwise by no means involved in the relevant market transaction,[85] is affected by either the production or consumption of a commodity, while these externalities do not impinge on the agents concerned by reason of failures in the price mechanism. An externality is

[77] AP Lerner, 'The Concept of Monopoly and the Measurement of Monopoly Power' (1934) 1(3) The Review of Economic Studies 165.

[78] PA Samuelson, 'The Gains from International Trade' (1939) 5(2) The Canadian Journal of Economics and Political Science 195.

[79] The assumption that any human being is an egoistic, utility maximizer who as a rule has purely selfish motives when she acts (*homo economicus*) constitutes the core of the public choice theory. JM Buchanan and G Tullock, *The Calculus of Consent: Logical Foundations of Constitutional Democracy*, 1974; also Ogus (n 37 above) 58; For a critical view on this theory, see SP Croley, 'Theories of Regulation: Incorporating the Administrative Process' (1998) 98(1) Columbia Law Review 34.

[80] J Bhagwati, 'Free Trade: Old and New Challenges' (1994) 104(423) The Economic Journal 232.

[81] Bhagwati (n 62 above) 69.

[82] See, however, MC Kemp and T Nagishi, 'Domestic Distortions, Tariffs, and the Theory of Optimum Subsidy' (1969) 77(6) The Journal of Political Economy 1012.

[83] *But* see J Le Grand, 'The Theory of Government Failure' (1991) 21(4) British Journal of Political Science 423; also AO Krueger, 'Government Failures in Development' (1990) 4(3) The Journal of Economic Perspectives 10; and C Wolf Jr, *Markets or Governments—Choosing between Imperfect Alternatives*, 1994, 36ff.

[84] Bhagwati (n 62 above) 76.

[85] Indeed, externalities 'are, by their nature, failures of participation'. NK Komesar, *Imperfect Alternatives—Choosing Institutions in Law, Economics, and Public Policy*, 1994, 102.

more usually defined as the effect of one person's decision on someone who is not a party to that decision.[86]

Depending on the kind of externality that a government has to cope with,[87] there is a variety of interventionist measures available, but in roughly all cases the first-best responses do not include trade restrictions (ie imposition of tariffs) because of the welfare losses associated with them. In the case of a negative production externality (ie a production process that has detrimental external effects on others, eg environmental pollution) the optimal intervention would entail a Pigouvian tax on production equal to the damage. If instead the consumers create the negative externality, then a tax on consumption will be called for as the optimal policy.[88] If, on the other hand, the externality were positive (eg the inability of an innovative firm to appropriate fully the knowledge and subsequently the technological spillovers it generates),[89] the optimal intervention would be a subsidy and not a tax.[90] Public goods such as parks, roads, or even clean air, lighthouse services, commercial-free TV and radio broadcasts, are all examples of positive externalities. The final aim of the governmental intervention is to instigate the full 'internalization' of the externality and thus correct the distortion without creating a new one.

Hence one of the most important contributions of the theory of domestic distortions (or theory of optimum subsidy) is the so-called 'targeting principle'. According to this principle, a production externality is best dealt with by a production tax or subsidy, a labour market distortion involving a wage differential is best countered by a wage subsidy to the high-wage sector, and so forth. The principle of targeting hence appears to be a powerful tool that allows a practical welfare-ranking of policies from first-best to *n*th-best when it comes to any market failure or non-economic objective.[91]

[86] RH Coase, *The Firm, the Market, and the Law*, 1988, 24; also JM Buchanan and WC Stubblebine, 'Externality' (1962) 29(116) Economica 373.

[87] The presence of externalities does not automatically render an intervention desirable. Ibid 381.

[88] AC Pigou, *The Economics of Welfare*, 1962. Unlike most taxes, which are inefficient because they result in a deadweight loss, Pigouvian taxes, such as on alcohol or cigarettes, improve overall economic efficiency. The Pigouvian approach will not always be sufficient, since it fails to consider that in a single externality relationship there are always two parties involved. Thus, there is a reciprocal bargain that must occur. As Coase pointed out, whenever transaction costs (ie all the costs necessary to carry out a market transaction) are low and property rights well-defined, people will make voluntary exchange for mutual benefits. Thus, a government intervention may not be necessary in order to correct the market failure associated with the externality. RH Coase, 'The Problem of Social Cost' (1960) 3 Journal of Law and Economics 1–44.

[89] P Krugman, 'Is Free Trade Passé?' (1987) 1(2) The Journal of Economic Perspectives 137.

[90] Deardorff (n 59 above) 75.

[91] D Rodrik, 'Policy Targeting with Endogenous Distortions: Theory of Optimum Subsidy Revisited' (1987) 102(4) The Quarterly Journal of Economics 903; also J Bhagwati and VK Ramaswami (n 69 above); also n 62 above.

(2) Foreign distortions

A distortion may also be of foreign origin. In that case it is accepted—albeit to a limited extent—that selected protectionism applied under certain circumstances can maximize national welfare. It could be suggested that such a proposition is contradictory to what has been pointed out earlier, that is, the inefficiency of the tariff. The reason for this conflict is that the standard trade models involve ideal markets, free of imperfect competition and, thus, market distortions are not present.

i. Optimal tariff Whilst a free-trade outcome—even unilaterally determined—would be the best policy to choose for a small country that cannot impinge on world prices, a tariff could under certain conditions improve national welfare for a large country.[92] This argument is commonly known as the 'terms-of-trade' (or 'optimal tariff') argument for protection, because the welfare betterment occurs on condition that the terms-of-trade gain exceeds the total deadweight losses.

Large exporting countries and large importing countries have a market imperfection present. 'Largeness' is to be conceived as the share that a country has in markets in which it exports and imports.[93] In the first case, the country has a monopoly power, whilst in the latter a monopsony power. The distortion here derives from the imperfect competitiveness of the international market and the optimal tariff is a means of offsetting this distortion.

According to this argument, a low tariff imposed by the importing country that has monopsony power prompts the decline of the world market price for the good, the international terms of trade (the price of imports relative to exports) shift in favour of the tariff-levying country, and thus raise national income. Conversely, a small export tax imposed by the export country that has monopoly power will force the international price up and will accrue benefits to the tax-levying country.

The essence of the optimum tariff is the exploitation of monopsonistic power. If a country can influence world prices due to its significance in terms of its share in global trade, it can force the prices down by restricting import demand. The tariff is the instrument through which this type of country manipulates the market. The optimum tariff argument is strictly an activist, nationalistic one. From a global point of view, the optimum rate of tariff is zero (ie amounting to free trade). With a higher-than-is-efficient tariff, however, the home country takes advantage of a terms-of-trade externality and inflicts a loss on the rest of the world, which exceeds the terms-of-trade gains that the tariff-levying country enjoys. From the imposition of such an import tariff a price effect (the home

[92] HG Johnson (n 76 above) 9ff; also J Bhagwati and TN Srinivasan (n 62 above) 27; J Bhagwati, VK Ramaswami, and TN Srinivasan, 'Domestic Distortions, Tariffs and the Theory of Optimum Subsidy: Some Further Results' (1969) 77(6) Journal of Political Economy 1005.

[93] Take the case of OPEC (Organization of Petroleum Exporting Countries).

country's terms-of-trade improvement) occurs which is accompanied by a volume effect (the restriction of market access to the home market).[94]

By and large, the terms-of-trade argument can be appealing only to a 'large' country (in the sense that I noted earlier) and only if other countries do not retaliate by raising tariffs themselves (tit-for-tat protectionism),[95] leading that way to Nash non-cooperative outcomes, ie to trade war.[96] But even in the case when other countries do not retaliate, this does not change the fact that optimal tariff constitutes a beggar-thy-neighbour policy because it decreases welfare abroad.

ii. Strategic trade policy Strategic trade policy is another argument in this regard, similar to the infant industry argument. The strategic trade policy argument postulates that, under certain circumstances, a government can raise national welfare at another country's expense if it deviates from the free-trade optimum and supports domestic firms in international competition.[97] Generally, strategic trade policy refers to cases of beneficial government intervention at the existence of imperfectly competitive markets (source of distortion). In this case, a benevolent and perfectly informed[98] government can aid a domestic company to reach a monopolistic position—or a stronger position than the one that it had before the governmental support—on the world market.

In their seminal work, Brander and Spencer[99] illustrated that, when international markets suffer from imperfect competition (eg foreign monopolist supplier), which, by the way, is always the case in the real world, export subsidies and import tariffs could deter foreign firms from competing for lucrative markets and, as a result, accrue benefits (or rents) to the domestic firms.[100] Hence, subsidies or protection might be used strategically[101] to extract rents from a foreign

[94] K Bagwell and RW Staiger, 'GATT-Think' (n 19 above) 19.

[95] Even in the case of retaliation, the tariff-levying country may still gain. HG Johnson, 'Optimum Tariffs and Retaliation' (1953–1954) 21(2) The Review of Economic Studies 142.

[96] G Grossman and E Helpman (n 13 above) 684.

[97] Japan followed a similar policy since the mid-1970s to promote the growth of the semiconductor industry. K Yamamura, 'Caveat Emptor: The Industrial Policy of Japan' in P Krugman (ed), *Strategic Trade Policy and the New International Economics*, 1986, 192.

[98] G Grossman and G Maggi, 'Free Trade vs. Strategic Trade: A Peek into Pandora's Box', 1997, 11; also SL Brainard and D Martimort, 'Strategic Trade Policy with Incompletely Informed Policymakers' (1997) 42 Journal of International Economics 33.

[99] JA Brander and BJ Spencer, 'Tariffs and the Extraction of Foreign Monopoly Rents under Potential Entry' (1981) 14(3) The Canadian Journal of Economics 371; JA Brander and BJ Spencer, 'Export Subsidies and International Market Share Rivalry' (1985) 18 Journal of International Economics 83. Also JA Brander, 'Strategic Trade Policy', NBER Working Paper No 5020, 1995.

[100] Such strategic policies could even *decrease* the costs of domestic firms and thus promote their exports ('protection-as-promotion'). P Krugman, 'Import Protection as Export Promotion: International Competition in the Presence of Oligopoly and Economies of Scale' in G Grossman (ed), *Imperfect Competition and International Trade*, 1994, 75.

[101] Government policy plays here the same role as 'strategic' moves, eg investment in excess capacity or research and development (R&D).

monopolist in a manner that enhances national income. In the case of 'strategic' subsidies, the profits rise by more than the amount of the subsidy, ie the cost to taxpayers is inferior to the benefit to the domestic firm.[102]

Such policies typically involve a shift of profits to the home country (rent shifting) at the expense of foreign countries and their firms whose losses more than offset the gains that are accrued to the home country.[103] 'Strategic policy' theory, just as the 'optimal tariff' theory, demonstrates that instruments other than tariffs can, depending on the circumstances, improve national welfare.

iii. Contingent protection (anti-dumping and countervailing measures, and safeguards) Lastly, another important argument that favours protectionist government interventions due to foreign distortions relates to trade remedies. Trade remedies aim to confront imports that injure the domestic firms. Imports have this effect if they are dumped (anti-dumping measures), subsidized (countervailing measures) or if they entered the domestic market in increased amounts (safeguards). These three types of temporary measures are the major types of contingent protection with anti-dumping being the most frequently used contingent protection tool with an increasing use over recent years.[104] A government uses all these instruments at hand to re-establish 'fair' trade[105] or 'symmetrical free trade',[106] ie allocation of resources based on strictly economic terms of efficiency.

Although there are various definitions of dumping,[107] the central point to all of them is the concept of price discrimination in different markets. No matter how justifiable this difference is from an economic viewpoint (business cycle, economies of scale, etc),[108] dumping is deemed particularly objectionable when it is genuinely identified as having been motivated by predatory intent (strategic

[102] J Brander, 'Rationales for Strategic Trade and Industrial Policy' in P Krugman (ed), *Strategic Trade Policy and the New International Economics*, 1986, 29.

[103] DG Tarr, 'Arguments For and Against Uniform Tariffs' in B Hoekman, A Mattoo, and P English (eds), *Development, Trade, and the WTO: A Handbook*, 2002, 527.

[104] In 1999 only the anti-dumping investigations reached an all time high of 356. See WTO, *Annual Report 2002*, 2002, p 34. Interestingly, a number of developing countries (eg Argentina, Mexico, Brazil) became major users of such practices in the same period. JM Finger and L Schuknecht, 'Market Access Advances and Retreats: The Uruguay Round and Beyond', PRWP No 2232, 1999, 36. This trend faded in subsequent years. In 2004, 239 investigations were initiated with the United States (42), India (37), and China (22) being the most active Members. WTO, *Annual Report 2005*, 2005, 39.

[105] R Hudec, 'Mirror, Mirror on the Wall: The Concept of Fairness in U.S. Foreign Trade Policy' in R Hudec (ed) (n 49 above) 227; also J Bhagwati, *The World Trading System at Risk*, 1991, 14.

[106] Ibid 13; also J Bhagwati, 'The Demands to Reduce Domestic Diversity among Trading Nations' in J Bhagwati and R Hudec (eds), *Fair Trade and Harmonization: Prerequisites for Free Trade?*, Vol 1: *Economic Analysis*, 1996, 21.

[107] M Matsushita, TJ Schoenbaum, and PC Mavroidis, *The World Trade Organization: Law, Practice and Policy* (2nd edition, 2006) 396.

[108] P Krugman and M Obstfeld, *International Economics: Theory and Policy* (7th edition, 2006) 131.

dumping). The latter type of dumping occurs when a foreign firm attempts to drive away the domestic competitors by following a low-price policy, then establishes a monopoly and subsequently increases the price.[109] Anti-dumping laws, which are permitted by WTO rules,[110] enable nations to impose offsetting duties on imports found to be dumped products in the domestic market and causing 'material injury' to a domestic industry[111] (causality between dumping and the material injury).

In addition, some countries may take action against imports that they suspect have been favoured with an export subsidy. In this case the domestic government intervention is superior to anti-dumping measures in that it is better targeted at the source of the perceived externality, that is, the foreign government intervention. These so-called 'countervailing duty' cases are also allowed under WTO rules and, if an investigation reveals that allegedly subsidized imports have injured 'materially' a domestic industry, then a tariff can be imposed on the products in question.[112]

Anti-dumping and countervailing duty laws are referred to as 'unfair trade laws', revealing the opinion that dumping and subsidization tilt the commercial playing field towards foreign firms. However, the more and more widespread resort to 'unfair trade laws' dilutes the gains from trade liberalization. In many cases it was demonstrated that the distinction between fair and unfair trade is only a legalism that was used as another instrument in the arsenal of possible measures for insulating domestic producers[113] from import competition and not in order to level the playing field,[114] as they were supposed to.

Nonetheless, disrupting surges in imports (even due to 'fair' practices)[115] can be far better tackled through the use of safeguard measures. In an incomplete contract such as the GATT with rigid bindings, safeguards constitute one of the escape mechanisms allowing for *temporary* import protection that this contract tolerates.[116] Safeguard measures are extraordinary, sovereign remedies to

[109] PA Messerlin and G Reed, 'Antidumping Policies in the United States and the European Community' (1995) 105(433) The Economic Journal 1565.

[110] Article VI GATT and the Anti-Dumping Agreement.

[111] This determination is crucial for all types of contingent protection. PKM Tharakan, 'Political Economy and Contingent Protection' (1995) 105(433) The Economic Journal 1556.

[112] H Marvel and E Ray, 'Countervailing Duties' (1995) 105(433) The Economic Journal 1576.

[113] Of course, the negative effects on consumer welfare have never been an issue of concern for the WTO. PC Mavroidis, 'Come Together? Producer Welfare, Consumer Welfare, and WTO Rules' in E-U Petersmann (ed), *Reforming the World Trading System—Legitimacy, Efficiency, and Democratic Governance*, 2005, 286ff.

[114] R Chrishna, 'Antidumping in Law and Practice', PRWP No 1823, 1997, 10; Also Bhagwati, *Protectionism*, 1988, 48. Several empirical studies suggest that strategic dumping occurred in at most 10%, and more probably at most 5% of the cases investigated. Nevertheless, even in these cases predatory intent might have been absent. Messerlin and Reed (n 109 above) 1568.

[115] Appellate Body Report, *US—Line Pipe*, para 80.

[116] H Horn, G Maggi, and RW Staiger, 'Trade Agreements as Endogenously Incomplete Contracts', 2006, 1; also K Bagwell and RW Staiger, *The Economics of the World Trading System*, 2002, 104.

be taken only in emergency situations.[117] Such measures afford domestic firms the chance to adjust to greater competition from abroad by reducing the pace of adjustment, but do so only for a fixed period of time. Because the import protection is temporary, trading partners know that their market access has not been permanently denied. Safeguards ensure an increased flexibility for the GATT to exogenous circumstances[118] and reduced aggregate adjustment costs due to a reduced pace of adjustment. By contrast, the anti-dumping and countervailing duty laws are implemented for as long as the dumping or subsidization continues. However, in numerous cases the sunset provisions have been misused and the anti-dumping or countervailing duties, though temporary measures in theory,[119] once imposed, have more often than not exceeded the five-year period as foreseen under Articles 11:3 of the Anti-dumping Agreement and 21:3 of the SCM Agreement.[120]

It follows that safeguards are not so 'appealing' for a protectionist government. Stringent conditions should be met to justify this type of action; inter alia, they should be applied on a non-discriminatory basis, exporting countries have the right to claim compensation or retaliate (this right is limited, though, pursuant to Article 8:3 of the Safeguards Agreement), and, above all, the injury should be 'serious' rather than 'material', ie the standard is higher in the case of safeguards.[121] The Appellate Body clarified the criteria that should be met for a Member to use safeguards: pursuant to Articles 2, 3, and 4 of the Safeguards Agreement, a Member must have determined that a product is being imported into its territory in such increased quantities and under such conditions as to cause or threaten to cause serious injury to the domestic industry. In addition, it should be demonstrated that there were 'unexpected' and, thus, 'unforeseen' circumstances which led to such increased imports pursuant to Article XIX GATT.[122]

[117] For an excellent analysis of the function of safeguards in the WTO, see AO Sykes, *The WTO Agreement on Safeguards: A Commentary*, 2006.

[118] As Roessler cogently put it, 'it is the combination of rigid market access rules with flexible safeguards and impairment procedures that permitted multilateral trade liberalization to proceed without any domestic policy harmonization'. F Roessler, 'Diverging Domestic Policies and Multilateral Trade Integration' in J Bhagwati and RE Hudec (eds), *Fair Trade and Harmonization: Prerequisites for Free Trade?*, Vol 2: Legal Analysis, 1996, 41.

[119] Appellate Body Report, *US—Carbon Steel*, paras 63 and 88, and Appellate Body Report, *US—Corrosion-Resistant Steel Sunset Review*, para 104 and fn 114. In these two cases the Appellate Body emphasized that Arts 11.3 of the Anti-Dumping Agreement and 21.3 of the SCM Agreement impose an 'explicit temporal limit' on the maintenance of anti-dumping or countervailing duties.

[120] For instance, in both the United States and the European Union more than the half of the anti-dumping cases subject to a sunset review exceeded the five-year standard in the period between 1998 and 2003. WTO, Negotiating Group on Rules, *Korea's View on the Improvement of the Sunset System—Submission of the Republic of Korea*, TN/RL/W/111, 27 May 2003, p 1.

[121] Appellate Body Report, *US—Lamb*, para 124.

[122] Appellate Body Report, *US—Line Pipe,* para 84; and Appellate Body Report, *Argentina—Footwear (EC)*, para 92.

3. Forms of protectionism (trade policy instruments)—Barriers to imports

As clarified earlier, an active trade policy redistributes income by transferring resources to specific industries and factors of production. It is exactly for that reason that protectionist pressures arise. Whether it is an industry's voting power, financial strength, political campaign contributions,[123] and so forth, that create pressures for protection, these pressures are powerful enough so that policy makers yield to protectionist pressures by imposing barriers to foreign imports to restrict market access. These barriers that a government imposes may be in principle either border measures or measures behind the border, ie internal measures that affect goods after they have entered the domestic market.[124]

The first category of these barriers usually includes import tariffs and other border measures based on price, hence import duties, tariff quotas (used mainly for agricultural products), and other border duties, levies, and charges. Even if tariffs distort international trade, they are generally deemed the least distortionary instruments compared with all the other trade-inhibiting commercial policies due to their transparency and readily quantifiable efficiency costs. The import tariff is in principle the sole instrument of protection allowed under GATT.

A second category could consist of measures that, even if lying at the border, are *non-price* instruments (non-tariff *border* measures), such as quantitative restrictions (import quotas, direct prohibitions, local content requirements, non-automatic import licensing), rules of origin, and contingency measures (anti-dumping, countervailing, and safeguard measures; in other words, 'administered protection').[125]

Finally, a third category entails 'behind-the-border' measures, ie internal regulations[126] and practices which may have protective effects if not applied uniformly to domestic and foreign goods and services. Here are classified measures and practices such as tax,[127] competition, credit, and investment policies, industrial and macroeconomic policies; price controls; fiscal incentives; government procurement policies; state trade monopolies; export subsidies and domestic support; technical barriers to trade (regulations, standards, testing and certification

[123] Claessens *et al* demonstrated that the higher the campaign contributions are the more probable it is to identify after the elections firm-specific political favours. S Claessens, E Feijen, and L Laeven, 'Political Connections and Preferential Access to Finance: The Role of Campaign Contributions', 2006.

[124] IMF and World Bank (n 40 above) 9.

[125] MJ Finger, KH Hall, and DR Nelson, 'The Political Economy of Administered Protection' (1982) 72(3) AER 452–466.

[126] Such regulations also embrace 'quasi-regulation' and soft law such as codes of conduct, advisory instruments or notes, etc, where there is a reasonable expectation of compliance.

[127] Article III GATT and its Interpretative Note, Annex I, *Ad* Art. III.

procedures); sanitary and phytosanitary measures (food, animal and plant health and safety);[128] and environmental policies.

In the literature, this last category tallies with the non-tariff barriers (NTBs), although into the latter fits literally any barrier to trade that is not a tariff,[129] such as quotas.[130] NTBs cover a broad array of government policies and practices that constitute import and export restraints on trade.[131] As quotas have been in principle eliminated and tariffs reduced, these 'behind-the-border' complementary policies have emerged as one of the most important remaining obstacles to international trade, as constituting a veiled form of protectionism that inhibits trade in many instances, and have thus become an increasingly significant issue in the WTO.[132]

Over the years, as nations have grown more interdependent and economic integration has intensified, the issues subject to international negotiations have expanded. It was not until the mid-1970s that NTBs appeared as an important source of protecting domestic markets. Before then, tariff levels were sufficiently high to conceal the NTB threat. Trade policy had for centuries been organized on the basis of the measures governments use at the border to define and defend national markets and domestic producers. It is notable that in the years before the Geneva Round of 1947, the tariffs of the industrialized countries were, on average, as high as about 40 per cent of the import value.

For that reason, trade negotiations principally revolved around tariffs and quantitative restrictions, and the major concern was the extension of MFN treatment, '"one of the pillars of the WTO trading system" which has consistently served as a key basis and impetus for concessions in trade negotiations'.[133] In the early years, the GATT rounds concentrated on further reducing tariffs. Then, the Kennedy Round in the mid-1960s brought about a GATT Anti-Dumping Agreement and a section on development. The Tokyo Round during the 1970s was the first major attempt to tackle NTBs through a series of side agreements

[128] The costs of product standards barriers may be much higher than tariffs to global trade. JS Wilson, 'Standards, Regulation, and Trade: WTO Rules and Developing Country Concerns' in B Hoekman, A Mattoo, and P English (eds), *Development, Trade, and the WTO: A Handbook*, 2002, 432.

[129] RE Baldwin, *Non-tariff Distortions in International Trade*, 1971, 5; also OECD, 'Overview of Non-Tariff Barriers: Findings from Existing Business Surveys', TD/TC/WP(2002)38/FINAL, 2003.

[130] For a list of the major NTBs, see AV Deardorff and RM Stern, *Measurement of Non-Tariff Barriers*, Studies in International Economics, 1998, 95.

[131] Some scholars distinguish between 'core' NTBs (quantitative restrictions or price controls on imports), which are considered to have clearly protective effects, and other NTBs. C Michalopoulos, 'Trade Policy and Market Access Issues for Developing Countries: Implications for the Millennium Round', PRWP No 2214, 1999, 25. Another distinction is made between formal and informal NTBs. Deardorff and Stern (n 130 above) 4.

[132] AO Sykes, 'The (Limited) Role of Regulatory Harmonization in International Goods and Services Markets' (1999) 1 JIEL 49.

[133] Appellate Body Report, *EC—Tariff Preferences*, para 101.

to GATT, known as the 'Tokyo Round Codes', and to improve the system.[134] By the mid-1980s the rapid growth of NTBs threatened the liberalization created by decades of hard-fought tariff reductions.

Overall, the eight rounds of trade negotiations that occurred under the auspices of the GATT have contributed to a substantial reduction of protection levels in most developed countries to a lower than five per cent average tariff rate for industrial products[135] and, thus, facilitated market access to international markets. The countries have undertaken liberalization commitments in successive rounds and, more often than not, honoured them.[136] Such binding multilateral commitments have offered a 'political cover' against domestic protectionist interests[137] which usually strive for subverting the trade regime and creating protectionist backlash to the detriment of the long-term national and global welfare.[138]

Whereas the level of tariffs and certain quantitative import restrictions have extensively declined and are programmed to abate further, there are concerns that NTBs to trade in general may be gaining greater import as a means of further protecting domestic producers of goods and services and impeding access to markets, and thus have a deleterious impact on international trade transactions.[139] Even when there is no protectionist intent on the part of trading policymakers, due to a lack of coordination, simple differences in regulatory or standard-setting regimes can function to hinder trade. Hence, it has become increasingly complicated to delineate the boundaries between a country's regulatory autonomy and its obligation to the international trading community not to restrict trade gratuitously.[140]

The GATT's two overarching objectives stated in its Preamble are a 'substantial reduction of tariffs and other barriers to trade' by means of reciprocal trade agreements and the abolition of discriminatory (both *de jure* and *de*

[134] RE Hudec, *Enforcing International Trade Law: The Evolution of the Modern GATT Legal System*, 1993, 24; also Hart (n 45 above) 321.

[135] DA Irwin, 'The GATT in Historical Perspective' (1995) 85(2) AER 326; also M Bacchetta and B Bora, 'Industrial Tariff Liberalization and the Doha Development Agenda', WTO Discussion Paper No 1, 2003, 15; Finger and Schuknecht (n 104 above) 7.

[136] As Bhagwati *et al* noticed, '... the smart way to keep freer trade going is to keep negotiating it: as with a bicycle [referring to the 'bicycle theory'], if you stop moving, you fall off'. J Bhagwati, A Krueger, and R Snape, 'Introduction' (1987) The World Bank Economic Review 1(4) 540; also J Bhagwati, *Protectionism*, 1988, 41; for the American perspective related to bicycle theory, see Bacchus (n 18 above) 429.

[137] Bacchetta and Jansen (n 72 above) 39.

[138] Maggi and Rodriquez-Clare demonstrated that a government may foreclose domestic lobbies by committing itself to free trade. Furthermore, they reached the paradoxical result that countries in which lobbies have more bargaining power are more likely to end up in a free-trade organization. G Maggi and A Rodriguez-Clare, 'The Value of Trade Agreements in the Presence of Political Pressures' (1998) 106(3) The Journal of Political Economy 574.

[139] D Vogel, *Trading Up—Consumer and Environmental Regulation in a Global Economy*, 1995, 3.

[140] RE Baldwin, 'Regulatory Protectionism, Developing Nations, and a Two-Tier World Trade System' in SM Collins and D Rodrik (eds), *Brookings Trade Forum: 2000*, 2001, 271.

facto)[141] treatment in international trade. In working towards the first objective, the results of reciprocal tariff-cutting negotiating rounds have been undeniably impressive. The second objective of the GATT, ie attaining non-discrimination, is the cornerstone of the Agreement.[142] Notwithstanding the fact that most of the GATT substantive provisions deal directly or indirectly with this principle, non-discrimination is primarily expressed through the MFN clause (Art I GATT) with regard to border measures, while with respect to internal measures—that is, measures that are applied once foreign like products have been cleared through customs procedures—the non-discrimination obligation is expressed through the national treatment obligation (Art III GATT).[143]

NTBs to trade are regarded in the GATT as unwelcome impediments that could thwart the expansion of world trade sought through reciprocal tariff reductions. Consequently, some NTBs are prohibited under the GATT. The two most important in this category are quotas (except when imposed in connection with balance-of-payments difficulties, domestic price support programmes in agriculture, and temporary domestic shortages of essential goods)[144] and export subsidies. It is fairly obvious that the GATT system tends, firstly, to ensure that discrimination against foreign products can only take the form of border measures, thus tariffs, with the intention of channeling protection into the policy instruments that do the least damage from an economic viewpoint,[145] and, secondly, it encourages the reduction of tariff rates through negotiating rounds.[146]

During the Uruguay Round, agreement was reached on new disciplines on NTBs which have led to a substantial reduction in the use of such measures over the years following the Uruguay Round.[147] The tariffication of all impediments in agricultural products;[148] the phase-out of the MFA by 2005; the outright prohibition of the so-called 'grey-area' measures (Art 11 of the Safeguards Agreement), including VERs, orderly marketing arrangements, and other similar measures

141 R Hudec, 'GATT/WTO Constraints on National Regulation: Requiem for an "Aim and Effects" Test' (1998) 32(3) The International Lawyer 623; also GATT Panel Report, *Japan—Alcoholic Beverages I.*

142 cf Appellate Body Report, *US—Section 211 Appropriations Act*, para 297.

143 'Article III protects expectations not of any particular trade volume but rather of the equal competitive relationship between imported and domestic products'. Appellate Body Report, *Japan—Alcoholic Beverages II,* p 16; also GATT Panel Report, *US—Superfund*, para 5.1.9. Furthermore this obligation concerns not only products that are bound in every country's schedule of concessions, but it 'also extends to products not bound under Article II'. Appellate Body Report, *Japan—Alcoholic Beverages II,* p 17.

144 Article XI GATT.

145 A Sykes, '"Efficient Protection" through WTO Rulemaking' in R Porter, P Sauvé, A Subramanian, and AB Zampetti (eds), *Equity, Efficiency and Legitimacy: the Multilateral System at the Millennium*, 2001, 123.

146 Hudec (n 134 above) 6.

147 Michalopoulos (n 131 above) 50.

148 The tariffication brought some transparency in the sector, but it did not bring about the desired level of liberalization. P Messerlin, 'Agriculture in the Doha Agenda', PRWP No 3009, 2003.

both on the export and import side; the new disciplines on import licensing; the TBT and SPS Agreements; other agreements concerning customs valuation procedures; pre-shipment inspection; rules of origin; and trade-related investment measures; all these arrangements created a more transparent and predictable environment for international trade[149] from which producers, consumers, and Members benefited.[150]

Decreasing tariff levels accompanied by lower transport costs and outstanding technology achievements have put aside many manmade and natural obstructions to trade, contributing to the levelling of the playing field to an extent never achieved before. This, however, means that the slightest tilt tends to affect extensively the efficient allocation of resources. As the influence of regulations on production and trade grows apace, regulatory diversity is gradually gaining an important position in the negotiators' agenda. Negotiators will be induced to look for responses deriving from arguments that favour liberalization, harmonization in specific issues, and/or mutual recognition solutions.

C. Protection in services industries

The evolution of services has led to a rising interest in their efficient supply. Nowadays, services can influence the international competitiveness of other parts of an economy including other traded services.[151] Tourism, for instance, hinges on the efficiency and international competitiveness of transport, telecommunications, etc. Financial service suppliers call for a proficient and innovative telecommunications industry.[152] National economies need an open and transparent financial services sector, as the Asian financial crisis has candidly showed a few years ago. More generally, services play an essential role in the overall functioning of markets, since they underlie the relations between producers and consumers. Services are an indispensable component of the information industry networks on which these relations between producers and consumers depend. Instantaneous interactive communication permits transactions in an

[149] P Low and A Yeats, 'Nontariff Measures and Developing Countries: Has the Uruguay Round Leveled the Playing Field?', PRWP No 1353, 1994; also SP Anderson and N Schmitt, 'Non-Tariff Barriers and Trade Liberalization, 2000, 3.

[150] *But* see JM Finger and LA Winters, 'Reciprocity in the WTO' in B Hoekman, A Mattoo, and P English (eds), *Development, Trade, and the WTO: A Handbook*, 2002, 58–59.

[151] B Hindley, 'Service Sector Protection: Considerations for Developing Countries' (1988) 2(2) World Bank Economic Review 207. See also Chapter I.B. above.

[152] These issues are associated with positive consumption externalities, the so-called 'network externalities'. For this notion, ML Katz and C Shapiro, 'Network Externalities, Competition, and Compatibility' (1985) 75(3) AER 424. For the effects of network externalities on trade negotiations, K Kubota, 'Trade Negotiations in the Presence of Network Externalities', PRWP No 2317, 2000. For a critical viewpoint regarding network externalities, SJ Liebowitz and SE Margolis, 'Network Externality: An Uncommon Tragedy' (1994) 8(2) The Journal of Economic Perspectives 133.

increasing number of services to occur at the same time but in different places. Furthermore, the growing interpenetration of services and goods, as regards both supply and demand, means that any policy seeking the optimal allocation of productive resources must now take into consideration both goods and services.

Gradually, consumers seek to access service inputs from the most cost-effective suppliers on the globe, whereas several service suppliers are selling their services worldwide. If a service supplier in one economy appears to have the required service-supplying capabilities, then a consumer, resident in another country, must in some way interact with that producer to acquire those services. Indeed, unless cross-border trade is feasible, the sale of services requires some proximity of the supplier and the receiver, and this means that at least one of them must change location for a transaction to go forward. In this event, the efficient supply of a service may call for establishment of some form in the vicinity of potential consumers. In the case of financial services, for instance, a form of establishment is usually necessary to carry out all the activities ordinarily linked to the supply of such services. In case the supply of a service is feasible through both commercial presence and traditional cross-border trade, it is the intensity of the barriers to trade in services which determines whether the two modes are substitutes or complements.

As detected above, in the case of trade in goods the main barriers appear in the form of tariffs. Although differences between tariff bindings and applied rates ('ceiling binding') and the existence of preferential trade agreements and subsidies hinder any attempts to analyse policymaking, the prevailing policies are relatively straightforward to identify. This is not the case with services. Since some form of interaction (either through direct physical contact or via a communications network) between the supplier and the receiver is necessary for most services transactions, barriers to services trade do not tend to take the traditional form of tariffs.

Putting up border barriers might be inexpedient for an interventionist government that wants to control services transactions. It would be 'shrewder' to raise barriers at a point where it can have control over the services transaction. For it is facile to restrict trade in services, so long as it is inextricably associated with factor mobility. Restricting any factor inflow could be a very effective weapon in order to impede trade in services. As Bhagwati shrewdly remarked, '...this weakens the traditional power of the border measures known by the trade in goods and goes beyond the conventional focus on border trade measures such as tariffs or non-tariff barriers for services'.[153] Consequently, many of the most effective barriers to international trade in services are restrictions on two important factors of production, ie commercial presence (capital) and labour movement (people).

In the case of many services, the fact that boundaries do not constitute anymore an insurmountable barrier to services transactions is more apparent

[153] Bhagwati (n 4 above) 453.

and has more direct implications than in merchandise trade. Policymakers around the world are grappling with these implications and how best to meet future policy objectives. Protection in the services sector consists almost entirely of non-tariff barriers. As the scope of border measures is fairly limited, the 'behind-the-border' regulatory measures have a much stronger influence on trade in services than on goods trade. In addition, NTBs in services—as opposed to goods—are much more difficult to 'tariffy', if only because governments do not really have knowledge of their existence, since many of these regulatory measures hampering trade were launched such a long time ago that it has become complex to acknowledge their deleterious effects on trade in services.[154] Contrary to tariffs and quotas, the identification and quantification of these 'behind-the-border' barriers is a daunting task. Consequently, liberalization of trade in services becomes a challenging assignment for negotiators.

As a result of the fact that services are frequently not tradable (in that the exchange sometimes requires the prolonged proximity of supplier and consumer), either firms and/or suppliers have to move to the location of the consumer of a service. In other cases, establishment (as well as its form, eg through branch, subsidiary, or a joint venture) may be the outcome of the preferences of particular suppliers, or even of the proximity of markets and customers that are often very important for the efficient supply of a service. It follows that any attempt to determine the overall policy stance of a given country towards services trade entails an examination of its regulatory regimes regarding temporary (eg ENTs[155] or restrictive visa requirements) or longer-term entry (eg policies governing FDI) of service suppliers.

[154] B Hoekman and PA Messerlin, 'Liberalizing Trade in Services: Reciprocal Negotiations and Regulatory Reform' in P Sauvé and RM Stern (eds), *GATS 2000: New Directions in Services Trade Liberalization*, 2000, 493. See, *however*, the comment of David W Leebron on Alan Sykes' Article in: R Porter, P Sauvé, A Subramanian, and AB Zampetti (eds), *Equity, Efficiency and Legitimacy: The Multilateral System at the Millennium*, 2001, 145. Leebron argues that a tariffication of services protection may still be achievable for two reasons: first, because imposing tariffs is similar to imposing income or sales taxes on services transactions, something that already is achieved and, second, because there are also sectors and forms of delivering a service where the transactions may be visible, eg in international shipping. Also, in the case of modes 3 and 4, an employment tax imposed on non-nationals could be substituted for investment, establishment, and immigration barriers. Deardorff also argues that the imposition of service tariffs is feasible. In his proposal, countries would be free to levy taxes on foreign service providers that will be additional to, and higher than, the taxes that apply to domestic service suppliers. His idea takes for granted that the GATS will be amended to allow the disregard of the national treatment principle in favour of the MFN principle. It also presupposes that Members will have the willingness to identify all barriers to trade in services and transform them into taxes that discriminate against foreign service suppliers. These taxes will be subject to reduction in future negotiating rounds, as has been the case in GATT. AV Deardorff, 'Tariffication in Services', Research Seminar in International Economics, Discussion Paper No 473, 2001.

[155] UNCTAD, 'List of Economic Needs Tests in the GATS Schedules of Specific Commitments', UNCTAD/ITCD/TSB/8, 1999, 2; OECD, 'Assessing Barriers to Trade in Services—The Scheduling of Economic Needs Tests in the GATS: An Overview', TD/TC/WP(2000)11/FINAL, 2000, 4.

At any rate, several studies have demonstrated that current levels of services protection are as high as—or higher than—those applied to goods twenty years ago. By way of illustration, it is suggested that in many instances, the level of protection equates to average *ad valorem* tariff equivalents ranging from 50 per cent to 100 per cent for large sectors[156]—obviously higher than rates observable for goods in OECD countries, but comparable to the rates existing in developing countries two decades ago.

An important eccentricity of the nature of protection in services industries is that most of the barriers to trade in services have quota characteristics. Consequently, such barriers tend to create economic rents for incumbent service suppliers. This is inevitable, since quantitative restrictions generate artificial scarcity, which in turn leads to inflated prices and hence the creation of rents. The presence of such a rent-creating process might in all probability induce incumbents to take action and it will strengthen their incentives to lobby in order to retain protection. The particularity in the services context is that this group of 'insiders' in the domestic market may include not only local firms/service suppliers but also *foreign* ones.[157] Then, oddly enough, it is likely to identify a formation of an alliance between domestic and foreign incumbents that opposes any change of the cartel-like *status quo*.[158]

In this regard, it bears mention that in several countries, export interests in services are weaker than in manufacturing or agriculture because some services are more difficult to trade and therefore any 'home-grown' reform initiative is very unlikely to appear. In OECD countries, for instance, the ratio of exports to output is on average over six times less for services than for goods.[159] Consequently, the number and political influence of import-competing sectors may significantly exceed that of export-oriented firms. Then, what is needed in order to buttress domestic reforms is a mobilization of exporters of goods who call for competitive service inputs. For example, this will be the case of potential foreign direct investors who may have such a strong export interest. In the case of services it seems more evident that those that liberalize first may have a strategic advantage, as employment opportunities can be expected to expand due to FDI.

[156] PA Messerlin, *Measuring the Cost of Protection in Europe: European Commercial Policy in the 2000s,* 2001, 46. Interestingly, the author reports that only in EU air transport services is the *ad valorem* tariff equivalent as high as 71 per cent.

[157] See also the case of Malaysia, where the entry restrictions in financial services benefited both national firms and foreign incumbents (Malaysia included in its Schedule so-called 'grandfathering provisions'). A Mattoo, 'Financial Services and the WTO: Liberalization in the Developing and Transition Economies', World Bank Paper, 16 March 1998, 23.

[158] J Francois and I Wooton, 'Market Structure, Trade Liberalization, and the GATS' (2001) 17 European Journal of Political Economy 395.

[159] CAP Braga, C Fink, and B Hoekman, 'Telecommunications-Related Services: Market Access, Deeper Integration and the WTO', Hamburgisches Welt-Wirtschafts-Archiv, Institut für Wirtschaftsforschung Discussion Paper No 158, 2002, 10.

Therefore, it is very likely that reforms might be more easily accepted than in the case of goods.[160] Again, this depends on the relative power of the incumbents.

D. Regulations as impediments to trade in services

Services have long operated in politically sensitive economic sectors. Many governments still own and directly or indirectly control the communications infrastructure and services. Other service industries such as banking and insurance are either government-owned or highly regulated; and this in spite of extensive structural reforms during the last decades that have entailed deregulation/ privatization policies in both developed and developing countries.[161] By tradition, many services were (or continue to be) supplied by the government, or, alternatively, a public institution directly associated with it, on the basis of a statutory monopoly. Since the 1980s many former government monopoly suppliers were transformed into private law companies whose shares were gradually sold to the public, and, thus, governments became minority shareholders.[162] Privatization efforts were often accompanied by liberalization policies to prevent the former government monopoly supplier from dominating the market, this time as a private monopoly. Special regulatory regimes were inaugurated in order to ensure the proper functioning of competition without putting in jeopardy the nature of those services as being supplied on a universal basis.

While the reform process in several service industries in recent years has involved a certain amount of deregulation, in most cases the decision is not whether to regulate, but rather the kind of regulation that is the most 'appropriate'.[163] For example, it is well known that the financial services sector is one of the most densely regulated sectors in an advanced economy. This is, first, due to the central economic role the financial system enjoys. What distinguishes the financial services sector, especially its banking component, from other service activities is its close links with the economy at large. Strong interdependence exists between,

[160] Hence, any demands for reciprocity, ie equivalent concessions by the trading partners, are likely to be less of a priority for countries than was the case in goods trade. Hoekman and Messerlin (n 154 above) 487.

[161] WTO, CTS 'Financial services', S/C/W/72, 1998, 5.

[162] Several governments, however, retain a so-called 'golden share'. 'Golden shares' may be defined as special rights or powers given to the government or other public institutions concerning influence over privatized companies regardless of the stake they hold in them. In order to retain control without having to keep a majority stake, governments set up golden share mechanisms that would allow them to interfere with key decisions such as the appointment of board members or the blocking of a hostile takeover. This practice became the object of a recent litigation before the ECJ. Case C-367/98 *Commission v Portugal* [2002] ECR I-4731; Case C-483/99 *Commission v French Republic* [2002] ECR I-4781; and Case C-503/99 *Commission v Kingdom of Belgium* [2002] ECR I-4809.

[163] C Findlay, 'Introduction to the Regulation of Services' in Productivity Commission/ Australian National University, *Achieving Better Regulation of Services,* 2000, 11.

on the one hand, macroeconomic management, financial regulation and supervision, and, on the other hand, the trade regime. Second, it is possible that problems arising in particular institutions or markets may, if allowed to spread, lead to a loss of consumer and stakeholders' confidence in that system[164] and therefore, prudential policies that pre-empt or reduce systemic risk and provide safety nets are vital for a safe and sound financial system that functions competitively.[165]

Depending on which services sector comes into focus, the extent of regulation varies. Several factors such as the extent of risk, the nature of the industry involved, or the need for flexibility or certainty in any regulatory arrangement can determine the form of governmental action. Fairly light-handed regulation, such as codes of good practice for an industry, is not expected to raise operational costs to a considerable extent, as it does not really affect the way the industry operates. On the contrary, highly interventionist regulation, like entry restrictions, prohibitions and burdensome controls for the 'newcomers' in a market, can change the structure and operation of an industry, and it is very probable that quite large economic costs are to be incurred.[166] Several governments attempt to ensure the strictest control at the national level, and for so long as such control is technically feasible, of all services activities liable to affect the short- and medium-term management of their economy. This partly answers why trade in services is regulated so heavily.

Nevertheless, regulating a services sector in a cost-effective manner so that legitimate objectives are met without negative effects on the sector at hand is of crucial importance. Market-oriented economists insist on avoiding governmental interference except when it comes to 'market failure'.[167] Since the financial sector is often considered *sui generis* in the sense that it provides certain services, which are considered as 'public goods',[168] and, in turn, public goods provide a set of market failure possibilities, it seems, in principle, to be justifiable that governments tend to intervene in various ways, also in order to ensure confidence in the system and its institutions. Another example where considerable heavy-handed regulation is

164 According to Benston, there are five reasons for regulating financial services: (a) benefits that can be generated for the government from direct or indirect taxation of financial institutions and services; (b) concerns about negative externalities, ie costs borne by people that did not deal directly with financial institutions that fail or perform poorly; (c) consumer protection, prevention of fraud and misrepresentation, unfair treatment and insufficient information; (d) benefits to elected officials to appear to have taken measures that benefit consumers; and (e) benefits to the regulated financial institutions and protection from competition. GJ Benston, *Regulating Financial Markets: A Critique and Some Proposals*, Institute of Economic Affairs, 1998, 28.

165 Also para 2(a) of the Financial Services Annex; and M Kono *et al*, 'Opening Markets in Financial Services and the Role of the GATS', WTO Special studies No 1, 1997, 27.

166 P Coghlan, 'The Principles of Good Regulation' in Productivity Commission and Australian National University, *Achieving Better Regulation of Services*, 2000, 37.

167 LJ White, 'Competition versus Harmonization—An Overview of International Regulation of Financial Services' in CE Barfield (ed), *International Financial Markets: Harmonization versus Competition*, 1996, 12.

168 WTO, CTS (n 161 above) 10; also OECD, 'Convergence in the Financial Services Industry', DAFFE/AS/WD(99)12, 1999, 48.

present is the professional services sector, since this is deemed necessary in order to maintain high professional standards, ensure the quality of services supply and the integrity of service suppliers, or to protect consumers.[169] Quite the opposite applies to the other categories of business services (also known as producer services or intermediate services), consulting and distribution services for which it is asserted that they are among the least protected sectors. Economic research has demonstrated that, in fact, the services sectors that are regulated the most are the ones that are deemed to clearly possess growth-generating characteristics.[170]

As a rule, governments tend to extensively regulate services industries in order to pursue an array of objectives, both economic and non-economic. In the former category, a benign government struggles to untangle problems associated with market failures, asymmetric information (including prudential requirements), monopoly (including natural monopolies),[171] public goods and externalities, protection of intellectual property, and the improvement of the terms of foreign trade and investment. Such terms would include the establishment of conditions for the operation of interconnected networks, including distribution, communication, transportation and public information systems networks; the protection of downstream suppliers against exploitation by firms with excessive market power; and the establishment of conditions for the operation of a market economy. This category of objectives deriving from economic arguments also embodies technical issues, eg dearth of radio frequency spectrum and integrity of networks.

Among the non-economic objectives are matters of distributional justice and equity considerations including universal availability,[172] access to essential facilities, supply of services to underserved regions or population segments, cultural and other social objectives (for instance, consumer and environmental protection), and national ownership.[173]

All the same, these newly established regulatory regimes can unduly constrain access to the supply of these services and hence services trade. In most cases, trade restrictions, by reducing competition in a services market, will reduce the efficiency of that market. As a result, national welfare will also decrease, as the extent to which service suppliers specialize in providing services according to their comparative advantage is limited, hampering in this way the optimal division of labour. Trade restraints interfere with the resources allocation in an economy

[169] For an early survey on the major professional services (legal, accounting, engineering, and architecture services), see WTO, WPPS, 'Work in the Area of Professional Services', Communication from the OECD, S/WPPS/W/4, 1995, and Addenda 1 and 2 (S/WPPS/W/4/Add.1, and S/WPPS/W/4/Add.2, 1996).

[170] A Mattoo, R Rathindran, and A Subramanian, 'Measuring Services Trade Liberalization and its Impact on Economic Growth: An Illustration' (2006) 21 Journal of Economic Integration 64.

[171] UNCTAD and World Bank, *Liberalizing International Transactions in Services: A Handbook*, 1994, 38.

[172] cf UNCTAD, 'Report of the Expert Meeting on Universal Access to Services', TD/B/COM.1/EM.30/3, 2006.

[173] This is the case, for example, in international aviation, which is not covered by GATS. RH Snape, 'Regulating Services Trade: Matching Policies to Objectives', 2000, 6.

benefiting the protected industry at the expense of other industries and consumers. In contrast, trade liberalization allows countries to pursue specialization commensurate with their comparative advantage. The employment of productive resources in those activities where they can be more efficiently utilized is likely to flourish in a liberal environment and this will have positive effects to consumers in the form of reasonable prices. In this setting, protected industries will have to adjust in response to international competition increase. Overall, the net welfare impact is expected to be positive (at least under competitive market conditions), as the concept of comparative advantage applies with equal force to international trade in services.[174]

Restrictions to trade in services may take the form of obscure licensing procedures; discriminatory taxation; discretionary qualification criteria; denial of the ability to establish a commercial presence, and so forth. Indeed, the complex structure of many services sectors provides numerous opportunities for effective discrimination and the imposition of opaque measures of ostensibly protectionist intent. Accordingly, foreign companies entering new markets often face formidable barriers. Although the policy instruments that affect international trade in services may be akin to those used in the goods context, consisting of measures such as subsidies, tariffs, taxes, quotas, and technical standards,[175] the most important barriers in the services context are generally embedded in arbitrary and non-transparent regulations imposed by the domestic regulatory institutions or authorities, and focused on the local provision or the local consumption of services.[176] The fact that such regulations can even be origin-neutral perplexes further. For that reason, it is often argued that liberalization of services is primarily a challenge for domestic (as opposed to trade) policy.

Such regulations very often nullify any ability of foreign companies to compete with domestic firms on an equal basis. They can effectively negate the benefits of trade liberalization commitments undertaken during multilateral negotiating rounds, where the countries explicitly promised to avoid reneging on their commitments. As noted, such barriers need not discriminate against foreigners. To be sure, market access barriers are often designed to protect incumbent firms from *any* new entry, be it domestic or foreign. The protection of consumers when it comes to shady practices connected with excessive competition, or the argument

[174] B Hindley and A Smith, 'Comparative Advantage and Trade in Services' (1984) 7(1) The World Economy 369. Messerlin argues that an explanation for the lack of progress in services negotiations is that Members have failed to identify their potential comparative advantages in services and experience shows that, in practice, developing countries may not have such an advantage in sectors where they believed they did. PA Messerlin, 'Non-Discrimination, Welfare Balances, and WTO Rules: A Historical Perspective' in E-U Petersmann (ed), *Reforming the World Trading System—Legitimacy, Efficiency, and Democratic Governance*, 2005, 300.

[175] Hindley (n 151 above) 220; also Hoekman and Braga (n 6 above) 5.

[176] T Warren and C Findlay, '"Sins of commission and omission": Measuring regulatory impediments to trade in services' in Productivity Commission and Australian National University, *Achieving Better Regulation of Services*, 2000, 358.

that the domestic market cannot physically and economically support more than a limited number of suppliers are rationales which are often provided to justify such self-defeating regulations.[177]

In more generalized terms, the regulatory regimes usually determine the very feasibility of trade in services. They also have an impact on the mode of supply that the service supplier chooses in order to provide its services (pattern of trade). In the case that a service supplier has the luxury of supplying her services through all four modes of supply, the decision on the mode will depend on the cost of using alternative modes.

Measuring the trade effects—positive and negative alike—of domestic regulations concerning the practice of medicine or law, capital requirements for financial institutions, data processing, advertising, construction services, supply of telecommunications to regions where it is difficult to get to, and so forth, is extremely complicated, since such 'within-the-border' laws, regulations, administrative decrees, and other legal instruments, are ingeniously created on a continuous basis by virtually all the domestic activities of government, at all levels of jurisdiction. Each regulatory act of a national government increases, at least potentially, the fragmentation of the world economy and, in this manner, might negatively encroach on the efficient delivery of services.

The problem of drawing a distinction between regulatory measures which are used as public policy instruments that assure the efficient supply of a service and protectionist measures that impede foreign competition also appears in the goods context. While NTBs in goods impede trade in goods in virtually the same way, the object of goods regulation is usually the product itself. Nevertheless, in service industries, due to the lack of extensive standardization, the object of regulation is concentrated not only on services *stricto sensu* but also on producers/service suppliers. Legislations often set out rules relative to the qualities of the service supplier. On the other hand, the content of the service itself is rarely stipulated. Consequently, not only can the regulatory authorities control the entry of producers/suppliers in the industry, but also their conduct once they are allowed to enter the domestic industry. Indeed, many of the most effective barriers to international transactions in the service sector concern both pre-establishment and post-establishment issues affecting the movement of capital and labour.

In various instances, however, regulation which limits competition is necessary to deal with 'market failure' and to meet particular social objectives. Regulation in service industries is widely pigeonholed as a justified instrument of public policy and as a prerequisite for the efficient delivery of the service concerned. Therefore, in reality, it is difficult most of the time to discern precisely where legitimate regulation ends and protection of domestic service industries against foreign rivals starts. Interest groups always strive for regulatory capture

[177] G Feketekuty, 'Assessing and Improving the Architecture of the GATS' in P Sauvé and RM Stern (eds), *GATS 2000: New Directions in Services Trade Liberalisation*, 2000, 91.

and hence their behaviour affects the efficiency of any regulatory measure and of the affected services sector overall. Regulations sometimes are put in place to protect domestic industries from foreign competition just as often as to meet public policy objectives.[178]

It is realistic to argue that there will always be a considerable number of possible non-trade-based policies which each Member can pursue and which will undermine the value of the negotiated legal disciplines with its trading partners. Such policies can take on the aspect of legitimate regulation for non-trade purposes.[179] At the same time, though, they may hamper effective market access, similarly to the explicit trade barriers which, however, Members have legally bound themselves to constrain or eliminate. This is why there exists the requirement that when a government decides to intervene through regulatory means it should seek those measures that are the least-trade-restrictive possible.[180]

The international ramifications of domestic regulations that have a negative impact on trade are likely to increase in importance as markets become more global. Given that the service sector is usually much more regulation-intensive than the goods sector, these negative side effects may be much more onerous and hard to overcome than in the case of goods. Contrary to goods, the alternative of arm's length trading between the parties to a transaction rarely occurs in services trade.[181]

Furthermore, barriers to trade in services are more onerous due to the widespread involvement of the public sector in providing services (especially key bottleneck facilities such as water or electricity supply) and the extensive role of private professional associations in the regulation of service industries (for instance, licensing requirements for engineers and doctors). Hence services are exposed to unduly burdensome domestic regulations more than goods. If these regulations are in addition non-transparent, foreign companies may be reluctant to undertake key commitments in the domestic market.

Of course, domestic authorities may prefer—or, they even might have got used—to consider some of the regulations that deal with trade in services as natural and inevitable precautions rather than as barriers to world trade. In some cases it is also possible that some domestic regulations have been in force for so long that governments are not always cognizant of their existence, or that the trade-restrictive effects emanate from official practice and not published domestic laws.[182] Even when governments are fully aware of the impediments that are in place, there lingers the issue of identifying their economic consequences. While

[178] Also Findlay (n 163 above) 10.

[179] Also M Trebilcock and R Howse, 'Trade Liberalization and Regulatory Diversity: Reconciling Competitive Markets with Competitive Politics' (1998) 6 European Journal of Law and Economics 6.

[180] See Chapter IV below.

[181] R Snape, 'The WTO Agenda: Next Steps' in C Findlay and T Warren (eds), *Impediments to Trade in Services: Measurement and Policy Implications*, 2000, 359.

[182] Feketekuty (n 1 above) 141.

the economic linkages and interdependencies between the goods sector and the rest of the economy are nowadays well understood, one cannot contend the same as far as the service sector is concerned.

Hence, such negative side effects on trade could be unintentional;[183] they could be the result of the regulatory authorities' long-time failure to realize the harmful trade impact of their domestic regulations[184] or imbued with an ethos that calls upon public interest or consumer protection. Insofar as they are non-discriminatory and necessary for the attainment of legitimate policy objectives, they should be endorsed, even though they may constitute a considerable burden on international trade *vis-à-vis* the domestic regulatory benefits. This is in line with the philosophy of the WTO Agreements. Notwithstanding the potential negative impact of domestic regulations on trade flows and domestic welfare, neither the stringency of a domestic regulation nor its adverse trade effects, as considerable as they may be, is of concern to the GATS and the WTO in general, insofar it satisfies the obligations set forth in the WTO agreements.

Nevertheless, while the ultimate objective of regulation should be to maximize domestic social welfare, international trade and investment considerations should not be overlooked. Infringing trade and investment may have important welfare repercussions.[185] Therefore, policymakers should cater for these 'chilling' effects when enforcing or evaluating a range of regulatory responses. Most of the time a juxtaposition of trade values with the domestic social values that are to be served by the regulations will be an appropriate aspect of the regulatory process.[186]

As odd as it may sound at first blush, a different treatment of foreign service suppliers is sometimes even necessary in order to attain a range of domestic regulatory objectives. In this category may fall, for instance, a regulation which obliges foreign insurance companies to preserve deposits and investments in local financial institutions, since a periodic audit of their books located abroad (for the identification of possible poor management) is not feasible. In this manner, they are within the reach of local regulatory authorities.[187] Such regulations, while discriminatory, are justified as a means for avoiding market failures brought about by the sheer lack of information and achieving a legitimate domestic goal, hence the protection of the average consumer. Besides, this type of regulation can be deemed part and parcel of a well-intentioned legislative prudential framework. At any rate, striking the right balance between legitimate domestic regulations that impose a necessary regulatory burden on the foreign service suppliers and

[183] DA Farber and RE Hudec, 'Free Trade and the Regulatory State: A GATT's-Eye View of the Dormant Commerce Clause' (1994) 47 Vanderbilt Law Review 1401.

[184] AO Sykes, 'Regulatory Protectionism and the Law of International Trade' in K Anderson and B Hoekman (eds), *The Global Trading System*, Vol 4: 'New' Issues for the WTO, 2002, 315.

[185] cf F Eschenbach and B Hoekman, 'Services Policy Reform and Economic Growth in Transition Economies, 1990–2004', PRWP No 3663, 2005, 15.

[186] J Trachtman, 'Trade and... Problems, Cost-Benefit Analysis and Subsidiarity' (1998) 9(1) EJIL 32. See also the discussion on cost–benefit analysis below.

[187] Feketekuty (n 1 above) 132.

regulations that constitute trade barriers may prove to be a very difficult task to accomplish when it comes to trade in services.

Nevertheless, it has been apparent on certain occasions that existing regulatory outcomes do not reflect the deliberative judgments of the polity. Governments sometimes misuse domestic regulations for protectionist purposes in order to disadvantage only foreign services and service suppliers or, alternatively, to confer on local industries a competitive advantage over their foreign competitors.[188] Regulatory protectionism may be defined as 'any cost disadvantage imposed on foreign firms by a regulatory policy that discriminates against them or that otherwise disadvantages them in a manner that is unnecessary to the attainment of some genuine, non-protectionist regulatory objective'.[189]

Crudely put, these types of regulations may be conceived as a service supplied to effective political interest groups.[190] This tendency is to be anticipated since the commercial interests of exporting firms in a given country have little or no representation in the political life of that country. Particularly in such cases, foreign interests have intrinsic disadvantages in influencing the domestic policies (and, consequently, the politicians) of the importing country; first and foremost, they are not eligible to vote.[191]

The rise of regulatory protectionism is to be expected, as the use of other protectionist policies like quotas or subsidies turns out to be more and more limited owing to significant obligations undertaken since GATT came into existence. In view of this, it has become very tempting to use regulations as protectionist devices since the GATT/WTO allows for their use which it does not for tariffs, quotas, or subsidies. Thus, regulations are a very appealing loophole for those Members that wish to cheat, undermining that way their commitments and the expectations of their trading partners. From a welfare-enhancing point of view, the deadweight losses deriving from protectionist regulations are much greater as compared to other protectionist instruments.[192]

The modern regulatory state inevitably produces burdens on trade, if only due to the lack of regulatory uniformity which usually is unavoidable.[193] The slightest differences in the form and/or level of regulation among national jurisdictions can result in restrictions to services trade. In this manner, domestic regulations

188 Or, in general, newcomers, be they foreign or national. See also Section C above.

189 Sykes (n 184 above) 315.

190 cf GJ Stigler (n 34 above) 11; also RA Posner, 'Theories of Economic Regulation' (1974) 5(2) The Bell Journal of Economics and Management Science 343. See also the discussion in Section B.2 above.

191 Such interest-group theories concentrate on the political dimensions of the regulatory process and can justify only partly (or even not at all) regulations in certain areas, such as health or environment, since regulation is not exclusively political. S Breyer, *Regulation and Its Reform*, 1982, 9 and fn 38.

192 For an economic comparison between alternative policies, see Sykes (n 184 above) 319, 330.

193 Also Farber and Hudec (n 183 above) 1402.

can affect the cost of providing a service and, consequently, the competition in trade in services both across borders and domestically.

Indeed, from an economic point of view, regulatory heterogeneity,[194] be it discriminatory or not, and remaining policy divergences pose substantial barriers to international trade in services already due to the cost of complying with multiple regulatory environments.[195] If, additionally, such discrepancies in regulations are unnecessarily burdensome, they can negatively affect competition in trade in services. Therefore, if such trade impediments can be reduced while at the same time allowing for the flexibility to protect legitimate regulatory objectives, global welfare will in principle increase.[196]

Of course, one should underscore here that overregulation of services or service suppliers does not necessarily mean that these services or service suppliers are at a comparative disadvantage vis-à-vis their foreign competitors providing, for example, their services in a cross-border way and thus escaping the strict national requirements. This is so, because, while the lightly regulated suppliers can offer their services at a lower price, the heavily regulated suppliers presumably provide their services with an assured minimum level of quality, even at a higher price. The latter may be preferable for consumers, especially when it comes to intermediation and knowledge-based services. This is also the case in financial and professional services; in other words, in sectors where information asymmetries exist. This does not refute the fact that national differences in domestic regulations and the conditions under which services can be legally supplied can indeed affect competition in a negative way and create barriers to trade in services.

The question that arises then is whether a need for harmonization in the field is desirable. The issue of harmonization versus regulatory diversity is not new. On the one side, some economists and many trade negotiators lean heavily towards substantial harmonization, citing the problem of levelling the playing field (the term 'level playing field' is arguably the metaphoric symbol of fairness in trade) and the danger that increased system friction will result in substantial disruption and weakening of the WTO.[197] On the other side, many economists and academics are sceptical as to the benefits of forced harmonization. For instance, Krugman argues that only differences in resources, tastes, technologies used, labour laws, etc can bring about trade gains (he calls this the 'back-to-basics

194 Sykes (n 132 above) 49.

195 Also R Howse and E Türk, 'The WTO Impact on Internal Regulations—A Case Study of the Canada-EC Asbestos Dispute' in G de Búrca and J Scott (eds), *The EU and the WTO: Legal and Constitutional Issues*, 2001, 285.

196 *But* see Sykes (n 132 above) 50.

197 For a review of the arguments in favour of reducing diversity, see J Bhagwati, 'The Demands to Reduce Domestic Diversity among Trading Nations' in J Bhagwati and R Hudec (eds), *Fair Trade and Harmonization: Prerequisites for Free Trade?*, Vol 1: Economic Analysis, 1996, 9. For some claims in favour of *legal* harmonization, see DW Leebron, 'Lying Down with Procrustes: An Analysis of Harmonization Claims' in J Bhagwati and RE Hudec (eds), *Fair Trade and Harmonization: Prerequisites for Free Trade?*, Vol 1: Economic Analysis, 1996, 51.

argument against the harmonization of standards').[198] It is further asserted that competition among national regulatory systems will ultimately produce a more efficient, as well as more equitable, system.[199]

In this regard, it has been argued that there is scope for creating optimum harmonization areas, ie sets of countries that exhibit similar regulatory preferences and broadly compatible regulatory institutions and thus can proceed to eliminate policy differences through harmonization. This can probably be the case in several Regional Integration Agreements (RIAs) which have achieved a relatively high level of integration and thus the possible aggregate adjustment costs of regulatory convergence and policy harmonization caused by the creation of such an area would be lower compared to other countries.[200] In such a case, regulatory harmonization would maximize aggregate welfare and mitigate adjustment costs.[201] Cost savings may be even higher in the case of mutual recognition agreements,[202] such as those described in Article VII GATS.[203]

However, endeavours to harmonize should be approached with caution. It is always possible that the call for harmonization comes from interests in maintaining the *status quo* (eg from incumbents who seek to preserve their strategic advantage by demanding more stringent standards so that they raise the costs of new entrants). In other cases, entering a harmonization agreement may not be beneficial for a country, as it could raise the costs of production (eg by requiring that a country apply stricter environmental or labour standards). Arguably, whether harmonization is preferable over regulatory competition or vice versa is an issue that should be determined on a case-by-case basis. In deciding which approach to follow, the principle of subsidiarity could serve as a valuable benchmark.[204]

198 P Krugman, 'What Should Trade Negotiators Negotiate About?' (1997) 35(1) Journal of Economic Literature 115.

199 LJ White, 'Competition versus Harmonization—An Overview of International Regulation of Financial Services' in CE Barfield (ed), *International Financial Markets: Harmonization versus Competition,* 1996, 30. For another approach which, however, leads to the same conclusion in favour of regulatory competition, see Trebilcock and Howse (n 179 above) 5.

200 OECD, 'The Relationship between Regional Trade Agreements and the Multilateral Trading System—Services', TD/TC/WP(2002)27/FINAL, 2002, 9; also SM Stephenson, 'Deepening Disciplines for Trade in Services', 2001, 11–20. For the difficulty of applying harmonization and/or mutual recognition schemes in services trade, see also A Mattoo in P Sauvé and RM Stern (eds), *GATS 2000: New Directions in Services Trade Liberalization*, 2000, 319.

201 A Mattoo and C Fink, 'Regional Agreements and Trade in Services—Policy Issues', PRWP No 2852, 2002, 23–24.

202 Also K Nicolaidis, 'Harmonization and Recognition: What Have We Learned? Some Preliminary Reflections' in OECD, *Trade and Regulatory Reform: Insights from Country Experience*, 2001, 105; and DW Leebron (n 197 above) 91.

203 See, in general, K Nicolaidis and JP Trachtman, 'From Policed Regulation to Managed Recognition in GATS' in P Sauvé and RM Stern (eds), *GATS 2000: New Directions in Services Trade Liberalization*, 2000, 264. The superiority of optimum harmonization areas *vis-à-vis* the GATS Art VII alternatives has been put into question, as the latter allows greater initial selectivity as regards the partners. See OECD (n 200 above) 12 and fn 12.

204 JP Trachtman, 'Regulatory Competition and Regulatory Jurisdiction' (2000) 3 JIEL 334; in the same direction, see AO Sykes, 'Regulatory Competition or Regulatory Harmonization? A Silly Question?' (2000) 3 JIEL 263.

To be sure, a total elimination of burdens on trade of both goods and services is at least utopian. This cannot be gainsaid. Consequently, in the case of services trade, multilateral attempts to create mutually acceptable rules have had to confront the same challenges that the GATT negotiators have coped with for more than fifty years, ie to make sure that protective policy changes will not invalidate market access expectations, to reduce the transaction costs associated with negotiations by convincing nations to use fewer or more efficient instruments of protection and to accentuate those that are transparent and predictable in their application, and, finally, to channel the remaining protection in services markets into the comparatively less profligate policy instruments.[205]

E. Typologies of barriers to trade in services

As it is clear by now, the concept of international trade in services encompasses traditional cross-border transactions, as well as consumption abroad, establishment in another jurisdiction, and temporary movement of labour. Consequently, any policy that hinders services producers and consumers to interact through any of these ways is considered as an impediment to trade in services.[206] The most common bifurcation of impediments that operate to distort international services transactions is the one that has been done at the multilateral level in the GATS context and distinguishes between restrictions of market access and derogations from national treatment.[207]

The market access barriers mainly encompass quantitative restrictions on entry,[208] regardless of whether such restrictions are imposed on foreign services or foreign service supplies on a discriminatory or non-discriminatory basis.[209] Manifold numerical ceilings, certain establishment requirements, discretionary application of ENTs, or zero quotas are only few examples of market access barriers.

Restrictions on national treatment, on the other hand, denote that foreign-owned firms are treated less favourably than domestic firms. Restrictions of such nature are discriminatory, since they alter the conditions of competition in favour of service suppliers of national origin. National treatment is defined in the

[205] For a potential ranking of instruments in the case of services trade, see A Mattoo, 'Shaping Future Rules for Trade in Services: Lessons from the GATS', 2001, 7.

[206] For an instructive consolidated list of cross-sectoral measures affecting services trade divided with reference to their restrictiveness (no/little, restrictive, prohibitive) and organized according to the four modes of supply, see OECD, 'Assessing Barriers to Trade in Services: Revised Consolidated List of Cross-Sectoral Barriers', TD/TC/WP(99)58/FINAL, 2001.

[207] UNCTAD and World Bank (n 171 above) Chapters IV–VII; also P Raworth, *International Regulation of Trade in Services*, Vol 1, Section II: Basic International Regulation of Trade in Services—II.A Basic Legal Issues Relating to Trade in Services, 2003, 7.

[208] For the different deadweight costs that such limitations may have, see Sykes (n 145 above) 129.

[209] For a more detailed analysis of Art XVI GATS, see Chapter III.D.2 below.

traditional GATT approach as the non-discriminatory application of domestic regulations to foreign services or service suppliers. This implies that *quantitative* limitations imposed on *foreign* services or service suppliers (a zero quota on entry by foreign banks may well be an example of a discriminatory quantitative limitation) fall under both the market access and national treatment provisions, thereby creating some muddle.[210] Nationality or residency requirements, special subsidies or tax privileges granted to domestic suppliers, differential capital requirements and special operational limits applying only to foreign suppliers' operations are typical examples of national treatment impediments.[211]

Even though GATT traditional notions influenced GATS structure and terminology, market access and national treatment are broader in scope in the services context than in the GATT. The GATS provision on market access, on the one hand, extends beyond the conventional notion of access for foreign service suppliers (tariff bindings in GATT) to embrace all policies which restrict access to a market (extending to a certain degree the multilateral trade disciplines into the area of domestic policy and regulatory reform). The GATS provision on national treatment, on the other hand, in lieu of distinguishing between border and domestic constraints and dealing with internal taxation and regulation only (as is the case in Article III GATT), embraces all policies (both border and non-border) which might discriminate—whether *de facto* or *de jure*—between domestic and foreign services *and* service suppliers. Thus, a potential parity of treatment in some services may equate to the complete absence of barriers. In a sense, full national treatment as a general obligation could be compared to an 'immediate, non-phased in zero-tariff situation'.[212]

A comprehensive typology of barriers in the realm of services, analogous with the one that exists for goods, has not yet been developed. This is partly due to the broad and complex nature of the barriers in the services area that overlap with policies and practices traditionally assumed to be within the purview of competition policy and law, and the fact that impediments to trade in services may vary from sector to sector, which alludes to the need of sectoral studies.[213]

[210] Feketekuty (n 177 above) 95. See the discussion on Art XX:2 GATS in Chapter III.D below.

[211] WTO, *2001 Scheduling Guidelines*, S/L/92, 2001, para 12 and p 16.

[212] WJ Drake and K Nicolaidis, 'Ideas, Interests, and Institutionalization: "Trade in Services" and the Uruguay Round' (1992) 46(1) International Organization 71; also Feketekuty (n 1 above) 216.

[213] A sectoral approach has been pursued in many international organizations in their attempts to identify some types of barriers to services trade. See, for example, the research that has been conducted in WTO and OECD, both available in their websites. Also Deloitte & Touche, 'Report Relating to the Industry Consultation in the Context of Preparatory Work for GATS 2000 via the "SIS"', 1999; also C Findlay and T Warren (eds), *Impediments to Trade in Services: Measurement and Policy Implications*, 2000. Worth noting also is the attempt by the Productivity Commission of Australia to establish a trade-restrictiveness index in order to estimate, based on the frequency of certain measures, the restrictiveness of an economy's trade policy for services based on the number and severity of restrictions. It classifies restrictions in examining, first, whether they impede establishment or ongoing operations and, secondly, whether they are discriminatory or not. For more

Indeed, barriers to trade in services may vary depending on the type of service at issue, the country imposing the barriers, and the sectors to which these barriers are incumbent.

Furthermore, the four modes of supply in GATS are not equally prominent; nor do all the detrimental measures affecting trade in services have the same protectionist effect.[214] An additional obscurity emanates from the difficulty in distinguishing whether the measures that may be canvassed in the services area (through the GATS Schedules), are applied in a discriminatory or in a non-discriminatory manner. Nevertheless, there have been studies identifying measures that apply frequently across the board and which are considered as barriers to services trade. An attempt to classify some types of such barriers was made by Hoekman and Braga.[215] In their survey, the authors identified four broad categories of such barriers:[216]

(a) Quotas, local content requirements, and prohibitions: QR-type policies are typically applied to service suppliers and not services per se. In many countries, there are also outright prohibitions directed against foreign suppliers as in the case of transport services. Restrictions on cross-border data flows and computer networks such as the internet may prove to impede market access and stymie services trade.
(b) Price-based instruments:[217] Such measures may take the form of visa fees and entry or exit taxes,[218] discriminatory airline landing or porting fees. Tariffs can also be important barriers to trade in goods that embody services (eg films, computer software) or goods that are necessary inputs into services production (eg computers, telecoms equipment).[219] Furthermore, certain services sectors are subject to government-sanctioned or -monitored price controls (eg financial services, telecom services), while other sectors benefit from government subsidies (eg construction, health, education, transport).
(c) Standards, licensing, and procurement: Licensing or certification requirements may be imposed on foreign service suppliers mainly in business and professional services (limitations on the 'right to practise'). Domestic

information and available data concerning such sectoral studies, see the Productivity Commission of Australia website at: <http://www.pc.gov.au>.

[214] Bacchetta and Jansen (n 72 above) 44; also WTO, *World Trade Report 2003*, 2003, 140.

[215] Hoekman and Braga (n 6 above) 6; also RM Stern, 'Quantifying Barriers to Trade in Services', 2000, 2.

[216] Also UNCTAD, 'Assessment of Trade in Services of Developing Countries: Summary of Findings', UNCTAD/ITCD/TSB/7, 1999, 11.

[217] If subsidizing the domestic services industries to protect them is not feasible, price-based restrictions on market access are to be preferred to quantity-based limitations, as the latter hamper competition. However, these price-based instruments should not be discriminatory. B Hoekman, 'Developing Countries and the Uruguay Round: Negotiations on Services', PRWP No 1220, 1993, 24.

[218] Measures that regulate the exit from a market may also operate as deterrents to entry in this market inducing firms to be cautious when they decide to invest.

[219] UNCTAD and World Bank (n 171 above) 119.

practices of granting a licence to a potential supplier may be highly restrictive, since in many instances the professional bodies concerned decide whether to accord market access or not. The fact that in such cases self-regulating professional bodies restrict access to their professions in order to maximize their income is deemed an exception to the general rule that impediments to international services tend to fall as income rises. In such cases, the incumbents may monopolize the authorization of professional licences to foreign service suppliers. The professional bodies have the absolute power to keep their income at high levels—and in most cases they use this power in order to shield the domestic industry from foreign competition. In other instances, environmental standards may have an impact on service suppliers, especially in the transport sector. Government procurement practices in the form of preference margins or outright prohibitions may also exclude any foreign service suppliers.

(d) Discriminatory access to distribution networks: Such access to distribution networks is subject to limitations in favour of domestic service suppliers in many countries in such sectors as air transport, telecom, advertising, and dealer networks. The issue of such discriminatory access is also inextricably bound up with public monopolies and the essential facilities regulation. Legislation on essential facilities is particularly critical in the services context and sometimes is explicitly limited to services. Potential entrants may not be able to compete with incumbent operators that control the natural monopoly components of the network within domestic services markets which do not have effective essential facilities legislation. In that case, ineffective regulation is as harmful as any licensing constraints.

The abovementioned classification portrays a significant part of the barriers restricting international trade in services and establishes that conventional NTBs such as QRs, price-based instruments, licensing and certification requirements, or discriminatory access to networks are also present in the services trade. The GATS deals with these barriers mainly through Articles VI, XVI, and XVII.[220] It is worth noting, however, that this classification identifies for the most part discriminatory measures, ie measures that *de jure* or *de facto* infringe the national treatment obligation and favour domestic service suppliers vis-à-vis foreign suppliers.[221] Even if the measures per se do not deliberately discriminate, they are considered to do so due to the discretionary *application* of domestic regulations and a lack of transparency in the criteria of the application of certain measures or tests, eg the implementation and maintenance of control bodies to scan services

[220] See Chapter III.D below.

[221] The aforementioned taxonomy, however, leads to relative measurements. While such measurements allow for a comparison among countries, they do not help in quantifying the importance of the differences in barriers, since they are not *ad valorem* equivalents. Therefore, they have only limited value. WTO (n 214 above) 141.

on the basis of cultural or social criteria, the exercise of monopoly power to hamper market access, government approval requirements, and the need for a local authority's prior approval for certain activities.

F. Possible gains from dismantling barriers to trade in services

Although the ranking of instruments in both goods and services is comparable, the GATS, unlike the GATT, did not create any hierarchy of instruments of protection.[222] Thus, quantitative restrictions, which have been discredited and prohibited with respect to trade in goods, thrive in trade in services.[223] Such restrictions, as stated above under Section C, create artificial shortage and thus incumbent firms earn significant rents. The dismantling of such tariff-like limitations and the ensuing elimination of rents to incumbent firms not only can improve allocative efficiency, but it will also have redistributive effects similar to the redistribution of tariff revenue in the context of goods.

In a nutshell, services are unique in some ways but familiar in others. The propositions about comparative advantage and the gains from trade apply equally in the services realm. Barriers to trade in services lead, as in the case of goods, to the loss of economic welfare.[224] Then, whatever eccentricities are present in the services trade, the general point that multilateral liberalization may facilitate the abolition of policies restricting market access is as valid in the context of services as in the context of merchandise trade.[225] According to World Bank estimates, the results from an abolition of trade barriers in services only in developing countries would be quite impressive: By 2015, an incremental income gain for developing countries of nearly $900 billion could be generated; in other words, some 4.5 times greater than their gains from global merchandise trade liberalization alone.[226]

Furthermore, an increasing awareness of the strong economy-wide case in support of services liberalization and the high costs that derive from the incessant protection that is accorded particularly to key infrastructure sectors has been

[222] This renunciation of a hierarchy of instruments comparable to GATT is to the detriment of the GATS and its welfare repercussions. PA Messerlin (n 174 above) 299–300.

[223] A Mattoo, 'Negotiating Improved Market Access Commitments' in B Hoekman, A Mattoo, and P English (eds), *Development, Trade, and the WTO: A Handbook*, 2002, 282; also Sykes (n 145 above) 126.

[224] The World Bank estimated the gains for the global income from the abolition of all trade barriers at $2.8 trillion by 2015. This would lift 320 million people out of poverty. World Bank (n 29 above) 176.

[225] For a comprehensive review of previous studies as to the potential gains of liberalization in several service sectors, see J Nielson and D Taglioni, 'Services Trade Liberalization: Identifying Opportunities and Gains', OECD Trade Policy Working Paper No 1, TD/TC/WP(2003)23/FINAL, 2004, 83ff.

[226] World Bank (n 29 above) 172.

established in the past decade.[227] In several instances, this protection can be vindicated on the grounds that services transactions penetrate much deeper into an economy than do goods transactions by reason of the nature of the interaction between supplier and consumer.

Despite the creation of GATS and the importance of services not only as indispensable sources of employment and income but also as vital intermediate inputs for the production of other goods and services, the removal of restraints on multilateral trade in services has been minimal to date. This, however, suggests that large welfare gains can be expected as liberalization efforts intensify given that the efficiency of the service sector greatly affects the efficiency of the economy overall. Various studies reveal that developing countries tend to have in place more restrictive regimes regulating trade in services than developed economies.[228] The greater openness of developed economies is the outcome of ongoing regulatory reform endeavours in several services sectors, with the most prominent examples being the financial and telecommunications service sectors.[229] In turn, domestic reforms are greatly associated with the fact that the role of the state as service supplier is constantly put into question in most developed economies.

As to the market access restrictions in developing countries, commercial presence is the most restricted mode. Given that many services require an on-the-spot local establishment so that they can be supplied, restrictions of that kind may exclude the possibility of supplying a service altogether. Restrictions on national treatment, on the other hand, may take different forms depending on the nature of the service at issue. For instance, in the case of construction services, national treatment limitations include licensing, standards, and qualifications in the presence of natural persons.[230]

More generally, restrictions on the movement of natural persons remain very important and affect suppliers not only from developing, but also from developed countries.[231] Several studies emphasized that the potential gains from mode 4 liberalization (even a partial one) can be of considerable magnitude. In a recent study, Winters *et al* demonstrated that an increase in mobility equivalent to

[227] G McGuire, 'Trade in Services—Market Access Opportunities and the Benefits of Liberalization for Developing Economies', UNCTAD, Policy Issues in International Trade and Commodities Study Series No 19, 2002, 21.

[228] N Dihel, 'Quantifying Costs to National Welfare from Barriers to Services Trade: A Review of the Literature' in OECD, *Quantifying the Benefits of Liberalizing Trade in Services*, 2003, 113ff. Of course, one should keep in mind that developing countries encompass an extremely heterogeneous group with differing characteristics and use of restrictions on the supply of services.

[229] A Lehmann, NT Tamirisa, and J Wieczorek, 'International Trade in Services: Implications for the IMF', IMF Policy Discussion Paper, PDP/03/6, 2003, 7.

[230] WTO, Council of Trade in Services, 'Construction and Related Engineering Services', Background Note by the Secretariat, S/C/W/38, 8 June 1998, para 26.

[231] Chaudhuri *et al* identified the following categories of barriers that affect Mode 4: a. Visa formalities; b. Prohibitions and quotas; c. Wage-parity conditions; d. General discriminatory treatment; and e. Non-recognition of professional qualifications and burdensome licensing requirements. S Chaudhuri, A Mattoo, and R Self, 'Moving People to Deliver Services: How Can the WTO Help?', PRWP No 3238, 2004, 2–3.

three per cent of the receiving countries' work forces would generate $156 billion a year in extra economic welfare.[232] Interestingly, these gains are equally distributed between developed and developing countries. Under this study, unskilled labour mobility appears to generate more benefits than the mobility of skilled personnel.[233]

Regarding other studies on the welfare gains of services liberalization, whilst different models using sundry modelling assumptions and input data can lead to differences in the range and quality of outcomes,[234] they all demonstrate that services liberalization can generate global effects of at least the same order of magnitude as those associated with full liberalization of merchandise trade.[235] According to other studies, the global gains from eliminating impediments to trade in services could even be of the same magnitude as those from abolishing all remaining barriers to trade in agriculture *and* manufacturing.[236] Nonetheless, the liberalization impact may differ significantly across countries,[237] since it seems that the economies with initial high protection levels tend to gain the most, ie the major benefits from liberalization accrue to developing countries because their restrictions on services are higher than those of developed economies.[238]

In order to reap the maximum gains, liberalization efforts should include all modes of supply. Any effort to liberalize partially can have adverse effects. For instance, dismantling barriers affecting establishment while retaining limitations on cross-border supply may lead to a transfer of rents to foreign firms and hence reduce national welfare.[239] Indeed, with the purpose of grasping the maximum net benefits from the removal of the barriers to trade in services, it appears to be preferable to negotiate gradual reductions in all types of barriers

[232] LA Winters, TL Walmsley, Z Kun Wang, and R Grynberg, 'Negotiating the Liberalization of the Temporary Movement of Natural Persons', 2002, under Section 3.

[233] Also LA Winters, 'The Economic Implications of Liberalizing Mode 4 Trade' in A Mattoo and A Carzaniga (eds), *Moving People to Deliver Services*, 2003, 59.

[234] OECD, 'Quantification of Costs to National Welfare from Barriers to Services Trade: A Literature Review', TD/TC/WP(2000)24/FINAL, 2001. For an overview of the methods used to measure restrictions on trade in services nowadays, G McGuire, 'Methodologies for Measuring Restrictions on Trade in Services' in OECD, *Quantifying the Benefits of Liberalizing Trade in Services*, 2003, 38.

[235] In some cases, like in network-related services, there is evidence that a global liberalization of trade in network-related services could accrue higher welfare gains than the liberalization of goods trade, and that irrespective of the country size. K Bhattarai and J Whalley, 'The Division and Size of Gains from Liberalization in Service Networks', NBER Working Paper No 6712, 1998, 14.

[236] P Dee and K Hanslow, 'Multilateral Liberalization of Services Trade', Productivity Commission Staff Research Paper, 2000, 17.

[237] For example, Dee and Hanslow point out that while China is expected to be the country that records the most significant gains from services liberalization, for the EU, Canada, the United States, Singapore, and Taiwan the impact of multilateral services liberalization is projected to be negative. Ibid 17.

[238] McGuire (n 227 above) 16.

[239] C Findlay, 'Services Sector Reform and Development Strategies: Issues and Research Priorities', UNCTAD: Policy Issues in International Trade and Commodities, Study Series No 8, 2001, 17.

simultaneously rather than to opt for partial liberalization and remove only some types of barriers in different periods of time. This latter option is likely to lead to inefficient outcomes.[240] Should, however, a government look for the best (in terms of world economic welfare) single type of liberalization, it must choose the elimination of non-discriminatory establishment restraints, which impede market access,[241] rather than the relaxation of foreign equity limitations.

The efforts aiming at the reduction of explicit and implicit protection that culminated in the adoption of the GATS did not take the desirable form. In many cases, the resultant provisions at the end of the Uruguay Round were considered weak, not concordant with the ends that they were supposed to meet at the beginning of the round. To be sure, as befits a multilateral agreement, the GATS has created an adequate framework to come to grips with explicit discrimination in the services context, but it fell short of generating the necessary negotiating impetus or the rules that would allow the reduction of such discrimination. Furthermore, the Agreement has been reprehended in that the trade-impeding impact of domestic regulations in the services realm has been one of the issues that were deemed, to the great disappointment of many, improperly developed.

240 Dee and Hanslow (n 236 above) 22.

241 Ibid 22.

III

Domestic Regulations and the GATS

A. Introductory remarks

The political compact which generated the post-war economic architecture hinged on a pledge that international canons and trade liberalization would not infringe upon domestic policy autonomy.[1] The ITO never came into being but one component of it, the GATT, successfully lived on. The primary mission of the GATT was the liberalization of trade, through successive multilateral negotiations with a view to reducing barriers at the border, and the creation of rules to govern and sustain the liberalizing momentum. The GATT reflected its origins in the post-war world, as it generated rules which were intended to provide a buffer or interface between the international objective of sustained liberalization and the domestic policy objectives.

Free trade rules were traditionally about constraining border measures such as tariffs and quantitative restrictions on imports. From this standpoint, the Uruguay Round was a landmark event in the evolution of the international trading system in that the policy focus has shifted from the border measures of the GATT to domestic regulatory and legal systems embedded in the institutional infrastructure of an economy.

During these first years of the WTO's existence, it has often been apparent that the degree of intrusiveness into national sovereignty bears little resemblance to the shallow integration of the GATT with its focus on border barriers and its buffers to preserve domestic policy autonomy.[2] Domestic policies in turn can no

[1] JG Ruggie, 'International Regimes, Transactions, and Change: Embedded Liberalism in the Postwar Economic Order' (1982) 36(2) International Organization 393ff.

[2] On sovereignty questions and the impact of the Uruguay Round results in the USA, see JH Jackson, *The Jurisprudence of GATT and the WTO: Insights on Treaty Law and Economic Relations*, 2000, 367; also JH Jackson, 'The Uruguay Round Results and National Sovereignty' in J Bhagwati and M Hirsch (eds), *The Uruguay Round and Beyond—Essays in Honour of Arthur Dunkel*, 1998, 294. The rhetoric of sovereignty nowadays fails to conceive sovereignty as an efficient reallocation of powers and thus decisionmaking authority. Also JH Jackson, *Sovereignty, the WTO, and Changing Fundamentals of International Law*, 2006. Then, before criticizing any sovereignty transfer to international institutions—like the WTO—the question that needs to be answered is 'whether the recipient of enhanced power and responsibility will exercise power and recognize its responsibility more effectively'. In other words, a cost–benefit analysis between the degree of local autonomy given up and the measure of influence over other sovereigns obtained should take place.

longer be insulated from the demands of global markets, unless the countries that keep them in force are prepared to pay for their discriminatory domestic regulations. Thus, the scope for domestic policy errors is diminished. It has even been alleged that, since the system is less about trade than about domestic policy and institutions, 'multilateral *trading* system' after the Uruguay Round is a misnomer.[3]

Accordingly, the WTO shifted in several instances from the GATT model of negative regulation/integration—what governments must *not* do—to positive regulation/integration—or what governments must do.[4] This is notable in the TRIPs, the TBT and SPS Agreements, as well as in Article VI GATS.[5] It is no coincidence that the trade remedies which were supposed to function as protective buffers (eg safeguards, anti-dumping, etc) seemingly have been increasingly used as protectionist tools in many instances after the Uruguay Round.[6] Such remedies have ostensibly been inappropriate as a means of safeguarding the diverse and changing concept of sovereignty.

What is the role that the GATS plays in this framework? To start with, the GATS is the first multilateral, legally enforceable agreement covering cross-border trade, investment, and movement of producers or consumers in the service sector. In the GATS, one can feel the first, tentative steps towards positive integration. Article VI notwithstanding, Articles VII, VIII, and IX GATS, as weak as they are for the moment, reveal this tendency. The GATS provides a single organizational and legal focal point for dealing with the various policy instruments that can impinge on the many different ways in which firms may supply services.[7] It is a liberalization-promoting forum, as it aims to minimize the negative trade effects of all governmental regulatory barriers, while preserving Members' right to regulate their economies to meet legitimate national policy objectives. This last principle is enshrined in the fourth recital of the Preamble to the GATS where national regulatory autonomy is explicitly reaffirmed:

> *Recognizing* the right of Members to regulate, and to introduce new regulations, on the supply of services within their territories in order to meet national policy objectives

J Trachtman, 'Reflections on the Nature of the State: Sovereignty, Power and Responsibility' (1994) 20 Canada-United States Law Journal 400; also CE Barfield, *Free Trade, Sovereignty, Democracy: The Future of the World Trade Organization,* 2001; JH Jackson, 'Sovereignty, Subsidiarity, and Separation of Powers: The High-Wire Balancing Act of Globalization' in DLM Kennedy and JD Southwick (eds), *The Political Economy of International Trade Law: Essays in Honor of Robert E. Hudec*, 2002, 22.

[3] S Ostry, 'Doha and After' (2002) 9(1/2) Canada Watch 52.

[4] cf E-U Petersmann, 'From Negative to Positive Integration in the WTO: The TRIPs Agreement and the WTO Constitution' in T Cottier and PC Mavroidis (eds), *Intellectual Property: Trade, Competition, and Sustainable Development,* 2003, 22.

[5] Nevertheless, but for these exceptions, WTO is still a negative-integration-type contract.

[6] See also the discussion in Chapter II.B on contingent protection above.

[7] RH Snape, 'Reaching Effective Agreements Covering Services' in AO Krueger (ed), *The WTO as an International Organization*, 1998, 285.

and, given asymmetries existing with respect to the degree of development of services regulations in different countries, the particular need of developing countries to exercise this right...

Concerns have been expressed over whether the Preamble of the GATS is legally binding in the same way as the main GATS text.[8] WTO case law reveals that Preambles do play a crucial role in the interpretation of a given WTO provision. In the *US—Shrimp* dispute, the Appellate Body underscored that a Preamble 'reflects the intentions of negotiators' and consequently it 'must add colour, texture and shading' to the interpretation of a given WTO provision by the WTO judiciary.[9] Thus, a correct interpretation of any GATS provision would give proper weight to the Preamble's affirmation of a Member's right to regulate and to introduce new regulations. Furthermore, it seems to be generally accepted that the entire GATS has been intentionally structured to protect the regulatory prerogatives of governments through its great flexibility in order to accommodate governmental policy needs.[10] Many of the stakeholders, however, seemingly remain sceptical.[11] Therefore, it is nowadays a challenge for the multilateral system and the GATS to accommodate these concerns originating in the fear of a purported and abstract loss of domestic regulatory sovereignty.

This chapter entails a comprehensive analysis of Article VI GATS, as it explores the objective function and the mechanics of this provision. The chapter starts with an examination of the basic rationales for regulating trade in services and the types of regulations that a government typically uses, sometimes to impede access to services markets. A thorough analysis of Article VI will follow. Section D attempts to shed light on the thorniest systemic issue in the GATS today—the relationship between Articles VI, XVI, and XVII GATS. It will be demonstrated that deciphering this relationship is essential for negotiators and policymakers, but also for the future of the GATS itself. Interpretations advanced by the WTO judiciary in the *US—Gambling* dispute as well as approaches put forward on this score in the aftermath of the ruling are also critically analysed. Section E will address the importance of good practices when regulating, notably the use of cost–benefit analysis and regulatory impact assessments as tools for evaluating the efficacy of domestic regulations. Section F concludes with an account of the current criticisms of GATS.

[8] See Australia's intervention in WTO, WPDR, 'Report on the Meeting Held on 29 November 2000', S/WPDR/M/9, 12 March 2001, para 17.

[9] Appellate Body Report, *US—Shrimp*, para 153.

[10] It has been alleged on several occasions that 'according to the GATS preamble, the national policy objectives as defined by Members were already legitimate and, therefore, did not need further clarification'. See the intervention of the European Communities in WTO, WPDR, 'Report on the Meeting Held on 20 March 2001', S/WPDR/M/10, 10 May 2001, para 30.

[11] S Sinclair, 'The GATS, Democratic Governance, and Public Interest Regulation' (2002) 9(1/2) Canada Watch 15. It is noteworthy that, in general, the Preamble of a treaty is qualified as 'context' when interpreting a treaty provision, in accordance with Article 31:2 of the *Vienna Convention*.

B. Snipping at the Gordian knot of domestic regulations

1. Why regulate in the first place?

Regulation is a particularly tempting means of protecting domestic service suppliers from foreign competition, taking into account the difficulty of imposing border restrictions on trade in services.[12] It is commonplace nowadays that the majority of the barriers to the development of the service sector are of regulatory, 'within-the-border' nature. Inefficient (using 'efficiency' as an expression of the maximum value attainable by a group of people with diverse preferences) domestic regulations arguably further limit growth and competition in services.

Traditionally, however, as accentuated earlier,[13] such regulations are designed by a well-intentioned government which, driven by public interest considerations, seeks to contend with perceived market failures, such as those typically associated with externalities, information inadequacies, or imperfect competition and misuse of market power.[14] Of course, interference with the market may be motivated by the need for accomplishing non-economic, social goals, such as redistribution of income, consumer protection, or universal service, in order to assure equity, or even for clearly paternalistic motivations.[15] All these regulatory goals are horizontal in nature; hence, they are applicable across the board to all services sectors. This fact can be decisive when determining the nature of the instruments (eg whether they should be specific to a certain sector or generally applicable).

To start with, the reason for regulating externalities (or spillovers) is that sometimes market prices do not fully capture the costs and benefits of the associated transactions. Provision of various services can generate important positive external effects, such as those deriving from health or education services. On the other hand, they can also have negative spillovers, such as negative environmental spillovers generated by suppliers of transport or tourism services. The rationale for regulation is then to avoid economic waste and compel the internalization of the spillover costs.[16]

Information plays a more central role in services than in goods. Information inadequacies mostly appear in intermediation and knowledge-based services. The nature of the services supply and the direct contact involved between

[12] See Chapter II above.

[13] See Chapter II.B above.

[14] C Gamberale and A Mattoo, 'Domestic Regulations and Liberalization of Trade in Services' in B Hoekman, A Mattoo, and P English (eds), *Development, Trade, and the WTO: A Handbook*, 2002, 290; also S Breyer, *Regulation and its Reform*, 1982, 15–35.

[15] A Ogus, *Regulation: Legal Form and Economic Theory*, 1994, 51.

[16] RA Cass and JR Haring, 'Domestic Regulation and International Trade: Where's the Race? Lessons from Telecommunications and Export Controls' in DLM Kennedy and JD Southwick (eds), *The Political Economy of International Trade Law: Essays in Honor of Robert E. Hudec*, 2002, 138–141; see also the discussion on domestic distortions under Chapter II above.

suppliers and consumers generate significant risks. The consequences of asymmetric information may not be easily reversible for consumers who lack information about the skills that a given service supplier has.[17] Since markets may not provide appropriate incentives for the acquisition and dissemination of information, appropriate legislation that requires disclosure of certain information could in theory remedy the problem. Nevertheless, it may be too expensive to communicate the necessary information to individual consumers. In such cases, instead of educating the consumers, it is more cost-effective to regulate suppliers.

Indeed, prudential regulation is often needed as a means of protecting consumers of financial services against suppliers who are rapacious or incompetent, or both. The imposition of minimum regulatory conditions on suppliers echoes a certain uniformity of preferences among consumers as regards the quality of services. For instance, the competent regulatory authorities ensure that all banks operating in the market meet a certain threshold of financial soundness or professionals a certain threshold of competence.[18] Moreover, the authorities may prefer to regulate inputs rather than outputs of a services industry, as the latter are often invisible. These types of regulations, however, can amount to unnecessary barriers to entry into the domestic market.

Hence, an important factor in the services context and, one that affects the extent of the regulatory intervention in a given case, is the information on qualitative characteristics of services and service suppliers. While the quality of some products such as milk or sugar can be ascertained on inspection prior to sale (*search* goods), others, including almost all types of services, cannot be evaluated until received, used or consumed (*experience* goods).[19] In extreme cases (eg a long-term alleged financial investment), the effects of use or consumption are made known only years later (*credence* goods).[20]

Therefore, since the market itself does not sufficiently protect the relevant values, in these cases, political decisionmaking proceeds to an evaluation of the situation in the market and, ultimately, it overrides it.[21] In particular, the

[17] UNCTAD and World Bank, *Liberalizing International Transactions in Services: A Handbook*, 1994, 40.

[18] In general terms, the asymmetric information problem has important implications for the financial services sector. First, because of the existence of asymmetric information the proximity to the consumer and *a fortiori* commercial presence becomes essential. Second, a credit institution acting as lender will probably prefer to lend to borrowers with whom it is familiar. LJ White, 'Unilateral International Openness: The Experience of the U.S. Financial Services Sector' in J Bhagwati (ed), *Going Alone: The Case for Relaxed Reciprocity in Freeing Trade*, 2002, 450ff.

[19] P Nelson, 'Information and Consumer Behavior' (1970) 78(2) Journal of Political Economy 311; also GA Akerlof, 'The Market for "Lemons": Quality Uncertainty and the Market Mechanism' (1970) 84(3) The Quarterly Journal of Economics 488.

[20] MR Darby and E Karni, 'Free Competition and the Optimal Amount of Fraud' (1973) 16(1) Journal of Law and Economics 67. The authors demonstrate that in the case of goods that have credence qualities, a governmental intervention would not lead to an efficient allocation of resources and thus it would be preferable to leave the market unregulated.

[21] If the market remains unregulated this would lead to a lowering of standards, as consumers would not be able to distinguish between low-quality and high-quality services. Ogus (n 15 above) 216.

governmental intervention will prescribe the type of information that needs to be provided and will aid potential buyers in evaluating the information that is being supplied. Licensure, certification procedures, setting of minimum standards, introduction of codes of practice and liability laws are governmental measures commonly used to ensure competence, performance, technical behaviour and accountability.[22] Thus, the primary advantage of regulation is that, due to its inherently coercive qualities, it can improve resource allocation or aid in obtaining other benefits in cases where the market is incapable of doing this alone.

Imperfect competition in the case of services usually stems from the existence of natural monopolies or oligopolies, such as those normally associated with networks (railways, water or energy supply pipelines, telecommunications, etc). Due to space constraints or large initial investments, it may be more efficient to give one firm a monopoly subject to regulation of matters such as prices and access to the network, rather than to have, say, three electricity companies laying separate networks and terminals. It is, however, possible to have services which can be provided in fully competitive conditions, but that at the same time should rely on services provided by a natural monopoly. Then, it is up to the regulator to ensure that any major supplier of essential facilities provides access to all new operators, national and foreign, at cost-based rates[23] and that cost-effective prices are charged. Sometimes, limiting the market power of large incumbents is also necessary to avoid oligopolistic behaviours.

Equity concerns may render regulatory intervention inevitable, as the market cannot always assure the socially desirable levels of availability and continuity of a service.[24] For example, it might be considered desirable that water services be made universally available. In an unregulated market this might not always be the case, since the supplier can decide not to supply poorer or more geographically dispersed groups of consumers because of the low profit margin or due to anticipated losses. Regulation is then justified as a means of generating socially desirable results. Traditionally, governments rely on public monopolies to pursue such goals, either through cross-subsidization across segments of the market or through transfers from the government (eg through government-controlled banks).[25] Re-distributional concerns and prevention of discrimination can justify regulation as well.

[22] Also OECD, 'Competition in Professional Services', DAFFE/CLP(2000)2, 2000, 18ff.

[23] cf Panel Report, *Mexico—Telecoms*, paras 7.160ff.

[24] R Baldwin and M Cave, *Understanding Regulation—Theory, Strategy, and Practice*, 1999, 12.

[25] It is noteworthy that Art VIII GATS, which prohibits actions undertaken by a domestic monopoly supplier that are inconsistent with the MFN principle or the specific commitments undertaken by a certain Member, should not be interpreted to outlaw cross-subsidization of such activities which relate to essential regulatory objectives such as the supply of essential facilities to geographically disadvantaged areas. Given the importance of the regulatory objectives that they serve, cross-subsidizations of this nature undertaken by monopoly suppliers via governmental encouragement or assistance cannot be deemed anticompetitive, notwithstanding provisions such as the one in para 1.2 of the Reference Paper on Basic Telecommunications.

By the same token, governments can intervene through regulation in order to transfer income from economic rents that are unjustifiable extra profit gained by producers or suppliers back to consumers. These rents represent a regressive income transfer from consumers to producers. A fairer income distribution justifies the control of rents in cases where they are large and occur suddenly.[26]

It goes without saying that domestic regulations are essential to attain legitimate policy objectives intertwined with the provision of services. Unfortunately, markets cannot always achieve the desired regulatory results by themselves; otherwise, no regulatory compulsion would be warranted. Given that markets do not always work perfectly, society's resources may be imperfectly or inefficiently used. For instance, there are imperative public goods aspects to many services sectors, such as telecommunications, education, or health, with a consequential need for extensive regulatory intervention. Of course, deliberation about the correct policy response is one thing, and deliberation about the management and the implementation of such responses is quite another, as pressure from interest groups occurs during this second phase of regulation.[27] The key question is how to address problems such as externalities or information asymmetries in ways that do not promote exploitation by interest groups which yearn to protract protection.[28]

In order to reduce the influence of interest groups on rulemaking, institutional choice and design becomes paramount. Institutions will transform a given social objective into public policy results. An allocation of authority to and among institutions (deciding who decides) determines what one views as the correct response to a particular problem. Indeed, goal choice is strongly associated with institutional choice since, first, institutional performance can be assessed only against the benchmark of some objective or set of objectives; and, second, institutional choice determines how an objective shapes public policy, given that any objective can be consistent with a wide array of public policies.[29] Each institutional process (regulating, adjudicating, or transacting), however, has its limitations, as it is everything but perfect or frictionless. Institutional choice is always a choice between highly imperfect alternatives. Depending on the setting, either the market or the political process (or even a combination of the two) may be better or

[26] Breyer (n 14 above) 21–23.

[27] See the analysis of the role of special interest groups in the regulatory process in Chapter II above.

[28] For example, there are cases where 'collective silence' in an industry is preferred in order to conceal information that would allow the regulators to make a decision harmful to the industry, eg to allow foreign competition. Indeed, an information asymmetry may refer not only to the relationship between producers and consumers, but also to the one between regulators and producers, ie between regulators and those that they regulate. This last asymmetry seems to be far more important because it will determine the making of regulatory policy. C Coglianese, R Zeckhauser, and E Parson, *Securing Truth for Power: Informational Strategy and Regulatory Policy Making*, 2004, 4.

[29] NK Komesar, *Imperfect Alternatives—Choosing Institutions in Law, Economics, and Public Policy*, 1994, 5.

worse than the available alternatives.[30] Therefore, the most important task in this context is to choose the least imperfect institution or combination of institutions. Recent research has demonstrated that institutions have a very significant impact on the performance of a given economy. More importantly, due to the idiosyncrasies of the service sector, institutions seem to matter even more for this sector than for the other areas of economic activity.[31]

2. Characteristics and types of regulations

Regulations consist of normative restraints upon otherwise free conduct and usually encompass measures that a government considers as an exercise of its authority to regulate its domestic affairs; in other words, an exercise of its sovereignty. Regulations involve internal measures that are intended to deal with a domestic inefficiency and, consequently, their primary purpose is not trade-related. In the broadest sense, regulations comprise a diverse set of instruments by which governments set requirements for firms and citizens.

Regulations may include laws, formal as well as informal orders, and subordinate rules issued by all levels of government, as well as rules enjoined by non-governmental or self-regulatory bodies to which governments have entrusted regulatory powers. Typical types of regulations in services may include: the establishment of standards for services and service suppliers; the use of fiscal incentives, subsidies and taxes for the promotion of certain non-economic goals; the establishment of rules for conducting business, including the legal establishment, financing, governance and conduct of corporations; and the establishment of property laws, including contract law.

Regulations as a general rule fall into three categories:[32] (a) economic regulations, which intervene directly in market decisions, such as pricing, competition, market entry, or market exit; (b) social regulations, which protect public interests such as health, safety, or the environment; and (c) administrative (or process) regulations, such as paperwork and administrative formalities through which governments collect information and intervene in individual economic decisions. Of course, combinations of such regulations are possible and in fact typical in most regulatory jurisdictions.

Historically, the politics of regulatory policy tackles two key questions—whether a government should regulate[33] and if so, what policy instruments it should use. Both choices seek the authoritative allocation of values. Of course,

[30] C Wolf, Jr, *Markets or Governments—Choosing between Imperfect Alternatives*, 1994, 155.

[31] M Amin and A Mattoo, 'Do Institutions Matter More for Services?', PRWP No 4032, 2006.

[32] RW Hahn, *Reviving Regulatory Reform: A Global Perspective*, 2000, 7.

[33] According to a World Bank study, income and legal origin are the most important factors in understanding the choice of a regulatory intervention level. The World Bank, *Doing Business in 2004—Understanding Regulation*, 2004, 84ff.

there are differences among several regulatory techniques depending on the extent to which the government intervention impedes freedom of activity. In economic regulatory policy, the decision as to the appropriate policy instruments is generally made among command-and-control regulation, economic incentives, and the provision of information.

With command-and-control regulation, the government both sets the objectives and stipulates the means to obtain those objectives while specifying the penalties for non-compliance; occupational safety regulations are a prime example. In an incentive-based regulatory regime a government sets goals and creates incentives to meet those goals; it is up to the individuals to decide how and when to respond. By economic incentives are meant financial penalties imposed on harm-causing behaviour, and financial rewards attached to harm-reducing behaviour.[34] Taxes are the majòr form of regulatory incentives; agricultural subsidies and tax credits can also be considered regulatory incentives. Finally, the disclosure of information (so-called 'disclosure regulation') can supplement or even replace other types of regulation, since it has the advantage of being less interventionist and still promoting economic efficiency. The logic of providing information, as in the case of financial services, is that consumers become capable of making an informed judgement in relation to the risk involved as well as to the benefits and costs of alternative behaviour.

In practice, however, the distinction between these regulatory strategies is not so straightforward. Furthermore, the competent authorities usually employ combinations of regulatory methods with a view to identifying the particular mixture of regulatory strategies that will best meet their objectives. Generally, the economic approach to regulation puts a premium on non-protectionist regulation that is transparent, consistent, coherent, and predictable not only in its objectives but also in its application. In turn, this implies that regulatory institutions should have a precise mandate to ensure the desired outcomes;[35] they should also be operationally independent of, but still accountable to, government.[36] This implies that regulation should be regularly reviewed and/or be subject to sunset clauses to pre-empt any anticompetitive use of regulation whether against domestic or foreign competitors, in other words regulatory capture by interest groups. Having said this, classical types of regulation are to be considered as the last resort.[37]

[34] Such penalties or rewards may supplement or displace command-and-control regulation.

[35] R Coase, 'The New Institutional Economics' (1998) 88(2) AER 73.

[36] JV DeLong, 'New Wine for a New Bottle: Judicial Review in the Regulatory State' (1986) 72(2) Virginia Law Review 405ff. The question of *quid custodiet ipsos custodes* (*in casu*, who regulates the regulators) becomes relevant in this context; also The World Bank, *World Development Report 2002: Building Institutions for Markets*, 2001.

[37] P Coghlan, 'The Principles of Good Regulation' in Productivity Commission and Australian National University, *Achieving Better Regulation of Services*, 2000, 38ff. In fact, there are studies that show a sharp negative correlation between regulatory intensity and productivity or even economic growth. JL Guasch and RW Hahn, 'The Costs and Benefits of Regulation—Implications for Developing Countries', PRWP No 1773, 1997, 10.

A 'least restrictive alternative' approach would consider regulation through a pro-competitive lens. If regulatory intervention is necessary, an incentive-based intervention would be advanced as the first instrument, followed by disclosure regulation, bargaining, or other less restrictive forms of interference before classical regulatory modes are applied.[38]

C. The obligations contained in Article VI GATS[39]

1. Negotiating history and *ratio legis*

Nearly 20 years ago, Feketekuty eloquently asserted:

> There has to be a process, however, for determining which regulations are negotiable and which regulations are not negotiable. The purpose of trade negotiations is to reduce barriers to trade, and by common consent this is to be achieved without infringing domestic regulatory objectives. In the words of the Uruguay Declaration, the objective of the negotiations is to achieve an expansion of trade 'under conditions of transparency and progressive liberalization', while at the same time the framework resulting from the negotiations 'shall respect the policy objectives of national laws and regulations applying to services'. It follows that the framework agreement should provide the means for identifying restrictive measures that are not essential for the achievement of domestic regulatory objectives.[40]

Negotiators' endeavours to detect such a process led to the creation of Article VI GATS. Members' regulatory autonomy did not prevent the inclusion in the GATS of provisions dealing with the minimization of the trade-distortive effects of domestic regulations which evade falling under the six categories of limitations in Article XVI GATS and which do not discriminate, *de jure* or *de facto*, against foreign services or service suppliers and thus are not captured by Article XVII GATS either.[41] The objective was to establish an effective mechanism which would ensure the betterment of regulations that are inequitable, excessively interventionist, and restrict trade more than is needed to achieve the desired non-economic objectives. Such provisions are to be found in Article VI, which ultimately consists of: (a) some legally binding provisions of procedural nature (paras 1–3, 6);[42]

[38] S Breyer, 'Analyzing Regulatory Failure: Mismatches, Less Restrictive Alternatives, and Reform' (1979) 92(3) Harvard Law Review 586.

[39] Also P Delimatsis, 'Due Process and "Good" Regulation Embedded in the GATS—Disciplining Regulatory Behaviour in Services Through Article VI of the GATS' (2007) 10 JIEL 13.

[40] G Feketekuty, *International Trade in Services: An Overview and Blueprint for Negotiations*, 1988, 212.

[41] Some regulations such as competition law fall under none of these Articles. A footnote to Art XVII makes it clear that there is no obligation to compensate for any competitive disadvantages which are inherent in the foreign character of foreign services or service suppliers—such as unfamiliarity with the local language or business culture.

[42] cf Panel Report, *US—Gambling*, para 6.432.

(b) a mandate for the development of multilateral disciplines associated with licensing, qualifications, and technical standards (para 4); and (c) a mechanism for the provisional application of the main principles underlying the future disciplines (para 5).

As depicted in the previous chapter, non-discriminatory (ie origin-neutral) regulations can create substantial barriers to international services transactions. Article VI GATS is one of the most important substantive provisions of the Agreement, as the liberalization of market access would not have any real value in the absence of a legal provision for coping with the detrimental effects of domestic regulations. Yet one of the paradoxes in the new multilateral framework dealing with services trade—and consequently one of its inherent problems—is that the provision tackling domestic regulations is among its weakest ones.

This may be justified by the strategic decision that Members took during the Uruguay Round to complete the work on finalizing the provisions on market access and national treatment before dealing more thoroughly with Article VI.[43] Members knew already in the early 1990s that a work programme for the coming years was needed to complete Article VI and therefore considered it inevitable to have an incomplete obligation in Part II of the GATS relating to General Obligations.[44]

Thus, Article VI has so far remained provisional in nature.[45] One good reason for this was that Members had great difficulty in developing multilateral disciplines in this area without seeming to interfere with national sovereignty and overly limiting regulatory autonomy.[46] *A priori*, strengthening Article VI could facilitate market access liberalization by committing countries to reforming regulations that impede market-oriented competition.

More than a decade ago, in a meeting of the Trade Negotiations Committee held on 20 December 1991, Arthur Dunkel, the then Director-General of the GATT, released the draft text of an agreement encompassing all the negotiating areas of the Uruguay Round, the so-called 'Dunkel Draft'.[47] The Dunkel Draft on services included 34 Articles and Annexes on MFN exemptions, movement of labour, financial services, telecommunications, and air transport services.[48] The final version of Article VI (and, for the most part, the GATS as a whole) is virtually identical to the draft Article VII contained in the Dunkel Draft of 1991.[49]

[43] GATT, 'Note of the Meeting of 10–25 July 1991', MTN.GNS/44, 28 August 1991, para 46.

[44] Ibid.

[45] Of course, as shown in Chapter I, other GATS Articles reflect unfinished business as well.

[46] A Mattoo, 'Developing Countries in the New Round of the GATS Negotiations: Towards a Pro-Active Role' in B Hoekman and W Martin (eds), *Developing Countries and the WTO: A Pro-active Agenda*, 2001, 88.

[47] GATT, 'Draft Final Act Embodying the Results of the Uruguay Round of Multilateral Trade Negotiations', MTN.TNC/W/FA, 20 December 1991.

[48] Also W Zdouc, *Legal Problems—Arising under the General Agreement on Trade in Services—Comparative Analysis of the GATS and GATT*, 2002, 72.

[49] JV Reyna, 'Services' in TP Stewart (ed), *The GATT Uruguay Round: A Negotiating History (1986–1992)*, Vol II: Commentary, 1993, 2429.

Although Article VI is entitled 'Domestic Regulation', its content concerns 'measures' as defined in Article XXVIII GATS; that is, it covers any measure taken by a Member, whether in the form of a law, regulation, rule, procedure, decision, administrative action, or any other form.[50] Article VI contains disciplines that have been applicable from the first day that the GATS entered into force. These are the due process requirements embedded in the provision. In addition, in paragraph 4, it mandated further work on the subject, which is currently taking place in the WPDR (the successor to the WPPS).[51]

Many of the obligations set out in the GATS take effect on the stipulation that Members schedule specific commitments based on one or more of the modes of supply set out in Article I:2.[52] On that basis, the intentions reflected in Article VI GATS are numerous. Nonetheless, its foremost purpose is to assure an objective and fair regulatory environment to complement the obligations that Members assume under Part III of the GATS, notably under market access and national treatment.

The *ratio legis* of Article VI has been Members' intention to set up a process that would allow the identification of trade-restrictive measures that are not essential for the achievement of the domestic regulatory objectives that Members have unilaterally defined in their jurisdiction. In the longer term, the trade-distortive effects of these measures should be minimized. The language used in Article VI reflects the need for transparency (transparency in trade-related domestic regulation encompasses regulatory decisionmaking, implementation, administration and enforcement) and due administrative process (including explicit recognition of the right of service suppliers to have access to information on regulatory and administrative decisions, and to judicial or administrative review and appeals processes) when regulating. In both respects, the GATS champions principles of good governance. To be sure, Article VI functions as a vector of regulatory reform and induces the adoption of 'good' regulatory practices, notably in sectors where specific commitments have been undertaken.

Though not stated, it is implicitly acknowledged that regulations may be unnecessarily burdensome or obscure and that they may have chilling effects—even unintentional—on foreign suppliers. The right to regulate notwithstanding, national laws and regulations that affect international trade in services have to be transparent, administered with due process, and impinge on trade as little as possible. In other words, Members should ensure that domestic regulation is responsive to the GATS principles of fairness (non-discrimination) and openness (transparency) and supports and upholds (rather than negating) negotiated GATS commitments (effectiveness).

[50] See Chapter I.E.1 above.

[51] WTO, CTS, 'Article VI:4 of the GATS: Disciplines on Domestic Regulation Applicable to All Services', S/C/W/96, 1 March 1999, p 2. See, *in extenso*, Chapter IV below.

[52] Article VI:2, however, is not conditioned upon scheduling.

Such an obligation would not jeopardize the sovereign right of Members to regulate their markets. The *US—Gambling* ruling was outspoken on this score. The Panel defined the limits of Members' regulatory sovereignty by emphasizing that '...Members maintain the sovereign right to regulate within the parameters of Article VI of the GATS. Members' regulatory sovereignty is an essential pillar of the progressive liberalization of trade in services, but this sovereignty ends whenever rights of other Members under the GATS are impaired.'[53] The Appellate Body endorsed the Panel's finding that Members' right to regulate trade in services forms part of the object and purpose of the GATS 'provided that they respect the rights of other Members under the GATS'.[54]

2. Article VI:1—Reasonable, objective, and impartial administration of measures of general application affecting trade in services

Paragraph 1 of Article VI GATS reads:

> In sectors where specific commitments are undertaken, each Member shall ensure that all measures of *general application affecting* trade in services are *administered* in a *reasonable, objective* and *impartial* manner. (emphasis added)

The first paragraph of Article VI thus calls for reasonable, objective, and impartial administration of those measures of general application that affect trade in services.[55] This provision establishes this general principle as a guide to understanding and interpreting the specific obligations contained in the other paragraphs of Article VI. Put differently, paragraph 1 constitutes part of the context of the other paragraphs of Article VI by embodying the sound regulatory principles of consistency and predictability.[56]

The principle of consistency, which has its roots in administrative law, is considered a key principle of 'best practices' in regulatory behaviour in order to inspire confidence in the regulatory regime and give a degree of predictability and legal certainty to those being regulated. This principle is linked to the provision of consistent and fair rules that do not have adverse effects on the business performance of a specific service supplier and it is believed to ensure greater confidence in the system, greater transparency in decisionmaking and promote greater efficiency across the various services sectors. In general terms, consistency and predictability may be seen as corollaries of the principles of transparency and due process.

[53] See Panel Report, *US—Gambling*, para 6.316.

[54] See Appellate Body Report, *US—Gambling*, para 235 and fn 271.

[55] cf Art 6 of the Reference Paper on Basic Telecommunications, which provides that 'any procedures for the allocation and use of scarce resources...will be carried out in an objective, timely, transparent and non-discriminatory manner'.

[56] cf Panel Report, *EC—Selected Customs Matters*, para 7.431 and fn 742.

The obligation of reasonable, objective, and impartial administration[57] is only concerned about measures which form part of a sector where a given Member has undertaken specific commitments. *A contrario*, then, a Member is not required to administer in a reasonable, objective and impartial manner those measures of general application affecting trade in services which do *not* relate to sectors where specific commitments are made. This approach deviates from Article X:3(a) GATT,[58] which is the counterpart of Article VI:1 GATS in the area of goods trade, where the reasonable, objective and impartial administration covers all measures specified in Article X:1 GATT.[59] Thus, unlike in the GATT, in the case of services a prominent feature of the principle of transparency under WTO law, ie the obligation of objective and impartial administration of trade regulations, applies differently from sector to sector, and from Member to Member, depending on the commitments undertaken.

Nonetheless, both Articles VI:1 GATS and X:3(a) GATT cover measures that apply to a broad spectrum of situations. Hence, measures addressing *specific* situations would not be subject to the obligation of due administration. In contrast, measures of general application, ie measures that affect 'an unidentified number of economic operators',[60] or else, cover 'a range of situations or cases, rather than being limited in their scope of application',[61] would fall under Article VI:1. Compared with Article X:3(a) GATT, Article VI:1 can be seen as both narrower and broader in scope, depending on the criterion used. It is narrower because the obligation for reasonable, objective and impartial administration refers only to

57 For a thorough analysis of the requirements of uniformity, reasonableness and impartiality as articulated in Art X:3(a) GATT, see Delimatsis (n 39 above) 24ff.

58 Art X:3(a) GATT provides:

Each Member shall administer in a uniform, impartial and reasonable manner all its laws, regulations, decisions and rulings of the kind described in paragraph 1 of this Article.

In *EC—Bananas III*, the Appellate Body found that the phrase of Art X:3(a) 'administer in a uniform, impartial and reasonable manner' is similar to the phrase 'neutral in application and administered in a fair and equitable manner' in Art 1.3 of the Import Licensing Agreement. The Appellate Body went on to find that these two phrases 'are, for all practical purposes, interchangeable' and concluded by stating that Art X:3(a) GATT and Art 1.3 of the Import Licensing Agreement 'have identical coverage'. See Appellate Body Report, *EC—Bananas III*, para 203. One could logically imagine a similar interpretation when it comes to a juxtaposition of Art X:3(a) with Art VI:1, since both provisions have the same function, ie they serve due process purposes regarding the administration of domestic measures.

59 See also Chapter V.C.2 below.

60 cf Panel Report, *US—Underwear*, para 7.65; and Appellate Body Report, *US—Underwear*, p 21. In *EC—Poultry*, the Appellate Body agreed with the Panel that the term 'of general application' laid down in Art X:3(a) GATT does not cover specific transactions (*in casu*, the treatment of a specific shipment). Appellate Body Report, *EC—Poultry*, paras 111 and 113. Furthermore, in *Japan—Film*, the Panel, in interpreting the term 'of general application', suggested that it should also cover administrative rulings in *individual* cases where such rulings establish or revise principles or criteria applicable in future cases. However, it is for the complainant to demonstrate that such rulings in *individual* matters which establish or revise principles applicable in *future* cases have not been published. Panel Report, *Japan—Film*, para 10.388.

61 Panel Report, *EC—Selected Customs Matters*, para 7.116.

those measures that are part of committed sectors. At the same time, it is broader because it also covers all measures that *affect* trade in services, ie measures that either directly govern or indirectly affect the supply of a given service.[62]

Nothing in Article VI seems to be intended to interfere with the way Members propose, prepare or adopt certain measures of general application; rather, the WTO judicial review, and consequently the multilateral obligation deriving from Article VI:1, focuses on the *administration* of such measures, or else, on how these measures are applied in practice.[63] Thus any measure, 'otherwise fair and just on its face', would come within the ambit of this provision if it is actually applied in an arbitrary, unreasonable, and biased manner.[64]

Consequently, the GATS recognizes Members' freedom to develop domestic laws and procedures that reflect their political, social, and economic conditions as well as their legal and constitutional systems in a manner that Members deem appropriate. Paragraph 2(b) of Article VI unequivocally leads to the same conclusion. Members are also free to determine for themselves how to achieve reasonable, objective and impartial administration, including the nature and level of entities that are charged with administration and the tools that are put in place to achieve administration that fulfils these requirements.[65] Hence, Article VI:1 is neutral with respect to the *means* that a Member may employ in order to achieve its desired level of administration.

In addition, any complaint relating to the *substantive* content of a Member's domestic regulations of general application and not to their administration should not be deemed as falling under Article VI:1.[66] The Appellate Body reached a similar conclusion regarding the *raison d'être* of Article X:3(a) GATT.[67] Hence, only the manner in which domestic regulations are *applied* or *administered* falls within the ambit of Article VI:1. This means that the generally applicable measures affecting trade in services *as such* are not required to be objective, impartial, or reasonable.[68]

However, the *Argentina—Hides and Leather* Panel found that a measure can still be challenged under Article X GATT if its substantive content is 'administrative in nature'. The Panel noted that, in such cases, the important question is whether the substance of the measure at hand is administrative in nature, ie whether it provides for a certain *manner of applying* substantive rules, or, rather, entails substantive issues that would be better tackled under other GATT provisions. The Panel went on to note that 'if the substance of a rule could not be

[62] See Chapter I.E.1 above.

[63] Appellate Body Report, *EC—Bananas III*, para 200.

[64] cf Appellate Body Report, *US—Shrimp*, para 160.

[65] Panel Report, *EC—Selected Customs Matters*, para 7.141.

[66] Panel Report, *US—Gambling*, para 6.432.

[67] Appellate Body Report, *EC—Poultry*, para 115.

[68] cf Appellate Body Report, *EC—Bananas III*, para 197; and Panel Report, *EC—Selected Customs Matters*, para 7.112.

challenged, even if the rule was administrative in nature, it is unclear what could ever be challenged under Article X'.[69]

More recently, the *EC—Selected Customs Matters* dispute touched upon this issue. The Panel disagreed with the approach advanced by the *Argentina—Hides and Leather* Panel. It started by ruling on the scope of the term 'administer' under Article X:3(a):

> the term 'administer' in Article X:3(a) of the GATT 1994 relates to the *application* of laws in particular cases and, particularly, to *administrative processes and their results*, since the application of the obligation of uniformity (and, for that matter, the obligations of reasonableness and impartiality) to such processes and their results pursuant to Article X:3(a) of the GATT 1994, helps to ensure that traders are treated fairly and consistently.[70] (emphasis in the original)

In this case, the complainant based its complaint merely on the assertion that several EC laws relating to customs matters[71] were not being administered in a uniform manner, thereby violating Article X:3(a) GATT. Interestingly, the complainant, based on *Argentina—Hides and Leather* case-law, contended that laws or regulations that can be interpreted as 'tools of administration' or 'administrative in nature' could be examined under Article X:3(a) GATT for their *substance* in order to determine whether they are evidence of non-uniform administration of domestic measures. Additionally, the United States argued that measures that do not fall in the category of 'tools of administration' or which are not 'administrative in nature' can still be scrutinized under Article X:3(a) to decide whether they are administered uniformly.

The Panel, correctly in my view, took issue with the *Argentina—Hides and Leather* ruling and consequently dismissed the United States' contention because it would 'blur' a distinction to be drawn, according to this provision, between the *instruments being administered* and the *acts of administration* of those laws, regulations, judicial decisions and administrative rulings. The Panel added that

> the text of Article X:3(a) of the GATT 1994 does not contemplate the possibility that laws and regulations can *simultaneously* qualify as laws, regulations, judicial decisions and administrative rulings of the kind described in Article X:1 of the GATT 1994 and

[69] Panel Report, *Argentina—Hides and Leather*, paras 11.70–11.71.

[70] Panel Report, *EC—Selected Customs Matters*, para 7.108.

[71] These included: The Community Customs Code, the Implementing Regulation, the Common Customs Tariff, the Integrated Tariff of the European Communities (TARIC) and related measures in the areas of customs administration, such as the classification and valuation of goods, procedures for the classification and valuation of goods, procedures for the entry and release of goods, procedures for auditing entry statements after goods are released into free circulation, penalties and procedures regarding the imposition of penalties for violation of customs rules and record-keeping requirements. Ibid para 7.23. The nucleus of the United States' complaint appears to have been the absence of any mechanism or procedure at the EC level to insure against divergences or to reconcile them promptly and as a matter of right when they occur. Appellate Body Report, *EC—Selected Customs Matters*, para 166.

as acts of administration within the meaning of Article X:3(a) of the GATT 1994.[72] (emphasis in the original)

The Panel went on to add that the United States' interpretation should be dismissed, as it would lead the WTO adjudicating bodies to examine whether the *substance* of laws or regulations that are 'tools of administration' or 'administrative in nature' is uniform throughout the territory of a given Member.[73] In the Panel's view, this interpretation would be contrary to the principle of effectiveness as laid down in Article 31 of the *Vienna Convention*.

The Appellate Body disagreed with the Panel in several respects. First, it found, contrary to the Panel, that the United States was entitled to challenge the EC customs administration 'as a whole or overall' and argue that this system, as administered collectively, results in non-uniform administration of EC customs law.[74] Second, the Appellate Body agreed with the Panel that Article X:3(a) GATT also covers administrative processes and their results, but it emphasized that this provision does not require uniformity of administrative processes leading to administrative decisions, or of the tools that might be used in the exercise of administration.[75]

More importantly, the Appellate Body, in a clear shift from its previous jurisprudence under Article X:3(a) GATT,[76] contended that:

> [w]hile the substantive content of the legal instrument being administered is not challengeable under Article X:3(a), we see no reason why a legal instrument that regulates the application or implementation of that instrument cannot be examined under Article X:3(a) if it is alleged to lead to a lack of uniform, impartial, or reasonable administration of that legal instrument.[77]

The Appellate Body qualified this by arguing that in this case the complainant will be obliged, first, to cite the provisions of that legal instrument, and, second, to demonstrate how and why those provisions necessarily lead to impermissible administration of the legal instrument of the type set out in Article X:1 GATT. Thus, the complainant should provide evidence (eg specific acts of administration) that demonstrates the causal relationship between this instrument and the lack of uniform, impartial or reasonable administration of the legal instrument that comes under Article X:1 GATT.[78]

For example, by contrast to the Panel, the Appellate Body declared that penalty laws and audit procedures do fall under the purview of Article X:3(a) GATT because they are 'instruments of implementation' of the EC customs

72 Ibid para 7.115.
73 Ibid para 7.117.
74 Appellate Body Report, *EC—Selected Customs Matters*, para 176.
75 Ibid paras 224–227.
76 See nn 63 and 67 above.
77 Ibid para 200.
78 Ibid para 201.

law. However, the complainant did not provide any evidence as to the causality between the divergences in national penalty laws or audit procedures within the European Union and the lack of uniform administration of EC customs law and, therefore, did not establish a *prima facie* case.[79]

On the basis of the analysis above, the Appellate Body dismissed the Panel's distinction between the *application* of laws and regulations, on the one hand, and the laws and regulations *as such*, on the other. The Appellate Body's approach appears to be more reflective of the Panel's view in the *Argentina—Hides and Leather* case. The Appellate Body, however, seems to contradict itself later on, as it agreed with the Panel, in its analysis of whether administrative processes come under Article X:3(a), that:

> the term 'administer' in Article X:3(a) refers to *putting into practical effect*, or *applying*, a legal instrument of the kind described in Article X:1. Thus, under Article X:3(a), it is the *application* of a legal instrument of the kind described in Article X:1 that is required to be uniform, but not the processes leading to administrative decisions, or the tools that might be used in the exercise of administration.[80] (emphasis in the original, footnote omitted)

The distinction that the Appellate Body proposed unnecessarily blurs the distinction between administration and the substantive content of measures falling under Article X GATT (and, by analogy, Article VI:1 GATS). If one were to follow this interpretation, a test of uniformity, reasonableness, or objectivity of the very *substance* of various domestic regulations that regulate the application or implementation of measures falling under Article X:1 would be implied. Nevertheless, Article X:3(a) (like Article VI:1), as it now stands, would suggest that only the *manner of administration* of the measures at stake is to be examined.

Regarding the conditions under which a Member can bring a claim based on Article VI:1 GATS, well-established case law with respect to Article X GATT suggests that a Member claiming a violation of this provision need not adduce evidence covering all three requirements of reasonable, objective/uniform and impartial administration. In other words, these requirements are not cumulative; rather, a complaining Member could merely put forward that the administration of the regulatory measure at stake is biased and this would already equate to a prima facie case of inconsistency with Article VI:1.[81] Of course, any claim that the conduct of a given Member is biased or unreasonable is serious and, therefore, should not be brought lightly, or in a subsidiary fashion. In the Appellate Body's words,

> a claim under Article X:3(a) of the GATT 1994 must be supported by solid evidence; the nature and the scope of the claim, and the evidence adduced by the complainant in

[79] Ibid paras 210–216.

[80] Ibid para 224.

[81] cf Panel Report, *Dominican Republic—Import and Sale of Cigarettes*, para 7.383. Establishing a *prima facie* case, however, should not be regarded as an easy task. See Appellate Body Report, *US—Gambling*, paras 138–141.

support of it, should reflect the gravity of the accusations inherent in claims under Article X:3(a) of the GATT 1994.[82]

This statement applies with equal force to Article VI:1 GATS. A breach of the obligations laid down in Article VI:1 may not only be the result of positive conduct, but may also be due to an omission in a case where an obligation to act in a specific manner is imposed.[83] On the other hand, with respect to a Member seeking to comply with Article VI:1, the standards of reasonableness,[84] objectivity and impartiality[85] are legally independent in that generally applicable measures affecting trade in committed services sectors must satisfy each of these three standards.[86]

As these requirements are legally independent, the standard of review is fairly lenient. Thus, Panels have the necessary leeway to examine each of the three requirements in the order that they deem appropriate. In the *Argentina—Hides and Leather* dispute, for instance, the Panel decided to examine the compliance of Argentina with the reasonableness requirement (that is, the third requirement of Article X:3(a) GATT), before turning to the requirement of impartial administration (that is, the second requirement of Article X:3(a) GATT).[87] Interestingly, the Panel analysed the obligation for impartiality, although it had earlier found a violation of the obligation for reasonableness within the meaning of Article X:3(a) GATT. Nonetheless, had the Panel concluded its analysis at that point, it would not have acted erroneously, since the three requirements of uniformity/objectivity, impartiality, and reasonableness are *not* cumulative.

The possibility should not be excluded that the requirement of reasonableness, objectivity and impartiality when administering measures of general application—especially its *reasonableness* prong—may be developed and used as a yardstick in WTO dispute settlement to impose substantive obligations in connection with domestic regulation in accordance with the principle of proportionality.[88] More specifically, even if the obligation contained in Article VI:1 focuses on the manner in which measures are *administered* and not generally on the regulations themselves, the *EC—Selected Customs Matters* case is the perfect example for illustrating the difficulty of attempting to draw in practice the dividing line between *substance* and *administration* of a given measure.

[82] Appellate Body Report, *US—Oil Country Tubular Goods Sunset Reviews*, para 217.

[83] cf Panel Report, *Dominican Republic—Import and Sale of Cigarettes*, para 7.379.

[84] WTO Panels had the opportunity to pronounce on the term 'reasonable application' when interpreting Art X:3(a) GATT. See Panel Report, *Argentina—Hides and Leather*, para 11.94; and Panel Report, *Dominican Republic—Import and Sale of Cigarettes*, paras 7.385–7.388.

[85] With respect to the term 'impartial administration' of regulations and rules within the meaning of Art X:3(a) GATT, see Panel Report, *Argentina—Hides and Leather*, para 11.100.

[86] Ibid para 11.86.

[87] Ibid.

[88] JP Trachtman, 'The "Necessity Test" in Domestic Services Regulation: How to Move Forward in the GATS?', APEC Group on Services, 2002, 12.

It would not be surprising if this construction were to bring about in the long run a general test of reasonableness, objectivity and impartiality of regulatory measures. A first attempt in this direction is considered to be the prospective necessity test of Article VI:4 with respect to measures relating to qualifications, licensing, and technical standards.[89]

Be that as it may, the focus on the way that domestic regulations are administered is deliberate; its underlying rationale is to ensure that foreign service suppliers can reap the benefits of the GATS without being frustrated in their work by administrative measures which are unreasonable, arbitrary or biased. As the Panel in *Argentina—Hides and Leather* ruled with respect to Article X:3(a) GATT, 'the focus is on the treatment accorded by government authorities to the traders in question'.[90] In an attempt to elaborate on this, the Panel suggested:

> Article X:3(a) requires an examination of the real effect that a measure might have on traders operating in the commercial world. This, of course, does not require a showing of trade damage... [b]ut it can involve an examination of whether there is a possible impact on the competitive situation due to alleged partiality, unreasonableness or lack of uniformity in the application of customs rules, regulations, decisions, etc.[91]

In *EC—Selected Customs Matters,* the Panel also underlined the importance of applying the obligation of uniformity, reasonableness and impartiality to domestic administrative processes and their results in order to ensure that 'traders are treated fairly and consistently'.[92]

Drawing from this case-law, Article VI:1 GATS, like Article X:3(a) GATT, requires Members to ensure that their laws are administered consistently and predictably. This requirement is not limited, for instance, to ensuring equal treatment with respect to Members, which is covered by the scope of Article II GATS (MFN principle). Under this provision, commercial fairness in everyday trading is expected. This means that due administration of the measures of general application between services or service suppliers and even with regard to the same service or supplier both over time and in different places is warranted.[93]

Given that the administration of the measures proves to be much more important than the measures themselves in many cases (eg relevant guidance given orally may nullify established legislation in force), this provision is of paramount importance and it should not be neglected by negotiators and policymakers. This is all the more so if one takes into account that in the aftermath of future negotiations the amount of the specific commitments that Members undertake in services sectors will inevitably multiply, as countries will gradually identify the possible gains of further liberalization of trade in services.

89 See Chapter IV.
90 Panel Report, *Argentina—Hides and Leather*, para 11.76.
91 Ibid para 11.77.
92 Panel Report, *EC—Selected Customs Matters*, para 7.108.
93 Panel Report, *Argentina—Hides and Leather*, paras 11.81–11.84.

3. Article VI:2—Prompt review of, and appropriate remedies for, administrative decisions

Article VI:2 GATS provides:

(a) Each Member shall maintain or institute as soon as practicable judicial, arbitral or administrative tribunals or procedures which provide, at the request of an affected service supplier, for the *prompt review* of, and where justified, *appropriate remedies* for, administrative decisions *affecting* trade in services. Where such procedures are not independent of the agency entrusted with the administrative decision concerned, the Member shall ensure that the procedures *in fact* provide for an *objective* and *impartial review*.

(b) The provisions of subparagraph (a) shall not be construed to require a Member to institute such tribunals or procedures where this would be inconsistent with its constitutional structure or the nature of its legal system. (emphasis added)

The second paragraph of Article VI introduces into the GATS the concept of recourse to judicial, arbitral or administrative review against unfavourable administrative decisions. It is required that each Member have (*de jure* or *de facto*) independent judicial, arbitral or administrative procedures for prompt, objective and impartial review upon request, and appropriate remedies for any GATS-inconsistent use of domestic laws and regulations which negatively affects trade in services.[94] Nonetheless, Members are free to decide on the institutional structure of a review mechanism that is commensurate with their specific needs and institutional traditions, since Article VI:2 does not contain any additional requirements on this score. This obligation is somewhat moderated in the second part of the paragraph which clarifies that this obligation does not require any Member to establish tribunals or procedures which would be incompatible with its constitutional structure or the nature of its legal system. The latter qualification renders the obligation laid down under Article VI:2(a) essentially facultative for those Members that come under this category. Thus, Article VI:2 guarantees

[94] cf Art X:3(b) and (c) GATT, which reads:

Each contracting party shall maintain, or institute as soon as practicable, judicial, arbitral or administrative tribunals or procedures for the purpose, *inter alia*, of the prompt review and correction of administrative action relating to customs matters. Such tribunals or procedures shall be independent of the agencies entrusted with administrative enforcement and their decisions shall be implemented by, and shall govern the practice of, such agencies unless an appeal is lodged with a court or tribunal of superior jurisdiction within the time prescribed for appeals to be lodged by importers; *Provided* that the central administration of such agency may take steps to obtain a review of the matter in another proceeding if there is good cause to believe that the decision is inconsistent with established principles of law or the actual facts.

The provisions of sub-paragraph (*b*) of this paragraph shall not require the elimination or substitution of procedures in force in the territory of a contracting party on the date of this Agreement which in fact provide for an objective and impartial review of administrative action even though such procedures are not fully or formally independent of the agencies entrusted with administrative enforcement. Any contracting party employing such procedures shall, upon request, furnish the CONTRACTING PARTIES with full information thereon in order that they may determine whether such procedures conform to the requirements of this sub-paragraph.

the review of and proper remedies for administrative decisions which *affect* trade in services. In the event of disagreement, all stakeholders should have recourse to the right to procedural review and to the provision of remedies (*ubi jus ibi remedium*), if applicable.

By and large, a proper regulatory system should recognize applicants' right to file complaints concerning their treatment or the refusal to consider an application, and the right to appeal if a licence application is dismissed. There shall be a mechanism that permits a challenge to the exercise of a discretionary power of a person or body in judicial (or another form of) review proceedings on the grounds that an abuse of discretion has taken place (an ultra vires[95] action of a national body), either because of the manner in which the discretion has been exercised or because of the failure of the designated person or body to exercise this discretion at all. Furthermore, service suppliers should be notified of regulatory enforcement proceedings, and allowed freely to choose their counsel and submit evidence. The individuals affected by such proceedings should be allowed to review all evidence and be heard before an appropriate forum, be it a judicial or other legally recognized review body.[96]

Judicial review is a valuable legal process. It is to be invoked in order to correct misunderstandings and potential abuses in the exercise of statutory powers by an administrative agency, a self-regulating body, or equivalent, and to ensure that discretionary powers have been exercised within the circumference of those powers in accordance with basic due process standards.[97] The recognition of the aforementioned rights is beneficial not only for the affected individuals but also for the regulatory bodies. It provides legitimacy and credibility to the regulatory body concerned (and, consequently, to the national regulatory regime as a whole) and enhances predictability and legal certainty. Viewed from this angle, it can generate a positive signalling effect to potential investors.

Thus, the procedural obligations of Article VI:2 amount to Members having to establish (or maintain) prompt review and appeal processes and an independent forum to judge in an impartial manner cases involving trade in services—and this is *irrespective* of any specific commitments undertaken. These are namely obligations that are not limited to the sectors in which Members undertook specific commitments, but apply unconditionally to all services sectors. Hence even though Article VI belongs to Part II of the GATS (General Obligations and Disciplines), Members have to avoid reneging on only the second paragraph of Article VI with respect to *all* services sectors.

[95] C Forsyth (ed), *Judicial Review and the Constitution*, 2000; also C Harlow, 'Global Administrative Law: The Quest for Principles and Values' (2006) 17(1) EJIL 192.

[96] Also R Baldwin and C McCrudden, *Regulation and Public Law*, 1987, 68.

[97] Judicial review essentially entails 'an assessment of the manner in which a decision has been made, it is not an appeal and the jurisdiction exercised is supervisory in nature'. H Delany, *Judicial Review of Administrative Action—A Comparative Analysis*, 2001, 5, 6, 267.

While Article VI:2 GATS has not been subject to review by the WTO judiciary, the *EC—Selected Customs Matters* Panel dealt with the scope of Article X:3(b) GATT, which foresees an identical obligation—albeit with respect to goods. This case touched upon highly sensitive issues relating to the supranational nature and the mechanics of the EC legal system as to the customs union and the EC common commercial policy. The complainant, *in casu* the United States, alleged that the decisions of the tribunals or procedures for the review and correction of administrative action regarding customs matters do not govern the practice of all EC agencies entrusted with administrative enforcement within the EC territory. Therefore, in the United States' view, the EC (and not its Member States) violated its obligations under this provision.[98]

The Panel started with an analysis of the terms included in Article X:3(b). Significantly, the Panel noted that tribunals and procedures can be deemed independent only if they 'have the ability to conduct the review provided for under Article X:3(b)...with freedom in institutional and practical terms from interference by the agencies whose decisions are being reviewed'.[99] It follows that, *arguendo*, under Article X:3(b) GATT, the *de facto* independence of the review mechanism in place would not be sufficient.[100] In contrast, Article VI:2(a) affirms that Members are allowed to maintain or establish review mechanisms which form part of the agency whose administrative decision is the subject of review on condition that Members ensure the objectivity and impartiality of this type of review. In fact, Article X:3(c) GATT also appears to consider as lawful any procedures or tribunals that are *de facto* or partially independent. It follows that the Panel's approach in *EC—Selected Customs Matters* seems to disregard Article X:3(c) GATT.

The Panel further submitted that this provision covers only *first* instance bodies or procedures[101] which should be independent from the administering authority that took the action that is subject to review. According to the Panel, this interpretation is also confirmed by the due process theme that underlies Article X GATT.[102] The wording of Article VI:2 GATS does not give any hint as to whether the prompt review requirement refers to first-instance review mechanisms as well. Negotiating history reveals that Members, when drafting Article VI:2 GATS found inspiration in Article X:3(b). The textual similarities between the two provisions are also striking. Therefore, Article VI:2 GATS should also be construed as requiring that Members ensure the review and correction of administrative decisions by first-instance review mechanisms, the rulings of which can be appealed through recourse to a second-instance review mechanism.

98 Panel Report, *EC—Selected Customs Matters*, para 7.495.

99 Ibid para 7.520.

100 Ibid; also fn 894 of the Panel Report on *Selected Customs Matters*.

101 Panel Report, *EC—Selected Customs Matters*, paras 7.521–7.522. The Appellate Body confirmed this view. Appellate Body Report, *EC—Selected Customs Matters*, para 294.

102 Panel Report, *EC—Selected Customs Matters*, para 7.538.

After reviewing the ordinary meaning of these terms contained in Article X:3(b) and the legal context thereof, the Panel admitted that no clear answer could be provided. Nevertheless, the Panel asserted that two important elements led it not to do justice to the United States' allegations.[103] First, it would be unreasonable to require that decisions of such tribunals and procedures bind all agencies across the territory of a federal Member, since Article X:3(b) refers to *first* instance review. Second, the due process objective merely seeks to ensure that negatively affected traders have the possibility to seek review of an administrative decision. The exigencies of due process would be exceeded in the existence of a requirement that reviews of this type would have an immediate effect throughout the territory of a federal Member.[104] Consequently, the Panel ruled that the EC acted in conformity with Article X:3(b) GATT, even though decisions regarding the review of administrative action relating to customs matters, which are taken by authorities in the EC Member States acting as EC organs, did not apply and have effect throughout the EC.[105]

In turn, the Appellate Body agreed with the Panel's reasoning in this regard. In its view, the ordinary meaning, the context, and the treaty's object and purpose support the conclusion that Article X:3(b) (and, by analogy, Article VI:2 GATS) allows, but does not require, that first-instance review decisions govern the practice of all agencies that are in charge of administrative enforcement within a Member's territory.[106] What this provision merely calls for is the possibility of an independent review and correction of the administrative action of every agency entrusted with customs enforcement, hence the existence of the Appellate Body.[107]

4. Article VI:3—Information by the domestic competent authorities and timely decision as regards an application

Paragraph 3 of Article VI states:

> Where authorization is required for the supply of a service on which a specific commitment has been made, the competent authorities of a Member shall, *within a reasonable period of time* after the submission of an application considered complete under domestic laws and regulations, inform the applicant of the decision concerning the application. At the request of the applicant, the competent authorities of the Member shall provide, *without undue delay*, information concerning the status of the application. (emphasis added)

Article VI:3 encompasses various transparency and due process obligations that apply only in sectors where specific commitments have been undertaken.[108]

[103] Ibid.
[104] Ibid para 7.539.
[105] Ibid paras 7.554, 7.556.
[106] Appellate Body Report, *EC—Selected Customs Matters*, para 304.
[107] Ibid para 302.
[108] Panel Report, *US—Gambling*, para 6.432.

This paragraph provides that where authorization is required to supply a service subject to a specific commitment, the regulatory authorities are obliged to communicate to the applicant the decision on her application within a reasonable period of time after the submission of this application is complete according to domestic laws and regulations. Additionally, at the request of the applicant, authorities should promptly provide information with respect to the status of the application.[109] Arguably, in the case that an application for an authorization has been rejected, the competent authorities should give reasons for such a decision.[110]

Article VI:3 GATS has no counterpart in the GATT. Including such a requirement in the GATS was deemed essential in order to oblige Members to abide by due process when granting authorizations. This requirement is a significant contour of the GATS, because authorizations constitute a very common instrument used by governments and domestic regulatory authorities (or self-regulating bodies) to streamline the supply of services and the entry of (domestic and foreign) service suppliers into the domestic market. This obligation, however, is weakened by the fact that it applies only to committed sectors.

Of course, in order for a Member to be required to comply with Article VI:3 GATS, it has to have in place a system that allows the granting of authorizations or, better, a system where an authority is in charge of examining applications for authorizations, providing information on their status, giving reasons for negative decisions, etc.[111] In *US—Gambling*, for instance, the complainant, *in casu* Antigua, based a claim of violation of Article VI:3 GATS against the United States on the fact that, while the supply of gambling and betting services was subject to a specific authorization, the United States had not put in place any procedures that would allow Antiguan suppliers to file an application for an authorization to supply such services in a cross-border manner.[112] Nevertheless, Antigua failed to identify the specific measures that impose such authorization requirements. Furthermore, it did not identify any such system of authorizations with respect to internet gambling in the United States which was purportedly accessible only to domestic gambling operators. Additionally, there was evidence that Antiguan suppliers had never applied for any authorization to supply gambling and betting services in the United States' market. On these grounds, the

[109] For suggestions on the further elaboration of Art VI:3 (eg scheduling examinations at reasonable intervals, reasonableness of licence fees and other charges, reasoned judgement in the case of rejecting the application etc), see WTO, CTS (Special Session), 'Transparency in Domestic Regulation', Communication from the United States, S/CSS/W/102, 13 July 2001, 3.

[110] cf Appellate Body Report, *US—Shrimp*, para 183.

[111] The requirement for giving reasons can also facilitate and improve the judicial review. M Shapiro, 'The Giving Reasons Requirement' (1992) University of Chicago Legal Forum 179. This has also been suggested by a landmark case in the EU. See Case 222/86 *Unected v Heylens* [1987] ECR 4097, paras 14–16.

[112] Panel Report, *US—Gambling*, paras 6.433–6.436.

Panel rejected Antigua's claim relating to a violation of Article VI:3 GATS by the United States.[113]

5. Procedural due process in Article VI GATS

Altogether, the first, second and third paragraphs of Article VI introduce in the GATS the concept of due process, a familiar principle from common law that goes back to the Magna Carta's '*per legem terrae*'.[114] They call for procedural justice in the national jurisdictions of all Members, and thus create a procedurally levelled playing field with respect to domestic administrative law provisions tackling trade in services. For instance, key principles from public law such as *nemo iudex in causa sua* (rule against bias) and *audi alteram partem* (right to a fair hearing and the principle of equality of arms that is implicated in it) are incorporated in the GATS framework regarding domestic regulations.

These principles are part and parcel of the 'natural justice' doctrine, renowned in English common law, which includes the notion of procedural fairness and relies on the premise that certain basic legal principles (such as the two mentioned above) are required by nature, or are so obvious that they should be applied universally without needing to be formalized in a legal code. By way of illustration, in the EU legal order, when the Court of First Instance refers to the obligation of the EU institutions to abide by the principle of equality of arms, it does not base this obligation on any Community rules or the European Treaties, but it considers it as a general principle of law.[115]

Although the concept of due process entails procedural and substantive matters alike,[116] Article VI arguably encompasses only the procedural due process in the sense of *minimum* standards of procedural fairness imposed on persons or bodies with judicial or quasi-judicial capacities or regulators in national jurisdictions.[117] To be sure, such standards of 'good' regulation form usually part of most Members' jurisdictions, as they are embedded in their national public laws. The

[113] Ibid para 6.437.

[114] Generally J Mashaw, *Due Process in the Administrative State*, 1985.

[115] Case T-30/91 *Solvay v Commission* [1995] ECR II-1775, para 83.

[116] According to US jurisprudence, due process '... is not a technical conception with a fixed concept...'. Nevertheless, when determining whether a process is constitutionally due, the US Supreme Court will balance a series of factors, which include (a) the private interest that will be affected by the official action; (b) the risk of an erroneous deprivation of such interest through the procedures used, and the probable value, if any, of additional or substitute procedural safeguards; and (c) the government's interest. See *Mathews v Eldridge*, 424 US 319, 334–335 (1976); see also the case *Planned Parenthood of Southeastern Pa. v Casey*, 505 US 833, 846, 849–850 (1992). The Supreme Court was criticized for its failure to establish a predictable and unproblematic mechanism regarding due process issues. H Delany, *Judicial Review of Administrative Action—A Comparative Analysis*, 2001, 239. For an analysis of due process requirements within the European Union and their interpretation by the ECJ, see K Lenaerts, '"In the Union We Trust": Trust-Enhancing Principles of Community Law' (2004) 41 CML Rev 317, 336ff.

[117] cf Panel Report, *US—Gambling*, para 6.432.

rule of law and principles such as participation, consultation, transparency, due process and independent administrative or judicial review are present in the public law of most Members, the only difference being the forms that they take.

Consequently, the GATS appears to be informed by the national legal traditions of Members and hence adopts at the *multilateral* level standards that we usually find at the *national* level.[118] Put differently, these multilateral standards of due process draw from existing standards in several national jurisdictions the universal value of which is generally acknowledged. These standards constitute minimum common denominators which can be identified in many Members' jurisdictions and be applied at the multilateral level.

Nevertheless, there is an important transformation of these due process standards when they are applied multilaterally: not only national suppliers but also suppliers coming from other Members can benefit from due process and procedural fairness. This non-discrimination element with respect to minimum due process rights is indeed very important for the everyday life of a service supplier. Then, the GATS creates multilaterally established private rights *vis-à-vis* national public administrators and regulators and adds a multilateral level of scrutiny regarding the adherence of the national regulatory and administrative authorities to the rule of law and due process in a non-discriminatory manner.[119] This two-way cross-fertilization is not original to the GATS; the same process is an intrinsic characteristic of the interaction between the EU and its Member States.[120]

As noted earlier, the resemblance of Article VI GATS to Article X:3 GATT is striking. Article X:3 GATT calls for the same 'rigorous compliance' with the minimum transparency and procedural fairness requirements in the application and administration of trade regulations with respect to trade in goods.[121] In *US—Shrimp*, the Appellate Body, when dealing with the issue of whether the application of the United States' measure in question could be considered as an 'arbitrary discrimination' within the meaning of the *chapeau* of Article XX, defined the scope of Article X:3 in the following terms:

> ...Article X:3 of the GATT 1994 establishes certain minimum standards for transparency and procedural fairness in the administration of trade regulations which, in our view,

[118] In more general terms, transplanting to the multilateral level certain principles of procedural fairness known from national administrative law has also been the subject of academic discussions. See, *inter alia*, B Kingsbury, N Krisch, and RB Stewart, 'The Emergence of Global Administrative Law' (2005) 68 Law and Contemporary Problems 15; also DC Esty, 'Good Governance at the Supranational Scale: Globalizing Administrative Law' (2006) 115 Yale Law Journal 1493ff. See also the very informative papers in the EJIL special issue (17:1, 2006) that hosted the Symposium on *Global Governance and Global Administrative Law in the International Legal Order*.

[119] Also S Cassese, 'Global Standards for National Administrative Procedure' (2005) 68 Law and Contemporary Problems 110ff.

[120] J Schwarze, 'The Role of the European Court of Justice in Shaping Legal Standards for Administrative Action in the Member States: A Comparative Perspective' in D O'Keeffe and A Bavasso (eds), *Judicial Review in European Union Law*, 2000, 447.

[121] Appellate Body Report, *US—Shrimp*, paras 180–183; also Appellate Body Report, *EC—Bananas III*, para 200.

are not met here. The non-transparent and *ex parte* nature of the internal governmental procedures applied by the competent officials in the Office of Marine Conservation, the Department of State, and the United States National Marine Fisheries Service throughout the certification processes under Section 609, as well as the fact that countries whose applications are denied do not receive formal notice of such denial, nor of the reasons for the denial, and the fact, too, that there is no formal legal procedure for review of, or appeal from, a denial of an application, are all contrary to the spirit, if not the letter, of Article X:3 of the GATT 1994.[122]

Recently, the Panel in *EC—Selected Customs Matters*, when dealing with the interpretation of Article X:3(a) and the requirement for uniform administration, confirmed that this provision has important due process dimensions.[123] More specifically, the Panel pointed out that this provision is 'aimed at ensuring that due process is accorded to traders when they import or export'.[124] According to the Panel,

> ... regardless of the form, nature and scale of administration at issue, ... administration should not fall below certain minimum standards of due process, which encompass notions such as notice, transparency, fairness and equity.[125]

The Panel added that such minimum standards originate in 'the broader due process context' of Article X:3(a).[126] Adhering to due process standards creates conditions of security and predictability for traders. Indeed, the administration of measures falling within the ambit of Article X:3(a) should not render the trading environment insecure and unpredictable without just cause because this would compromise the underlying due process objective of Article X GATT.[127] Whether a trader's treatment is insecure and unpredictable should be evaluated by taking account of the *overall* pattern of administration and not on the basis of individual instances of administration.[128]

Clearly, when compared to goods trade, due process, transparency, and procedural fairness play, an equally—if not more—significant role in the services trade, so long as they imply legal obligations to Members to which they should conform when regulating. I can see no reason that would prevent the WTO adjudicating bodies from following the same line of reasoning in the services realm

[122] Appellate Body Report, *US—Shrimp*, para 183.

[123] cf Appellate Body Report, *US—Underwear*, p 21.

[124] Panel Report, *EC—Selected Customs Matters*, para 7.107.

[125] Ibid para 7.134. In this respect, the Panel endorsed the EC's view that Art X:3(a) GATT is a 'minimum standards provision', which provides Members with minimum guarantees when it comes to the administration of domestic measures. Ibid paras 4.213, 4.401.

[126] This type of due process should be distinguished from the due process that governs the WTO dispute settlement proceedings. For a discussion on procedural due process regarding dispute settlement procedures, see Appellate Body Report, *US—Gambling*, paras 269–273 and the Appellate Body jurisprudence mentioned therein. For a more general review, see JC Thomas and D Palmeter, 'The Need for Due Process in WTO Proceedings' (1997) 31(1) JWT 45.

[127] Panel Report, *EC—Selected Customs Matters*, para 7.431.

[128] cf the EC's response to the Panel's Question No 48 in the *EC—Selected Customs Matters* dispute, p A-49.

when examining the consistency of national regulatory measures (or their administration) falling under Article VI GATS with the obligations originating therein. Moreover, as is the case with Article X:3 GATT dealing with goods, a violation complaint against a certain trade regulation affecting services can be based on Article VI alone, that is, the complainant need not look for violations of additional GATS legal obligations to support its request for the establishment of a panel.

Procedural due process and fairness as described above go beyond the concept of due process in the American legal system[129]—where this concept was first developed—and do not purport to have any great differences from other legal systems of civilized countries. In fact, it is generally reflected in the formulation of the two primary rules of the fair-trial guarantee articulated in Article 6 of the European Convention on Human Rights—namely, a tribunal must be independent and impartial, and the parties be given adequate notice and an opportunity to be heard (right to a fair trial).[130] Then, while it would not be accurate to argue that due process and its constituents were conceived and have been developed under identical historical, political, or institutional circumstances in the EU and the United States, it is true that the concept of due process displays nowadays manifold functional similarities in the two jurisdictions.[131]

Finally, it is worth emphasizing the dialectical process established between the GATS and the Members' public laws. These two levels of governing trade in services are expected to inform one another. Where this process will lead (perhaps to a global set of sound administration rules?) also depends on the interpretations that the WTO judicature will advance with respect to core principles of administrative law that may, or may not, be explicitly mentioned in the text of the WTO Agreements. In any event, the implementation of Article VI shows that important standards of 'efficient' or 'good' regulation flow into the GATS.

6. Article VI:4—The substantive obligation

Notwithstanding the procedural obligations enclosed in the aforementioned paragraphs of Article VI, a substantive obligation is laid down in Article VI:4 GATS which provides:

With a view to ensuring that measures relating to *qualification requirements and procedures, technical standards and licensing requirements* do not constitute *unnecessary* barriers

[129] JP Gaffney, 'Due Process in the World Trade Organization: The Need for Procedural Justice in the Dispute Settlement System' (1999) American University International Law Review 14 1175.

[130] Art 6 of the Convention for the Protection of Human Rights and Fundamental Freedoms of the Council of Europe; also Art 41:1 of the Charter of Fundamental Rights of the European Union, which summarizes the ECJ jurisprudence on due process and sound administration to date and which provides in the relevant part: 'every person has the right to have his or her affairs handled impartially, fairly and within reasonable time by the institutions, bodies, offices and agencies of the Union'. See OJ 2000, C 364/18.

[131] Also Harlow (n 95 above) 204–207.

to trade in services, the Council for Trade in Services shall, through appropriate bodies it may establish, develop any necessary disciplines. Such disciplines shall aim to ensure that such requirements are, *inter alia*:

(a) based on *objective* and *transparent* criteria, such as competence and the ability to supply the service;
(b) not more burdensome than necessary to ensure the quality of the service;
(c) in the case of licensing procedures, not *in themselves* a restriction on the supply of the service.[132] (emphasis added)

The GATS contains a soft mechanism in the form of a legal mandate that has been brought into play to ensure that specific regulatory disciplines will be developed with regard to measures relating to licensing, qualifications, and technical standards.[133] In particular, the fourth paragraph of Article VI aims to ensure that such measures 'do not constitute unnecessary barriers to trade in services'. To this effect, the CTS is directed to develop disciplines which would guarantee that these types of measures are, *inter alia*, based on objective and transparent criteria, such as competence and the ability to supply the service; are not more burdensome than necessary to ensure the quality of the service; and, as far as licensing procedures are concerned, are not in themselves a restriction on the supply of the service.

The criteria mentioned under Article VI:4(a), (b), and (c) amount to an *indicative* list of characteristics that the new rules relating to qualifications, licensing, and standards should have as *a minimum*. Article VI:4, then, envisages positive integration and minimum harmonization attempts in these areas in the long run, since Members negotiate at the multilateral level with a view to establishing a common regulatory framework on these specific regulatory areas. This provision demonstrates the strong legislative capacity that Members have in services vis-à-vis other WTO agreements.

Rationae materiae, Article VI:4 covers measures that are meant to serve regulatory or other public policy objectives. Consequently, their purpose is not to hamper trade. Nevertheless, domestic rules are normally established to respond to local conditions and therefore it is possible that they lead to trade friction, even if unintentionally. In the case where they have restrictive effects on trade in services—either unintentionally or as disguised protectionism—Article VI calls for these effects to be the minimum possible without jeopardizing the achievement of the desired policy objective. Such measures would be deemed GATS-consistent on condition that they meet the three aforementioned requirements of paragraph 4. Clearly, it is neither the intention nor the purpose of the potential disciplines to prescribe or impose certain regulatory approaches, much less the substance of any domestic regulations.

132 See, in more detail, Chapter IV below.

133 WTO, WPDR, 'Report on the Meeting Held on 15 May 2003', S/WPDR/M/21/Rev.1, 25 June 2003, para 16.

Thus, Article VI:4 merely requires that Members create appropriate bodies which will negotiate disciplines in designated sectors or horizontally, ie for *all* services sectors, to ascertain that measures relating to qualifications, licensing or technical standards do not unduly constitute a barrier to trade in services. The reader of Article VI:4 might be taken aback by the fact that this provision contains a mandate for the development of disciplines rather than a straightforward binding rule similar to that enclosed in the first draft of the GATS presented by Arthur Dunkel in 1991.[134] This first draft was very simple but it apparently covered the core of what is stated in the form of a mandate in Article VI:4 in its present form. Indeed, a simple transformation of the principles listed in VI:4 into binding rules/disciplines would bring domestic regulations within the GATS framework.

Nevertheless, such a rule of general application was deemed to be too broad and to provide insufficient guidance for the settlement of potential disagreements or disputes about particular measures. The purpose of transforming these general principles into disciplines is to make these principles sufficiently specific so that they are effective, enforceable and operationally useful.[135] Hence, it was and continues to be problematic to determine the extent to which regulatory principles can, amidst considerable sectoral diversity, be pursued through the creation of coherent and meaningful horizontal (ie non-sector-specific) disciplines.

During the Uruguay Round negotiations on services, governments had not been able—due also to time constraints—to set out criteria to guide them in the application of such measures to ensure that they 'are not more burdensome than necessary'. Instead, they agreed to a work programme geared in part to prolonging discussions, which would add greater precision to the definition of what constitutes 'an unnecessary burden'. A germane task assigned to the negotiators involves confronting the reality that domestic regulations, even when they do not discriminate, can undermine any substantive value of the market access commitments undertaken at the multilateral level, if they are non-transparent, unfair, or unduly burdensome. This work programme set out in Article VI:4 presumes that no services sector is excluded *a priori* from the application of the future rules on domestic regulations.

The work programme was originally implemented by the *Decision on Professional Services* adopted by the CTS in March 1995, which established the

[134] GATT, 'Draft Multilateral Framework for Trade in Services', MTN.GNS/35, 23 July 1990. In Art VII, the draft text of the GATS reads: 'Parties may require that services or suppliers of services of other parties meet certain regulations, standards or qualifications. Such requirements shall be based upon objective criteria, such as competence and the ability to provide such services, and not be more burdensome than necessary to achieve the national policy objectives.'

[135] WTO, WPPS, 'Background Information on the Agreement on Technical Barriers to Trade and the Agreement on Import Licensing Procedures', S/WPPS/W/6, 29 February 1996, para 2.

WPPS pursuant to Article XXIV GATS.[136] It called on the Working Party to carry out work on the liberalization of professional services.[137] Priority was accorded to the accountancy sector and taken up by the WPPS in April 1995. In particular, the mandate had three parts: (1) the development of disciplines on domestic regulation; (2) the possible use of international standards; and (3) the establishment of guidelines for the recognition of qualifications.

The *Decision on Professional Services* establishing a work programme on accountancy services was perceived as an attempt to satisfy the strong interest manifested by the industry itself, but also to minimize the frustration brought about by the imperfect results of the Uruguay Round in the services domain and the limited scope of commitments in the national Schedules. At the core of the mandate was the development of disciplines necessary to ensure that measures relating to qualifications, licensing, and technical standards in the field of professional services do not constitute unnecessary barriers to trade in services.

Members' basic concerns associated with the accountancy sector, as with other professional services, were to ensure the professional competence of the individual service supplier, to monitor professional performance, and to address any lapses of professionalism. Indeed, domestic standards and procedures may constitute unreasonable barriers to trade in that they unnecessarily discriminate against foreign suppliers (accountants in this case), or unnecessarily restrict entry (be it by nationals or foreigners) into the profession.

It bears mention that, while the *Decision on Professional Services* called upon the WPPS to develop the necessary disciplines for professional services on a sector-by-sector basis,[138] thus reflecting the view that any across-the-board approach towards domestic regulation could be complex due to the special character of many services sectors or sub-sectors, Article VI:4 purports to favour the solution of developing disciplines on domestic regulation for all services sectors, thus horizontally.[139] Then, while the approach followed does not match the ordinary meaning of paragraph 4, horizontal and sectoral disciplines are not necessarily mutually exclusive,[140] but reinforcing; put differently, there is a certain degree of complementarity between the development of horizontal disciplines and the

[136] WTO, Trade in Services, 'Decision on Professional Services', S/L/3, 4 April 1995.

[137] Professional services are deemed to be part of the business services category and include: legal services, accounting, auditing and bookkeeping services, taxation services, architectural services, engineering services, integrated engineering services, urban planning and landscape architectural services, medical and dental services, veterinary services, services provided by midwives, nurses, physiotherapists and para-medical personnel, and a residual 'other' category. WTO, *2001 Scheduling Guidelines*, S/L/92, 2001, p 35.

[138] WTO, Trade in Services (n 136 above) para 1.

[139] See the informative discussions during earlier meetings of the CTS on whether a horizontal or sector-specific approach should be followed with regard to future work under Art VI:4 in WTO, CTS, 'Report of the Meeting Held on 22 and 23 March 1999', S/C/M/34, 16 April 1999, paras 52–53.

[140] See also the intervention of Japan in WTO, WPDR (n 133 above) para 48.

work on professional services.[141] For instance, horizontal rules could be used to decide what aspects of a regulatory system would have to be negotiated on a sectoral basis.

At the first WTO Ministerial Conference (Singapore, 9–13 December 1996), Members reiterated their commitment to materializing the Article VI:4 mandate in the CTS for all services and, at the same time, completing the work in the WPPS on the development of disciplines in the accountancy sector. The broader Article VI:4 work programme was discussed by the CTS after the Singapore Ministerial Conference and it was suggested that the WPPS work on accountancy disciplines should be accomplished before beginning the work on the development of domestic regulation rules for all services sectors.

The WPPS concluded its work relative to the development of disciplines on domestic regulation in the accountancy sector at the end of 1998 and the CTS approved the text on 14 December 1998. The WPDR replaced the WPPS and was assigned the task of carrying out the work in line with the mandate under Article VI:4,[142] ie giving priority to the development of horizontal disciplines on domestic regulation.

As a final remark, paragraph 4 of Article VI has the same power as paragraph 2 thereof, since it should apply to all services sectors, regardless of commitments undertaken. Indeed, when one peruses Article VI, it is only in its second and fourth paragraphs that the usual caveat, ie the phrase 'in sectors in which a Member has undertaken specific commitments' or phrases with the same meaning, does not appear. Nevertheless, the WPDR has not yet opted for the development of horizontal disciplines applicable to *all* sectors, ie regardless of commitments undertaken. It is still unclear whether or not Members would wish to limit the applicability of horizontal disciplines only to committed sectors, following the example of the accountancy disciplines.[143] It seems plausible to argue that such expansion of horizontal disciplines to non-committed sectors would not be accepted so easily and, consequently, it should be renegotiated.[144]

It is clear by now that differences in regulatory measures for services industries across countries, even when such measures apply in a non-discriminatory manner, may lead to undesirable results from a trade-friendly point of view. To alleviate this, governments can be biased in favour of a minimum harmonization of regulatory practices and methods. In this regard, Article VI:4 calls for the creation of positive rules relating to licensing, qualifications, and technical standards. These rules would in all likelihood lead to a minimum harmonization

[141] While the horizontal and the sector-specific approaches are not mutually exclusive, one cannot refute the existence of a tension 'between being too specific, with a risk for the result not to be multilaterally acceptable, and being too generic, without adding value to the current text of Article VI:4.' WTO, WPPS, 'Note on the Meeting Held on 24 March 1997', S/WPPS/M/8, 5 May 1997, para 5.

[142] WTO, Trade in Services, 'Decision on Domestic Regulation', S/L/70, 28 April 1999.

[143] WTO, Trade in Services, 'Decision on Disciplines Relating to the Accountancy Sector', S/L/63, 15 October 1998, para 1

[144] WTO, WPDR (n 10 above) p 8.

of regulations regarding licensing, qualifications, or standards.[145] For many, the GATS is the natural, multilateral forum in the field of trade in services to promote minimum harmonization efforts, lend credibility to the results achieved through legally binding commitments and to the consequential domestic regulatory reform endeavours, and to alleviate domestic opposition. Finally, strengthened rules on domestic regulations can be conducive to the promotion and consolidation of domestic regulatory reform and to the abolition of restrictive regulatory barriers. Hence, it needs to be assured that the gains from liberalization are not undermined by inadequacies in policy choice and regulation. The main value of Article VI:4 is that it sets up the framework for achieving such an outcome.

7. Article VI:5—The substantive obligation of transitional nature

Prior to the agreement and entry into force of more specific rules under Article VI:4, Article VI:5 provides for the application of the main principles contained in paragraph 4 to licensing and qualification requirements and technical standards so that a country's measure does not lead to nullification or impairment[146] of its commitments in a manner not anticipated by the WTO Membership. More specifically, this provision reads:

(a) In sectors in which a Member has undertaken specific commitments, *pending the entry into force* of disciplines developed in these sectors pursuant to paragraph 4, the Member shall not apply licensing and qualification requirements and technical standards that *nullify or impair such specific commitments* in a manner which:
   (i) does not comply with the criteria outlined *in subparagraphs 4(a), (b) or (c)*; and
   (ii) *could not reasonably have been expected of that Member at the time the specific commitments in those sectors were made.*

(b) In determining whether a Member is in conformity with the obligation under paragraph 5(a), *account shall be taken* of international standards of relevant international organizations[147] applied by that Member. (emphasis added)

The disciplines established by Article VI:5 are transitional in nature and apply only to measures in areas in which a Member has undertaken specific commitments. The key objective of paragraph 5 is to ensure that the standards that were set in Article VI:4(a)–(c) with respect to qualifications, licensing and technical standards will not be neglected and undermined by their absence while negotiations under Article VI:4 are taking place.[148] It is the protection of the benefits

[145] For more details, see the analysis in Chapter IV below.

[146] For these concepts and their origin, see F Roessler, 'The Concept of Nullification and Impairment in the Legal System of the World Trade Organization' in E-U Petersmann (ed), *International Trade Law and the GATT/WTO Dispute Settlement System*, 1997, 125.

[147] [Original footnote] The term '*relevant international organizations*' refers to international bodies whose membership is open to the relevant bodies of at least all Members of the WTO.

[148] Indeed, 'Article VI:5 was an effort to operationalize the objectives stated in VI:4, the most important of which was the necessity test', according to the WTO Secretariat in WTO, WPDR, 'Report on the Meeting Held on 11 May 2001', S/WPDR/M/11, 7 June 2001, para 29.

from negotiated rights and contractual obligations that should be reassured.[149] Again, the scope of Article VI:5 is narrower than that of Article VI:4, as the former covers licensing, qualifications, and technical standards, but *not* measures relating thereto.

In order for these disciplines to apply, two sets of criteria must be cumulatively satisfied, ie the licensing and qualification requirements and technical standards must nullify or impair specific commitments in a manner that

(a) is (i) not based on objective and transparent criteria, or (ii) more burdensome than necessary to ensure the quality of the service, or (iii) in the case of licensing procedures, in itself a restriction on the supply of the service; *and*
(b) could not reasonably have been expected at the time the specific commitments were made.

These conditions apply cumulatively; in other words, any Member shall ensure that, for instance, a specific licensing requirement that comes under a sector where that Member made a specific commitment complies with *all* three criteria set out in paragraph 4(a), (b), and (c), and, in addition, does not nullify or impair that Member's specific commitments in a manner that could not have been reasonably anticipated by its trading partners. For the disciplines in Article VI:5 to come into play, not only must the *application* of licensing and qualification requirements and procedures, or technical standards fall short of meeting the transparency, objectivity, and necessity criteria outlined in Article VI:4, but it must also nullify or impair specific commitments in a way that could not reasonably have been expected.

A careful reader would also observe that Article VI:5(a) does not refer to licensing and qualification *procedures*, as is the case in the *chapeau* of paragraph 4. Nonetheless, this should not be taken to mean that those procedures are not subject to Article VI:5 disciplines. There are two elements that lead to this conclusion: the first is related to the text of the provision. Article VI:5(a)(i) also refers to Article VI:4(c) which exclusively deals with licensing procedures. The second is based on the object and purpose of Article VI:5: the negotiating history of the Uruguay Round demonstrates that Members sought, through the creation of Article VI:5, to operationalize Article VI:4 until the development of specific disciplines under the latter provision and procedures are an important part of the Article VI:4 mandate. Both of these elements lead plausibly to the conclusion that licensing and qualification procedures are also covered by Article VI:5(a).

Article VI:5 could be considered as including some guidance with respect to the minimum to be achieved under VI:4 disciplines, that is, implementing the three criteria of VI:4(a), (b) and (c).[150] The formulation of Article VI:4 (inter alia)

[149] According to the WTO Secretariat, '...Article VI:5 had been conceived basically as a temporary solution during the Uruguay Round to secure the value of commitments'. WTO, WPDR, 'Report on the Meeting Held on 3 December 2003', S/WPDR/M/24, 22 January 2004, para 7.

[150] See the intervention of Hong Kong, China, in WTO, WPDR (n 133 above) para 31.

leads to the same conclusion, ie that this is the minimum to be sought pending the implementation of the Article VI:4 mandate.

The scope of application of Article VI:5 encompasses measures that nullify or impair specific commitments. Article VI:5 would provide the basis for complaints about measures in the areas of licensing, qualification, and technical standards which were believed to nullify or impair a specific commitment in an unforeseeable manner. The impact of the disciplines is further weakened by subparagraph (ii) of Article VI:5(a) which exempts measures which could reasonably have been expected of a Member *at the time that the specific commitments in the relevant sectors were made*. Subparagraph (ii) would, therefore, seem to exempt from Article VI:5(a) at least all those measures which were already in place in 1995, as those measures most likely were expected by the negotiating partners. Thus, this provision has the effect of grandfathering pre-existing domestic regulations, but it applies to licensing and qualification requirements and procedures as well as technical standards that were adopted *after* the entry into force of the GATS.[151] In this case, the principle of predictability apparently prevails over that of non-discrimination in a situation of pre-existing conditions.[152]

Furthermore, new measures, ie those that entered into force *after* January 1995, that are more trade-friendly than the measures in force before that date are equally excluded from the scope of Article VI:5(a), since such measures are presumably along the lines of Members' reasonable expectations and the spirit of the GATS. For that reason, Article VI:5 can also be viewed as a type of 'standstill' obligation, since there is no Article VI:5-consistent way to implement a qualification or licensing requirement or a technical standard that leads to the deterioration of the supply of a given service in a sector where specific commitments were undertaken.[153] In other words, a Member is expected to ensure that, in committed sectors, the application of any *new* licensing and qualification requirements and procedures, and technical standards does not nullify or impair specific commitments in a manner that could not have been reasonably expected of that Member.

As Article VI:5(a) entails the notion of 'nullification or impairment', it may be appropriate to examine the meaning of this concept in the WTO law. By virtue of Article XXIII of GATT, a remedy is only available in the case of nullification or impairment. In the event of an infringement of an obligation assumed under one or more agreements covered by the DSU, nullification or impairment is presumed in accordance with Article 3:8 DSU (prima facie nullification or

[151] WTO, WPDR, 'Report on the Meeting Held on 1 July 2003', S/WPDR/M/22, 22 September 2003, para 16.

[152] SM Stephenson, '"Deeper" Integration in Services Trade in the Western Hemisphere: Domestic Regulation and Mutual Recognition' in OECD, *Trade and Regulatory Reform: Insights from Country Experience*, 2001, 81.

[153] Also D Luff, 'Regulation of Health Services and International Trade Law' in A Mattoo and P Sauvé (eds), *Domestic Regulation and Service Trade Liberalization*, 2003, 203; and WTO, WPDR (n 151 above) para 30.

impairment), this placing the burden of rebutting the existence of nullification or impairment (in other words, the *onus probandi*) on the respondent. Hence, there is a presumption that a breach of the rules has an adverse impact on other Members, and in such cases, it is up to the Members against whom the complaint has been brought to rebut the charge.[154] This presumption, however, has never been rebutted and hence has operated as an irrefutable presumption.[155]

Nullification or impairment may still serve as the basis for a successful complaint even in the absence of an actual violation of a WTO provision.[156] In this case, an allegation of a violation of a WTO obligation is not required.[157] Therefore, in such cases one speaks of 'non-violation nullification or impairment'.[158] The basic premise is that Members should keep away from applying measures—even if they are consistent with the letter of the WTO Agreements—or acting in a manner that might undermine the reasonable expectations of other Members[159] and the negotiated balance of concessions between Members.[160] As market access cannot be deemed a guarantee against changes in market conditions and thus a guarantee of trade volumes, the introduction of a non-violation clause was deemed essential, as it is expected to provide protection of market access expectations.

The concept of the 'non-violation remedy' was first elaborated in the context of Article XXIII:1(b) of GATT.[161] Non-violation is an exceptional remedy within the WTO dispute settlement system,[162] which has its roots in the public international law tenet of '*pacta sunt servanda*'.[163] In this regard, the complaining party bears the burden of presenting a 'detailed justification'[164] of the complaint pursuant to Article 26:1(a) DSU and to demonstrate the following:[165]

(a) An application of a measure by a Member;
(b) A benefit accruing to the complainant under the relevant agreement;[166] and

[154] Appellate Body Report, *US—Wool Shirts and Blouses*, p 14. also Appellate Body Report, *EC—Hormones*, para 98.

[155] Roessler (n 146 above) 127; also GATT Panel Report, *US—Superfund*, para 5.1.7.

[156] Of course, as the coverage of WTO rules expands to include new areas and thus WTO becomes a more complete contract, the scope for raising non-violation complaints will diminish.

[157] Appellate Body Report, *India—Patents (US)*, para 39.

[158] Also H Horn, G Maggi, and RW Staiger, 'The GATT/WTO as an Incomplete Contract', 2005, 26, 33ff.

[159] For the interpretation of the 'reasonable or legitimate expectations' concept in *non*-violation cases, see WTO, *WTO Analytical Index—Guide to WTO Law and Practice*, Vol 1, 2003, p 375, para 557.

[160] Appellate Body Report, *India—Patents (US)*, para 41; also GATT Panel Report, *EEC—Oilseeds I*, para 144.

[161] For the relationship between Arts XXIII:1(a) and XXIII:1(b), see Appellate Body Report, *EC—Asbestos*, paras 185–188.

[162] Panel Report, *Japan—Film*, para 10.36.

[163] Panel Report, *Korea—Procurement*, para 7.93.

[164] Panel Report, *Japan—Film*, paras 10.30–10.31.

[165] Ibid para 10.41, and Panel Report, *Korea—Procurement*, para 7.86.

[166] With only one exception (unadopted GATT Panel Report, *EC—Citrus*), in all the previous cases where a non-violation complaint arose the claimed benefit was that of legitimate expectations

(c) Nullification or impairment of the benefit as the result of the application of a measure that could not have been reasonably expected by the exporting Member[167] (causal relationship between the measure and the nullification, or impairment, or impeding of objectives).[168]

In the case where the challenged measures were introduced *after* the end of the negotiations, it is suggested that the *complaining* party should not be held to have anticipated these measures. It is then for the *respondent* to rebut the established presumption.[169] In contrast, for measures adopted *before* the conclusion of the negotiations, it is presumed that the *complainant* could have reasonably foreseen these measures and hence it is for the latter to rebut that presumption.[170]

It follows that, while nullification or impairment could be relevant for violation *and* non-violation cases, this concept has typically been associated with the latter. This is not surprising: as already pointed out, in a violation case there is a (*de facto* irrefutable) presumption of nullification or impairment pursuant to Article 3:8 DSU. Therefore, the application of this concept to violation cases '*cannot fulfil a useful function*'.[171] In non-violation cases, the concept of nullification or impairment was equated to 'upsetting the competitive relationship' which existed between domestic and imported products as a result of the relevant tariff concessions.

Article VI:5 GATS incorporates the concept of nullification or impairment by requiring that Members do not apply qualification and licensing requirements and procedures or technical standards that nullify or impair specific commitments in a manner that could not reasonably be anticipated by the WTO Membership at the time that the commitments were scheduled. It is worth noting that Article VI:5 was negotiated intensively.[172] Members started dealing with its drafting after having finalized the drafting of Article VI:4, as they felt that, in the absence of rules under Article VI:4, there was a need for a provision that would allow interim operationalization of the objectives endorsed in Article VI:4(a)–(c) and would secure the value of the commitments undertaken.

of improved market access opportunities resulting from the relevant tariff concessions. Panel Report, *Japan—Film*, para 10.61 and fn 1528.

167 Contrary to violation cases, where the WTO adjudicating bodies will seek to establish the mutual understanding, or else the common intentions, of the negotiating parties, in a *non*-violation case the Panel or the Appellate Body will be only interested to identify the reasonable expectations of the *complainant*. Panel Report, *Korea—Procurement*, para 7.75.

168 Hence, the complainant is expected to show a clear correlation between the measures and the adverse effect on the relevant competitive relationships. Panel Report, *Japan—Film*, para 10.82.

169 The *EC—Asbestos* Panel, however, noted that this presumption should not apply for a measure that was adopted *after* the conclusion of the negotiations, but which falls under the Art XX GATT exceptions. Panel Report, *EC—Asbestos*, para 8.291.

170 Panel Report, *Japan—Film*, paras 10.79–10.80; also K Nicolaidis and JP Trachtman, 'From Policed Regulation to Managed Recognition in GATS' in P Sauvé and RM Stern (eds), *GATS 2000: New Directions in Services Trade Liberalization*, 2000, 258.

171 Roessler (n 146 above) 141.

172 WTO, WPDR (n 133 above) para 23.

At the same time, several elements that were added in the body of Article VI, such as the nullification or impairment concept or that of reasonable expectations that allowed the grandfathering of existing measures, clearly reveal the Members' reluctance to commit themselves to a strong provision the implications of which could not be anticipated at that time, or to a provision that would interfere with the regulatory flexibility that they had enjoyed until then with respect to important domestic regulatory areas in services such as qualifications, licensing, and technical standards.

Against this backdrop, Article VI:5 appears to cover a *non*-violation nullification or impairment case.[173] As noted earlier, this provision includes elements that are constituents of a non-violation nullification or impairment case under WTO law and jurisprudence: it disciplines the application of the measures rather than the measures per se; it mentions nullification or impairment in the text of the provision; and, most importantly, it includes the reasonable expectations concept, which has been linked to non-violation complaints.[174]

Nevertheless, other elements seem to exclude the possibility of a non-violation nullification or impairment case under Article VI:5. First and foremost, is the fact that Article XXIII:3 GATS already includes the non-violation nullification or impairment concept adopting a wording identical to that of its GATT counterpart, Article XXIII:1(b).[175] Even if it is argued that Article VI:5 is an interim provision that will become void after the entry into force of the disciplines generated in accordance with Article VI:4 and hence non-violation complaints will be covered exclusively by Article XXIII:3, it is still inconceivable what reason could possibly lead Members to put two *non*-violation provisions in the GATS text in the first place. To my mind, there is simply no logical or convincing answer to this remark that identifies the overlap between Articles VI:5 and XXIII:3. Therefore, it is only the latter, and not Article VI:5, that should be considered as covering non-violation complaints, as it is broader in scope than Article VI:5. Indeed Article XXIII:3 GATS covers the nullification or impairment of *any* benefit reasonably expected as a result of the application of *any* measure. Additionally, it is not expected to expire after the adoption of any disciplines, as is the case under Article VI:5.

Furthermore, after a careful examination of provisions that foresee non-violation complaints, one observes that such provisions are procedural in character. This is, for instance, discernible when one reads Articles XXIII GATS or XXIII GATT. Both of them foresee that a Member is deemed to have violated

[173] Trachtman (n 88 above) 13.

[174] cf Appellate Body Report, *India—Patents (US)*, para 36.

[175] In two WPDR meetings, the Secretariat attempted to clarify the relationship between Arts VI:5 and XXIII:3 GATS in its interventions. It seems, however, that the Secretariat took contradictory views, as from the first meeting one concludes that Art VI:5 foresees a non-violation case, while from the second meeting the opposite impression is gained by the reader. cf WTO, WPDR (n 133 above) para 23, and WTO, WPDR (n 151 above) paras 33–34.

its obligations (and *not* a specific WTO provision) if it nullified or impaired, through the application of *any* measure, *a benefit* that another Member reasonably expected to accrue to it based on previous tariff concessions or specific commitments (under GATT and GATS, respectively) that this Member made. Nonetheless, Article VI:5 is substantive in nature and entails a clear legal obligation. It provides for specific requirements that a Member should abide by in order to avoid a challenge to its measures before the WTO or, viewed from the complainant's side, the substantive elements that the latter has to establish if it wants its complaint to be successful.

And this brings me to my main argument regarding Article VI:5. As this provision entails a substantive obligation, any complaint based on it can only be a *violation* complaint. Whether Article VI:5 covers violation or, rather, *non*-violation cases may have important ramifications. For instance, if it covers only *non*-violation cases, a salient implication is that the respondent is not obliged to withdraw the measure(s) at issue pursuant to Article 26 DSU. Therefore, given that only *violation* complaints can be founded under Article VI:5, if a Member plans to bring a complaint based on this provision, it would have to demonstrate that the respondent violated the substantive elements of Article VI:5 and hence establish a *prima facie* case of inconsistency with this provision. Hence a Member bringing a complaint must establish that:

(i) a Member made a specific commitment in a specific sector;
(ii) this Member applies a certain measure, ie licensing or qualification requirements (or procedures), or technical standards, in this sector;
(iii) the application of this measure nullifies or impairs the specific commitment undertaken;
(iv) this nullification or impairment occurs in a manner that does not comply with one of the criteria laid down in Article VI:4(a)–(c); *and*
(v) such nullification or impairment could not have been reasonably expected of that Member when it undertook specific commitments.

If the complainant demonstrates all these elements, then the inconsistency of the measure at issue with Article VI:5 is established and there is a presumption that a nullification or impairment occurred (in that the violation of this provision had an adverse impact on the complainant's trade opportunities); then it is for the respondent to rebut the charge. Hence, nullification or impairment comes into play only after the WTO adjudicating bodies have ascertained the infringement of Article VI:5.

Therefore, Article VI:5 has a peculiar nature when it comes to nullification or impairment. This peculiarity resides in the fact that nullification or impairment arises in two different instances: in the first instance, nullification or impairment of specific commitments which could not have been reasonably expected of a Member at the time that this Member made such commitments is deemed a starting point, or else a substantive element of Article VI:5 that needs to be demonstrated in order to establish a violation of this provision. In the second instance, nullification or impairment need not be demonstrated, but it is the *presumed result* of Article VI:5 violation, which has proven to be irrefutable at all times.

To summarize as to Article VI:5(a), it would be accurate to contend that Article VI:5, while enclosing several elements well known from non-violation nullification or impairment cases, foresees a violation case and, *a fortiori*, any complaint based on this Article will be a violation complaint. Of course, because of the several substantive elements that the complainant has to demonstrate in order to support its complaint, the establishment of an Article VI:5 violation would definitely be a daunting task. Indeed, the presence of a nullification or impairment clause in Article VI:5 will make it difficult for a complaining party to challenge longstanding non-discriminatory measures under this Article. As the complaining party must demonstrate that the measure at issue could not reasonably have been expected, established regulatory practices or circumstances are protected. At the end of the day, this may be what Members seeking to protect their regulatory flexibility initially wanted.

Furthermore, Article VI:5(b) GATS requires that due account be taken of international standards of relevant international organizations applied by a Member in evaluating whether its domestic regulations are in compliance with the principles of necessity, transparency, and objectivity established in Article VI:5(a). The term 'relevant international organizations' refers to international bodies whose membership is open to the relevant bodies of all Members. The International Association of Insurance Supervisors (IAIS), the International Organization of Securities Commissions (IOSCO), or the International Civil Aviation Organization (ICAO), for instance, would probably qualify for taking their standards into account in determining whether a Member is in conformity with Article VI:5(a). Conversely, the OECD would not, in all likelihood, qualify, since accession to it does not seem to be open to all Members.

Article VI:5(b) provides a benchmark for determining the transparency, objectivity, and necessity of regulatory requirements. It constitutes a safe harbour for Members whose licensing and qualifications requirements and procedures, and technical standards conform to international standards, by essentially implying that those Members which use international standards in their domestic regulatory processes can keep these domestic regulations intact. This provision, however, is not expected to produce any major incentives for the adoption of international standards by Members owing to the weakness of Article VI:5(b). This weakness has its roots in the lack of any presumption of compliance, contrary to Article 2.5 TBT and Article 3.2 SPS.[176]

[176] The TBT and SPS agreements go even further in two respects: First, they contain important provisions requiring Members to use international standards as a *basis* for their technical regulations (Arts 2.4 TBT and 3.1 SPS). More importantly, both agreements require that Members become involved in the work of international standardizing bodies (Arts 2.6 TBT and 3.4, 3.5 SPS).

To be sure, Article VI:5(b) was inspired by other WTO Agreements in the area of goods, especially the TBT and SPS Agreements, with respect to the use of international standards to determine the necessity and reasonableness of non-discriminatory measures.[177] Nevertheless, Article VI:5(b) GATS falls short of going as far as the TBT or the SPS Agreement in establishing a general obligation for Members to apply international standards when they are available. These Agreements establish a presumption, albeit rebuttable, that any measure which is consistent with international standards would be considered not to unnecessarily impede trade.[178] This can be justified by the fact that standards in the area of services trade are scarce. Nevertheless, the demand for such standards has increased recently due to several factors, including the deregulation and privatization of public, 'bottleneck' services; the delocalization of the supply of various services; the pressure by consumers regarding quality, the environment, and safety, with a corresponding enhancement of the legislation that covers consumer protection in services; and the expansion of internet-based services.[179]

Depending on the long-term objectives of the GATS, the absence of a TBT/SPS-type presumption in favour of international standards can be deemed either a weakness or a potential asset for the GATS. It can be viewed as a weakness because a presumption of compliance would induce Members to adopt international standards in the area of services also in order to avoid litigation. In its current state, Article VI:5 is a weak negative integration provision that provides fewer incentives for harmonization under the GATS than under the SPS and TBT Agreements and cannot serve to reduce gratuitous regulatory diversity, as the respective provisions of the latter Agreements do.[180] This weakness, of course, may be attributed to the lack of international standards to date in many services sectors when compared with international standards in the goods area. But, even in the areas in which international standards exist, Members generally do not endorse them. It could be argued that Article VI:5, by not embodying a presumption of compliance, is partly to blame for this attitude. In addition, Members have no incentive to create international standards. Members are merely encouraged, wherever appropriate, to work in cooperation with relevant intergovernmental

Also JP Trachtman, 'Lessons for the GATS from Existing WTO Rules on Domestic Regulation' in A Mattoo and P Sauvé (eds), *Domestic Regulation and Service Trade Liberalization*, 2003, 70.

177 WTO, WPDR (n 149 above) para 7.

178 WTO, WPPS, 'The Relevance of the Disciplines of the Agreements on Technical Barriers to Trade (TBT) and on Import Licensing Procedures to Article VI.4 of the General Agreement on Trade in Services', S/WPPS/W/9, 11 September 1996, para 22.

179 WTO, WPDR, 'Report on the Meeting Held on 22 June 2005', S/WPDR/M/30, 6 September 2005, para 166.

180 It is worth noting that the decision on accountancy disciplines deviates somewhat from Art VI:5(b) by providing that account must be taken of internationally recognized standards applied by a Member to determine whether that Member acted in conformity with the requirement that technical standards be prepared, adopted and applied only to fulfil legitimate objectives. WTO, Trade in Services, 'Disciplines on Domestic Regulation in the Accountancy Sector', S/L/64, 17 December 1998, para 26.

and non-governmental organizations towards the establishment and adoption of common international standards for the practice of relevant services trades and professions.[181] The WPPS that was assigned, *inter alia*, to give full effect to paragraph 5 of Article VII GATS did not live up to expectations although considerable work had been undertaken in several international organizations dealing with the accountancy sector.[182] In any case, the WPDR, the heir to the WPPS, can assume this responsibility,[183] both across all services sectors and in a sector-specific base.

On the other hand, the GATS approach as to the relevance of international standards can also be deemed advantageous, as in many instances, the adoption of international standards is not necessarily the result of a multilateral consensus on the universality of a given standard. Sometimes, a given standard may not even represent the absolute majority of Members in a standard-setting body. This fact, however, may still lead the WTO judiciary to uphold the validity of such standards. In *EC—Hormones*, for instance, this issue was at the heart of the dispute. The Codex Alimentarius Commission did not reach a consensus with respect to standards related to growth-promoting hormones in cattle, but the standard was finally approved with a very narrow majority of 33 votes to 29, with seven abstentions.[184] Nevertheless, the Panel, in a finding not reviewed by the Appellate Body, ruled that, for the purposes of Article 3.1 SPS, it was irrelevant whether the standard at stake was adopted by consensus or by a wide or narrow majority.[185] Likewise, in the Explanatory Note of paragraph 2 of Annex 1 to the TBT Agreement it is explicitly noted that standards that are *not* based on consensus are still to be considered as international standards for the purposes of the Agreement.[186]

In addition, most standard-setting bodies clarify that the standards that they develop are voluntary. In fact, in paragraph 2 of Annex 1 to the TBT Agreement a standard is defined as a 'document approved by a recognized body... with which compliance is not mandatory'. Nevertheless, a presumption of compliance like the one included in the TBT and SPS Agreements essentially transforms such standards to *de facto* mandatory, as Members feel compelled to abide by them in order to avoid litigation. This can definitely distort Members' preferences, especially in case where a Member has expressed its disagreement and voted against the adoption of a given standard by the respective standard-setting body.[187]

Viewed from this angle, the approach that the GATS endorses regarding international standards appears to be the most satisfactory one, because, by requiring

[181] Article VII:5 GATS.
[182] Also Chapter IV.B below.
[183] WTO, Trade in Services (n 142 above) para 2.
[184] DA Motaal, 'The "Multilateral Scientific Consensus" and the World Trade Organization' (2005) 38(5) JWT 866.
[185] Panel Report, *EC—Hormones*, para 8.69.
[186] Also Appellate Body Report, *EC—Sardines*, paras 222–225.
[187] DA Motaal (n 184 above) 871–872.

that 'due account' of international standards be taken, Article VI:5(b) leaves sufficient space for manoeuvre for the WTO adjudicating bodies to examine the background of the adoption of the international standard at stake, its degree of acceptance and other relevant factors.[188] Again, Members could agree to clarify what they understand by the term 'due account' so that the WTO judiciary has a benchmark when called upon to interpret Article VI:5(b). Given that Article VI:5 is transitional in nature and hence will have no reason to exist after the adoption of the disciplines under Article VI:4, Members should reflect on the possibility of incorporating in the prospective disciplines a provision that would clarify the role of international standards when the objectivity, necessity, and transparency of a domestic measure is scrutinized. Provided that the 'due account' language is adopted, Members should also adopt criteria that would concretize what 'due account' entails.

8. Article VI:6—Adequate procedures for verifying competence of professionals

The last paragraph of Article VI: entails another obligation of procedural nature:

> In sectors where specific commitments regarding *professional services* are undertaken, each Member shall provide for *adequate* procedures to verify the competence of professionals of any other Member. (emphasis added)

Thus, Article VI:6 requires Members that have adopted specific commitments regarding professional services to adopt or maintain adequate procedures to verify the competence of professionals of any other Member. The verification of the competence of foreign professionals usually entails the review of qualification and licensing requirements that these professionals had to meet in their home jurisdiction. This review allows the host authorities to satisfy themselves that the foreign supplier demonstrates an equivalent level of competence to that of a like supplier originating in the host country. A mechanism for the verification of competences would also allow the identification of the main material differences that may have to be compensated for between the qualification and licensing requirements in the two jurisdictions. The completion of this process can proceed through recognition of professional titles, recognition of education, recognition of licences to practise, etc.

Article VI:6 amounts to an attempt on the part of the GATS to facilitate trade in services through the movement of natural persons and, consequently, is of paramount importance to developing countries for the further liberalization of

[188] In the current WPDR negotiations it has been proposed that Members consider international organizations as relevant only provided that they adopt international standards by consensus and/or that they follow the 'one country–one vote' principle. WPDR, 'Disciplines on Domestic Regulation Pursuant to GATS Article VI:4—Consolidated Working Paper', JOB(06)/225, July 2006, fn 3 to para 2.

mode 4, which will positively affect their export interests in professional services. It provides valuable baseline, MFN treatment in the sense that where specific commitments are undertaken, there must be a procedure appropriate to confirm the competence of service suppliers from all other Members.[189]

Hence, a minimum means is provided to facilitate the provision of services by suppliers from Members which do not participate in a mutual recognition agreement (MRA). Of course, the guarantees or automaticity of an MRA are not present, but, through this provision, Members can seek information from their trading partners concerning such verification procedures during the request-offer-type negotiations on services, and perhaps to insist on improvements to those procedures.[190] In this sense, Article VI:6 differs from Article VII GATS, but it still offers an alternative option to Article VII disciplines and contains some elements similar to recognition under the latter.[191] In fact, the two provisions are complementary, as the implementation of Article VI:6 should facilitate the effective application of Article VII and the recognition of professional qualifications.

Although Article VI:6 is not directly related to recognition, it is contiguous to it, as it refers to the establishment of 'adequate procedures' for verifying the competence of professional services suppliers without, however, defining what 'adequate procedures' might constitute. It is clear that Article VI:6 aims at materializing any specific commitment that a Member may have undertaken with respect to professional services, thereby preventing them from undermining market access granted for professionals by failing to establish a mechanism for evaluating their competences which are ostensibly required in order for the foreign professionals to actually supply their services.

Again, it is for each Member to determine the type of procedures that it intends to use, since Article VI:6 is limited to process and does not deal with substantive issues of domestic regulations nor does it include any instructions associated with the content of the procedures for the verification of professional competences. Thus, all that paragraph 6 of Article VI requires is the availability of a mechanism for assessing competences of professionals wishing to be granted market access to domestic professions for which specific commitments have been undertaken. This mechanism should be 'adequate'. Clarifying what the 'adequate procedures' requirement may entail would allow Members to come to a common understanding on an issue intertwined with mode 4 liberalization. In any event,

[189] OECD, 'Service Suppliers on the Move: Mutual Recognition Agreements', TD/TC/WP(2002)48/FINAL, 2003, 5.

[190] Ibid 30.

[191] See the intervention of Japan in WTO, WPDR, 'Report on the Meeting Held on 30 September 2003', S/WPDR/M/23, 27 November 2003, para 56, where two differences in terminology are pointed out: first, that the verification provided for in Art VI:6 was not used as a condition for a services licence of the host country and, second, Art VII is, contrary to Art VI:6, a permissive provision, ie it permits derogation from MFN.

it is noteworthy that Article VI:6 requires neither recognition nor the negotiation of MRAs.[192]

Article VI:6, when implemented,[193] is expected to facilitate the effective application of Article VII of the GATS and the recognition of professional qualifications, as it would elucidate differences and similarities between diverse national systems relating to qualifications, licensing, education, or titles. All Members interested in the further development of services supply through mode 4 should appreciate the value of this provision and strive for its full implementation sooner rather than later. For instance, in order to expedite the implementation of this provision, developing countries could seek an agreement among Members as to what 'adequate procedures' within the meaning of this provision entail and adopt guidelines for the recognition of professional qualifications.[194] Additionally, and for the sake of transparency, it could be agreed that any procedures for verification of the competences of foreign professionals that are already in force or that Members establish have to be inscribed in the 'Additional Commitments' column of Members' Schedules pursuant to Article XVIII GATS. In more general terms, the disciplines to be developed under Article VI:4 with respect to qualifications, licensing, and technical standards, together with the implementation of Article VI:6 and the further development of Article VII, may allow an unprecedented development of mode 4. Clearly, the discussions within the WPDR could potentially deliver far-reaching results, but not necessarily during the current negotiating round.

In sum, paragraph 6 of Article VI, in connection with the other paragraphs of Article VI (notably paragraph 4 due to the disciplines that are expected to be developed thereunder with respect to qualifications and licensing) and Article VII GATS, may constitute the first tentative steps towards further liberalization in the temporary movement of natural persons in the framework of GATS. Mode 4 continues to be the least-developed mode of supply in terms of trade flows and the volume of meaningful commitments recorded under the GATS.[195] This strongly contradicts not only the great value that especially developing and least-developed countries attach to this mode of supply but also the results of several

[192] WTO, WPDR (n 151 above) para 77.

[193] New Zealand is one of the few Members that implemented the Art VI:6 obligation by establishing such verification procedures for foreign engineers, a sector wherein it undertook specific commitments during the Uruguay Round. WTO, WPDR (n 149 above) paras 69ff.

[194] This has already been the case with respect to the accountancy sector, but the text is of non-binding nature. WTO, 'Guidelines for Mutual Recognition Agreements or Arrangements in the Accountancy Sector', adopted by the CTS on 28 May 1997, S/WPPS/W/12/Rev.1 and S/L/38.

[195] WTO, 'Market Access: Unfinished Business—Post-Uruguay Round Inventory and Issues', Special studies No 6, 2001, 105. For the major problems arising in the ongoing negotiations on labour mobility, see AM Young, 'Where Next for Labor Mobility under GATS?' in P Sauvé and RM Stern (eds), *GATS 2000: New Directions in Services Trade Liberalization,* 2000, 185; also The World Bank, *Global Economic Prospects 2006—Economic Implications of Remittances and Migration,* 2006, 73–76.

empirical studies regarding potential benefits of further liberalization of factor mobility.[196]

D. The relationship of Article VI with Articles XVI, XVII, and XVIII GATS—A conciliatory approach

1. Introductory remarks

Since Article VI on domestic regulation is to be strengthened in order to be effectively applicable, the most important principles in the GATS for the time being are its provisions on MFN treatment, transparency, market access, and national treatment. While the obligations regarding MFN and transparency apply across the board, the GATS does not impose any market access or national treatment obligations on Members unless a Member decides to list that service in its Schedule.[197] Indeed, the scope of the obligations laid down in Articles XVI and XVII is, for each Member, determined by the contents of its Schedule.

Thus, the operative part of the GATS deviates from the relative simplicity of the GATT regime on market access and national treatment to the extent that a Member undertakes specific obligations on a purely voluntary basis. It follows that the GATS rules operate on two levels: there is a set of rules that apply generally to all measures affecting trade in services (ie independently of whether a Member has undertaken specific commitments in a particular sector) and a second set of sector-specific commitments that denote the degree of liberalization that each Member deems optimal for its own market.

Consequently, the mere existence of general obligations in the GATS does not necessarily guarantee market access to any Member. For instance, a country can respect the transparency or the MFN obligation and still keep its market inaccessible. Members are free (subject, of course, to pressures from their trading partners or domestic industries) to open their service markets in the sectors where they wish to do so and with the reservations they value that are commensurate with their current state of development. Thus, both the concepts of market access and national treatment in the GATS are closely related to the concept of progressive liberalization.

No matter how limited in scope market access and national treatment under the GATS might be, these two provisions constitute the main liberalizing tools of the GATS. While the full achievement of national treatment equals for the most part the elimination of all discriminatory measures against foreign services or foreign service suppliers, the inclusion of a market access obligation in

[196] See Chapter II.F above.
[197] See Chapter I.E.3 above.

the Agreement is aimed to remove non-discriminatory (mostly quantitative) measures that impede trade in services and the opening of services markets.[198]

As to the relationship of these two principles with the MFN principle in the GATS, it should be underlined that both market access and national treatment accorded in the Schedules must be extended to all foreign service suppliers on a non-discriminatory basis, regardless of whether a country had also listed any MFN exceptions. In other words, an MFN exemption can provide legal cover only for better treatment for some trading partners, while all other Members receive at least the minimum standard of market access and national treatment appearing in a Member's Schedule.[199]

It follows that the impact of the GATS depends to a considerable extent on the coverage and the nature of the commitments that Members assumed. Notwithstanding this departure from GATT, the liberalizing tools of the GATS are potentially broader in scope (albeit limited in coverage) than the corresponding GATT provisions on market access and national treatment for the reasons mentioned above.[200]

2. The market access obligation of Article XVI[201]

Market access is a concept peculiar to the GATS and has no GATT counterpart. Whereas both Articles XI GATT and XVI GATS deal with quantitative trade restrictions, they can hardly be considered as analogous. Article XI GATT is more comprehensive, as it contains a per se prohibition regarding the use of quotas or 'other measures' resulting in a restriction or prohibition on the importation or exportation of any product.[202] Article XVI GATS can instead be regarded as a requirement to schedule market access limitations. In this respect, the spirit of Article XVI GATS is closer to Article II GATT 1994 on schedules of tariff concessions. At the same time, Article XVI GATS covers both discriminatory and origin-neutral quantitative limitations and, in this sense, has a broader scope than Article XI GATT. For similar measures regulating trade in goods, the GATT provides that Article III GATT should rather be applicable, by virtue of the *Ad Note* to Article III GATT.

Hence, Article XVI GATS on market access extends beyond traditional concerns of access for foreign service suppliers to encompass policies that hamper access to a market, irrespective of whether these policies favour the domestic suppliers. Multilateral trade rules are thereby extended into the realm of government

198 European Commission, *GATS 2000—L'Ouverture des Marchés de Services*, 1998, 31ff.

199 WTO (n 137 above) para 21; also Panel Report, *US—Gambling*, para 6.265 and fn 821.

200 See the discussion in Chapter II. E above.

201 For a thorough analysis of the market access obligation in the GATS, see P Delimatsis and M Molinuevo, 'Article XVI GATS' in R Wolfrum, P-T Stoll, and C Feinäugle (eds), *Max-Planck Commentaries on World Trade Law, Volume 6: WTO-Trade in Services*, 2008.

202 Panel Report, *India—Autos*, paras 7.246–7.249.

regulation and can have extensive implications particularly in conjunction with competition policy and attempts to re-regulate domestic services markets.[203]

The GATS does not define market access. The first paragraph of Article XVI solely obliges Members to grant the same (or a higher)[204] degree of market access to scheduled sectors as specified in their respective Schedules.[205] This provision points to the link that exists between Members' market access obligation in committed sectors, and the 'terms, limitations and conditions' inscribed in Members' Schedules.[206] In other words, the market access obligation is subordinate to, and qualified by, the relevant 'terms, limitations and conditions' inscribed in the Schedules.[207]

The second paragraph consists of an exhaustive list of six different types of limitations on market access.[208] Hence, these limitations, which cannot be maintained or adopted unless a Member decides to schedule them, exhaust the types of market access restrictions prohibited by Article XVI. Then, 'paragraph 2 of Article XVI complements the first paragraph of that Article'[209] in that it defines the scope of the obligation set out in Article XVI:1 to provide 'no less favourable treatment', the benchmark being 'the terms, limitations and conditions agreed and specified' in each Member's Schedule.

The relationship, however, between paragraphs 1 and 2 of Article XVI is not so straightforward. For instance, it is not clear whether a market access commitment undertaken by a Member would constrain that Member from introducing any measure that might inhibit market access even if that measure was not among those listed in Article XVI:2.[210] Based on the above, it appears opportune to answer this question in the negative.[211] Article XVIII GATS also supports this

[203] It is asserted that by outlawing non-discriminatory quotas the GATS confuses trade liberalization with internal deregulation, thereby providing fuel for criticism. P Raworth, *International Regulation of Trade in Services*, Vol 1, Section II: Basic International Regulation of Trade in Services—II.A Basic Legal Issues Relating to Trade in Services, 2003, 27.

[204] Panel Report, *US—Gambling*, paras 6.263–6.264.

[205] cf Art II:1(a) GATT.

[206] Appellate Body Report, *US—Gambling*, para 214.

[207] cf Appellate Body Report, *Canada—Dairy*, para 134.

[208] WTO (n 137 above) para 8. Also Panel Report, *US—Gambling*, paras 6.298, 6.318.

[209] Panel Report, *US—Gambling*, para 6.298.

[210] WTO, CTS (Special Session), 'Technical Review of GATS Provisions', Informal Note by the Secretariat, JOB(01)/17, 16 February 2001, p 3.

[211] See, however, para 4 of the *1993 Scheduling Guidelines* where it is stated that 'a Member grants *full* market access in a given sector and mode of supply when it does not maintain in that sector and mode any of the types of measures listed in Article XVI' (emphasis added). This point of view was held by the United States in the *Mexico—Telecoms* dispute. Panel Report, *Mexico—Telecoms*, para 4.109. Nevertheless, the *1993 Scheduling Guidelines*, which have been considered as supplementary means of interpretation in the *US—Gambling* case, should *not* prevail over the textual elements within the GATS *itself*, ie fn 8 to Art XVI as well as Art XVIII, which both appear to support the view that the absence of the limitations listed in Art XVI in a Member's Schedule does not *ipso facto* mean that this Member allows for full market access. Also DE Siegel, 'Legal Aspects of the IMF/WTO Relationship: The Fund's Articles of Agreement and the WTO Agreements' (2002) 96(3) AJIL 598 and fn 151.

view, as it acknowledges that there are measures (including, but *not* limited to, measures with respect to qualifications, standards, or licensing) that affect market access and which are not subject to scheduling under Article XVI.[212] Then, even in the case of an unlimited market access commitment ('None' in the market access column), a Member is not obliged to provide unlimited, unfettered access to its market. This interpretation is also consistent with the principle of progressive liberalization and Members' right to regulate,[213] both explicitly established in the GATS Preamble.[214] Thus, 'market access' under GATS is a legally defined concept that encompasses a limited set of situations, described by Article XVI, and is not to be equated with common terms, such as entry, admission, establishment, etc, that imply the general ability to perform business activities in a given market.

In *US—Gambling* both the Panel and the Appellate Body failed to answer this question in an unambiguous manner. The WTO adjudicating bodies merely ruled that a Member cannot maintain any of the types of measures that are listed under Article XVI:2 if it undertook a full market access *commitment* under Article XVI ('None' in the Schedule).[215] But the question remains whether in the case of a full market access *commitment* a Member is also obliged to allow *total* market openness in a given sector. As noted above, answering this question in the affirmative would neglect important textual elements entrenched in the text of the GATS.[216]

The bulk of the limitations referred to in Article XVI:2 involves non-discriminatory measures of quantitative nature and comprises measures that place a limitation on:

(a) the number of services suppliers;[217]
(b) the total value of services transactions or assets;
(c) the total number of service operations or the total quantity of service output;
(d) the total number of natural persons who may be employed in a certain service sector;
(e) the forms of legal entity or joint venture through which a service may be delivered; and
(f) the participation of *foreign* capital.

[212] Also Panel Report, *US—Gambling*, para 6.311.

[213] Ibid paras 6.313–6.317.

[214] Arguably, this interpretation is further supported by the Panel in *US—Gambling*, paras 6.279, 6.304.

[215] Panel Report, *US—Gambling*, para 6.318, and Appellate Body Report, *US—Gambling*, para 215.

[216] Also P Delimatsis, 'Don't Gamble with GATS—The Interaction between Articles VI, XVI, XVII and XVIII GATS in the Light of the *US—Gambling* Case' (2006) 40(6) JWT 1064.

[217] In *US—Gambling*, the Panel dismissed Antigua's argument that the measures enumerated under Art XVI:2(a), ie numerical quotas, monopolies, exclusive service suppliers or requirements of an economic needs test, are part of an *indicative* list of measures that can limit the number of service suppliers. Instead, the Panel suggested that 'the word "whether" identifies an exhaustive list of limitations that are covered by Article XVI:2(a) . . .'. Panel Report, *US—Gambling*, paras 6.325, 6.341.

The GATS negotiating history reveals that Members construed market access under GATS as extending beyond any notion of access for foreign service suppliers (tariff bindings in GATT) to encompass all policies, mostly of *quantitative* nature, that restrict market access; and this even in a *non*-discriminatory manner.[218] Having said this, Article XVI:2(e) is not a quantitative restriction, as it refers to the *form* of legal entity, whereas Art. XVI:2(f) relates to *foreign* equity participation and, thus, is a discriminatory quantitative limitation. The measure that requires the creation of a joint venture is also discriminatory, as this type of establishment typically involves cooperation between a domestic and a foreign company.[219]

The quantitative limitations of Article XVI may be expressed either in numerical terms or through the criteria established in subparagraphs (a)–(d).[220] In *US—Gambling*, the Appellate Body confirmed that 'the thrust of sub-paragraph (a) is not on the form of limitations, but on their numerical, or *quantitative*, nature' (emphasis added).[221] In so saying, the Appellate Body rejected the United States' view that the 'market access limitations' within the meaning of Article XVI can only include the precisely defined limitations set out in Article XVI:2.[222] The Appellate Body noted, instead, that the words of Article XVI:2 (*in casu*, subparagraphs (a) and (c)) should not be interpreted as prescribing a 'rigid mechanical formula'[223] nor can limitations covered thereunder take a single form or be 'constrained in a formulaic manner'.[224]

All market access limitations on services and service suppliers which fall under Article XVI:2 are addressed under the rubric of market access and thus should be scheduled in the market access column, independent of whether such limitations are origin-neutral or not,[225] ie even in cases where they also violate the national treatment standard under Article XVII.[226]

[218] See, *inter alia*, GATT, Note on the Meeting of 27 May to 6 June 1991, MTN.GNS/42, 24 June 1991, 1–3; GATT, Note on the Meeting of 24–28 June 1991, MTN.GNS/43, 15 July 1991, paras 34–36, and GATT (n 43 above) para 45; also GATT, *1993 Scheduling Guidelines*, MTN. GNS/W/164, para 4.

[219] cf Appellate Body Report, *US—Gambling*, paras 214, 248; also Panel Report, *US—Gambling*, para 6.327.

[220] WTO (n 137 above) para 8.

[221] Appellate Body Report, *US—Gambling*, para 232. As to subpara (c), the Appellate Body reached a similar conclusion. Ibid para 247.

[222] United States' appellant's submission in the *US—Gambling* case, para 111, available at: <http://www.ustr.gov>.

[223] Appellate Body Report, *US—Gambling*, para 231.

[224] Ibid para 247.

[225] It has been argued that the objective function of Art XVI is to cover measures concerning *exclusively* foreign services or service suppliers. PC Mavroidis, 'Highway XVI Re-visited—The Road from Non-Discrimination to Market Access in GATS' (2007) 6(1) World Trade Review 10ff. For the counterarguments, see Delimatsis and Molinuevo (n 201 above). In *US—Gambling*, the WTO adjudicating bodies followed the prevailing opinion, ie that Art XVI covers *both* discriminatory and non-discriminatory measures.

[226] See Section D.4 below.

By entering a market access limitation in their Schedules, Members commit to maximum 'ceilings'.[227] Of course, these 'ceilings' should be regarded as *minimum* guarantees rather than maximum quotas.[228] If, for instance, a Member wishes to allow entry to *more* suppliers than it had initially guaranteed in its Schedule, it is free to do so. Moreover, provided that it has an unbound commitment with regard to national treatment, a Member could also require that all new suppliers be nationals. These ceilings do not reveal existing levels of protection. This lack of precision damages the quality of the Schedules and abates their importance. Greater transparency, maximum liberalization and greater certainty require a higher degree of precision when scheduling.

In *US—Gambling*, the WTO adjudicating bodies confronted the question as to whether a total prohibition on the cross-border supply of a service in respect of which a full market access commitment has been undertaken (*in casu*, gambling and betting services) can be considered as a market access limitation under Articles XVI:2(a) and XVI:2(c); and even if this prohibition does not contain any express reference to numbered units. The complainant, Antigua, argued that this total prohibition amounts to a zero quota in that it altogether forbids the market access through mode 1 to service suppliers and hence limits their number to zero.[229] The Appellate Body gave justice to the Antiguan argument and hence endorsed the Panel's assertion that

> [t]he fact that the terminology [of Article XVI:2(a)] embraces lesser limitations, in the form of quotas greater than zero, cannot warrant the conclusion that it does not embrace a greater limitation amounting to zero. Paragraph (a) does not foresee a 'zero quota' because paragraph (a) was not drafted to cover situations where a Member wants to maintain full limitations. If a Member wants to maintain a full prohibition, it is assumed that such a Member would not have scheduled such a sector or sub-sector and, therefore, would not need to schedule any limitation or measures pursuant to Article XVI:2.[230]

Thus, the Appellate Body answered the question in the affirmative by accepting that a maximum limit in the form of a numerical quota (the first of the limitations covered by Article XVI:2(a)) can also include a *maximum* limit of zero (zero quota).[231] The Appellate Body further turned to the *1993 Scheduling Guidelines*,[232]

[227] WTO (n 137 above) p 4 at para 11.

[228] A Mattoo, 'National Treatment in the GATS: Corner Stone or Pandora's Box?' (1997) 31(1) JWT 110; also Panel Report, *US—Gambling*, paras 6.263–6.264.

[229] cf Mexico's arguments as regards zero quotas under Art XVI GATS in the *Mexico—Telecoms* case. Panel Report, *Mexico—Telecoms*, paras 4.105, 4.118, 4.124, 4.127. In this dispute, the Panel had to deal, *inter alia*, with a measure that limited to zero the number of suppliers that wished to deliver their services in a cross-border manner. Hence, this measure effectively prevented any supply by mode 1; also Panel Report, *Mexico—Telecoms*, paras 7.85–7.86.

[230] Panel Report, *US—Gambling*, para 6.331; and Appellate Body Report, *US—Gambling*, para 234.

[231] Ibid paras 227–233.

[232] GATT, *1993 Scheduling Guidelines*, MTN.GNS/W/164, 1993.

the same way as the Panel did,[233] to confirm the view that any measure equivalent to a zero quota falls under Article XVI:2(a).[234] The Panel had found earlier, and the Appellate Body subscribed to this view, that the United States' allegation that only restrictions explicitly expressed in numerical terms fall within Article XVI:2(a) would lead to absurdity.[235]

An important issue in the *US—Gambling* dispute was the legal value of two negotiating documents, the *1993 Scheduling Guidelines* and the WTO Document W/120 on the classification of services sectors.[236] According to the Appellate Body, these documents do not constitute context within the meaning of Article 31 of the *Vienna Convention*, as the Panel had suggested, but mere preparatory work and thus can be used only as supplementary means of interpretation[237] in accordance with Article 32 of the *Vienna Convention*.[238] It is worth noting that recently, in *EC—Chicken Cuts*, the Appellate Body contradicted itself by classifying as context within the meaning of Article 31:2 of the *Vienna Convention* the Harmonized Commodity Description and Coding System of the World Customs Organization (the 'Harmonized System'), a document that is germane to the classification of goods and has a function similar to that of the W/120 in the context of services.[239]

In any case, the Appellate Body relied on the *1993 Scheduling Guidelines* and the examples mentioned therein, as the Panel had done previously.[240] Hence, the Appellate Body followed in essence the Panel's reasoning by concluding that a limitation equivalent to a zero quota is a measure of quantitative nature and falls within the scope of Article XVI:2(a), as it limits to zero the number of suppliers of a service in respect of which a full market access commitment has been undertaken.[241]

[233] Panel Report, *US—Gambling*, para 6.332.

[234] Appellate Body Report, *US—Gambling*, para 237.

[235] Ibid para 250, and Panel Report, *US—Gambling*, para 6.332.

[236] GATT, 'Services Sectoral Classification List', MTN.GNS/W/120, 1991.

[237] Appellate Body Report, *US—Gambling*, paras 178, 196–197; also Panel Report, *Mexico—Telecoms*, para 7.44; and Mavroidis (n 225 above) 7. A careful reader would identify a subtle divergence between the two Reports regarding the legal qualification of the *Guidelines* according to Art 32 of the *Vienna Convention*. The *Mexico—Telecoms* Panel qualified the *Guidelines* as part of the 'circumstances of the conclusion' of the GATS. Nevertheless, the Appellate Body in *US—Gambling* was less consistent in its interpretation. While it qualified the *Guidelines* as supplementary means of interpretation (para 196), in a footnote it argued that the *Guidelines* are *both* preparatory work *and* 'relevant circumstances relating to the conclusion of the GATS' (fn 244 to para 196). Later, however, it qualified the same *Guidelines* only as preparatory work (paras 237, 249).

[238] See also Chapter I.A above, at n 9; also Panel Report, *Mexico—Telecoms*, para 7.122, and Appellate Body Report, *EC—Computer Equipment*, para 86.

[239] Appellate Body Report, *EC—Chicken Cuts*, paras 194–199.

[240] Also Appellate Body Report, *US—Gambling*, paras 236–237.

[241] Ibid paras 238–239. This would be in accordance with the views expressed by the EC and Japan. Appellate Body Report, *US—Gambling*, paras 98, 101, 107. During the Panel proceedings, the EC argued that '... the fact that Article XVI:2(a) refers to "limitations on the number of service suppliers ... in the form of numerical quotas" does not in itself indicate that a particular

In other words, the different qualification of the *1993 Scheduling Guidelines* that the Appellate Body adopted did not alter the conclusion that the Panel had earlier arrived at. The Appellate Body reached the same conclusion with respect to Article XVI:2(c) as to service operations and service output[242] and hence upheld the Panel's finding, albeit modifying somewhat the Panel's analysis relating to subparagraph (c).[243] Regardless of the legal classification of the *Guidelines*, ie whether they constitute context within the meaning of Article 31 of the *Vienna Convention* (as the Panel suggested) or supplementary means of interpretation pursuant to Article 32 of the *Vienna Convention* (as the Appellate Body ultimately ruled), both WTO adjudicating bodies relied on this document so extensively that one could reasonably argue that, but for the existence of the *Scheduling Guidelines*, this dispute would necessitate a high degree of judicial creativity in order to be resolved. Hence, the *Scheduling Guidelines* ended up constituting a crucial interpretative instrument of the GATS and the obligations laid down therein.[244]

To my mind, especially in its interpretation of Article XVI:2(a) with respect to a limitation on the number of service suppliers, the Appellate Body attempted to strike a balance between a formalistic interpretation of Article XVI supported by the United States and an approach which would allow measures that *have the effect of* limiting the number of service suppliers (or, in the case of Article XVI:2(c), the number of service operations or the total quantity of service output) to be covered by the prohibition of Article XVI:2.[245]

Delimiting between these two approaches has not been a walkover and this is no doubt due to the ambiguities of the GATS itself when it comes to the demarcation between the core provisions of the GATS—Articles VI, XVI, XVII, and XVIII. Having to interpret the wording of Article XVI:2, the Appellate Body attempted to clarify the issue in the least intrusive manner possible.[246]

number or ceiling of providers, operations or output must be expressly indicated in a measure in order for it to be caught by such provision. Otherwise, it would indeed not be difficult for Members to fashion their measures in such a way as to escape the prohibition in Article XVI:2(a)'. Panel Report, *US—Gambling*, para 4.35. Mexico also agreed with the EC during the Panel proceedings that a blanket prohibition of cross-border supply of gambling and betting services falls under Art XVI:2(a), as in such cases 'the number of service suppliers that can supply a service through that mode is zero'. Panel Report, *US—Gambling*, p C-82.

242 Appellate Body Report, *US—Gambling*, paras 251–252.

243 Importantly, the Appellate Body, when interpreting Art XVI:2(c), made a statement of general value by emphasizing that 'a prohibition on the supply of services in respect of which a full market access commitment has been undertaken is a quantitative limitation on the supply of such services'. Appellate Body Report, *US—Gambling*, para 250.

244 cf Panel Report, *US—Gambling*, para 6.345; and Appellate Body Report, *US—Gambling*, paras 237, 249.

245 cf Appellate Body Report, *US—Gambling*, paras 232, 246 and 247.

246 Several quotes in the Appellate Body Report on *US—Gambling* show the difficulties that the Appellate Body faced in attempting to reject an interpretation that would allow measures that have the *effect* of limiting market access to be considered a violation of Art XVI:2. See, for instance, para 237: 'This example confirms the view that measures *equivalent to* a zero quota fall within the

Ultimately, while dismissing the second, fairly sweeping approach, the Appellate Body preferred (as did the Panel) to interpret Article XVI broadly enough to prevent a Member that has undertaken a *full* market access commitment from designing a measure that would escape the prohibition laid down in that Article. Indeed, an attentive reading of the Panel and Appellate Body Reports reveals that both bodies took seriously into account the fact that the United States had made a full market access commitment with respect to gambling and betting services that did not differentiate as to the mode of supply.

The Appellate Body made it clear that, when scrutinizing the compatibility of a measure with Article XVI:2, the important question to be answered does not refer to the form that this measure takes.[247] Rather, the important question is whether this measure limits the number of service suppliers, the value of services transactions, the number of service operations or the quantity of service output, or the number of natural persons that can be employed in a given services sector. Thus, it is not the *form* of the measure that is decisive as to the applicability of Article XVI:2, but rather the *quantitative nature* of the measure at issue, even when this nature is not expressed in numbers.[248]

This reading of the Appellate Body report is also confirmed by the fact that the Appellate Body did not bother to legally classify the full prohibition of gambling and betting services in a remote manner, ie to decide whether it is a numerical quota, a monopoly etc under Article XVI(a), or a designated numerical unit in the form of a quota or the requirement of an ENT under Article XVI(c).[249] On the contrary, the Appellate Body was satisfied that the measures at issue were *quantitative* measures limiting to *zero* the number of service suppliers that could provide their gambling and betting services in a cross-border way or the

scope of Article XVI:2(a)'; also para. 238: '...we are of the view that limitations *amounting to* a zero quota are quantitative limitations and fall within the scope of Article XVI:2(a)'; also para 251: '...the measures at issue...*amount* to a zero quota on services operations or output...'; also para 252: '...such a ban *results in* a "zero quota" on one or more or all means of delivery included in mode 1'. In due course, the Appellate Body will probably be forced to explain the difference between, on the one hand, the phrases 'has the effect of' and, on the other hand, the phrases 'is equivalent to', 'amounts to', and 'results in', which, at first blush, would seem to have the same meaning.

[247] This interpretation appears to be consistent with the interpretations that GATT/WTO panels advanced with regard to Art XI GATT, the provision tackling quantitative restrictions in the area of goods. These panels had equally underlined the irrelevance of the explicit numerical form of a measure when evaluating the impugned measure under Art XI GATT. cf GATT Panel Report, *Japan—Semi-conductors*, paras 117–118, and Panel Report, *India—Autos*, paras 7.270–7.272.

[248] The Appellate Body clearly rejected the United States' view on that point because the latter would not cover, for instance, 'a limitation expressed as a percentage or described using words such as "a majority"'. Appellate Body Report, *US—Gambling*, para 250. For the opposite view, see United States' appellant's submission in the *US—Gambling* case, paras 122–133, and J Pauwelyn, 'Rien ne Va Plus? Distinguishing Domestic Regulation from Market Access in GATT and GATS' (2005) 4(2) World Trade Review 159ff; also F Ortino, 'Treaty Interpretation and the WTO Appellate Body Report in US—Gambling: A Critique' (2006) 1 JIEL 135–146; also Markus Krajewski, 'Playing by the Rules of the Game? Specific Commitments after *US—Gambling and Betting* and the Current GATS Negotiations' (2005) 32(4) Legal Issues of Economic Integration 417.

[249] Delimatsis (n 216 above) 1068.

service operations and the output with respect to such services.[250] The fact that the Appellate Body did not feel compelled to proceed to a legal classification of the measures at stake vis-à-vis the categories of measures identified under Article XVI(a) and (c) GATS is meaningful.

The *US—Gambling* ruling has been criticized on the basis that the WTO judiciary erred by not scrutinizing the measures in question under Article VI rather than Article XVI.[251] First, these critiques fail to note that the United States did not in fact argue the case of the measures at issue falling under Article VI.[252] Thus, the WTO judiciary could not make the claim on behalf of the United States.[253] Second, and more importantly, a closer look at the three federal laws of the United States at stake[254] does not support this view. These measures provide in essence that whoever supplies gambling services in a remote (ie also cross-border) manner shall be fined or imprisoned and thus establish a total prohibition on the cross-border supply of gambling and betting services.

Such a prohibition can never be regarded as falling under the types of measures that Article VI:4/5 covers. Indeed, the latter provision refers to *minimum* requirements that aim to ensure the quality of the supplied service with respect to licensing, qualifications, or technical standards. Conversely, a total prohibition entails a *maximum* requirement, where the maximum is equal to zero. A blanket prohibition that limits the potential service suppliers to zero with respect to a certain mode of supply (in this case, cross-border) can never be intended to ensure the *quality* of the service. Excluding the supply of Internet gambling in order to protect minors, morality, or public order, or to avert fraud does not ensure the quality of the service *per se*, but is simply a means for achieving a legitimate objective; and this should be examined under the Article XIV exceptions.

Neither can such a prohibition be regarded as a technical standard, as it was alleged,[255] because it does not define or describe the apposite way of supplying a gambling service in a remote (and, *a fortiori*, cross-border) manner, but merely excludes this mode of supplying gambling and betting services. A proper technical standard would define minimum technical requirements that a service supplier should adhere to or rules according to which remote (and, *a fortiori*, cross-border) gambling and betting must be performed in order for the supplier to be allowed to supply gambling and betting services. Hence, under this approach, a technical standard would set technical requirements that *at least one* supplier

[250] This becomes particularly apparent in the Appellate Body's analysis under subpara (c). Appellate Body Report, *US—Gambling*, para 247.

[251] Pauwelyn (n 248 above) 159; Ortino (n 248 above) 135; and Krajewski (n 248 above) 417. For the counterarguments, see Delimatsis (n 216 above) 1059.

[252] Some weak references are to be found in paras 22 and 26 of the Appellate Body Report on *US—Gambling*.

[253] cf Appellate Body Report, *Japan—Agricultural Products II*, para 129.

[254] That is, the Wire Act, the Travel Act, and the Illegal Gambling Business Act (IGBA).

[255] Pauwelyn (n 248 above) 161ff.

can meet and not exclude altogether a specific mode of supplying gambling and betting services.

Another track of criticism in the aftermath of the *US—Gambling* ruling has focused on the relevance of the objective of the measure at issue when distinguishing between Articles XVI and VI.[256] In particular, it was argued that a measure that serves a legitimate objective such as the United States' blanket prohibition of remote gambling cannot be a measure falling under Article XVI. Nevertheless, nothing prevents a quantitative restriction from equally aiming at serving a legitimate objective. For instance, take the case of a limitation of the number of TV channels to ten due to a lack of frequencies or in order to ensure the quality of the transmission. In other words, the quantitative characteristic of a measure does not necessarily imply that this measure is protectionist. And this was the case in the *US—Gambling* case, where the Appellate Body correctly identified the legitimate policy concerns of these federal laws and consequently had recourse to the exception of Article XIV relating to public morals and public order to justify the federal laws otherwise inconsistent with Article XVI. Therefore, the WTO adjudicating bodies were correct in their decision not to classify the United States' laws under Article VI:4/5.

3. The national treatment obligation contained in Article XVII

Turning to the national treatment obligation, Article XVII prohibits any form of discrimination (ie frontier and non-frontier, as well as pre- and post-establishment discriminatory measures)[257] against foreign services and service suppliers. In *EC—Bananas III*,[258] the Panel clarified that a three-prong test determines whether or not there has been a breach of the national treatment obligation: (i) the Member has made a commitment in the sector and mode of supply at issue; (ii) the measure that the Member has adopted or applied affects the services supply in the relevant sector and/or mode of supply; and (iii) that measure accords to services or service suppliers of any other Member treatment less favourable than that it accords to the domestic *like* services or service suppliers. The last element requires the establishment of likeness between domestic and foreign services or service suppliers.[259]

[256] Ortino (n 248 above) 135.

[257] WTO, Committee on Specific Commitments, 'Revision of Scheduling Guidelines', S/CSC/W/19, 5 March 1999, para 15.

[258] Panel Report, *EC—Bananas III (US)*, para 7.314.

[259] Establishing likeness between services or—worse—service suppliers is much more challenging than in the goods realm. Mattoo argued that only the 'end-uses' criterion can give satisfactory results in a comparison between services. In other words, what ultimately matters is whether the consumer treats the two services or service suppliers as substitutable. Nonetheless, regulators can make further distinctions that would render any full national treatment commitment meaningless. Therefore, Mattoo suggests that the burden of proof should be reversed in this case to require that the *responding* party proves why the two services or service suppliers are *not* like. A Mattoo,

It is worth noting that the less favourable treatment may involve not only measures that impose costs or other competitive disadvantages on foreign service suppliers in the domestic market but also measures that provide a direct cost *advantage* to domestic suppliers such as direct subsidies to local service suppliers. The concept of national treatment may be expressed in terms of the principle of equal opportunity in that it ensures that the effect of regulations is equal in terms of the opportunities provided to foreign suppliers and hence can be interpreted as equality of access to a particular market.[260]

No exhaustive list similar to Article XVI GATS of measures inconsistent with the national treatment principle is provided in Article XVII. This fact, however, does not have any negative effect on the broad coverage of the principle of national treatment, since paragraphs 2 and 3 of Article XVII GATS make plain that limitations on national treatment cover cases of both *de jure* and *de facto* discrimination. According to Article XVII:2, a Member has to accord 'either formally identical or formally different treatment to that it accords to its own like services and service suppliers'. Hence it is possible that positive action may be required by a Member in order to meet its obligations under the national treatment obligation.[261] Paragraph 3, on the other hand, serves as an interpretative note to paragraph 2 of Article XVII.[262] This latter provision brings the GATT jurisprudence pertaining to non-discrimination[263] into the realm of the GATS.[264]

4. The overlap between Articles XVI and XVII GATS and possible solutions

According to Article XVII:1, the national treatment obligation applies to *all* measures *affecting the supply of services*;[265] hence, it also includes *any* discriminatory

'MFN and the GATS' in T Cottier and P Mavroidis (eds), *Regulatory Barriers and the Principle of Non-Discrimination in World Trade Law*, 2000, 78; also Nicolaidis and Trachtman (n 170 above) 252; and M Cossy, 'Determining "Likeness" under the GATS: Squaring the Circle', WTO Staff Working Paper ERSD-2006–08, 2006.

[260] cf GATT Panel Report, *US—Section 337*, para 5.11.

[261] Ibid.

[262] Mattoo correctly points out that 'the phrase "if it modifies the conditions of competition" is somewhat misleading in that it may suggest that the obligation is to preserve the *status quo*. On the contrary, national treatment must be interpreted as an obligation not to disadvantage foreigners at all rather than as an obligation not to worsen historical disadvantages. In this respect, it would perhaps have been more appropriate to use the words "if it creates unequal conditions of competition"'. Mattoo (n 228 above) 111, fn 9.

[263] GATT Panel Report, *US—Section 337*, para 5.11 and GATT Panel Report, *Italy—Agricultural Machinery*, para 12. The Appellate Body summarized the legal standard in the Appellate Body Report, *Korea—Various Measures on Beef*, paras 133–138. See also Chapter II.B.3 above.

[264] Panel Report, *EC—Bananas III (US)*, para 7.327.

[265] It is not clear whether the distinction between 'measures affecting the supply of a service' (Arts XVII:1 and XXVIII(b) GATS) and 'measures affecting trade in services' (Arts I:1 and XXVIII(c) GATS) is intentional. Nevertheless, from the wording of Art XXVIII(b) and (c) and

measure of the types referred to in Article XVI:2. This means that in certain cases an overlap may emerge between Articles XVI and XVII. Identifying the potential problems as regards the scheduling of discriminatory quantitative restraints, the drafters of the GATS included in the Agreement a technical, bookkeeping[266] convention laid down in Article XX with a view to avoiding duplication and confusion.[267] Hence, Article XX:2 GATS provides that:

> Measures inconsistent with both Article XVI and XVII shall be inscribed in the column relating to Article XVI. In this case the inscription will be considered to provide a condition or qualification to Article XVII as well.

Thus, in accordance with the scheduling rule of Article XX:2 GATS, discriminatory quantitative limitations, which fall under both Articles XVI and XVII, should be scheduled in the market access column of each Member's Schedule and will be understood to provide a condition or qualification to the national treatment standard as well. It follows that the market access column in a Schedule may contain measures that are inconsistent either with Article XVI alone or with both Articles XVI and XVII. Thus, only discriminatory measures *other than* the six types of quantitative limitations specified as covered by market access would be scheduled as national treatment limitations, assuming commitments have been made. However, this should not be taken to suggest that a commitment on national treatment is not an independently negotiated commitment. Such commitments are operative regardless of whether a market access commitment was made.[268]

Article XX belongs to Part IV of the GATS, which contains the operational aspects of liberalization. It determines the manner according to which liberalization commitments under Part III of the GATS should be negotiated, scheduled, and possibly modified or withdrawn. The negotiating history evinces that, initially, Members had assumed that commitments would normally be established with respect to *both* market access and national treatment and, therefore, the prevalent issue seems to have been the creation of a scheduling convention that would determine where such measures should belong in a Schedule.[269] Thus, while it is true that when scheduling sectoral limitations, a Member must first

the relevant jurisprudence it can be argued that the two phrases are used interchangeably. cf Panel Report, *EC—Bananas III (US)*, para 7.281 and Appellate Body Report, *EC—Bananas III*, paras 220–221.

[266] WTO, CTS, 'Report of the Meeting Held on 17 July 2002', S/C/M/61, 23 September 2002, para 6.

[267] See also the relevant discussion in R Adlung, 'The GATS Turns Ten: A Preliminary Stocktaking', WTO Staff Working Paper ERSD-2004–05, 2004, p 12.

[268] G Feketekuty, 'Deepening Sectoral Disciplines for Services Regulation: How to Move Forward in the GATS', Paper for APEC Group on Services Workshop, 2002, 5.

[269] WTO, Committee on Specific Commitments, 'Consideration of Issues Relating to Article XX:2 of the GATS', JOB(03)/213, 20 November 2003, para 11 (attached as Annex I to the document WTO, CTS, 'Consideration of Issues Relating to Article XX:2 of the GATS', Report by the Chairman of the Committee on Specific Commitments, S/C/W/237, 24 March 2004).

determine whether the measure at issue falls under the market access provision due to the scheduling convention of Article XX:2 and hence there is a hierarchy as to *scheduling*, nevertheless, there is nothing in this Article that can be interpreted to establish a hierarchy with respect to *substance* between market access and national treatment.[270]

As noted, the overlap between market access and national treatment obligation lies in the fact that any measure of the types referred to in Article XVI:2(a)–(d) in their discriminatory form, as well as discriminatory restrictions relating to the legal entity (subparagraph (e)) or those referring to foreign equity participation under subparagraph (f), would fall within the scope of both the market access and national treatment provisions. As a result, the scope of the obligations laid down in Articles XVI and XVII is nebulous.[271] Article XX:2 GATS appears to protect Members from unintended commitments on national treatment, since a limitation under Article XVI would be considered as limiting national treatment as well, in the absence of any stipulation to the contrary.

In an attempt to resolve this problem, Members added a sentence to the revised *2001 Scheduling Guidelines*[272] requesting that Members indicate in their Schedules the measures that, while scheduled in the market access column, are inconsistent with both market access and national treatment. This constitutes, of course, no obligation whatsoever for Members when they prepare their Schedules. In addition, this sentence deals only with the case where a limitation on market access *and* national treatment is to be entered in the column relating to market access. Nonetheless, Members did not tackle the situation where, with respect to any mode of supply, commitments are undertaken under one of the obligations (eg national treatment), but not under the other (eg market access, and *vice versa*). In this case, it is correct to argue that because there is a full commitment under Article XVII (by entering 'None' in the national treatment column), no measure inconsistent with this Article could be maintained, *including* those discriminatory measures falling within the scope of Article XVI (even if the Member entered 'Unbound' in the market access column)?

Article XX:2 does not give an answer to this question, as it was conceived in order to deal with situations where commitments are made under *both* market access and national treatment. Nevertheless, one could logically argue that it is technically feasible for a Member to maintain discriminatory quantitative restrictions in accordance with Article XVI, even in the case that it scheduled a *full* national treatment commitment ('None' inscribed in the national treatment column). In this case, national treatment would apply to all measures *other*

[270] WTO, CTS, 'Proposals for a Technical Review of GATS Provisions—Article XX:2', JOB(02)/89, 16 July 2002, p 2.

[271] P Low and A Mattoo, 'Is There a Better Way? Alternative Approaches to Liberalization Under the GATS' in P Sauvé and RM Stern (eds), *GATS 2000: New Directions in Services Trade Liberalization,* 2000, 450.

[272] WTO (n 137 above) para 18.

than those covered by Article XVI. Under this setting, the scope of a national treatment commitment in circumstances in which market access measures may actually be conceded to be discriminatory is ambiguous. Arguably, the opposite could equally apply, ie that in the case that full national treatment is granted, no discriminatory measure, even if it falls under the types of Article XVI:2, can be maintained.

Consequently, the important issue for Members is deciding, in the case of unbound market access, whether overlapping measures inconsistent with both market access and national treatment are governed by the commitment under national treatment, or rather by the *absence* of a commitment under market access, and, conversely, in the case of unbound national treatment, whether the measures that overlap, and which are inconsistent with both market access and national treatment, should be ruled by the commitment under market access, or rather by the *absence* of a commitment under national treatment.

This is not a purely theoretical problem; on the contrary, it has important practical repercussions, as it can greatly undermine the scope of existing and future commitments with regard to effective market access. Especially with regard to mode 3 (commercial presence), which is influenced by both pre- and post-establishment issues, the scope of market access and national treatment needs to be clarified sooner rather than later, and preferably through negotiations rather than dispute settlement,[273] since it concerns fundamental traits of the GATS. Moreover, the existent GATS commitments would imply a greater extent of liberalization under some interpretations than under others and hence Members would not necessarily have the same interests if they were called upon to favour one interpretation over another.[274]

A possible solution to the question of overlap and the problems that may result from it would be to consider Article XVI as *lex specialis* in relation to Article XVII and hence affirm that the measures mentioned under Article XVI:2(a)–(f), even in their discriminatory form, would be treated *exclusively* under the scope of the market access obligation. This approach would also be consistent with the fact that the GATS allows Members to undertake commitments on market access and national treatment *independently*.[275] Nevertheless, this solution implies a hierarchy between Articles XVI and XVII that has no legal basis in the GATS

[273] It holds true that the DSU can accelerate the process of opening up markets and the effective implementation of the covered agreements. J Bhagwati, 'After Seattle: Free Trade and the WTO' in R Porter, P Sauvé, A Subramanian, and AB Zampetti (eds), *Equity, Efficiency and Legitimacy: the Multilateral System at the Millennium*, 2001, 52. Nevertheless, when the legal provisions and their interplay are not clear, this opening up may be undesirable and unintended.

[274] See, for instance, the revealing discussion of issues relating to the Arts XVI/XVII overlap in WTO, Committee on Specific Commitments, 'Report of the Meeting Held on 4 December 2003', S/CSC/M/31, 14 January 2004, paras 31–74.

[275] Also M Krajewski, *National Regulation and Trade Liberalization in Services—The Legal Impact of the General Agreement on Trade in Services (GATS) on National Regulatory Autonomy*, 2003, 115.

text. Even if one could establish such a hierarchy, because Article XVI:2 already includes a discriminatory measure under subparagraph (f), more elements would be needed to found a primacy of Article XVI over Article XVII.

A second possible solution to the problem would allocate to Article XVI only the types of measures listed in Article XVI:2 in their *non-discriminatory* form. Consequently, national treatment would cover all discriminatory measures, including the Article XVI:2 measures provided that they discriminate against foreign services or service suppliers. This option would be in line with Article XVII:1, which provides that its scope includes 'all measures affecting the supply of services', and not only measures other than those falling under Article XVI. This option also appears to be confirmed by the *2001 Scheduling Guidelines* where it is suggested that '[r]egardless of what is inscribed in the market access column, a "no limitations" entry in the National Treatment column (expressed as "None") would mean that national treatment is bound for the entire mode; it is not limited to what may be bound in a market access commitment with limitations.'[276] This interpretation would imply a strong national treatment obligation to cover both the right of establishment *and* post-establishment issues.[277] Consequently, in accordance with this option, the issue of discrimination *in its entirety* would be dealt with under Article XVII.[278]

This solution, however, would require the exclusion of the measures that can be applied only in a discriminatory form, such as joint-venture requirements and foreign equity limitations (Articles XVI:2(e) and XVI:2(f), respectively), from the scope of Article XVI, and would thus require a change in the wording of Article XVI:2. Hence, provided that this option favours the supremacy of the national treatment column *vis-à-vis* the market access column, the question that inevitably arises is why then are foreign equity limitations mentioned in Article XVI rather than in Article XVII. In any case, if either of these two solutions is advanced, the GATS should be amended to reflect the clear separation of the scope of the two Articles, confirming at the same time that they are mutually exclusive.

A third option would be to accept that an 'Unbound' entry prevails over the entry making a commitment. Under this option, a Member would be allowed to introduce discriminatory measures falling under the overlap notwithstanding the entry in the other column. Under this scenario, an 'Unbound' entry in the national treatment column and a 'None' in the market access column would permit a Member to apply measures in a discriminatory form, including those that fall under Article XVI:2. Thus, under this option any measures which are inconsistent with both Articles XVI and XVII would be allowed, while some

[276] WTO (n 137 above) para 43.

[277] Mattoo (n 228 above) 115.

[278] In this direction, Pauwelyn (n 248 above) 150, fn 65.

restrictions to market access would be allowed inspite of inscribing 'None' in the market access column.

The reverse would also be conceivable, ie that the entry that contains a commitment prevails over the 'Unbound' entry. In this case, the measure falling under the overlap could not be maintained or introduced unless scheduled in either the market access or national treatment columns. For instance, having scheduled a 'None' entry in the market access column and an 'Unbound' entry in the national treatment column, a Member could apply measures restricting market access only so long as it scheduled them. But since it grants full market access, this means that discriminatory measures are allowed only to the extent that they do not compromise the market access commitment.[279] Under this approach, overlapping measures would be scheduled in both the market access and national treatment columns. For the sake of streamlining the Schedules, both Article XX:2 and paragraph 18 of the revised *Scheduling Guidelines* would appear to have a clear *raison d'être*. This option ensures the protection of granted commitments and appears to favour the progressive liberalization of services trade.

Another approach would call for sufficient clarity when scheduling commitments, rather than any changes to the text of the GATS itself.[280] Members could thereby be requested to introduce into their Schedule any necessary clarifications as to the intended scope of their commitments. For instance, in the case of a 'None' entry in the national treatment column, a Member, wishing to allocate the overlap area to the area covered by the commitment, could enter in its market access column 'Unbound, except for measures falling also under Article XVII'. This option would not, however, resolve the problem of overlap in its entirety.[281]

Even so, additional transparency when scheduling is always useful. Unfortunately, Members often do not indicate in their Schedules (in fact, they are not obligated to do so, as pointed out earlier) whether the measures at issue are discriminatory (within the meaning of the national treatment provision) or not. This lack of transparency hampers the identification of remaining barriers and hinders the trade liberalization process. To be sure, a simple clarification of whether such measures, which are inscribed under the market access column of the Schedules, are also inconsistent with the national treatment discipline would greatly enhance transparency.

In addition, the overlap of the market access and national treatment disciplines amounts to the intermingling of commitments on discriminatory and non-discriminatory barriers, which seemingly combines two separate objectives: the objective of liberalizing trade and that of reforming the domestic regulatory

[279] According to Switzerland, this approach would be the most appropriate. WTO, Committee on Specific Commitments, 'Consideration of Issues Relating to Article XX:2 of the GATS', Communication from Switzerland, JOB(03)/214, 27 November 2003, para 19 (attached as Annex II to WTO, CTS (n 269 above)).

[280] See the intervention of Hong Kong, China in WTO, CTS (n 266 above) para 7.

[281] WTO, Committee on Specific Commitments (n 269 above) para 20.

regime. While trade liberalization amounts to removing discrimination, be it in its quantitative or qualitative form, domestic regulatory reform typically entails the removal of non-discriminatory restraints which may unduly hamper trade. The use (and abuse) of such restraints usually mirrors a country's approach when it comes to the regulation of its service sector.

This intermingling may be interpreted to mean that trade liberalization and regulatory reform at home should take place at the same time.[282] The current GATS scheduling technique does not allow Members to underscore their progress on either trade liberalization or regulatory reform.[283] Policy monitoring becomes more difficult and countries do not have any incentive to move forward with trade liberalization or regulatory reform. As a result, their trading partners face difficulties when they try to identify discriminatory regulatory measures in other markets and they cannot insist on the dismantling of these barriers to trade in services.

All in all, the GATS widens the traditional concepts of market access and national treatment endorsed in the GATT, but at the same time incorporates concepts associated with domestic regulation and competition policy. The GATS' variable geometry consists of permitting Members to make their own decisions with respect to their domestic regulations while also allowing the exercise of voluntary commitments in the form of national, sector-specific Schedules in which only the bound thresholds necessary for a specific activity are in fact pre-specified.[284] Clearly, in the services context the level as well as the form of protection emanate from negotiations between Members.[285]

With reference to market access and national treatment in the GATS, the following problems seem to be in need of attention:

- The overlapping of market access and national treatment obligations;
- The lack of any consideration of non-quantitative measures which restrict market access (eg fiscal measures are not covered);
- The insufficient legal security for service suppliers, who only tend to be familiar with the bound commitments of Members, which, however, do not reflect actual levels of liberalization;
- The covert discrimination arising from the implementation of discretionary decisions due to the lack of transparency and commonly agreed international standards.

282 G Feketekuty, 'Assessing and Improving the Architecture of the GATS' in P Sauvé and RM Stern (eds), *GATS 2000: New Directions in Services Trade Liberalisation,* 2000, 96.

283 Ibid. Therefore, Feketekuty suggests that the scheduling rule of Art XX:2 should be reversed, so that discriminatory quantitative restrictions are listed in the national treatment column. In this case, the countries could show their progress on trade liberalization by scheduling commitments under the national treatment column, and shed light on their progress on regulatory reform by scheduling commitments under the market access column.

284 WTO, *The Future of the WTO—Addressing Institutional Challenges in the New Millenium* ('The Sutherland Report'), 2004, 63–65.

285 A Mattoo, 'Shaping Future Rules for Trade in Services: Lessons from the GATS', World Bank Paper, 2001, 8.

5. The role of Article XVIII

As to Article XVIII GATS, it seems that Members wanted, through this provision, to cover all types of trade restrictions *other than* those covered by the disciplines laid down in Articles XVI and XVII.[286] Such restrictions would escape Article XVII, as they would be non-discriminatory, and Article XVI, as they would not be of the six types of measures identified in subparagraphs (a)–(f) of Article XVI:2. As stated earlier, such restrictions would relate (but would not be limited) to qualifications, standards and licensing issues. Hence, Article XVIII offers a legal basis for Members to negotiate and undertake specific commitments 'which they would define, on a case-by-case basis, in relation to any measures which do not fall within the scope of Article XVI or XVII'.[287] Article XVIII, however, can overlap with Article VI:4/5, as it may also include measures that fall under the scope of the latter. For instance, the regulatory disciplines of the Reference Paper on Basic Telecommunications were negotiated as additional commitments under Article XVIII and Members (66 out of 69 participants in the negotiations) inscribed them in their Schedules.[288]

In this regard, Article XVIII appears to be linked to Article VI:4 which establishes a work programme for the development of disciplines relating to qualification requirements and procedures, technical standards, and licensing requirements and procedures. The types of obligations that can be contained in such disciplines can be very similar to the types of commitments that may be negotiated under Article XVIII. In fact, the scope of Article XVIII is even broader as it can also engender commitments on areas other than qualifications, standards, or licensing. In the latter case, however, unlike Article VI:4 GATS, there is no legal mandate that forces Members to identify these areas and make positive commitments.

6. Exploring the relationship between Articles VI, XVI, and XVII

Given the magnitude of the regulatory facet in the liberalization process with respect to trade in services, Article VI on domestic regulation plays a key role in the liberalization of trade in services. The completion of Article VI, however, was not among the priorities of the Group of Negotiations on Services during the Uruguay Round. Members felt fairly comfortable with the decision in the early 1990s to complete the drafting of the market access and national treatment obligation before turning to Article VI. The participants in the negotiations were envisaging the creation of a 'standards-related work programme'[289] to be dealt

[286] WTO, Committee on Specific Commitments, 'Additional Commitments under Article XVIII of the GATS', S/CSC/W/34, 16 July 2002, para 3.

[287] Ibid. Also Panel Report, *US—Gambling*, paras 6.310–6.311.

[288] WTO, Committee on Specific Commitments (n 286 above) para 17.

[289] GATT (n 43 above) para 46.

with in the negotiating rounds to come. Article VI, again, would be construed as preventing any circumvention of the Members' market access concessions.[290]

Hence, while the GATS does not appear to establish or imply a hierarchy as to the scope of Articles XVI, XVII, and VI,[291] there was nevertheless a chronological order according to which Members decided to tackle the issues relating to the new multilateral framework on trade in services. At that time, Members judged that liberalization of trade in services should precede the negotiations on non-discriminatory domestic regulations relating to the quality of the service supplied, or the ability of the supplier to supply a given service. This decision, however, affected the overall balance of the GATS disciplines governing Members' regulatory behaviour.[292]

Modelled on corresponding provisions in existing WTO Agreements (particularly the TBT Agreement), Article VI can be seen as the third, complementary dimension of a three-pronged approach with regard to effective access to services markets, along with Articles XVI and XVII GATS. While Article XVI primarily addresses the use of discriminatory and non-discriminatory quantitative restrictions affecting trade in services, and Article XVII comes to grips with any measure that discriminates against foreign services and service suppliers in favour of like services or service suppliers of national origin, Article VI aims to deal with non-discriminatory veiled impediments to trade in services. Such impediments are concealed in domestic regulations (or the administration thereof)[293] and have, for the most part, a *qualitative* character[294] (as opposed to the *quantitative* character of the limitations under Article XVI:2) because they ostensibly aim to ensure the quality of services supply.

Furthermore, whereas Articles XVI and XVII belong to Part III of the GATS (Specific Commitments), Article VI belongs to Part II (General Obligations and Disciplines). Accordingly, the elimination of restrictions on market access and national treatment hinges on the negotiations of specific commitments among Members through the request-and-offer approach in connection with both current and future services negotiations. Nonetheless, the obligation to minimize the trade-restrictive elements of domestic regulatory measures that may undermine the value of market access or national treatment commitments freely entered into by a Member is a general obligation which is subject to the disciplines to be developed under Article VI:4.

Moreover, the legal prominence of these measures differs substantially, since measures hampering market access and national treatment are outlawed, unless

290 GATT, 'Note of the Meeting of 17–27 September 1991', MTN.GNS/45, 18 October 1991, para 16.

291 cf Panel Report, *US—Gambling*, para 6.307.

292 See also Chapter IV.

293 G Feketekuty (n 282 above) 101; also WTO, WPPS, 'Report to the Council for Trade in Services on the Development of Disciplines on Domestic Regulation in the Accountancy Sector', S/WPPS/4, 10 December 1998, p 9; also WTO, WPDR, 'Domestic Regulation: Necessity and Transparency', Communication from the European Communities and their Member States, S/WPDR/W/14, 1 May 2001, p 2.

294 GATT (n 43 above) para 46.

scheduled, in sectors where specific commitments have been undertaken, while they can be maintained in sectors which remain unscheduled. Nevertheless, the right to preserve origin-neutral regulatory measures which are adopted in pursuit of public policy objectives is explicitly recognized and will be subject to the disciplines to be developed under Article VI with the aim of minimizing their trade-inhibitory burden. The non-discriminatory, *non*-quantitative measures covered by Article VI include non-negotiable regulations intended for consumer protection and other legitimate objectives. Members retain the right to create additional measures of this type at any time, while the market access and national treatment limitations inscribed in a Member's Schedule are essentially limited.

To ensure correct scheduling within the meaning of GATS, if a regulation entails a market access constraint, the measure should be scheduled under the market access column. On the other hand, if a non-quantitative measure has a discriminatory component, then it should be inscribed under the national treatment column. In all other cases, Article VI comes into play. For example, *minimum* requirements (eg licensing or capital adequacy requirements in the banking sector) cannot be inscribed under Article XVI. Unless they impose an additional burden on foreign services or service suppliers (and, consequently, should be scheduled as a limitation on national treatment), such measures of a *qualitative* nature[295] (eg relative to the quality of the service supplied, to technical standards or qualifications of the service supplier, etc) will be subject to the disciplines of Article VI and need not be scheduled as limitations. If they cannot be justified as an exception, and taking into account that Article VI:4 disciplines are yet to be established, these measures should conform to the disciplines of Article VI:5.[296] Alternatively, such measures can be scheduled as positive undertakings under the additional commitments column in a Member's Schedule in accordance with Article XVIII GATS.

Thus, when scheduling, Members ought basically to have the following diagram in mind:

Types of measures	Market access (XVI)	National treatment (XVII)	Domestic regulation (VI)	Additional commitments (XVIII)
Discriminatory quantitative	X	X		
Discriminatory non-quantitative		X		
Non-discriminatory quantitative	X			
Non-discriminatory non-quantitative (or non-discriminatory quantitative beyond the six categories of Art. XVI:2 GATS)			X	X

[295] GATT (note 43 above) para 46.
[296] WTO (n 137 above) para 11.

The abovementioned method of distinguishing between the GATS provisions at hand that may overlap is convenient for trade officials and negotiators, as it theoretically allows differentiation between measures that hamper market access, nullify national treatment, or do not meet the Article VI requirements, and seems to be well founded from a legal point of view. Nevertheless, no matter how easy this appears to be in theory, it is not always easy to make such a distinction in practice. Sometimes the boundaries between Articles XVI, XVII, and VI are at best opaque when one attempts to identify where to classify specific measures affecting trade in services.[297]

In *US—Gambling*, the Panel examined the relationship between Articles XVI, XVII, XVIII, and VI:4/5 as context in order to determine the scope of the obligations laid down in Article XVI,[298] although it did not seem necessary to raise this issue. This very question has stimulated intense discussions during the ongoing negotiations in the Working Party of Domestic Regulation, highlighting the continuing importance and the sensitivity of the matter in the aftermath of the Uruguay Round. In a finding not reviewed by the Appellate Body,[299] the Panel concluded that 'Articles VI:4 and VI:5 on the one hand and XVI on the other hand are mutually exclusive'. It is true that an overlap is more likely to exist between these two provisions, since both of them, contrary to Article XVII which deals with services trade liberalization, are linked to regulatory reform in the service sector. Nonetheless, the Panel, *au lieu* of bringing forth arguments against the existence of a real overlap in line with corresponding work in the relevant WTO bodies, misguidedly opted for the mutual exclusivity as the only trait of the relationship between Article VI and XVI.

The Panel based its finding on the *1993 Scheduling Guidelines*[300] and was guided by the tentative results of the discussions in the WPPS,[301] which considered as unacceptable any overlap between these provisions. By examining, however, the negotiating history, one realizes that Members thought that it was one thing to say that these two provisions do not (or should not) overlap but quite another to state that they are mutually exclusive. The second proposition has

[297] See, for instance, the Secretariat's response in WTO, WPDR (n 10 above) para 8.

[298] Panel Report, *US—Gambling*, paras 6.301–6.313.

[299] In fact, the Appellate Body emphasized that 'it is neither necessary nor appropriate for us to draw, in the abstract, the line between quantitative and qualitative measures'. Appellate Body Report, *US—Gambling*, para 250. As emphasized in Section D.2 above, the United States did not actually insist on classifying the measures at issue under Art VI GATS. Therefore, the Appellate Body was correct not to draw the line between Arts VI/XVI in this case, in accordance with the *non ultra petita* maxim. cf Appellate Body Report, *Chile—Price Band System*, Para 173. Thus, the Panel's view cannot be regarded as also expressing the Appellate Body's opinion on the Arts VI/XVI relationship. Appellate Body Report, *Canada—Periodicals*, p 19, fn 28.

[300] GATT, *1993 Scheduling Guidelines*, MTN.GNS/W/164, 1993, paras 4–5.

[301] WTO, WPPS, 'Discussion of Matters Relating to Articles XVI and XVII of the GATS in Connection with the Disciplines on Domestic Regulation in the Accountancy Sector', Informal Note by the Chairman, Job No 6496, 25 November 1998 (Attachment 4 of Annex 2 of the *2001 Scheduling Guidelines*, p 25).

never been expressed by a Member or the Secretariat in a WTO body and thus, to my mind, the Panel incorrectly confused the two.[302] What the Panel seemed to overlook in supporting its theory of 'mutual exclusivity' is the possibility of having a measure which may yield sundry effects and hence raise at the same time several issues with respect to market access, national treatment, and/or domestic regulation as defined in the GATS. Accordingly, a more holistic approach to the issue would be more appropriate and indeed necessary in such a case.

For instance, let us take the case of a licensing procedure/system. Such a procedure/system can be composed of measures falling under both Articles XVI and/or XVII, and Article VI:4; alternatively, it can be simply composed of measures which fall exclusively under Article VI and, thus, it need not be scheduled. In neither case is there an overlap.[303] The restrictions or the discriminatory effects of the components of the licensing procedure/system would be evaluated under Articles XVI and XVII, while transparency, administration, and other non-discriminatory burdens of that procedure/system would be a matter for Article VI; that is, the market access/national treatment aspect of the system would be addressed by Articles XVI and XVII, while the regulatory/procedural aspects (eg the burdensomeness of the procedure in administering the licensing requirements) would be tackled by the disciplines laid down in Article VI:4. In other words, the system itself can fall under the scope of Article VI while the restrictions it administers may be subject to Articles XVI and XVII. Then, what appears to be of vital importance is the distinction between a licensing system and its several components, in terms of their different requirements and different measures.

When looking at the discussions of the relevant WTO bodies,[304] the intentions of Members which participated in the GATS negotiations to avoid any overlap between Articles XVI and XVII on the one side, and Article VI, on the other side, become apparent.[305] Although there have been voices underlining the existence of a certain overlap between Article VI and Articles XVI/XVII measures,[306] the approach ultimately considering such an overlap between these

[302] In this direction, see the United States' appellant's submission in the *US—Gambling* case, paras 132–133.

[303] See the Secretariat's intervention in WTO, WPDR, 'Report on the Meeting Held on 4 December 2002', S/WPDR/M/19, 29 January 2003, para 12, and WTO, WPDR, 'Report on the Meeting Held on 3 July 2001', S/WPDR/M/12, 16 August 2001, para 44; also WTO, WPDR, 'Relationship of Regulatory Disciplines with National Treatment', Communication from Hong Kong, China, JOB(04)/24, 31 March 2004, p 2. Pauwelyn also argues that measures governed by Art VI can still be market access restrictions within the meaning of Art XVI and thus rejects the 'mutual exclusivity' finding made by the Panel on the *Gambling* case, but he falls short of identifying the merits of the decision that Members largely met to exclude any possibility of overlap between these provisions. Pauwelyn (n 248 above) 155.

[304] See, for instance, WTO, WPPS (n 301 above); also WTO, WPDR, 'Report on the Meeting Held on 4 December 2002' (n 303 above) p 3.

[305] Also WTO, CTS (n 51 above) p 3.

[306] cf WTO, WPDR, Report on the Meeting Held on 3 July 2001 (n 303 above) paras 42–43; see also WTO, WPDR (n 148 above) paras 14, 21, 32. Compare also the *2001 Scheduling Guidelines* which provide: 'If approval procedures or licensing and qualification requirements contain any of

provisions as undesirable seems to be generally accepted among Members.[307] The endeavour to avoid any overlap does not concern the measures (which sometimes do have diverse effects, touching upon several GATS provisions), but the GATS disciplines under the provisions at hand in that the disciplines to be developed under Article VI:4, just as with the other Article VI disciplines, should not overlap with those laid down in Articles XVI and XVII.[308]

Thus, the Panel set up a false dichotomy between Articles VI and XVI. The Panel was wrong to end its analysis at that point once it had raised the issue in the first place. Rather, it should have continued to demonstrate that, in the absence of an overlap, Articles XVI and VI are complementary. More generally, the relationship between Articles VI, XVI, and XVII is one of complementarity with all three provisions tackling restrictions on trade in services. These provisions are necessary for an exhaustive description of situations relating to trade in services restrictions.

These restrictions, however, have a distinct nature, as pointed out earlier. Their complementarity is not in the scope of the measures to which they apply, but rather in their functions. Accordingly, whereas Article VI was not designed to cope with measures scheduled in line with Articles XVI and XVII,[309] any procedures administering quantitative restrictions of Article XVI (eg number of licences granted to service suppliers) or discriminatory requirements scheduled under Article XVII column (eg separate certification required for foreign suppliers) could still be subject to Article VI disciplines as regards their regulatory elements (eg for being non-transparent). Hence, the fact that a measure has been scheduled in the market access or national treatment column in accordance with the *Scheduling Guidelines* does not shield it from the scrutiny of Article VI as to the regulatory aspects of that measure. In fact, it is possible that a given measure may comply with a Member's commitments as to Articles XVI or XVII, but the administration of the same measure may still raise a question of incompatibility with Article VI. Then a given measure can raise issues, which do not overlap, under both Article VI and Article XVI/XVII GATS.

The proposition that these provisions should be regarded as complementary is also confirmed by Article VI:1 GATS. This provision requires that Members ascertain, in sectors where they undertook specific commitments, the reasonable, objective, and impartial administration of *all measures of general application* affecting trade in services and not only those not falling under Articles XVI and/or XVII. Consequently, since a measure can have several facets, it would be

the limitations specified in Article XVI, they should be scheduled as market access limitations'. WTO (n 137 above) para 10.

[307] WTO, CTS (Special Session), 'Report of the Meeting Held on 5, 8 and 12 October 2001', S/CSS/M/12, 28 November 2001, para 299; also WTO, WPDR, 'Report on the Meeting Held on 2 October 2001', S/WPDR/M/13, 21 November 2001, para 10.

[308] WTO, WPDR, Report on the Meeting Held on 3 July 2001 (n 303 above) paras 42–43.

[309] WTO, WPDR (n 307 above) para 9.

erroneous to contend that such a measure can fall under only one of the Articles VI, XVI, or XVII. This, of course, does not mean that the disciplines themselves should not be distinct, legally speaking.[310]

Admittedly, while such an approach adds to the desired level of legal certainty, it is not easy to follow in practice. Although, for instance, it is possible to examine whether licensing standards fulfil the requirements of the market access and national treatment obligations, and examine separately whether the same standards are consistent with Article VI disciplines, it is also possible that a failure to apply licensing standards reasonably, objectively, or transparently can itself have implications for market access or national treatment.[311] Accordingly, a parallel, more comprehensive interpretational approach would be much more helpful in this regard. This could also be very helpful for the whole GATS framework, because if Articles XVI and XVII overshadow Article VI, then the indispensable symmetry between liberalization process and regulatory reform vanishes, something that is not desirable at all. Rather, liberalization and regulatory reform should be encouraged to progress simultaneously.[312]

E. To regulate, or not to regulate? That is the question—But not the only one: A primer on the tools for evaluating the domestic regulatory regime

The previous discussion on domestic regulations and services trade liberalization brings to the forefront the issue of regulatory reform. Taking into account the positive effects that such a reform may have on investment flows and the overall efficiency of a regulatory system, this endeavour can be worthwhile and rewarding in terms of a long-term increase in aggregate welfare of an economy. As implied earlier, however, reforming a domestic regulatory system can be a daunting task for regulators. It is not only an issue of how to intervene and regulate in a given market, but also one of whether a regulatory intervention is necessary. Once the latter question has been answered in the affirmative, it is suggested in this section that a government should undertake an evaluation of the regulatory regime it actually has in place. Cost–benefit analyses or regulatory impact assessments can be very helpful tools in such an evaluation.

It is economically plausible to suggest that in the absence of a market defect the unregulated market should be relied upon.[313] Furthermore, even if a market failure exists and depending on its nature, an appropriate response for a government

[310] WTO, WPDR, Report on the Meeting Held on 3 July 2001 (n 303 above) paras 42–43.

[311] R Janda, 'GATS Regulatory Disciplines Meet Global Public Goods: The Case of Transportation Services' in A Mattoo and P Sauvé (eds), *Domestic Regulation and Service Trade Liberalization*, 2003, 119ff.

[312] Low and Mattoo (n 271 above) 456.

[313] Breyer (n 14 above) 184.

might still be not to intervene at all and to leave the distortion to the market to resolve, either because there is always the possibility of a costly government failure when intervening[314] or because market mechanisms will emerge or market processes will develop in order to solve the distortion by themselves due to lower transaction costs/low-cost bargaining, in accordance with the Coase theorem.[315] Thus, market failure, in and of itself, is a necessary, but not a sufficient reason for regulation.

As noted earlier, it is possible that protectionism emanating from domestic regulations may not be intentional. In fact, due to investment considerations or international obligations, protection against foreign competition nowadays is seldom the only or even the primary objective when regulating a services sector. As a rule, a governmental intervention is initially aimed at dealing with market failures or achieving social objectives. In that case, it is of paramount importance to reassess (and probably put in a hierarchical order) the instruments that a government or the delegated regulatory authority has at its disposal when dealing with a problem, since regulation is not the only possible policy response available to a government.[316] In this regard, the determination of the appropriate level of government to be charged with acting in order to achieve more effectively the intended goals becomes crucial.[317]

The aforementioned approach, ie putting the available instruments into a hierarchy may require two prerequisites to be fulfilled: first, it requires an assessment of the costs (for instance, the compliance costs associated with the adherence to the regulatory measure at issue) as compared with the benefits of the imposition of every instrument (eg positive externalities); and, second, it requires a very detailed specification of the objectives with periodic screening of the policies applied (eg through regulatory impact assessments[318] or international benchmarking studies[319]). For instance, a set of regulatory arrangements might initially be built up to deal with a problem associated with information asymmetries. Regulations can become outdated or more stringent and substitute for a barrier to entry in due course, as the regulatory instruments are captured by the industries negatively

314 Breyer (note 38 above) 553.

315 RH Coase, 'The Problem of Social Cost' (1960) 3 Journal of Law and Economics 1. See also the relevant analysis under Chapter II above, in the section referring to domestic distortions.

316 See also the comments by A Mattoo in Productivity Commission/Australian National University, *Achieving Better Regulation of Services,* 2000, 54.

317 G Feketekuty, 'Regulatory Reform and Trade Liberalization in Services' in P Sauvé and RM Stern (eds), *GATS 2000: New Directions in Services Trade Liberalization,* 2000, 235.

318 See, in general, D Rodrigo, 'Regulatory Impact Analysis in OECD Countries—Challenges for Developing Countries', South Asian—Third High level Investment Round Table, 2005; also RW Hahn and RE Litan, 'Counting Regulatory Benefits and Costs: Lessons for the US and Europe' (2005) 8 JIEL 486ff. For the application of RIAs in the European Union, see European Commission, 'Communication of the Commission on Impact Assessment', COM(2002) 276 final, 5 June 2002; also European Commission, 'Impact Assessment Guidelines', SEC(2005) 791, 15 June 2005.

319 Such a study would seek to identify best practices at the *international* level and implement them in order to improve performance of a *domestic* institution.

affected. As a result, a source of inefficiency arises from regulations that were initially an appropriate policy response to a problem of asymmetric information.

Therefore, a continuous evaluation of the impact of public policies on economic action and on the economy overall must be established. Through this evaluation process one can perceive that policies recreate circumstances over time; that is, governments exert influence on markets and their structure, behaviour, and performance. This influence brings about new problems and thus new policies are usually needed. Constant review of domestic regulations is indispensable to ensure effective, well-functioning competition in sectors that are liberalized and to achieve important legitimate public policy objectives over time, such as consumer protection and universal access to a service.

Moreover, new technologies and other changes in the market might render some earlier concerns about market failure redundant. Indeed, regulatory instruments intended to suit an earlier period may later have perverse effects due to scientific advances. Many such tools no longer make sense; altered circumstances make them obsolete or, worse, counterproductive. Domestic regulation cannot and should not be static; an appropriate regulatory framework can have dynamic aspects which necessitate close monitoring. Accordingly, regular reviews of regulatory policy are valuable to ensure that objectives remain valid over time and that the initially implemented policies remain the most appropriate way of achieving those objectives.

By meeting the two aforementioned requirements, ie the juxtaposing of the costs and the benefits of the available instruments and the specification of objectives with periodic reviews of applied measures, the likelihood increases that the instrument which directly tackles the distortion/market failure will be chosen.[320] Whilst the second of these requirements is associated with the economic theory of domestic distortions[321] in that it requires an intervention that will be appropriate to face the market failure directly (in accordance with the theory of first-best), the first requirement essentially entails a cost–benefit (and, consequently, a cost-effectiveness)[322] analysis.

Cost–benefit analysis is a technique for thoroughly and consistently evaluating the incremental advantages and drawbacks associated with all relevant alternatives to both the *status quo* and the prospective policy changes. It provides a government with information needed in order to ameliorate the quality of public policies with a view to eliminating the possibility of unwanted losses; such quality is defined according to the change in social well-being (hence, in the aggregated welfare of individuals) that these policies engender.[323]

[320] C Findlay and J-D Kim, 'Issues in Domestic Regulation of Services', APEC Group on Services Paper, 2001, 5.

[321] See Chapter II.

[322] CR Sunstein, 'The Cost–Benefit State', University of Chicage, John M. Olin Law and Economics Working Paper No 39, 1996, 21.

[323] Cost–benefit analysis uses as a metric a monetary measure of the aggregate change in individual welfare due to a policy decision. Individual welfare depends on the satisfaction of individual preferences and monetary measures of welfare change are drawn by observing how much

Since the total elimination of unwanted losses such as damages and harmful risks is neither feasible nor desirable, first and foremost because of the amount of money that would be needed, cost–benefit analysis entails an assessment of government intervention which asks whether the benefits of regulation justify its costs. Cost–benefit analysis can serve specific purposes—*inter alia*, enable better priority-setting, advance market-oriented incentives in lieu of command-and-control regulation, exempt *de minimis* risks, help with cognitive distortions and take account of reflective and informed public judgments, spur voluntary and least-cost compliance, as well as concentrate on ultimate results rather than methods and processes (performance standards as opposed to design standards).[324]

The main criticism of this type of analysis is that the quantifiable effects will typically prevail, since the qualitative effects, though usually more important, are very difficult to quantify in monetary terms. This will lead to a bias in favour of market outcomes rather than regulation, for the simple reason that the quantifiable costs will tend to outweigh the quantifiable benefits. If, however, the regulatory intervention is absolutely necessary, then non-monetary consequences should also be influential when conducting a cost–benefit test. On the other hand, trying to include a predominantly qualitative effect in a quantitative framework (in order to be able to quantify the costs and the benefits) involves a certain degree of subjective judgment.[325] Thus, while conceptually straightforward, the soundness of empirical cost–benefit analysis rests upon the availability of reliable estimates of elements such as social benefits and costs.

More generally, there appears to be some disagreement as to the need for taking into account concerns associated with economic efficiency when regulating. The argument against cost–benefit analysis would be that regulations are typically established in order to satisfy values other than economic efficiency.[326] Especially with reference to distributional issues, efficiency in itself is not the answer and the

individuals are willing to give up in terms of other consumption opportunities (willingness-to-pay). Cost–benefit analysis appears to be particularly germane to regulatory areas where the avoidance or reduction of risk is central. Nevertheless, such an approach can be equally applied to non-market public goods (eg environmental quality) and market goods and services. The measurement of non-market values is, however, more exacting. RJ Kopp, AJ Krupnick, and M Toman, 'Cost–Benefit Analysis and Regulatory Reform: An Assessment of the Science and the Art', Resources for the Future Discussion Paper 97–19, 1997, 2.

[324] Regulatory tools such as performance standards and economic incentives accomplish regulatory objectives at lower cost. In general, governmentally prescribed means of achieving desired ends are prone to producing inefficiencies. Such inefficiencies are likely to arise from stifling innovation on the supply side (innovation costs) and reducing choice on the demand side of the market as well as raising direct costs associated with inspection.

[325] RW Hahn and CR Sunstein, 'A New Executive Order for Improving Federal Regulation? Deeper and Wider Cost–Benefit Analysis', 2002, 34; for the existence of bias in economic policy analysis, see RG Noll, *The Economics and Politics of the Slowdown in Regulatory Reform*, 1999, 26.

[326] Baldwin and Cave (n 24 above) 87.

pursuit of efficiency may in fact conflict with legislative statements on distributional matters.[327]

As a result, in spheres of regulation where addressing distributive concerns is essential, the appropriateness of economic efficiency claims, which are inherent in cost–benefit analysis, may be at least problematic. Therefore, cost–benefit analysis may not provide any answers and, hence, will be unhelpful when authorities seek a regulatory response to reflect non-welfare considerations eg deontological or distributive considerations, since social welfare might be promoted by regulations that do not pass the cost–benefit test.[328] Thus, the main objection to a purely economic approach is an ethical one. But nothing should prevent regulatory institutions from using other methods of regulatory decisionmaking, alone or in combination with cost–benefit analysis. Again, if the costs are grossly disproportionate to the benefits, there should be a strong presumption against regulation overall, unless the distributive argument is compelling.

Even in the latter case, however, cost–benefit analysis proves to be a very effective tool for streamlining the domestic regulatory environment and certainly a practical and administrable proxy for an enquiry into the social welfare question. Regulators could adjust the analysis for any distributional biases by re-evaluating certain variables when they are first assigned or by undertaking a separate distributional assessment. In this case, one would start with the ordinary cost–benefit balancing and take distributional considerations into account at a later stage of the analysis.[329] The lack of information and the existence of uncertainties as to the consequences should not cause policy paralysis, as they do not constitute a rationale for neglecting the already known pros and cons of policy. It is in this very case that policy analysis can be particularly useful.[330]

Arrow *et al* list eight principles for the appropriate use of cost–benefit analysis.[331] They are the following:

(1) Cost–benefit analysis is useful for comparing the favourable and unfavourable effects of policies;
(2) Decisionmakers should not be precluded from considering the economic costs and benefits of different policies in the development of regulations. Agencies should be allowed to use economic analysis to identify regulatory priorities;

[327] Sykes advocates a reconciliation of Kaldor-Hicks efficiency and redistributional concerns. AO Sykes, 'Comparative Advantage and the Normative Economics of International Trade Policy' (1998) 1 JIEL 58–59.

[328] MD Adler and EA Posner, 'Rethinking Cost-Benefit Analysis', University of Chicago, John M. Olin Law and Economics Working Paper No 72 1999, 81.

[329] RH Pildes and CR Sunstein, 'Reinventing the Regulatory State' (1995) 62(1) University of Chicago Law Review 46.

[330] WK Viscusi, 'Regulating the Regulators' (1996) 63(4) University of Chicago Law Review 1439.

[331] KJ Arrow *et al*, *Benefit–Cost Analysis in Environmental, Health, and Safety Regulation—A statement of principles*, 1996.

(3) Cost–benefit analysis should be required for all major regulatory decisions;
(4) Much as agencies should be required to conduct cost–benefit analyses for major decisions and to explain why they have selected actions for which reliable evidence indicates that expected benefits are significantly less than expected costs, those agencies should not be bound by strict cost–benefit tests. Other factors such as equity or fairness may be significant in some decisions;
(5) Benefits and costs of proposed policies should be quantified wherever possible. Best estimates should be presented along with a description of the uncertainties;
(6) The more external review that regulatory analyses receive, the better they are likely to be. Peer review of economic analyses and periodical retrospective assessments of selected regulatory impact analyses can prove to be important instruments in this respect;
(7) A core set of economic assumptions should be used in calculating benefits and costs. Key variables include the social discount rate, the value of reducing risks of premature death and accidents, and the values associated with other improvements in health; and
(8) Although cost–benefit analysis should focus primarily on the overall relation between benefits and costs, a good analysis will also identify important distributional consequences.

Implicit in Arrow *et al*'s suggestions on the use of cost–benefit tests is the importance of institutional choice. Given the advantages of using cost–benefit analysis, it may be advisable for regulatory institutions to commit themselves more seriously to such analysis in regulatory policy as a way of drawing attention to the possible effects of alternative courses of action. As trade becomes more liberalized and multilateral obligations multiply, the burden on regulatory institutions becomes greater. This implies a qualitative and quantitative betterment of the institutions at stake. Resources for this may be scarce so that any such effort needs to be accompanied by capacity building programmes.

As a tentative conclusion, one could reasonably argue that regulations should not be judged according to the benchmark of economic efficiency alone. Qualitative elements are indispensable in any cost–benefit balancing,[332] although requiring an assessment of costs and benefits is definitely most easily warranted on economic grounds, as a way of advancing Kaldor-Hicks economic efficiency[333] and, thus, diminishing superfluous and profligate public and private expenditures. Most importantly, however, the justifications of cost–benefit analysis may be based on considerations associated with democracy. Indeed, cost–benefit analysis may be promoted to a central feature of the regulatory programme of a government with a view to diminishing interest-group pressures on regulation

[332] Hahn and Sunstein (n 325 above) 8.
[333] FH Stephen, *The Economics of the Law*, 1988, 59.

and ensuring that the consequences of regulation are not shrouded in mystery but instead are transparent and available for public inspection and review.[334]

As a general rule, such cost–benefit analysis neglects the international impact that domestic regulations may have. Thus, any detriment to trade is not taken into consideration during the evaluation of domestic regulations. It has been argued that cost–benefit analysis as it currently stands must be changed to include international concerns, thereby taking into account not only trade concerns, but also 'issues of externalization and the desire of explicit or implicit co-operation with other states'.[335]

Of course, this 'global' cost–benefit analysis ('thinking globally and acting locally') takes into consideration a cost dimension not normally included in the ordinary cost–benefit analysis, ie adverse effects of *domestic* regulations on *foreign* persons either in the form of non-pecuniary or pecuniary externalities. Therefore, it would strike down as too costly some regulations that would not otherwise fail such a test. Adding this global dimension to the cost–benefit analysis conducted domestically may be the result of international commitments undertaken. It may also occur due to the existence of cross-border externalities that can be tackled only if each national government takes into account transboundary effects, or due to the ascertainment that the struggle against barriers to trade that are entrenched in domestic regulations can be more efficient at the national level, or, better still, at the smallest domain at which they can yield results. This is also what the application of the principle of subsidiarity, as applied by the European Union, would suggest.[336] Indeed, depending on the problem at issue, a centralization or, inversely, decentralization of the regulatory jurisdiction may be needed.[337]

A cost–benefit analysis of this type, undertaken by national courts, the legislature, or the markets, would therefore oblige domestic institutions first to identify and subsequently to compare the local benefits with any possible burden on foreigners that the regulation at issue may yield. Non-protectionist laws may still be costly when applied to foreigners and these external costs may even override local benefits. Those foreigners, however, by definition, did not participate in the formal political process that led to the legislation under review. Therefore, it is argued that after the adoption of a domestic law, foreign interests that have not been represented in the legislature should be given virtual representation at the time of the judicial review, provided that it would be more costly to have those interests represented in other preference-revealing mechanisms such as politics or markets.[338]

[334] Sunstein (n 322 above) 22.

[335] J Trachtman, 'Trade and... Problems, Cost–Benefit Analysis and Subsidiarity' (1998) 9(1) EJIL 41.

[336] Thus, the EC institutions will act only when the comparative efficiency calculus comes out in favour of an action at the Community level. P Craig, *EU Administrative Law*, 2006, 423.

[337] Trachtman (n 335 above) 37.

[338] In this regard, it is interesting to follow the discussion between Regan and Trachtman regarding the competence of the judiciary to engage in cost–benefit analysis. Trachtman seems

A global cost–benefit analysis undertaken on a mandatory basis by domestic authorities would be in the interest of the proponents of free trade, as it would facilitate identifying whether domestic regulatory measures promote efficiency or, rather, distort trade.[339] By the same token, one could correctly argue that an international agreement on the use of common analytical methods (or, in other words, a common efficiency metric) for evaluating regulatory proposals such as cost–benefit analysis would serve to drive domestic regulations towards more efficient policies, and thereby promote market openness and hence trade. This agreement would, of course, mainly concern international regulatory distortions, ie inefficient domestic regulations that have significant international repercussions; in fact, few distorting regulations have purely domestic negative effects. The WTO judiciary would probably welcome an agreement about methods for evaluating regulations as well, since it can contribute to the identification of ultimate purposes and effects of domestic regulations.[340] In *US—Gasoline*, the Appellate Body, in examining the conformity of the baseline establishment rules of the US Gasoline Rule with the *chapeau* of Article XX GATT implied that domestic authorities are required to take account of the costs that the adopted measures may have for foreign producers. Otherwise, the application of such measures may constitute unjustifiable discrimination and a disguised restriction

to suggest that this 'global' cost–benefit analysis (which D Regan calls 'virtual representation') could be made by the adjudicative bodies fairly effectively. In any case, his argument runs, this analysis of local benefits *vis-à-vis* external trade costs should be conducted at a level that will, too, be the result of a cost–benefit analysis so that it is assured that the final choice of the institution which will conduct the 'global' cost–benefit analysis best reflects constituent interests. Trachtman (n 335 above) 46–50, 84. Regan, on the other side, attempts to demonstrate that there is no such thing as judicial competence to engage in cost–benefit analysis. DH Regan, 'The Supreme Court and State Protectionism: Making Sense of the Dormant Commerce Clause' (1986) 84 Michigan Law Review 1131. According to Regan, foreign interests, even not represented in the regulating state's legislature, are fully accounted for when regulating in the case of a non-protectionist regulation and thus any judicial virtual representation is unnecessary. DH Regan, 'Judicial Review of Member-State Regulation of Trade within a Federal or Quasi-Federal System: Protectionism and Balancing, Da Capo' (2001) 99(8) Michigan Law Review 1855. Regan goes on to argue that, unless there is a failure in the political process regarding the treatment of local interests, the legislature does better at optimizing overall interests (ie local and foreign alike) than courts due to the fact that local interests are normally represented in the political process. If the legislature does indeed do better, then there is no need for the courts to intervene and second-guess the legislature to protect local (and consequently, according to Regan, out-of-state) interests. Ibid pp 1860–1861.

339 However, few countries as yet take into account such trade concerns in their domestic regulatory review processes. K Iida, 'Trade and Regulatory Reform: Insights from the OECD Country Reviews and Other Analyses' in OECD, *Trade and Regulatory Reform: Insights from Country Experience*, 2001, 15. The EU, for instance, when it assesses the impact of its legislation proposals or the legislation in force, does take into account the economic, environmental and social impact of its regulatory measures. Within the rubric 'economic impact' the European Commission is required to take into account the EU trade policy and its international obligations, including those deriving from WTO law. European Commission, 'Impact Assessment: Next Steps—In Support of Competitiveness and Sustainable Development', Commission Staff Working Paper, SEC(2004)1377, 21 October 2004, 11.

340 RG Noll, 'Regulatory Reform and International Trade Policy' in T Ito and AO Krueger (eds), *Deregulation and Interdependence in the Asia-Pacific Region*, 2000, 44–45.

to trade and thus not be in conformity with the requirements of the *chapeau* of Article XX GATT.[341]

F. Put the blame on the GATS: liberalization, deregulation, regulatory reform . . . or something else?

Interestingly, one of the major fallacies, which has led to significant scepticism and muddle over the role of the GATS, is that the objective of this Agreement is the deregulation of services. Yet the GATS calls for the liberalization of services and the management of the existing regulatory diversity among the Members' domestic laws in a mutually advantageous manner. The fact that the pursuit of freer trade requires the evaluation of Members' regulatory policy and the possibility of negotiating regulatory reform in parallel with trade negotiations does not refute this. The case for liberalization of trade and investment should not be confounded with the need for regulation and regulatory reform. The right to regulate is one of the fundamental tenets in which the Agreement resides. The GATS does not prejudice this right by any means.[342]

The majority of the services sectors are highly regulated, frequently for good reasons, among which the protection of public health and safety, the rights of consumers, and maintaining the high quality of services provided are the most apparent. Thus, regulations cannot merely be assimilated to trade restrictions. National measures that achieve such legitimate objectives should be in place and be properly synchronized with liberalization efforts. Whereas there are justifications for deregulation (or demonopolization) and regulatory reform,[343] putting in place new regulations and as a way to tackle problems related to networks, consumer protection (including data protection), and provide equitable access to essential facilities.[344] All Members attach great importance to the right to regulate services.[345] Nevertheless, reform equates to change and hence opposition from domestic vested interests is expected to arise. Such opposition is usually political, as in many services sectors governments are implicated as suppliers, investors, or

[341] Appellate Body Report, *US—Gasoline*, pp 28–29.

[342] cf Panel Report, *US—Gambling*, para 6.316.

[343] OECD, *The OECD Report on Regulatory Reform—Synthesis*, 1997, 6; also G Feketekuty (n 317 above) 226.

[344] Regarding health services, see WHO and WTO, *WTO Agreements and Public Health*, 2002, 121.

[345] The existence of this right was once more reaffirmed during the Doha Ministerial Conference and explicitly mentioned in the Doha Ministerial Declaration that launched the new round, the ninth in a row. WTO, *Doha Ministerial Declaration*, adopted on 14 November 2001, WT/MIN(01)/DEC/W/1, para 7. At the last Ministerial Conference, Members reiterated that trade in services negotiations shall proceed 'with due respect for the right of Members to regulate'. *Hong Kong Ministerial Declaration*, adopted on 18 December 2005, WT/MIN(05)/DEC, para 25.

regulators. Therefore, managing the politics of reform can be as important as the reform itself.

The liberalization of international trade in services involves processes whereby measures are enforced which expand market access for foreign service suppliers wishing to enter a market or diminish discrimination against them compared with domestic suppliers.[346] To be sure, market access in services may be denied not only by the imposition of restrictive border policies (in fact, this is rarely the case in services), but also through the existence of domestic regulatory policies, often non-discriminatory, that distort trade and have anticompetitive effects. In addition, barriers to trade in services not only affect the 'product', as in the GATT, but also the supplier and the way the service is supplied. Since these measures are found primarily in domestic regulations, the GATS more directly impacts domestic regulatory regimes than the GATT. Such an impact may call for reform, which from this perspective will inevitably mean rationalization, re-regulation, and sometimes deregulation to make sure that the opening of the market achieves its objectives without affecting legitimate policies.[347]

For example, a revision of domestic standards and qualifications may be necessary for countries that would like to export professional services, as low standards and differences in domestic training or examinations can impede foreign recognition. Such inadequacies, thus, may legitimize barriers that hamper entry to a certain domestic market.[348] This reform process would probably call for a broad set of policies and involve various regulatory instruments, institutions, and constituencies, domestic and foreign, public and private. The GATS, however, cannot ensure or enjoin any complementary action that is needed to deliver liberalization with positive welfare effects.[349]

Again, deregulation in the service sector is not necessarily associated with liberalization. Whereas deregulation efforts may result in reforms in ownership schemes of domestic service suppliers and may reduce bureaucratic delays and red tape, deregulation does not automatically lead to any parity with the opening of the domestic market to foreign service suppliers, given that a country can deregulate a services activity without allowing foreign competition (eg by replacing a former public monopoly with a private monopoly). This also suggests that deregulation may be futile from a domestic welfare perspective, if its outcome does not enhance the competitiveness and openness of markets. Any benefits in consumer welfare are expected to result not from a change in ownership, but rather from increased competition and economically meaningful regulation.

[346] J Hodge, 'Liberalization of Trade in Services in Developing Countries' in B Hoekman, A Mattoo, and P English (eds), *Development, Trade, and the WTO: A Handbook*, 2002, 222.

[347] A Crosby and JT Vielma, 'Trade in Services, the GATS and Sustainable Development' (2000) 4 BRIDGES 11.

[348] Gamberale and Mattoo (n 14 above) 298.

[349] The World Bank, *World Development Report 2004: Making Services Work for Poor People,* 2003, 105.

When liberalizing, a strengthening of some regulations may be indispensable to deal with problems related to market failures such as natural monopoly or asymmetric information. Most services sectors require efficient regulatory principles and measures in order to guarantee consumer welfare, but also aggregate welfare by avoiding market abuse and restrictions to market entry. Often, therefore, in order to reap the benefits from services trade liberalization, a central policy issue can entail the identification of the right mixture between regulation and competition. The regulatory intensity of services industries complicates such a task.

The GATS can be the appropriate medium to allow negotiators and regulators to find the best way to harness rulemaking endeavours at the multilateral level with an eye to encouraging sound regulatory institutions and practices domestically. Because of characteristics peculiar to services, such as asymmetric information in business services or high fixed costs in bottleneck services, and the greater danger of market failure, effective regulatory supervision of both domestic and foreign operators can be significant.[350] More generally, when the domestic regulatory framework is inappropriate, sound domestic regulation (for instance, prudential regulation that ensures safety and soundness of the financial system, or pro-competitive regulation in network-based services) is more often than not a necessary complement to the opening up of a country's foreign trade and investment regime in order for a country to reap the benefits of services liberalization.[351] In the absence of a proper sequencing of regulatory reform and liberalization, national welfare may decrease.

Economic theory suggests that, in the absence of cross-border externalities, countries should avoid seeking solutions at an international forum, as regulations that meet locally defined needs and preferences and protect any domestic comparative advantage would probably be the most efficient and legitimate ones. Accordingly, in the absence of non-pecuniary cross-border externalities or economies of scale in production and distribution that create optimum regulatory areas, the imposition of one set of standards across different regulatory domains could nullify trade possibilities and be, generally, inefficient and counterproductive.[352] Thus, in accordance with the principle of subsidiarity, there is little justification on efficiency grounds for not allocating the regulatory jurisdiction to the lowest-level repository of authority possible, ie national/regional bodies.[353]

[350] F Eschenbach and B Hoekman, 'Services Policy Reform and Economic Growth in Transition Economies, 1990–2004', PRWP No 3663, 2005, 16.

[351] Mattoo (n 46 above) 76.

[352] It could be added here that multilateral disciplines are desirable in the case of a specific market failure, which is the natural monopoly/oligopoly, due to the direct trade concerns that it raises. The adoption of the Reference Paper on Basic Telecommunications paved the way for other sectors where significant monopolies remain, eg transport and energy services. Gamberale and Mattoo (n 14 above) 293. See, for example, WTO, CTS (Special Session), 'Postal/Courier: Proposal for a Reference Paper', Communication from the European Communities and their Member States, TN/S/W/26, 17 January 2005.

[353] But see JH Jackson, 'Sovereignty-Modern: A New Approach to an Outdated Concept' (2003) 97(4) AJIL 792–793.

What multilateral disciplines could ensure, however, is that domestic measures, including those intended to achieve social objectives, do not have unnecessary trade-restrictive effects.[354] The GATS can function as a forum that could eventually yield strengthened multilateral disciplines on domestic regulation with a view to promoting and consolidating domestic regulatory reform. For instance, one cannot fully reap the benefits from market access and national treatment commitments undertaken under mode 4 unless unduly trade-restrictive licensing or qualifications requirements are set aside in accordance with Article VI. In addition, allocating the decisionmaking power to an international body such as the WTO may prove to be very helpful in terms of neutralizing competing interests which cannot be dealt with otherwise at the national level. The GATS can provide additional assistance against backsliding. Furthermore, an international trade negotiations arena is a first-rate opportunity for increasing the benefits of domestic regulatory reform by pairing them, on the basis of reciprocity, with foreign reforms that grant domestic suppliers greater access to external markets.

Clearly, the GATS does not call for harmonization of domestic regulations; this is, in fact, not desirable at all. What is expected in the aftermath of the GATS is that regulators see the public interest and the concept of regulation in a wider context that takes into account the growth of international trade, and notably trade in services. According to the GATS, it is feasible for a regulator to guarantee a certain minimum level of quality of the supply of a service and thus protect the public interest domestically, or achieve its national policy objectives, and still have a not-more-trade-distortive-than-necessary attitude. The following chapter will provide an in-depth examination of the necessity test under Article VI GATS as well as its potential ramifications.

[354] Feketekuty (n 317 above) 236.

IV

Creating a Horizontal Necessity Test for Services

A. Introductory remarks

At the end of the Uruguay Round, Members had to a great extent finalized the incipient institutional framework that would cover the international liberalization of trade in services. Until then, the GATS founding fathers had attempted, inter alia, to define restrictions to trade in services in legal terms. This task has proven to be insurmountable for measures that are not captured by Article XVI and XVII and thus Members failed to reach consensus on the treatment that *non*-discriminatory *non*-quantitative measures affecting trade in services should have under the GATS. For many Members, the provision tackling such measures, that is, Article VI GATS, seemed to severely impinge on the Members' regulatory sovereignty. Many Members felt that crucial prerogatives that they have had in order to regulate in 'sensitive' policy areas such as standards or qualification and licensing requirements in their jurisdictions were threatened. For others, their sovereign right to regulate was diminished.

Not surprisingly, then, Article VI was one of those provisions that Members decided to put aside and leave their finalization for the years to come. That was so, not only because of its intrinsic difficulties, but also due to the fact that it was touching, more than any other Article in the GATS, upon the relationship between trade liberalization and domestic policy flexibility. Leaving this provision unfinished, together with the decision to make the national treatment principle conditional upon scheduled commitments, has harmed the potential 'bite' of the GATS itself. This was so because domestic services regulations and barriers entrenched in them can have a considerable impact on trade in services more than in any other sector of economic activity. Overall, in the absence of a strong provision addressing domestic regulations, the GATS framework governing regulatory behaviour constitutes an unbalanced outcome.[1]

Nonetheless, Members acknowledged the potentially trade-inhibiting effects of even non-discriminatory measures interwoven in Members' domestic

[1] Also P Delimatsis, 'Determining the Necessity of Domestic Regulations in Services—The Best is Yet to Come' (2008) EJIL (forthcoming).

regulations. They also were cognizant of the fact that Members have an incentive to circumvent multilateral obligations, as their preferences associated with their domestic regulatory activities are not put into question either by the GATS or by any other WTO agreement.[2] Hence, the formulation of a mediating principle or principles between the international trade values, on the one side, and the domestic policy values, on the other, was of overarching importance. Willing to develop precise disciplines to ensure that domestic regulations were not unduly burdensome or trade-restrictive, Members decided to rather create a work programme for the coming years as envisaged under Article VI:4, which would bestow on the CTS the decision of whether there was a need to develop disciplines 'with a view to ensuring that measures relating to qualification requirements and procedures, technical standards and licensing requirements do not constitute *unnecessary* barriers to trade in services'. If so, the CTS had the freedom to establish the bodies that it considered appropriate for the development of any necessary disciplines with respect to the aforementioned types of regulation, ie licensing, qualifications, and standards.

Thus, Article VI:4 does not entail a direct, horizontally (ie across sectors) applicable necessity test; it rather entreats Members to negotiate any disciplines considered essential to ensure that measures within the scope of this Article (qualification requirements and procedures, technical standards, licensing requirements and procedures) do not create unnecessary barriers to trade in services. Notably with respect to necessity, the prospective disciplines should additionally ensure, pursuant to the work programme set out in Article VI:4 and subparagraph (b) thereof, that such measures are not more burdensome than necessary to ascertain the quality of the supplied service. The final outcome of this work programme is expected to provide the appropriate legal instruments to ensure that services trade expansion continues apace without impinging on Members' right to regulate and to adopt new regulations to attain legitimate policy objectives. Hence, Article VI:4 qualified the otherwise broad regulatory sovereignty that Members enjoy by requiring that Members do not unduly restrict trade through the use of origin-neutral domestic regulations.

In this regard, it seems foreseeable to construct a regulatory framework of general applicability that would be as detailed as feasible,[3] and then base sector-specific rules in the national regulatory jurisdictions on principles entrenched in the general, horizontal framework created at the multilateral level. As is logical in any negotiation, Members do not necessarily share the same views with respect to the issues at stake. Particularly with respect to the development of a horizontal necessity test, consensus cannot be considered as a *fait accompli* in the WPDR. There are Members that are of the view that several sectoral specificities of certain

[2] cf Appellate Body Report, *US—Shrimp*, para 121.

[3] The level of detail will also affect the efficiency of a trade agreement, since the more detailed a contract is the more costly the negotiations (and higher the transaction costs) are.

services sectors are intractable and hence a sectoral approach, similar to the one endorsed with respect to accountancy disciplines, has considerable advantages and would be a more appropriate way to move forward.

This chapter focuses on the most significant and contentious[4] aspect of the GATS Article VI:4 legal mandate, that is, the creation of a meaningful, coherent, and enforceable necessity test that would apply to all services sectors. This test would allow validating the GATS consistency of national measures relating to qualifications, licensing, or technical standards provided that they are not more trade-restrictive than necessary to fulfil the objectives of a given Member. Most importantly, this chapter attempts to demonstrate that creating disciplines under Article VI:4 will have no value unless a necessity test forms part of these disciplines. This is so for the reason that necessity is a key proxy for drawing the fine line between legitimate regulatory interference and protectionism.

B. The establishment of the WPPS and the development of disciplines on domestic regulation with respect to accountancy services

1. The WPPS mandate

With its *Decision on Professional Services* of 1 March 1995, the CTS created the WPPS, which was assigned the task of continuing the work on liberalization of professional services. The mandate of the WPPS was twofold: first, the WPPS was instructed to focus on the examination and report, with recommendations, of any possible disciplines, which would ensure that measures regarding qualifications, licensing, and technical standards do not unduly distort trade in professional services. Second, as a matter of priority, the WPPS had to concentrate on the elaboration of multilateral disciplines in the accountancy sector to give operational effect to specific commitments.

Professional services had already been tackled in a working group that was established on 11 May 1990 during the Uruguay Round negotiations, along with working groups on financial, transport, and tourism services.[5] Within the broad range of professional services, the decision to start with accountancy services was intentional. Two factors are considered to be determinative for this choice: First, the relevant industry had a great interest in the development of a sector that was expanding rapidly worldwide and was deemed a crucial infrastructural element of

[4] For the opposition against the adoption of a necessity test because of its allegedly negative effects on Members' policy space and regulatory flexibility, see, *inter alia*, Institute for Agriculture and Trade Policy and Polaris Institute, 'Five Danger Signs—The GATS Assault on Sovereignty and Democracy', 2006.

[5] JV Reyna, 'Services' in TP Stewart (ed), *The GATT Uruguay Round: A Negotiating History (1986–1992)*, Vol II: Commentary, 1993, 2373.

financial services.[6] It was not accidental that already during the Uruguay Round the United States had proposed the endorsement of an Annex on Professional Accountancy Services.[7] The second factor relates to the level of integration that the accountancy services demonstrated at that point of time, which was considerable if compared to other professional services.[8]

According to the Ministerial *Decision on Professional Services*, in preparing its recommendations, the WPPS had to focus on:[9]

a. developing multilateral disciplines relating to market access so as to ensure that domestic regulatory requirements are based on objective and transparent criteria, such as competence and the ability to supply the service, and are not more burdensome than necessary to ensure the quality of the service, thereby facilitating the effective liberalization of accountancy services;
b. using international standards and, in doing so, encouraging cooperation with the relevant international organizations as defined under paragraph 5(b) of Article VI, so as to give full effect to paragraph 5 of Article VII. By 'international organizations' the CTS probably meant the International Federation of Accountants (IFAC) and the International Accounting Standards Committee (IASC); and
c. facilitating the effective application of paragraph 6 of Article VI of the Agreement by establishing guidelines for the recognition of qualifications.

The analysis that follows takes these three sets of issues in reverse order. By recognizing the important role that recognition of qualifications plays particularly with respect to professional services, the WPPS first produced tangible results in the third set of issues of its mandate, ie the elaboration of voluntary guidelines for the recognition of professional qualifications that would facilitate the effective application of Article VI:6 GATS. The essential task of those guidelines would be to provide some practical guidance that would assist the negotiation and conclusion of mutual recognition agreements or arrangements among Members while ensuring the transparency of such agreements and arrangements.

At this stage, Members preferred to create provisions of *non*-binding nature ascribing to the guidelines a soft law status.[10] Consequently, these guidelines do not preclude the use of alternative methods.[11] This was deemed an appropriate

[6] LJ White, *Reducing the Barriers to International Trade in Accounting Services*, 2001, 4.

[7] MTN.GNS/PROF/W/2 of 2 October 1990.

[8] WTO, WPPS, 'Functions of the Working Party on Professional Services in Relation to Accountancy', S/WPPS/W/1, 27 June 1995, para 4.

[9] WTO, WPPS, Trade in Services, 'Decision on Professional Services', S/L/3, 4 April 1995, para 2. For the full list of issues for consideration that the WPPS had agreed on, see WTO, WPPS, 'Report of the Meeting of 16 January 1996', S/WPPS/M/3, 30 January 1996, p 4. See also WTO, CTS, 'Accountancy Services', S/C/W/73, 4 December 1998, pp 12–13.

[10] WTO, WPPS, 'Note on the Meeting Held on 2 October 1996', S/WPPS/M/6, 12 November 1996, para 4.

[11] This was made explicit in WTO, WPPS, 'Recommendation of the Working Party on Professional Services to the Council for Trade in Services', S/WPPS/W/14/Rev.1, 15 May 1997.

method for facilitating the realization of bilateral MRAs, which remain the most common way to achieve recognition, via multilateral rules guiding the establishment of such valuable agreements. The final version of the *Guidelines for Mutual Recognition Agreements or Arrangements in the Accountancy Sector* that Members had agreed upon was adopted by the CTS on 28 May 1997.[12]

At the outset, the Guidelines acknowledge the existence of differences in education and examination standards, experience requirements, regulatory influence, etc, which hamper the implementation of recognition on a multilateral level. According to the Guidelines, MRAs should clearly identify: the participants; the purpose of the agreement; the details of the mutual recognition provisions, including eligibility requirements for recognition and specification of the conditions under which any additional supplementary requirements may be applied; the mechanisms for implementation; any further licensing or related requirements; and the conditions under which the agreement may be revised. The Guidelines also reiterate the notification obligations under Article VII GATS that each Member has to adhere to when it negotiates and concludes an MRA.[13]

With respect to the second set of issues included in the WPPS mandate, that is, the focus on the use of international standards, the results were disappointing. Indeed, the WPPS did not devote much time and effort to the issue of technical standards and the relevant work of international bodies after the end of the first year of negotiations within the WPPS, during which two symposia with standards-setting bodies in the accountancy sector were organized. Members seem to have felt that the circumstances had not been sufficiently mature to fulfil the mandate in this field. Members ultimately limited themselves to affirming their support regarding the successful completion of international standards in the accountancy sector by IFAC, IASC, and IOSCO during the Singapore Ministerial Conference.[14]

Work on the accountancy sector was completed on 14 December 1998 with the adoption by the CTS of the *Disciplines on Domestic Regulation in the Accountancy Sector* (henceforth, 'the accountancy disciplines').[15] In this manner, the WPPS accomplished the third requirement of its mandate regarding accountancy

[12] S/WPPS/W/12/Rev.1 and S/L/38.

[13] For a critique on the actual value of these Guidelines, see also C Trolliet and J Hegarty, 'Regulatory Reform and Trade Liberalization in Accountancy Services' in A Mattoo and P Sauvé (eds), *Domestic Regulation and Service Trade Liberalization*, 2003, 151.

[14] *Singapore Ministerial Declaration*, adopted on 13 December 1996, WT/MIN(96)/DEC, para 17. According to J Trachtman, this statement 'signals the WTO's deference and, in effect, delegation (at least in part), to these organizations. Thus, the WTO has "delegated" to specific functional organizations the task of establishing standards to facilitate the free movement of accountancy services'. JP Trachtman, 'Accounting Standards and Trade Disciplines—Irreconcilable Differences?' (1997) 31(6) JWT 70. This optimistic assessment, however, seems to be overridden by the subsequent circumstances within the WPPS that demonstrated Members' reluctance to work constructively on the preparation of international standards.

[15] WTO, Trade in Services, 'Disciplines on Domestic Regulation in the Accountancy Sector', S/L/64, 17 December 1998.

services. The WPPS was assigned the task of tailoring the criteria of Article VI:4, which countries needed to respect when regulating, to the specificities of professional services and particularly of the accountancy services so that the disciplines become readily applicable.

2. The accountancy disciplines *in concreto*–Strengths and weaknesses

As stated earlier, the *Decision on Professional Services* and, more generally, the outcome of the work in the WPPS did not fully respond to the Article VI:4 mandate in that it advanced a sector-specific solution which was against the letter and spirit of this provision.[16] What is more, the WPPS discussed at length whether the disciplines on domestic regulation with respect to accountancy services should constitute conditional or rather unconditional obligations.[17] In the end, Members decided to limit the application of the accountancy disciplines only to those Members that undertook specific commitments on accountancy services in their Schedules.[18] If anything, this is also against the Article VI:4 mandate, which does not make the application of disciplines to be established dependent on whether Members undertook specific commitments in a given sector.

Indeed, the fact that four other paragraphs in this Article are specifically declared to apply only in the case that commitments are undertaken strongly implies that, *a contrario*, the absence of any such limitation in Article VI:4 was deliberate. Therefore, the application of any disciplines developed under Article VI:4 should not be denied even in sectors where *no* commitment has been undertaken. The fact that Article VI:5, which, for want of anything better in the aftermath of the Uruguay Round, is considered as the *alter ego* of Article VI:4, provides for the temporary application of the Article VI:4 principles only in sectors in which Members undertook specific commitments should not confuse the reader. The main objective of Article VI:5 was to ensure that, pending the entry into force of the disciplines foreseen under Article VI:4, specific commitments should not be undermined by the absence of such disciplines.

Apparently, the source of this limitation with respect to the accountancy sector is to be identified in the *Decision on Professional Services*. Already the second recital of the Preamble of the Decision provides: 'Desiring to establish multilateral

16 Members, however, restated at the 1996 Singapore Ministerial Conference their commitment to pursuing the mandate foreseen under Art VI:4 in the CTS for all services and in the WPPS for the accountancy sector. *Singapore Ministerial Declaration* (n 14 above) para 17. The Art VI:4 work programme was discussed by the CTS after the Ministerial Meeting and Members agreed to conclude the work on accountancy within the WPPS before dealing with the development of horizontal disciplines.

17 WTO, CTS, 'Article VI:4 of the GATS: Disciplines on Domestic Regulation Applicable to All Services', S/C/W/96, 1 March 1999, para 15.

18 WTO, Trade in Services, 'Decision on Disciplines Relating to the Accountancy Sector', S/L/63, 15 October 1998, para 1.

disciplines with a view to ensuring that, *when specific commitments are undertaken,* such regulatory measures do not constitute unnecessary barriers to the supply of professional services'. Furthermore, paragraph 2 of the Decision provides: 'as a matter of priority, the Working Party shall make recommendations for the elaboration of multilateral disciplines in the accountancy sector, *so as to give operational effect to specific commitments*' (emphasis added).[19] In any case, the ultimate scope of application of the horizontal disciplines to be developed is still open and can be subject to future negotiations.[20]

What is more, *de lege lata*, the accountancy disciplines do not address measures that are subject to scheduling under Articles XVI and XVII GATS. Hence, a domestic regulatory measure that *de facto* denies market access or national treatment will not be automatically negated when the disciplines enter into force, but must rather be addressed through future negotiations. Accepting the opposite would be a 'liberalization vector', as it would have brought about generally applicable rules for behind-the-border issues.

With respect to the accountancy disciplines, they consist of eight sections: Objectives, General Provisions, and Transparency (five measures); Licensing Requirements (six measures); Licensing Procedures (five measures); Qualification Requirements (three measures); Qualification Procedures (three measures); and Technical Standards (two measures). These disciplines have no legal effect for the time being. They are expected to be integrated into the GATS at the end of the current negotiations, along with any other disciplines that may be developed before the end of the current round.

As noted, once the current round of negotiations comes to an end, the disciplines will be legally binding only for those Members that have undertaken specific commitments in the accountancy sector.[21] Meanwhile, all Members have agreed to abstain from introducing new measures in the accountancy sector which will contravene the established disciplines (standstill).[22]

The accountancy disciplines constitute a useful indication of the focus and possible outcome of the ongoing work on domestic regulations, first and foremost due to the fact that they contain, for the first time, a binding sector-specific necessity test, which, compared to Article VI:4, articulates further and tightens the principle of necessity. More generally, the accountancy disciplines are expected to assist Members as they consider the possible scope, content and structure of horizontally applicable disciplines on domestic regulation.

The accountancy disciplines include detailed provisions with respect to licensing requirements and procedures, qualification requirements and procedures,

[19] See, for example, Uruguay's intervention in WTO, WPDR, 'Report on the Meeting Held on 22 October 2002', S/WPDR/M/18, 3 December 2002, para 15.

[20] WTO, WPDR, 'Report on the Meeting Held on 20 March 2001', S/WPDR/M/10, 10 May 2001, p 8.

[21] WTO, Trade in Services (n 18 above) para 1.

[22] Ibid para 3.

and technical standards, and take fully into account the Article VI:4 criteria of objectivity, transparency, and necessity. More generally, they encompass various important elements deriving from the concept of due process. For instance, licensing authorities should base their decisions on pre-established, publicly available objective criteria, acknowledge receipt of applications, process applications in a reasonable timeframe, and provide reasons in the case of rejecting an application.

The accountancy disciplines make explicit that their scope does not cover measures that restrict access to the domestic market or limit the application of national treatment to foreign suppliers.[23] The latter measures, subject to scheduling, are addressed by Articles XVI and XVII, while Article VI:4 covers non-discriminatory regulatory measures that usually aim at ensuring the quality of services rendered to the public, but still may constitute unnecessary barriers to trade in services.[24] The right of adopting or maintaining domestic regulatory measures is specifically acknowledged, the task of GATS being the minimization, through the application of the necessity test, of their negative impact on services trade.

The disciplines do not tackle the substantive content of qualifications or standards in accountancy. Setting the level of qualifications or the content of technical standards of any kind to be required of suppliers of accountancy services essentially remains a prerogative for each Member or the delegated national authority.[25] Nevertheless, these disciplines do envisage, for the most part, the need to ensure procedural transparency in matters of licensing and qualification.

In addition, the disciplines endorse principles of good governance by requiring, for the first time in the services context, that Members: (a) explain upon request the specific objectives intended by their domestic regulatory measures in accountancy services (Section III, para 5); and (b) provide an opportunity for trading partners to comment on proposed new measures that significantly affect trade in accountancy services before their adoption, and to give consideration to such comments (Section III, para 6).

The first provision endorses the same principle of procedural transparency to the administration of domestic regulations as is reflected in Article 2.5 TBT[26] and

[23] WTO, CTS, 'International Regulatory Initiatives in Services', S/C/W/97, 1 March 1999, para 9.

[24] WTO, WPPS, 'Discussion of Matters Relating to Articles XVI and XVII of the GATS in Connection with the Disciplines on Domestic Regulation in the Accountancy Sector', Informal Note by the Chairman, Job No 6496, 25 November 1998, para 3 (Attachment 4 of Annex 2 of the *2001 Scheduling Guidelines*, p 25).

[25] With regard to qualification requirements, the disciplines indicate that they may include education, examinations, practical training, experience, and language skills (Section IV, para 20). This provision, however, can be deemed more as an indicative one than a provision which interferes with national regulatory autonomy.

[26] Art 2.5 TBT provides in part:

A Member preparing, adopting or applying a technical regulation which may have a significant effect on trade of other Members shall, upon the request of another Member, explain the justification for that technical regulation in terms of the provisions of paragraphs 2 to 4.

enhances the necessity test that domestic regulatory measures should not fail, by requiring that Members spell out the link that connects the regulatory measure and the policy objective pursued that is listed in paragraph 2 of the accountancy disciplines. Both the first and the second provision on the opportunity of prior comment could be relevant in the process of developing horizontally applicable disciplines, as they are crucial for the effective administration of any necessity test to be applied across services sectors.

The second principle is, however, weakened by the use of best-endeavour language and counterbalanced by the qualification that the right of prior comment concerns only domestic legislation that 'significantly' affects trade in accountancy services. In a more general sense, the formulation that the drafters of the text endorsed is, in some important instances, non-prescriptive; in addition some obligations use 'best-efforts' language (eg by using phrases such as: 'in principle', 'shall endeavour', 'wherever possible', 'shall consider whether', etc).

It may also be considered as a weakness of the created disciplines with respect to the qualification requirements (included in Section VI) the fact that the inclusion of a presumption against full requalification—or in support of a test of competence—proposed by India did not find broad support.[27] It is all the more so, because the requirement to requalify is considered as one of the most important barriers to the supply of services, which usually weighs more heavily on potential suppliers stemming from developing countries.

Additionally, it can be deemed a weakness the fact that Members did not agree to use internationally agreed standards on accountancy[28] as a benchmark for determining whether national standards are more burdensome than necessary to achieve a legitimate policy objective. Even if an agreement among Members to

Actually the obligation in the accountancy disciplines is even stronger than the one included in the TBT, since there is no requirement that the domestic regulatory measures have a 'significant effect on trade of other Members'.

[27] WTO, WPPS, 'Note on the Meeting Held on 4 December 1998', S/WPPS/M/24, 18 December 1998, paras 3–5; and WTO, WPPS, 'Note on the Meeting Held on 29 July 1998', S/WPPS/M/21, 29 September 1998, paras 5–6.

[28] The IASC (now International Accounting Standards Board—IASB) established the International Accounting Standards (IASs) in December 1998. Moreover, it continuously improves existing standards and issues new ones. The IFAC, on the other hand, produces the International Standards on Auditing (ISA) and the International Code of Ethics for Professional Accountants. It is also involved in the preparation of international education guidelines. Both institutions have also worked on the interpretation of the (for the most part, voluntary) standards that they issue. As to IOSCO, it endorsed a core set of IASs for financial statements used in all cross-border offerings and foreign listings. The application of this set of standards is now mandatory in the European Union. Also Trolliet and Hegarty (n 13 above) 157; also WTO, CTS (n 9 above) para 36, and WTO, WPPS, 'The Relevance of the Disciplines of the Agreements on Technical Barriers to Trade (TBT) and on Import Licensing Procedures to Article VI.4 of the General Agreement on Trade in Services', S/WPPS/W/9, 11 September 1996, paras 24–25. In addition, the International Organization for Standardization (ISO) deals with the development of standards in the services area. Importantly, about 30% of all ISO quality and environmental management standards relates to services. WTO, WPDR, 'Report on the Meeting Held on 22 June 2005', S/WPDR/M/30, 6 September 2005, para 170.

make mandatory the use of international standards would be impossible to reach, Members could still agree that such use would establish a rebuttable presumption that the measure at stake does not constitute an unnecessary obstacle to trade in services. Such a TBT-type approach could have strengthened the voices that demand betterment of regulatory approaches and methods in the accountancy sector. Instead, Members adopted a lighter obligation in paragraph 26 of the accountancy disciplines by agreeing that account must be taken of internationally recognized standards applied by a Member in order to determine whether that Member acted in conformity with the requirement that technical standards be prepared, adopted and applied only to fulfil legitimate objectives. Of course, the advantage of the approach that was finally adopted is that it allows the WTO judiciary to consider several factors when determining whether Members abide by the requirement that the preparation, adoption, and application of technical standards lead to the fulfilment of legitimate objectives.[29]

3. The necessity test as foreseen under paragraph 2 of the accountancy disciplines

The most important achievement of the disciplines is the creation of a binding necessity test in the form of an obligation. Paragraph 2 of the disciplines provides:

> Members shall ensure that measures not subject to scheduling under Articles XVI or XVII of the GATS, relating to licensing requirements and procedures, technical standards and qualification requirements and procedures are not prepared, adopted or applied *with a view to* or *with the effect of* creating *unnecessary* barriers to trade in accountancy services. For this purpose, Members shall ensure that such measures are *not more trade-restrictive than necessary to fulfil a legitimate objective.* Legitimate objectives are, inter alia, the protection of consumers (which includes all users of accounting services and the public generally), the quality of the service, professional competence, and the integrity of the profession. (footnote omitted; emphasis added)

As a result, Members are required to ensure that domestic regulatory measures relating to licensing, qualifications, and technical standards do not generate unnecessary barriers to trade in accountancy services and are not more trade-restrictive than necessary to fulfil a legitimate objective. The scope of this provision is expressly limited to those measures which escape the reach of Articles XVI and XVII GATS.

Importantly, paragraph 2 of the accountancy disciplines, while not requiring the scrutiny of all domestic regulations on accountancy services through the lens of necessity, gives the opportunity to Members to challenge other Members' requirements or standards that they believe are unduly trade-restrictive, either

[29] See also the discussion on Art VI:5 under Chapter III.C.7 above.

because they intended to or because they produce this effect when they are applied in practice. It stems that trade-restrictiveness should be neither the *intent* nor the *effect* of the regulatory measure at stake.[30] In addition, with reference to technical standards (Section VIII, para 25), the disciplines require that they be prepared, adopted, or applied only to fulfil legitimate objectives in accordance with paragraph 2 of the disciplines. Hence the accountancy disciplines apply a necessity test to technical standards as well.[31]

Furthermore, paragraph 2 contains an open-ended list of four legitimate objectives that a government may be willing to pursue when it intervenes in the domestic market. Thus, the measure at issue should be deemed necessary to fulfil a legitimate objective, *inter alia,* the protection of consumers, the quality of the service, professional competence, and/or the integrity of the profession.

Compared to paragraph 2, Article VI:4 does not provide a definition or a list of public policy objectives, save a mere reference to 'not more burdensome than necessary *to ensure the quality of the service*' pursuant to subparagraph (b) thereof (emphasis added). Thus, according to Article VI:4, the only objective that could be deemed legitimate and justify the burdensomeness of a licensing requirement or procedure, a qualification requirement or procedure, or a technical standard is the desire of the regulatory authorities to ensure the quality of the service supplied. Consequently, already due to the fact that it broadens the list of public policy objectives deemed legitimate, the necessity requirement of the accountancy disciplines is substantially stronger than the one contained in Article VI:4/5 GATS.

Of course, 'quality' could be interpreted in a broad manner to cover not only the delivery to the consumer, but also reliability, efficiency, comprehensiveness or issues associated with externalities and public goals.[32] After all, it is for each Member to decide whether it would like to maintain or seek a high(er) level of quality and perhaps adopt a broad interpretation of the term 'quality' to cover more than the intrinsic technical quality of the service in question.[33] The latter

[30] The necessity test in the accountancy disciplines was inspired by the necessity test laid down in Article 2.2 TBT. See Section D.3 below.

[31] See the Secretariat's intervention in WTO, WPDR, 'Report on the Meeting Held on 22 November 2004', S/WPDR/M/28, 25 January 2005, para 25.

[32] WTO, WPDR, 'Communication from Australia', S/WPDR/W/1, 19 July 1999, para 7; also DW Leebron, 'Regulatory Discrimination in Domestic United States Law: A Model for the GATS?' in A Mattoo and P Sauvé (eds), *Domestic Regulation and Service Trade Liberalization,* 2003, 52.

[33] In the EU context, for instance, it is clear that 'quality' can relate to a range of issues. Chapter V of the EU Services Directive sets a framework that aims to improve the level of quality of the services supplied within the EU. Notably service suppliers are encouraged to allow for certification and assessment of their activities by independent or accredited bodies, and to establish 'quality charters' or, if they already exist at a Community level, participate therein. Assessments by consumer associations, transparency on quality labels and regular testing are also part of this framework. In addition, subscription to professional liability insurance can be required by suppliers whose services present a 'direct and particular risk to the health or safety' of the consumer or a third party. In addition, the Directive foresees the development of voluntary standards at the European

statements, however, do not refute the former for at least one reason: in the case of paragraph 2 of the accountancy disciplines, Members have expressly agreed on at least four legitimate objectives that they consider as being legitimate when it comes to the supply of accountancy services. Thus any Panel or the Appellate Body, after the endorsement of the accountancy disciplines as legally binding at the end of the Doha Round, will be obliged to take these objectives into account and examine the link between the measure adopted and the objective that it seeks to pursue.[34]

Quite the opposite applies in the case of Article VI:4 (and, *a fortiori*, Article VI:5) as it stands now, since one cannot anticipate whether the interpretation that the WTO adjudicating bodies advance with respect to the notion 'quality of the service' will be broad or rather narrow. To date, the Appellate Body has advanced a rather rigid interpretation of the concept of necessity entailed in provisions providing for an *exception*, such as Article XX GATT.[35]

Quid with the outcome of a case where the Appellate Body would be called upon to deal with an appeal involving the 'necessary to ensure the quality of the service' concept envisaged in an *obligation* provision as it is Article VI:4? One should not attempt to ascertain such an outcome in advance, even though the Appellate Body has generally avoided encroaching on Members' regulatory autonomy to date. Under the current structure of Article VI:4, one could legitimately argue that licensing and qualification requirements and procedures, or technical standards that are not related *stricto sensu* to the quality of the service would be outlawed when examined against the stipulations of Article VI[36] and thus the respondent would have recourse to the exceptions of Article XIV, where, however, the list of legitimate objectives is exhaustive.

Therefore, a pragmatist reader would underscore that even a narrow interpretation of the term 'quality of the service' and of the measures adopted thereunder would not have significant ramifications, since the responding Member will always have recourse to Article XIV GATS, the 'ultimate resort'. Under this

level which would facilitate compatibility between services supplied in different Member States, information to the consumer, and the quality of service provision. Directive (EC) 2006/123 on services in the internal market [2006] OJ L376/36, Chapter V, notably Arts 24 and 26.

34 One could draw a parallel here with Arts 2.5 and 2.2 TBT to demonstrate the importance of the explicit reference to specific public policy objectives. In TBT, Art 2.2 provides that technical regulations should not be more trade-restrictive than necessary to fulfil a legitimate objective. It goes on by enumerating in an *indicative* list four legitimate objectives, ie national security, prevention of deceptive practices, protection of human health or safety, animal or plant life or health, and the environment. In Art 2.5, however, the rebuttable presumption covers *only* the technical regulations which are prepared, adopted or applied for one of the legitimate objectives *explicitly* mentioned in Art 2.2. *A contrario*, then, all the other possible legitimate objectives implied in Art 2.2 through the use of the phrase '*inter alia*', but not explicitly mentioned, are not protected by the presumption that they do not create an unnecessary obstacle to trade.

35 Appellate Body Report, *Korea—Various Measures on Beef*, para 161.

36 Also R Adlung, 'Public Services and the GATS', WTO Staff Working Paper ERSD-2005-03, July 2005, 23.

scenario, a domestic measure pursuing a regulatory goal set out by a benevolent government would plausibly be justified without considerable difficulties.

So, too much ado about nothing? Not really. It does make a difference and has important legal implications whether the issue will have been solved already under Article VI or rather under Article XIV GATS. Under the requirements and conditions of Article VI, it would be incumbent on the plaintiff to bear the burden of proving the claimed violation. In contrast, if a narrow definition of quality is advanced to outlaw all regulatory measures relating to qualifications, licensing, or technical standards that do not aim directly at ensuring the quality of the service at stake, the burden of proof would shift to the *respondent* to justify the measure at issue under the broader criteria of Article XIV. Case-law under Article XX GATT, which is the counterpart of Article XIV GATS when it comes to trade in goods, demonstrates that complying with the requirements of this provision is not an easy task.

Thus, it was correctly emphasized that Article VI:4(b) is in urgent need of revision to clarify that the concept of quality does not only refer to the reliability of the service from the perspective of an individual consumer, but that it also entails regulations aiming to achieve the full range of social objectives, such as safety, network integrity, the provision of service to underserved regions, affordability of the service at issue, etc.[37]

Of course, absent any attempt by Members to define the quality of a service, one could delve into the other side of the coin. In this regard, the concept of ensuring quality can arguably be interpreted very narrowly by the WTO adjudicating bodies to consider as burdensome and hence outlaw any domestic regulatory measure that does not aim at ensuring the quality of a service supply. Indeed, what would be the interpretation of a measure that does not directly relate to ensuring the quality of a service? Furthermore, how close or strong should the relationship be between the measure taken and the betterment of the quality in providing a service? One cannot be sure of the outcome. Hence, this clause entailed in Article VI:4(b) can be too precarious for domestic regulators in that it can limit the instruments that a government has at its disposal to achieve a regulatory objective as well as the types of regulatory objectives that are allowed to be sought and consequently needs to be a focal point of the negotiations in progress.[38]

[37] G Feketekuty, 'Regulatory Reform and Trade Liberalization in Services' in P Sauvé and RM Stern (eds), *GATS 2000: New Directions in Service Trade Liberalization,* 2000, 237. For a discussion on this issue with respect to health services, see D Luff, 'Regulation of Health Services and International Trade Law' in A Mattoo and P Sauvé (eds), *Domestic Regulation and Services Trade Liberalization*, 2003, 204–206.

[38] cf K Nicolaidis and JP Trachtman, 'From Policed Regulation to Managed Recognition in GATS' in P Sauvé and RM Stern (eds), *GATS 2000: New Directions in Services Trade Liberalization*, 2000, 260.

In a nutshell, the adoption of the *Disciplines on Domestic Regulation in the Accountancy Sector* was a success in some respects (eg the adoption of a binding necessity test) and a failure in others (eg the absence of a presumption for a test of competence; the limited elaboration on existing GATS provisions such as Article III on transparency; and the use of weaker language for specific rules than the language used for the necessity test). But this is what Members could agree to at that point in time and hence these disciplines reflect a balanced political compromise.[39]

Besides, Members' reluctance to yield to a process that would result in binding commitments was all the more evident due to the fact that their preference has predominantly been for voluntary and unilateral changes in the accountancy sector. To be sure, one should wait for the disciplines to become legally binding at the end of the ongoing negotiations in order to evaluate their impact on domestic regulations and regulatory reform with regard to the accountancy sector. It is certain, however, that the accountancy disciplines, and notably the necessity test, will influence the work currently in progress on the feasibility of the development of horizontally applicable disciplines under the auspices of the WPDR[40] and will serve as a useful parameter in this regard.

C. The establishment of the WPDR

1. The WPDR mandate

In the aftermath of the adoption of the accountancy disciplines by the CTS, the Council had to face again the problem of reconciling the two mandates under Article VI:4 that seemed to overlap: the first, contained in Article VI:4 itself, urged the Council to develop disciplines on domestic regulation in *all* services sectors; the second, contained in the *Decision on Professional Services*, called upon the WPPS to fulfil the same task with respect to professional services, but to give priority to the accountancy sector.[41]

The CTS decided to establish a new subsidiary body that would be responsible for accomplishing the Article VI:4 mandate, including the remains of the WPPS mandate.[42] Moreover, Members appeared to incline towards giving priority to the development of horizontal disciplines which would apply to all service sectors without prejudice to the still remaining option of developing sector-specific

[39] See, for instance, WTO, WPPS (n 27 above) paras 17–19; also Trolliet and Hegarty (n 13 above) 152, 159.

[40] cf WPDR, 'Chairman's Note', 14 September 2001, JOB(01)/130, para 14.

[41] WTO, CTS, 'Report of the Meeting Held on 26 April 1999', S/C/M/35, 17 May 1999, para 19.

[42] These remains also entailed the development of general disciplines for professional services. See WTO, Trade in Services, 'Decision on Domestic Regulation', S/L/70, 28 April 1999, para 2.

disciplines.[43] Accordingly, the CTS adopted the *Decision on Domestic Regulation* that established the WPDR.[44]

The WPDR was urged to submit its final recommendations to the CTS at the conclusion of the current round of services negotiations at the latest. After the establishment of the *Negotiating Guidelines and Procedures* by the Special Session of the CTS,[45] this time-limit was shortened, as Members were requested to complete the negotiations under Article VI:4 *prior* to the conclusion of negotiations on specific commitments (which, in turn, should obviously precede the end of the negotiations round).

The task of the WPDR has been the development of horizontal disciplines applicable to all service sectors, while preserving the option of developing further disciplines applicable to specific sectors or clusters of sectors,[46] including the development of general disciplines for professional services as required by paragraph 2 of the *Decision on Disciplines Relating to the Accountancy Sector*.[47] The latter was a task that the WPPS did not manage to carry out. The language used in the *Decision on Domestic Regulation* confirms that the horizontally applicable measures foreseen under Article VI:4 are meant to 'provide Members with a framework which would ensure, amongst other things, that domestic regulations are based on objective and transparent criteria and are not more burdensome than necessary to ensure the quality on the service'.[48] The WPDR reports annually to the CTS as to the progress on accomplishing its mandate.

Hence, the WPDR is called upon to focus primarily on the development of generally applicable disciplines to ensure that measures relating to licensing, qualifications, and technical standards do not unnecessarily hamper trade in services. The Council Decision on the establishment of the WPDR mandates further that the activities of the previous WPPS be incorporated into those of the WPDR.

[43] Also WTO, WPPS, 'Note on the Meeting Held on 9 February 1999', S/WPPS/M/25, 5 March 1999, para 2.

[44] WTO, Trade in Services (n 42 above).

[45] WTO, 'Guidelines and Procedures for the Negotiations on Trade in Services', S/L/93, 29 March 2001, para 7.

[46] WTO, Trade in Services (n 42 above) paras 2–3. On the option of negotiating disciplines on clusters of interrelated sectors, see WTO, CTS (Special Session), 'The Cluster Approach', Communication from the European Communities and their Member States, S/CSS/W/3, 22 May 2000.

[47] WTO, Trade in Services (n 42 above) para 2. Paragraph 2 of the *Decision on Disciplines Relating to the Accountancy Sector* provides in part: '... [T]he Working Party shall aim to develop general disciplines for professional services, while retaining the possibility to develop or *revise sectoral disciplines, including accountancy*' (emphasis added). Arguably, then, the WPDR would have the authority not only to revise the accountancy disciplines before the end of the current negotiations round (in order to avoid any problems of inconsistency between the accountancy disciplines and the horizontally applicable disciplines on domestic regulation), but also to decide that the accountancy disciplines apply to *all* Members rather than only to Members that undertook specific commitments in the accountancy sector. WTO, Trade in Services (n 18 above) para 2; see also WTO, CTS (Special Session), 'Report of the Meeting Held on 26 May 2000', S/CSS/M/3, 26 June 2000, para 159.

[48] WPDR, 'Chairman's Note', JOB(01)/59, 27 April 2001, para 7.

Consequently, the work of WPDR encompasses the continuing development of disciplines for professional services.

As a general preliminary remark, one would argue that the progress of the work within the WPDR has been slower than anticipated.[49] This is due to the conscious decision by a few Members to put services low in their negotiating agenda with respect to the priorities that they have for this round of negotiations (it has never been a secret that without substantive progress in agriculture, this round may never conclude)[50] or use the services liberalization as a negotiating chip (eg concessions in services and notably mode 3 commitments in return for significant concessions in agriculture). Furthermore, the sensitivities associated with the issue of disciplining domestic regulations, such as the implications for the regulatory autonomy; the possibility of developing (and, thus, having to abide by) regulatory disciplines even in sectors where no specific commitments were made; the complexity of the issues related to federal/sub-federal competence and delegated authorities; or even the lack of general capacity to participate actively in the WPDR discussions are also to blame for the lack of progress. Even when there is no problem of technical capacity to participate actively in the negotiations, there is a lack of active involvement of domestic regulators in the WPDR negotiations. This growing disconnection between the negotiating cycle and the cycle that entails regulators and service suppliers may seriously damage the quality of any disciplines to be developed, or, even worse, render such disciplines inapplicable and hence useless.

2. Organization of the work within the WPDR relative to the development of horizontal versus sectoral disciplines

As to the organization of their work programme, Members decided to consult on a voluntary basis with their domestic professional associations concerning the potential applicability of the accountancy disciplines to their professions, as the latter are considered by many Members to be an excellent starting point at least for the creation of new, general disciplines covering professional services. At the same time, the Secretariat was assigned the remit to consult with relevant international professional services organizations, open to the entirety of the WTO Membership, to be identified by Members[51] regarding the suitability of the accountancy disciplines for other professions.

[49] In Hong Kong, however, Members acknowledged that domestic regulation was the only area of the still open regulatory fronts in the GATS (the others being subsidies, safeguards, and government procurement) where the adoption of a text appeared the most likely. See *Hong Kong Ministerial Declaration*, adopted on 18 December 2005, WT/MIN(05)/DEC, para 5.

[50] This has also been the case during the Uruguay Round. See Reyna (n 5 above) 2420.

[51] WTO, WPDR, 'Report on the Meeting Held on 14 July 1999', S/WPDR/M/2, 2 September 1999, paras 8–9.

While paradoxical at first sight, this approach of proceeding simultaneously with the remits of developing horizontally applicable disciplines and sector-specific disciplines for professional services demonstrates the interdependence of these two tasks. Indeed, Members appear to endorse the view that the work on horizontal disciplines and the work on sectoral disciplines are reinforcing and complementary rather than mutually exclusive.[52]

To be sure, negotiations, discussions, and contributions in one area can inform and facilitate the respective negotiations, discussions, and contributions in the other area. This is also in line with the WPDR mandate contained in the *Decision on Domestic Regulation*. Indeed, the Council Decision could have established two separate work programmes; the fact that it did not should mean something. Members preferred that the development of sector-specific disciplines with respect to professional services be part of the more general work on the development of horizontal disciplines pursuant to Article VI:4. This would allow a cross-fertilization to occur.

Accordingly, the discussions within the WPDR have adopted the following structure with respect to the development of regulatory disciplines under Article VI:4: the first part would entail a discussion of concepts relating to the development of horizontal disciplines for all service sectors, while the second would be dedicated to discussions on the development of general disciplines for professional services. It is true that the latter, while not ruled out, has been largely neglected for the sake of the development of horizontally applicable disciplines on domestic regulation.

The preference of giving priority to the development of horizontal disciplines for the management of regulatory practices, while being part of the deal that Members reached after the conclusion of the draft accountancy disciplines, does make sense from a trade-policy perspective. In Mattoo's words, 'even though services sectors differ greatly, the underlying economic and social reasons for regulatory intervention do not'.[53] As noted in the previous chapters, these reasons identified horizontally, ie across sectors, are usually associated with market power, information asymmetries, externalities, or social distributive objectives motivated by equity considerations. They constitute the underpinnings of any horizontally applicable disciplines.

A generic approach can be preferable *vis-à-vis* a sectoral one for several reasons: it can achieve a broad impact and hence allows economizing on negotiating effort (as it would also automatically cover new services or new modes of supply) and reduces negotiation and other transaction costs as well as the risk of regulatory capture and undue influence by narrow sectoral interest groups. Importantly, a

[52] WTO, WPDR, 'Report of the Meeting Held on 11 May 2001', S/WPDR/M/11, 7 June 2001, para 6.

[53] A Mattoo, 'Developing Countries in the New Round of the GATS Negotiations: Towards a Pro-Active Role' in B Hoekman and W Martin (eds), *Developing Countries and the WTO: A Pro-active Agenda*, 2001, 88.

horizontal approach can further ensure consistency of process across all service sectors and improve efficiency as it is less apt to risks of over-regulating sectors where technological innovations expand rapidly.[54] It can also stimulate reform of all services sectors rather than only the ones put in the political agenda and aids avoiding mercantilist policy linkages.

Sectoral disciplines on the other hand can have important positive effects in the short term because of their specificity. Disciplines established on a sector-by-sector basis provide higher predictability, both *ex ante* and *ex post*, as the language used is also less ambiguous than the language used in the creation of general disciplines. They are also less costly to comply with. Sectoral disciplines usually involve fine-tuned instruments which are commensurate with any given sectoral specificities. As a general rule, sectoral disciplines may be preferable in sectors where extensive regulatory intervention by national governments is present, as it is the case in financial services.

In addition, sectoral disciplines are perhaps easier to achieve, since individual, sometimes powerful domestic suppliers (like it was in the case with the United States' financial industry) may hasten governments to collaborate with other Members with a view to developing powerful disciplines sooner rather than later. This may not necessarily be the case with horizontal disciplines that aim to create rules applicable across sectors, as in the latter case the interests of a given individual service industry are harder to identify. Then, this service industry may prefer to free-ride, or worse, not be interested at all, rather than lobby for the expeditious development of horizontal disciplines at a multilateral level that will affect it anyway only marginally. In the case of long-lasting negotiations, of course, the transaction costs multiply.

Clearly, Members have been correct to regard their twofold task of developing horizontal and sector-specific disciplines as rather reinforcing and complementary. There are, for instance, principles that are horizontally applicable such as those about the value of an independent regulator or the importance of pro-competitive regulation accompanied by competitive safeguards (eg ensure access to essential facilities at cost-based rates) already endorsed in the Reference Paper on Basic Telecommunications.[55] Such principles could with no trouble be applied to all network services or, more generally, services that have 'natural monopoly' characteristics, as the language used in the Reference Paper is indistinct enough to cover more sectors. Furthermore, when developing a horizontally applicable framework negotiators could identify the features of a given regulatory system that would need to be negotiated sectorally. In other sectors, however, the nature

[54] WTO, WPDR, 'Report on the Meeting Held on 2 October 2000', S/WPDR/M/8, 17 November 2000, para 4; also A Sidorenko and C Findlay, 'Issues in Domestic Regulations of Services: Horizontal versus Sectoral Disciplines', Asia Pacific School of Economics and Management—The Australian National University, February 2002.

[55] M Matsushita, TJ Schoenbaum, and PC Mavroidis, *The World Trade Organization: Law, Practice and Policy*, 2nd edition, 2006, 680ff.

of the production process or the technology involved would call for negotiations on a sectoral basis to ensure appropriate regulatory structures.

A propos of the development of horizontal regulatory disciplines which would apply to all sectors, Members organized their discussions in accordance with an informal *Checklist of Issues*[56] that the Secretariat prepared at the request of the Membership, containing the main elements and issues under discussion within the WPDR,[57] ie necessity, transparency, equivalence, and international standards. These policy areas have been identified by the Secretariat in a Note.[58] In the Secretariat's view, the development of disciplines with respect to domestic regulation in services in these four areas was the most likely to occur.

In addition, the *Checklist* entailed a list of five general issues that the WPDR had to take into consideration: Examples of actual regulatory issues; the linkage between transparency and necessity; the relationship between Article VI:4 and Articles XVI/XVII; the scope of Article VI:4; and the possible administrative burden of the regulatory disciplines under development. In the list of general issues was also added the issue of the potential need to develop a definition of regulations and the issue of whether the prospective disciplines should be applicable at a federal *vs* sub-federal level.

While Members have held extensive discussions on all the aforementioned issues, they requested the Secretariat to list examples of the types of regulatory measures that would be addressed by the future disciplines under Article VI:4.[59] In preparing the requested document the Secretariat would benefit from two sources of information, that is, contributions by Members and WPPS materials on accountancy (mainly the accountancy questionnaires and the previous drafts of the accountancy disciplines). The Secretariat was further instructed to pinpoint measures which were covered neither by the accountancy disciplines nor by Articles XVI/XVII measures.

The Secretariat consequently presented the first version of its informal paper, *Examples of Measures to be Addressed by Disciplines under GATS Article VI:4*

[56] WPDR, 'Checklist of Issues for WPDR', Informal Note by the Secretariat, JOB(01)/92 (5067/Rev.1), 19 June 2001. Initially the *Checklist* circulated as JOB No. 5067, dated 17 August 2000, and was subsequently revised to include issues related to equivalence and international standards. Members requested that an informal summary of the discussions relative to the *Checklist* be added as an Annex to the minutes of each WPDR meeting. WTO, WPDR (n 54 above) para 2 and Annex. In a formal meeting, Members decided to separate the summary of the discussions from the Minutes of the formal meetings. WTO, WPDR, 'Report on the Meeting Held on 29 November 2001', S/WPDR/M/14, 29 January 2002, paras 15ff. During the subsequent meeting, Members agreed to merge into one document the *Checklist* and the summary of discussions thereon. WTO, WPDR, 'Report on the Meeting Held on 12 March 2002', S/WPDR/M/15, 10 April 2002, paras 28–29.

[57] WTO, WPDR, 'Report on the Meeting Held on 25 May 2000', S/WPDR/M/6, 29 June 2000, para 9; and WTO, WPDR, 'Report on the Meeting Held on 12 July 2000', S/WPDR/M/7, 19 September 2000, paras 13–15.

[58] WTO, CTS (n 17 above) para 16.

[59] WTO, WPDR, 'Report on the Meeting Held on 29 November 2000', S/WPDR/M/9, 12 March 2001, paras 4ff.

(the *Examples* paper).[60] This phase of the WPDR discussions was fairly educational[61] in that it has allowed Members to make significant progress towards better understanding the various concepts interwoven with the development of regulatory disciplines under Article VI:4 as well as the options that could be available for the consideration of any disciplines that might be required to address such regulatory issues.

Moving from the abstract to the concrete, ie focusing more on the regulatory barriers and issues that service suppliers actually face in their attempts to access a market, the WPDR dealt with the question of whether Article VI:4 was the most appropriate means for dealing with certain regulatory measures. Following the WPDR Chairman's suggestions, Members decided to proceed with an examination of concrete regulatory measures as reflected in the *Examples* paper prepared by the Secretariat based on contributions by Members in order to clarify which of those measures could fall within the scope of Article VI:4 as opposed to other GATS provisions, such as Articles XVI and XVII. This examination of the *Examples* paper has continued in tandem with the discussion of the proposals that Members have submitted henceforth.

In this respect, Members would ask the following questions when considering each measure individually:[62] (a) whether the measure is already covered by Articles XVI and/or XVII; (b) if not, whether it is addressed by any other GATS provisions (eg Articles II, III, VIII, IX); (c) if not, whether it falls within the scope of Article VI, in particular VI:4 (licensing requirements and procedures, qualification requirements and procedures, and technical standards); (d) if so, whether it is adequately addressed by the relevant provisions of the accountancy disciplines, or modifications are required.

Whereas the *Checklist of Issues* and the *Examples* paper constitute the resource documents with respect to the development of horizontal disciplines, the process of developing general disciplines for professional services has benefited from two sources. The first source entailed the voluntary consultations that Members conducted with their domestic professional services associations with respect to the potential applicability of the accountancy disciplines to other professions. In the formal WPDR meeting of 2 October 2000, Members asked the Secretariat to come back with a compilation of Member responses up to that date.[63] On 29 November 2000 the Secretariat introduced its *Synthesis* paper which has been subsequently revised to reflect additional reports submitted by Members with respect to their domestic consultations with professional services associations.[64]

[60] WTO, WPDR (n 52 above) para 33. The *Examples* paper circulated as JOB(01)/62, dated 10 May 2001. A more representative paper of examples of regulatory measures is to be found in the JOB(02)/20/Rev.10, dated 31 January 2005.

[61] WTO, WPDR, 'Report on the Meeting Held on 12 March 2002' (n 56 above) para 27.

[62] WTO, WPDR (n 19 above) para 8.

[63] WTO, WPDR (n 54 above) paras 10 and 12.

[64] WPDR, 'Synthesis of Results to Date of the Domestic Consultations in Professional Services', Informal Note by the Secretariat, Job No. 7667, 29 November 2000. A recent version of this document is to be found in JOB(02)/204/Rev.1, dated 21 February 2003.

While the idea of applying the accountancy disciplines to other professional services found considerable support, some professions were of the view that additional disciplines were needed to accommodate their requirements.[65] The up-to-date responsiveness of Members with respect to the conclusion of consultations with domestic professional services associations has not met the eye, to say the least. It is unclear whether this is happening because Members undervalue this procedure or, rather, because there is a lack of technical capacity that does not allow the majority of Members to conclude such consultations.

To be sure, the latter cannot justify the fact that less than 20 Members to date have reported on their consultations with domestic professional associations. In addition, with such a low rate of Members' responses, any attempt to draw some conclusions relating to the willingness of domestic professional services associations to accept the accountancy disciplines as applicable to their professions would be precipitate. In any case, Members agreed to initiate an examination of the *Synthesis* paper.[66] In the meantime, Members could always submit for discussion by the WPDR the results of the domestic consultations that they have held.

The second source assisting the progress of the work on the development of general disciplines for professional services has been the Secretariat's paper on the results of the consultations with international professional services organizations.[67] As already mentioned, the WPDR, during its meeting of 14 July 1999, requested the Secretariat to consult with relevant international professional services organizations with respect to the suitability of the accountancy disciplines for other professions. These organizations, however, had to be designated by Members. Members finally agreed, during the meeting on 22 October 2002 (that is three years later), on Secretariat consultations with 22 international professional services organizations, as selected by Members.[68] To facilitate the ongoing discussions in the WPDR, the Secretariat was asked to regularly summarize the information that it received through those consultations.[69]

Recently, Members have decided to organize the WPDR work on a thematic basis rather than on a proposal-by-proposal basis that had been the working method until then. The issues selected for being at the heart of the WPDR discussions are drawn from previous Members' negotiating proposals, including

[65] WTO, WPDR (n 54 above) para 12.

[66] WTO, WPDR, 'Report on the Meeting Held on 4 and 7 June 2002', S/WPDR/M/16, 8 July 2002, para 77.

[67] WPDR, 'Results of Secretariat Consultations with International Professional Services Associations', Informal Note by the Secretariat, JOB(03)/126, 25 June 2003.

[68] WTO, 'Report of the Working Party on Domestic Regulation to the Council for Trade in Services (2002)', S/WPDR/4, 6 December 2002, para 5. The list of the organizations is to be found in JOB(01)/98, dated 28 June 2001. Until the sixth revision of the Secretariat's Note (JOB(03)/126/Rev.6, dated 15 September 2005) there were 17 (out of 22) organizations that provided the Secretariat with answers.

[69] WTO, WPDR, 'Report on the Meeting Held on 15 May 2003', S/WPDR/M/21/Rev.1, 25 June 2003, para 83.

the five categories of measures identified in the *chapeau* of Article VI:4 as well as other issues such as transparency, objectives, scope, application, and definitions.

3. The scope of Article VI:4 as defined within the WPDR

Regarding the scope of Article VI:4 GATS and the necessity test to be developed, Members have not yet reached a consensus as to whether the horizontal disciplines, when finalized, would be applicable only to sectors where specific commitments have been undertaken or rather they would be conditional upon the existence of specific commitments. The *Decision on Domestic Regulation* that delineates the mandate of the WPDR remains silent on this issue,[70] as it does not prejudice in any way the outcome of the discussion relating to the applicability of the disciplines to be developed.[71] *A priori*, nothing in Article VI:4 advocates that its disciplines were to be limited to cover only services on which specific commitments are scheduled.

Taking a close look at the Members' statements before the WPDR, it becomes apparent that the scope of application is an issue for negotiations, and that there are several options on the table to choose from, including horizontal application, application only where specific commitments were undertaken (both of these options could find expression in the form of an Annex on domestic regulation), or application in the form of a reference paper that would allow Members to undertake additional commitments pursuant to Article XVIII GATS.

The implications of choosing the option of an Annex over a reference paper and vice versa are paramount: an Annex would require consensus and probably an amendment of the GATS, whereas a reference paper would not. A reference paper, on the other hand, would not ensure the uniform application that an Annex can ensure after having been adopted. An option similar to a reference paper would be to allow those Members that would like to make commitments with respect to horizontal disciplines to undertake such commitments in the form of additional commitments under Article XVIII GATS.[72] The latter option would hinge on the efficiency of the request–offer negotiating method.

Another interesting option that has been advanced by the Chairman in a Note submitted to the WPDR[73] would allow each Member to decide whether any horizontal disciplines would also apply to those sectors where specific commitments have not been made and this decision could be made clear in the horizontal sector of each Member's Schedule. While it is clear from the above that the scope of application of a prospective horizontal necessity test is an issue for negotiations,

70 WTO, Trade in Services (n 42 above) para 2.

71 Also WTO, CTS (n 41 above) para 20.

72 Several examples of commitments of this type can be found in WTO, Committee on Specific Commitments, 'Additional Commitments under Article XVIII of the GATS', S/CSC/W/34, 16 July 2002, p 23.

73 WPDR, 'Chairman's Note', JOB(01)/159, 22 November 2001, para 6.

one could already extrapolate a propensity towards an application of such disciplines only under the prerequisite that specific commitments have been undertaken in the sector in question.[74]

As noted earlier in the discussion on the accountancy disciplines, the fact that paragraph 2 and paragraph 4 of Article VI are the only unqualified paragraphs in Article VI, ie their application is not made dependent on whether a Member scheduled specific commitments, is not fortuitous and this omission of a reference to specific commitments should have some meaning in accordance with the *expressio unius est exclusio alterius* principle of interpretation. Put differently, if the GATS founding fathers wanted to put a qualification on the application of Article VI:4, they would have done so, as they did in four out of the six paragraphs of Article VI. Since Article VI belongs to Part II of the GATS, which is entitled 'General Obligations and Disciplines', any obligation should be considered to apply in all sectors regardless of specific commitments undertaken, *unless* Members have specified otherwise. And this occurred only with respect to paragraphs 1, 3, 5, and 6 of Article VI GATS.

It has been argued during the WPDR discussions that Article VI:1 speaks for the application of the disciplines only to measures where specific commitments have been made.[75] Nevertheless, this argument does not take into account that Article VI:1 has a broader reach than Article VI:4, as the former refers to all measures of general application affecting trade in services, while the latter covers only measures with respect to licensing, qualifications, and technical standards. Hence, with respect to paragraph 1 it is logical to assume that Members were not really fond of the idea of applying the possible far-reaching criteria of reasonableness, objectivity, and impartiality to *all* measures of general application with an effect on trade in services regardless of the scheduling of commitments, but rather preferred to narrow down this obligation only with regard to their commitments already undertaken. This argument is not sustainable under paragraph 4 whose scope is fairly specific.

In addition, paragraph 1 of Article VI is of limited ambit in that it refers to the *administration* of the measures of general application and *not* the measures *themselves*. What is more, paragraph 1 is, for the most part, a provision aiming to enhance procedural transparency. On the other hand, the disciplines to be developed under paragraph 4 will deal with the *preparation*, *adoption*, and *application* of measures relating to licensing requirements and procedures, qualification requirements and procedures, and technical standards. It is only for those

[74] WTO, CTS (Special Session), 'Report of the Meeting Held on 3–6 December 2001', S/CSS/M/13, 26 February 2002, para 93; also WTO, WPDR, 'Report on the Meeting Held on 4 December 2002', S/WPDR/M/19, 29 January 2003, para 15. The most recent draft submitted by the WPDR Chairman confirms this tendency. WPDR, 'Disciplines on Domestic Regulation Pursuant to GATS Article VI:4', Informal Note by the Chairman, Room Document, 18 April 2007, para 10.

[75] WTO, WPDR, 'Report on the Meeting Held on 29 November 2001' (n 56 above) para 14.

measures that Members should ensure that they do not constitute *unnecessary* barriers to trade in services. It follows that, while paragraph 1 informs the other paragraphs of Article VI,[76] it cannot be considered as a guide with respect to the issue of whether the prospective disciplines would be conditional on specific commitments or not. In fact, it is clear that Article VI:1 is, at best, irrelevant for deciding on this issue.

Furthermore, it seems awkward to associate the application of Article VI:4 with the application of Articles XVI and XVII in a particular sector. This seems to contravene the structure and the spirit of the GATS. Theoretically, domestic regulations are created and applied regardless of market access considerations. To be sure, domestic regulations are enforced to protect legitimate policy objectives and ensure policies are in line with good governance and the public interest. Then Article VI:4, on the one hand, and Articles XVI and XVII are designed to deal with different aspects of measures with respect to trade in services and consequently it would not be appropriate to hinge Article VI:4 disciplines on commitments scheduled in accordance with Part III of the GATS. The application of any horizontal disciplines regardless of the scheduling of specific commitments would help to streamline disguised market access restrictions entrenched in domestic regulations.[77]

On the other hand, it has correctly been argued that in certain cases, the absence of specific commitments liberalizing trade in services can render ineffective and without any practical value any regulatory disciplines developed under Article VI:4. For that reason, the argument goes, such horizontal disciplines should be made conditional upon the existence of specific commitments.[78]

The *chapeau* of Article VI:4 clarifies that it applies to measures *taken by Members*. This should be understood to cover measures adopted by regional or local governments, ie all levels of government, as well as non-governmental bodies with delegated powers (notably professional associations benefiting from the right to be self-regulated), as foreseen under Article I:3(a) GATS.[79] In this case, each Member is expected to take any reasonable measures that are available in order to ensure that local governments and authorities and non-governmental bodies do abide by this Member's WTO obligations and commitments.[80] While

[76] Also Chapter III.C.2 above.

[77] cf WTO, WPDR, 'Report on the Meeting Held on 29 November 2001' (n 56 above) paras 12ff.

[78] P Low and A Mattoo, 'Is There a Better Way? Alternative Approaches to Liberalization Under the GATS' in P Sauvé and RM Stern (eds), *GATS 2000: New Directions in Services Trade Liberalization,* 2000, 455–456.

[79] cf WTO, WPDR (n 28 above) para 147; also J Wouters and D Coppens, 'Domestic Regulation within the Framework of GATS', Working Paper No. 93, Institute for International Law, KU Leuven, 2006, 37.

[80] Article I:3 GATS, then, would cover those measures taken at the local level or by a non-governmental body which the federal government cannot control because they fall outside its jurisdiction under the constitutional distribution of powers. Several GATT Panels reached this conclusion when interpreting Art I:3 counterpart under GATT, that is, Art XXIV:12 GATT.

internal distribution of competences is to be respected by the WTO judiciary, Members with federal structure are obliged to secure the implementation of the WTO provisions, which are applicable to all levels of government. This would imply that Members that fall under this category would be treated more favourably than unitary Members with respect to possible problems of implementation of WTO obligations at a sub-federal level. It follows that Article I:3 GATS (just as Article XXIV:12 GATT) foresees an exception to the general principle of international law that a party to a treaty may not invoke the provisions of its internal law, including its constitutional law, as justification for the failure to perform the treaty (Article 27 of the *Vienna Convention*).[81] An exception to the above-mentioned principle is also to be found in Article VI:2(b) GATS. For the sake of clarity, however, it bears mention that Article I:3 GATS, just like Article XXIV:12 GATT, cannot justify a derogation from the WTO substantive obligations.[82]

Regarding the scope of Article VI:4, the WPDR reflected on the question of whether Article VI:4 extends beyond the five items listed in this provision, ie qualification requirements and procedures, technical standards, and licensing requirements and procedures.[83] Given the language of Article VI:4, as well as the WPDR mandate, the statements of most Members that the disciplines to be developed should not extend beyond these five categories of measures seem to be appropriate, as there is no reference indicating an illustrative list of categories of regulatory measures.[84] To be sure, the coverage of these five categories of measures can be vast, as it also covers measures *relating to* qualifications, licensing, and technical standards.[85] Again, a considerable range of regulatory measures fall outside the scope of measures which purport to be addressed by Article VI:4, such as the question of the independence of the regulatory authority, universal service provisions, and access to networks as well as to essential facilities.[86]

In addition, it appears that most Members feel comfortable with the definitions of these sub-categories of measures provided by the WTO Secretariat in a Background Note,[87] keeping open the possibility of reviewing these definitions if deemed necessary. The Secretariat defined the aforementioned categories of measures in the following way:[88]

See unadopted GATT Panel Report, *Canada—Gold Coins*, para 56; and GATT Panel Report, *US—Malt Beverages*, para 5.79.

81 Ibid.

82 cf Panel Report, *EC—Selected Customs Matters*, para 7.145.

83 Also WTO, WPDR (n 32 above) para 2, where Australia answers the question in the affirmative.

84 WPDR (n 40 above) para 9.

85 WTO, WPDR, 'Report on the Meeting Held on 29 November 2001' (n 56 above) para 8.

86 Such issues can be tackled through a reference paper, as the example of the Reference Paper on Basic Telecommunications demonstrates.

87 WTO, WPPS (n 28 above) para 4.

88 These definitions were formulated by the Secretariat with respect to professional services and, thus, are not necessarily applicable to all sectors. For an alternative set of definitions, see WTO, WPDR, 'Definitions of Qualification Requirements, Qualification Procedures, Licensing

(i) *Qualification requirements:* these comprise substantive requirements relating to the competence to supply a service that a service supplier (natural person) is warranted to fulfil in order to obtain certification or authorization to supply a service. Usually, these requirements relate to matters such as education, examination requirements, practical training, experience or language requirements, and registration requirements;

(ii) *Qualification procedures:* these are rules of administrative or procedural nature that a natural person must abide by in order to demonstrate compliance with qualification requirements with a view to obtaining authorization to supply a given service. They encompass procedures that candidates wishing to acquire a qualification must comply with to obtain authorization to supply a service, including the administrative requirements to be met, and rules relating to the verification of the compliance of the candidates with qualification requirements. This covers, inter alia, where to register for education programmes, conditions to be respected to register, documents to be filed, fees, mandatory physical presence conditions, alternative ways to attend an educational programme (eg distance learning), alternative routes to gain a qualification (eg through equivalences), and organizing of qualifying examinations, etc.

(iii) *Licensing requirements:* these are substantive requirements, other than qualification requirements and technical standards, that a service supplier (natural *or* juridical person) is required to conform to in order to obtain, amend, or renew authorization to supply a service.[89] They include measures such as fees, establishment requirements, registration requirements, etc.

(iv) *Licensing procedures:* these are administrative or procedural rules associated with the submission and processing of an application for an authorization to practise or renewal thereof, entailing such matters as timeframes for the processing of a licence, and the number of documents and the amount of information required in the application for a licence. They can relate to both natural and juridical persons seeking to supply services.

(v) *Technical standards:* these are requirements, be they mandatory or voluntary, which may apply both to the characteristics or definition of the service itself and to the manner in which it is supplied.[90] This can be exemplified by considering a standard that may stipulate the content of an audit, which is akin to definition of the service; another standard may lay down rules of ethics

Requirements, Licensing Procedures and Technical Standards', Communication from the Separate Customs Territory of Taiwan, Penghu, Kinmen and Matsu, S/WPDR/W/37, 6 October 2005, para 9. Nevertheless, horizontal proposals sometimes adopt these same definitions with minor changes. WPDR, 'Disciplines on Domestic Regulation Pursuant to GATS Article VI:4—Consolidated Working Paper', JOB(06)/225, July 2006, p 4. In fact, these definitions appear to be accepted as being applicable *across* services sectors by now. WPDR (n 74 above) paras 5–9.

[89] cf WTO, Trade in Services (n 15 above) para 8.

[90] cf the TBT definitions in TBT, Annex 1.1 and 1.2.

or conduct to be observed by the auditor. Hence, technical standards may relate either to the service characteristics or to the service supplier. In addition, under this category also come procedures relating to the enforcement of such standards.

a) Qualification requirements and procedures

Qualification requirements and procedures comprise substantive and procedural rules with respect to three principal areas, ie education, examinations, and experience.[91] It is commonplace that marked differences in national laws or traditions exist between countries in terms of the content, length, and rigour of educational and examination systems, the nature and extent of required experience, and the level of qualifications needed to supply a service.[92] Such differences, however, are usually non-discriminatory and typically result from objective factors, such as the complexity of each economy, its structure with differing levels of governments and thus different systems, or the nature and difficulty of the functions required of the service suppliers/professionals in question under national law. For instance, the same function may be assigned to substantially different professions from country to country.[93]

To be sure, such differences might make it difficult for potential entrants to meet the qualification requirements and hence may constitute a barrier to the movement of natural persons. The fact that such differences may be deemed necessary complicates any attempt to compare national systems and reach a common, detailed definition of excessive burdensomeness with regard to all Members as far as particular services are concerned.[94] Given that such differences can additionally be very difficult to identify due to the obscurity and complexity of the national or sub-national system pertaining to education, examination, training, or experience, any potential service supplier can be discouraged from exploring the possibility of supplying her services abroad.

Against this backdrop, it is, however, likely that Members can, at a minimum, ensure transparency and objectivity with respect to domestic qualification requirements or procedures as a first step leading to greater openness and improved market access for foreign service suppliers. For instance, in the absence of mechanisms that would determine the equivalence of foreign qualifications,

[91] cf WTO, Trade in Services (n 15 above) para 19.

[92] See the relevant discussion on a room document submitted by Chile, India, Pakistan, and Thailand entitled *Proposed Elements for Disciplines on Qualification Requirements and Procedures* in WTO, WPDR, 'Report on the Meeting Held on 7 and 18 February 2005', S/WPDR/M/29, 11 July 2005, paras 44ff. Interestingly, the proponents introduced the idea of creating a 'harmonization exam' to establish the equivalence of qualifications in the case that educational systems are found to be comparable. This proposal circulated subsequently as JOB(05)/50, dated 30 March 2005. Bolivia and Mexico also joined as co-sponsors of the proposal. WTO, WPDR (n 28 above) paras 96ff.

[93] WTO, WPPS (n 8 above) para 8.

[94] Also WTO, WPPS (n 28 above) paras 13–15.

education, training, and experience, any market access commitments may remain without any precise value. In this respect, the creation or betterment of such national mechanisms providing for objective verification of qualifications, including educational qualifications and professional competence, as Article VI:6 GATS also stipulates, is of paramount importance for effective market access, notably as regards mode 4,[95] taking into account that qualification requirements and procedures only refer to natural (as opposed to juridical) persons. Notably with respect to Article VI:6 GATS, the prospective disciplines aim to expand on its scope. The latter will cover *all* types of services (ie not only professional services, as is the case in Article VI:6) where qualification procedures exist to ensure that adequate procedures exist for verifying and assessing the qualifications of service suppliers of other Members seeking authorization to supply services.

Greater transparency could also allow Members to identify potential similarities between education or examinations systems that would otherwise have remained unknown and hence encourage Members to use a powerful liberalizing instrument, ie the conclusion of MRAs. Alternatively, Members could agree to ensure that their national systems relating to qualification requirements and procedures are non-discriminatory in every sense, and use a necessity test as the benchmark for ensuring the less-burdensomeness of the relevant national legislation. For instance, a requirement for a foreign experienced engineer to requalify instead of sitting an examination of competence would fail to satisfy the necessity test, as it can be deemed unduly burdensome. Transparency can also allow the scrutiny of qualification requirements and procedures with a view to eliminating any unreasonable or burdensome provisions.[96]

The only proposal to date tackling exclusively this category of Article VI:4 measures was submitted by Chile *et al.*[97] According to the proponents, the proposed disciplines should apply only to committed sectors and bind all levels of government. What is more, a necessity test is proposed with respect to qualification requirements and procedures. Regarding qualification requirements, the proposal expands on the related disciplines agreed for the accountancy sector. It requires the establishment of mechanisms that would verify and, if applicable, recognize the equivalency of qualifications of foreign service suppliers through the application of equivalent criteria for the recognition of qualifications obtained at home or abroad.

[95] WPDR, 'Proposed Elements for Disciplines on Qualification Requirements and Procedures', Communication from Bolivia, Chile, India, Mexico, Pakistan and Thailand, JOB(05)/50, 30 March 2005.

[96] WTO, WPDR, 'Report of the Chairman of the Working Party on Domestic Regulation to the Special Session of the Council for Trade in Services', JOB(05)/280, 15 November 2005, p 4.

[97] WPDR (n 95 above). For the revised proposal, see WTO, WPDR, 'Proposed Disciplines on Qualification Requirements and Procedures', Communication from Chile, India, Mexico, Pakistan, Peru and Thailand, JOB(06)/160, 30 May 2006. My analysis refers to this latter proposal.

Issues such as the fulfilment of additional requirements relating to course work, training or work experience, the membership of domestic professional associations, the content of examinations verifying the competences of the supplier and their relevance to the activities for which authorization is sought, the required language skills, and the linkage to the service supplied, are addressed in the paper in a fairly comprehensive manner. Importantly, the proposal would allow the fulfilment of additional educational requirements in the home or in a third country, unless overriding reasons call for their fulfilment in the host country. Importantly, the latest comprehensive drafts on prospective rules on domestic regulation endorse the latter proposition.[98] If ultimately adopted, this provision would greatly enhance labour mobility.

With respect to qualification procedures, the proposal extends the application of Article VI:4(c) to qualification procedures. Thus, Members shall be in a position to ensure that *both* licensing and qualification procedures do not in themselves constitute a restriction on the supply of services.[99] According to the proposal, transparency, public availability, and the reasonableness of timeframes regarding verification of qualifications and the organization of examinations shall be ascertained. Members shall also strive to ensure that fees are proportional to the administrative costs and thus are not prohibitive.[100] Enhanced transparency provisions regarding the current legal framework as well as any modifications are also included in this proposal. For developing countries and LDCs, the proponents put forward several special and differential treatment provisions, allowing, for instance, longer timeframes for compliance or technical assistance on mutually agreed terms. The latter disciplines, however, are rather abstract and, consequently, Members that have an interest in strong obligations of this nature should seek the betterment of these provisions so that they become more precise.

b) Licensing requirements and procedures

Licensing requirements are extensively employed in the service sector, as countries often require a licence for professionals to practise a regulated activity in their jurisdiction. Licensing is a precondition for the performance of certain tasks by certain service suppliers on condition that they fulfil certain qualifications pre-established by the domestic authorities. Hence, the number of the suppliers that will receive the licence is, by its nature, limited. Viewed from that angle, licensing reduces consumer choice and shrinks competition by restricting entry.[101]

[98] WPDR (n 74 above) para 32.

[99] This is actually an extension that will most likely form part of the prospective rules on domestic regulation. WPDR (n 74 above) para 30.

[100] This appears to be a view that all Members share. The issue of concessionary fees for developing countries and LDCs has also been discussed within the WPDR as part of the development-friendly aspects of the future disciplines. WPDR, 'State-of-Play in the Negotiations on Regulatory Disciplines under GATS Article VI:4', JOB(06)/37, 3 March 2006, para 14.

[101] For this reason, licensing should be used only in cases of important information asymmetries or where the harm potential is high. N Byron, L Gropp, and K Gusberti, 'Principles for Regulating

Depending on the jurisdiction and the activity at issue, non-discriminatory licensing requirements may include an establishment requirement, membership of a local professional association, subscription to a professional indemnity insurance, evidence of sound moral and financial standing, absence of criminal records, and/or the taking of an oath.

It bears mention that licensing requirements, contrary to qualification requirements, apply to both natural and juridical persons. Even so, licensing requirements are regarded as a *residual* category covering measures that do not fall under qualification requirements. It follows that licensing requirements and qualification requirements are mutually exclusive in the sense that a given measure can fall within the ambit of only one of these categories of measures. At the same time, the fulfilment of qualification requirements may be part of the requirements for acquiring a licence. It could be argued that this distinction between qualification and licensing requirements is artificial. By way of comparison, the recently adopted EU Services Directive does not encompass such a distinction. On the contrary, it uses the term 'requirement' to cover the scope of *both* qualification and licensing requirements. More specifically, it defines 'requirement' as 'any obligation, prohibition, condition or limit provided for in the laws, regulations or administrative provisions of the Member States or in consequence of case-law, administrative practice, the rules of professional bodies, or the collective rules of professional associations or other professional organizations, adopted in the exercise of their legal autonomy'.[102]

Whereas licensing, authorization, or mandatory membership requirements are usually deemed part and parcel of domestic regulation, they can bring about significant problems for foreign suppliers, especially where they are accompanied by the independent requirement of possessing host-state qualifications. This last requirement may oblige a potential service supplier coming from abroad to requalify in order to meet the host-state requirements. In addition, certain requirements can impede the supply of a service via a particular mode of supply. For instance, an establishment requirement as a proviso for granting a licence can render impossible the cross-border supply of a service.[103]

Residency requirements can also fall under licensing requirements. The issue is not, however, very straightforward, since in many cases such requirements may constitute *de facto* discriminatory measures and hence be tackled by the national treatment provision of Article XVII.[104] Arguably, those requirements can pertain to Article VI:4 provided that they treat nationals and foreigners identically, not

the Professions' in Productivity Commission/Australian National University, *Achieving Better Regulation of Services,* 2000, 191.

[102] Dir (EC) 2006/123 (n 33 above) Art 4:7.

[103] WTO, WPPS (n 8 above) para 10.

[104] Also Committee on Specific Commitments, 'Discussion of Residency Requirements in the Context of the Development of the Accountancy Disciplines and Scheduling Guidelines', JOB(06)/159, 30 May 2006.

only *de jure*, but also *de facto*.[105] In the case of residency requirements not subject to Article XVII, the accountancy disciplines encourage Members that create or maintain such requirements with respect to licensing to consider whether less restrictive means can be used to achieve the objectives that these requirements purport to serve, taking into account costs and local conditions. Moreover, when it comes to qualification procedures the accountancy disciplines rule out any residency requirements that are a precondition in order to sit an examination.[106]

In the draft text on domestic regulation that the WPDR Chairman recently circulated to Members, only residency requirements *not* subject to scheduling under Article XVII are part of the disciplines. The latter text essentially adopts this difference in the treatment of residency requirements relating to *licensing* versus residency requirements relating to *qualifications* that the accountancy disciplines also exhibit. More specifically, Members are requested to consider alternative less trade-restrictive methods to achieve their objectives if they impose residency requirements for licensing. However, when it comes to qualification requirements, Members are asked to abolish any residency requirement if it is a prerequisite in order for the competent domestic authority to assess and verify the competence of a foreign service supplier.[107]

As to licensing procedures, they refer to procedures of administrative nature and thus do not touch upon the regulatory intensity or the substance of domestic regulations with respect to the granting or the renewal of a licence. In other words, they constitute the means to handle an application for a licence. Having said this, licensing procedures can become unnecessary barriers to the supply of services and this is already recognized in the text of Article VI in an implicit manner through the wording of Article VI:4(c).[108] One should bear in mind that, whereas in some cases the grant of a licence may be a formality and hence a provider can obtain it in a quite automatic manner, in some other cases licensing procedures are designed in order to administer substantive regulatory requirements or trade restrictions such as those falling under Article XVI (eg a limitation on the number of service suppliers). What the GATS seeks to ensure is that licensing procedures do not become an instrument of trade restriction in their own right, that is, they should not restrict or distort trade any more than would be expected from the measures that they administer.[109]

[105] WTO, WPPS, 'Synthesis of the Responses to the Questionnaire on the Accountancy Sector', S/WPPS/W/11, 5 May 1997, para 62; also WTO, WPDR, 'Report on the Meeting Held on 16 July 2002', S/WPDR/M/17, 1 October 2002, para 8.

[106] WTO, Trade in Services (n 15 above) paras 9 and 24.

[107] WPDR (n 74 above) paras 17, 28.

[108] cf the objective of the Agreement on Import Licensing Procedures, ie that licensing should not become a trade-restrictive instrument in its own right.

[109] In the Agreement on Import Licensing Procedures, this is achieved through several disciplines, eg through minimizing the scope for discrimination and administrative discretion in licensing decisions and procedures, ensuring that the administrative burden of licensing is no greater than what is necessary to achieve the relevant policy objective, and requiring that all licensing procedures be carried out in a timely, transparent, and impartial manner.

In a proposal submitted for consideration to the WPDR, the European Union utilized a fairly sweeping definition; in the European Union's view, licensing procedures are the administrative procedures 'to be followed for the submission and processing of applications under a licensing or other authorization regime requiring the submission of an application or other documentation to the relevant administrative/regulatory body as a prior condition for the supply of a service in the territory of a Member'.[110]

In its proposal the European Union focused on three issues: transparency procedures, potential trade-restrictiveness of licensing procedures, and procedures related to the review of administrative decisions (as provided by Art VI:2). According to the European Union, licensing procedures should be pre-established, publicly available, and based on objective criteria. These procedures should delineate activities for which a licence would be required, and the terms and conditions under which a licence can be obtained, including all critical information for the completion of an application, relevant timeframes and critical deadlines.

Furthermore, such procedures should identify the competent authority and the appeal procedures that applicants have at their disposal. The EC proposal draws upon provisions and wording already used in the accountancy disciplines, the Reference Paper on Basic Telecommunications, and the Import Licensing Agreement.[111] A number of Members considered the EC proposal as a good starting point for developing disciplines relative to licensing procedures.[112]

Discussions within the WPDR on licensing procedures addressed the issue of whether onerous or non-transparent visa procedures would fall under the scope of Article VI:4, ie whether such procedures could fit within one of the sub-categories of domestic regulatory measures foreseen in paragraph 4 of Article VI, probably the sub-category of licensing procedures.[113] A Member, for instance, was of the view that visa procedures could fall under Article VI:4 provided that one could prove that they are directly related to competence, ability to supply the service, and quality of the service, in accordance with Article VI:4(a) and (b).[114] In elaborating on this statement, a number of Members suggested that visa

[110] WTO, WPDR, 'Proposal for Disciplines on Licensing Procedures', Communication from the European Community and its Member States, S/WPDR/W/25, 10 July 2003, para 19. The European Union adopts a wide concept of the term 'licence' to cover licences, authorizations, permits, for which certain requirements have to be fulfilled in order to obtain permission to supply a service, as well as automatic authorization procedures, that is, where approval for the supply of a service is granted in all cases. Additionally see the resemblance of this definition with the one used in Art 1:1 of the Agreement on Import Licensing Procedures.

[111] WTO, WPDR, 'Report on the Meeting Held on 1 July 2003', S/WPDR/M/22, 22 September 2003, para 51.

[112] WTO, WPDR, 'Report on the Meeting Held on 30 September 2003', S/WPDR/M/23, 27 November 2003, paras 12ff.

[113] WPDR, 'Examples of Measures to be Addressed by Disciplines Under GATS Article VI:4', JOB(01)/62, 10 May 2001, para 5; also WTO, WPDR (n 74 above) para 17.

[114] WTO, WPDR, 'Report on the Meeting Held on 12 March 2002' (n 56 above) paras 39ff.

procedures could be relevant when examining the scope of Article VI:4 so long as they are directly related to one of the five items, eg to the domestic administrative procedures for issuing a licence.

On the other hand, several Members, notably developed countries, feel that the scope of Article VI:4 cannot be extended to cover these kind of procedures, which go well beyond Article VI:4, as they may relate to immigration policies. According to these Members, the WPDR, if anything, cannot be regarded as the most appropriate forum to discuss this issue. Normally, visa procedures, while being of an administrative nature, provide a supplier the right to *enter* a market, and not the right to *supply* a service.[115] Furthermore, one can arguably contend that the issue is already addressed by paragraph 4 of the GATS *Annex on Movement of Natural Persons*,[116] subject to the proviso that such measures were not applied in a manner that nullifies or impairs benefits accruing to a Member due to specific commitments undertaken.[117]

It would be congruous with a correct interpretation of Article VI:4 to suggest that visa procedures can fall under the scope of this provision if the complexity of the formalities, the lack of transparency, and the unreasonableness of delays concerning their issuance is directly related to the issuance of a work permit or a licence.[118] Such measures, however, can equally fall under Article XVII, as they usually are discriminatory measures with respect to mode 4. Alternatively, and depending on the circumstances of each case, they could fall under Articles II, VI:1, or VI:6.

Regarding the issue of whether the scope of Article VI:4 encompasses visa procedures, much will depend, inter alia, on how sweeping or narrow will be the definition of the term 'a restriction on the supply of the service' in the case of a licensing procedure, as required in Article VI:4(c), that Members will endorse. The discussions within the WPDR are pending[119] and are also pursued within

[115] See Australia's intervention in WTO, WPDR, 'Report on the Meeting Held on 24 June 2004', S/WPDR/M/26, 8 September 2004, para 26.

[116] Para 4 of the Annex provides :

> The Agreement shall not prevent a Member from applying measures to regulate the entry of natural persons into, or their temporary stay in, its territory, including those measures necessary to protect the integrity of, and to ensure the orderly movement of natural persons across, its borders, provided that such measures are not applied in such a manner as to nullify or impair the benefits accruing to any Member under the terms of a specific commitment. (footnote omitted)

In the footnote it is stated that the mere fact of discriminating when requiring a visa for natural persons cannot be deemed a nullification or impairment of a benefit under a specific commitment. See also the intervention by the European Communities in WTO, WPDR, 'Report on the Meeting Held on 24 September 2004', S/WPDR/M/27, 15 November 2004, para 33.

[117] See Australia's intervention in WTO, WPDR (n 92 above), paras 108–112.

[118] WTO, WPDR, 'Examples of Measures Relating to Administrative Procedures for Obtaining Visas or Entry Permits', Communication from Colombia, S/WPDR/W/29, 7 July 2004.

[119] It is noteworthy that the Secretariat classified the issues associated with burdensome visa procedures under the rubric of licensing procedures in the last version of the *Examples* paper. See WPDR, 'Examples of Measures to be Addressed by Disciplines under GATS Article VI:4', JOB(02)/20/Rev.10, 31 January 2005, pp 27–28.

the Special Session of the CTS in the framework of the broader discussions on the liberalization of mode 4.

Finally, Members appear to give considerable weight to the simplification of procedures relating to licensing as well as qualifications. In this respect, the future disciplines will require that in each jurisdiction only one domestic authority is tasked with qualification procedures or is in charge of processing applications for a licence.[120] While the language used will in all probability be hortatory, this development demonstrates Members' propensity towards more simple and transparent structures. Additionally, this reminds one of the new EU Services Directive, which also requires that EU Member States establish points of single contact where authorizations to supply a service can be sought, if possible through electronic means.[121]

c) *Technical standards*

Technical standards are developed in most jurisdictions to respond to evolving social, legal, and economic environments and to guarantee a consistent level of quality in the service at issue in a given market. These standards vary from country to country (sometimes even within a country, as a sub-federal government may deviate and apply its own standards), thereby reflecting differing conditions and preferences throughout different markets. Thus, any attempt that aims at the mutual recognition of services or the identification of corresponding or like services can be a difficult task not only for a regulator but also for an adjudicating body.

Similarly, attempts to create horizontal disciplines applicable to all services sectors with respect to technical standards may prove to be particularly complex. Standards in the area of trade in services apply to the technical characteristics of the service itself (for instance, by specifying methods of financial reporting) and to the rules according to which the service must be performed (eg rules of conduct in a particular profession). This distinction is similar to the one made in the TBT between product standards and standards relating to production and process methods.

Theoretically, all technical standards are created and applied in order to serve legitimate objectives, a concept that has already been codified in the TBT Agreement and is also part and parcel of the intrinsic logic of Article VI:4. Having said this, the potential burdensomeness of such standards, bringing

[120] WPDR (n 74 above) paras 18, 30.

[121] Dir (EC) 2006/123 (n 33 above) Arts 6, 8. Interestingly, in order to define the types of procedures that a supplier must go through to supply her services, the Directive uses the all-encompassing notion of 'authorization schemes' which includes 'any procedure under which a provider or recipient is in effect required to take steps in order to obtain from a competent authority a formal decision, or an implied decision, concerning access to a service activity or the exercise thereof'. Ibid Art 4:6. In addition, Art 13 aims to ensure the objective, impartial, and expedited character of the authorization procedures that Member States may enact. On the rationale behind the attempts for administrative simplification, see Ibid, point (43).

about regulatory asymmetries and market fragmentation, is well recognized in trade in both goods and services. As in the goods area, ensuring that the preparation and application of such standards do not unnecessarily restrict trade in services while fulfilling their legitimate goals becomes an objective of the services negotiations. Absent any meaningful standards in the services domain developed by international organizations, the TBT Agreement can provide useful guidance in this respect, as it establishes rules governing the drafting, adoption and certification of standards-related activities at the national level.[122]

It seems that Members within the WPDR have a decision to make regarding their goals with reference to technical standards. Their work could be limited to the creation of rules to govern intergovernmental consultations over technical barriers with respect to trade in services. Alternatively, they could delegate this task to international standard-setting bodies. Another, rather far-reaching option would be a broad mandate that would aim to develop common disciplines to cover all stages of the process that leads to the creation of standards.

Work on technical standards within the WPDR has been limited to date. The most comprehensive proposal that has been brought to Members' attention was submitted by Switzerland.[123] From the subsequent discussions within the WPDR one can infer that the main controversial issues raised by the proposal have been:[124]

- the relevance of various elements of the TBT Agreement and their applicability to the service sector: some Members were reluctant to consider such elements as readily applicable in the services context;
- the issue of mandatory versus voluntary standards: contrary to the TBT Agreement, where technical standards are voluntary, the Swiss proposal identifies technical standards as measures that can be either voluntary or mandatory;
- the role of the non-governmental standardizing bodies and the value of their standards, especially when their authority is not delegated: according to the proposal, voluntary standards developed by such bodies can be very influential in certain professions and for that reason should be covered by the disciplines to be developed. Some linkage to governmental authority, the proposal runs, would still be necessary in the sense that a government should at least authorize such private standard-setting activities by non-governmental bodies.

[122] Mexico, for instance, has established a standards-related regulatory framework which is common for both goods and services following the example of international standardizing bodies such as the ISO not to distinguish between goods and services with respect to their definitions of technical regulations and standards. Mexico's regulatory framework with respect to standards draws upon the TBT agreement in several instances. WTO, WPDR, 'Mexico's Experience of Disciplines on Technical Standards and Regulations in Services', Communication from Mexico, S/WPDR/W/30, 24 September 2004, para 6.

[123] WTO, WPDR, 'Proposal for Disciplines on Technical Standards in Services', Communication from Switzerland, S/WPDR/W/32, 1 February 2005.

[124] WTO, WPDR (n 92 above), paras 12ff; also WTO, WPDR (n 28 above) paras 120ff.

The Swiss proposal was subsequently revised and presented as a joint proposal sponsored by Switzerland and Mexico.[125] This proposal also reflects enhanced transparency and good regulation concepts already well known from other WTO Agreements, such as the TBT or the SPS. Importantly, with respect to standards created by non-governmental bodies with no implicit or explicit delegated power, the proponents request that Members encourage these bodies, such as business associations, to conform to the principles enclosed in the TBT Code of Good Practice.[126]

However, Members do not appear to be prepared to discuss and accept wide-ranging disciplines with respect to technical standards in the area of services. The case of the accountancy disciplines inexorably leads to this conclusion: as explained earlier, despite the relevant sector-specific work already accomplished in several international organizations, Members ultimately reached an agreement on adopting only two paragraphs in the final text of the accountancy disciplines. This reveals Members' fear that their regulatory autonomy is under threat.[127] *A fortiori*, Members may be even more reluctant to accept disciplines relating to technical standards in sectors where no international standards exist or at a horizontal level.

Indeed, recent developments within the WPDR reveal Members' reluctance to advance work on technical standards. It appears that Members will ultimately endorse a requirement that measures relating to technical standards be pre-established, based on objective criteria and relevant to the supply of the service to which they apply. This obligation will be coupled with a best-endeavour provision encouraging Members to ensure transparency when *non*-governmental bodies develop and apply domestic or international standards. Apart from this soft obligation for transparency, voluntary standards will not be subject to the future disciplines on domestic regulation.

More importantly, an obligation similar to Article 2.4 TBT,[128] first proposed by Switzerland, has been considered as relevant in the discussions on technical standards. This provision foresees that Members, when they are in the process of formulating their technical standards, should take into account relevant international standards (or parts of them) that already exist or the completion of which is imminent, unless these standards (or the relevant parts) are deemed an 'ineffective and inappropriate means for the fulfilment of national policy objectives'.

[125] WTO, WPDR, 'Proposal for Disciplines on Technical Standards in Services', Communication from Switzerland and Mexico, S/WPDR/W/32/Rev.1, 28 October 2005.

[126] Ibid para 4. By way of comparison, the new EU Services Directive encourages the creation of EU-wide Codes of Conduct by professional bodies, organizations and associations which would facilitate the provision of services or the establishment of a supplier in another Member State. The Directive makes clear the purpose of this encouragement is to achieve minimum harmonization by establishing minimum standards of conduct which would not override Member States' legal requirements. Dir (EC) 2006/123 (n 33 above) Art 37 and point (115).

[127] Also WTO, WPDR (n 31 above) para 25.

[128] WTO, WPDR (n 123 above) para 20.

The important difference with Article 2.4 TBT is that the latter requires that Members use such standards as a basis for their technical regulations, instead of merely taking them into account.[129] Even so, the proposed provision is stronger than Article VI:5(b) or paragraph 26 of the draft accountancy disciplines.

D. Towards the development of a horizontal necessity test applicable to all services sectors as foreseen in Article VI:4 GATS

Many of the issues that are related to the development of the Article VI:4 disciplines are quite familiar to Members from work undertaken in other sectors, such as basic telecommunications and accountancy services. Common threads can indeed be identified through an examination of the Reference Paper on regulatory disciplines for basic telecommunications, the additional commitments concerning regulatory matters undertaken by several Members in the financial services negotiations and the draft accountancy disciplines.[130] This accumulated experience is expected to assist Members in building coherent horizontally applicable disciplines on domestic regulation.

As stated earlier, in organizing their prospective work programme, Members found guidance in a Secretariat's Note that identified necessity, transparency, equivalence, and international standards as the four policy areas where disciplines with respect to domestic regulation in services could be developed.[131] According to the Secretariat's paper, 'the first two areas, necessity and transparency could help to develop rules on domestic regulation applicable to all types of measures listed in Article VI:4: qualification and licensing requirements and procedures and technical standards. The last two areas, equivalence and international standards could instead help to develop rules limited to some of the measures listed in Article VI:4: qualification and licensing requirements and technical standards.'

Members agreed to focus first on the issues of necessity and transparency,[132] leaving the issues of equivalence and international standards for a later date. Even when the two latter issues finally became part of the regular WPDR discussions, Members continued to give priority to issues related to necessity and transparency.[133] Importantly enough, necessity has been on an equal footing with transparency,

[129] For an analysis of Art 2.4 TBT and the relevant WTO case-law, see Chapter IV.D.3.c.

[130] cf WTO, CTS, 'Article VI:4: Possible Disciplines on Domestic Regulation', S/C/W/66, 17 November 1998, para 4.

[131] WTO, CTS (n 17 above).

[132] WTO, WPDR, 'Report on the Meeting Held on 17 May 1999', S/WPDR/M/1, 14 June 1999, para 6.

[133] WTO, WPDR (n 52 above) para 8.

something that demonstrates the importance that Members attribute to transparent regulatory regimes for their services exporters.[134]

Members have used as basis for the discussions of substantive issues within the WPDR the *Checklist of Issues* that the Secretariat drew up, in response to a request by Members. In the *Checklist of Issues*, the Secretariat identified three issues that Members appeared to consider pertinent when it comes to the issue of necessity: legitimate objectives, criteria for the necessity test, and the so-called 'third aspect' of the necessity test.

1. Legitimate objectives

Under this sub-category, Members have had to deal with two questions: first, whether there is a need to create a positive list of legitimate objectives, as it was the case of the accountancy disciplines, which contain an illustrative, open-ended positive list of four objectives which Members specifically considered as being legitimate. If so, the second question that Members needed to consider was how concise, or alternatively, how broad such a list would be.

As to the first question, a consensus is still to be reached as to whether a positive list enumerating legitimate objectives is needed. Some Members contended that, according to the GATS Preamble, the national policy objectives that a government chooses to pursue were presumably legitimate. Importantly, it has been proposed not to list any legitimate objectives at all not only due to practical reasons, as it would be too difficult to strike the balance between being overly specific and being broad enough to provide guidance for the domestic regulators when they intervene in exercising their powers, but also because of some Members' concern that any listing, even in an illustrative manner, could yield unexpected legal ramifications.[135] According to some Members, it could even allow the WTO adjudicating bodies to assess the legitimacy of policy objectives. Nevertheless, the necessity test would not aim to question the necessity or legitimacy of objectives, but rather the necessity of a given measure to achieve its objectives. Consequently, there may be no reason to limit what can be classified as a legitimate objective, but the determination of policy objectives should be Members' prerogative in accordance with the GATS Preamble.

As to the second question, a long listing could dilute the effect of the disciplines, while reaching a consensus on any list, be it small or long, cannot be considered a doddle with such a wide range of Members' preferences and specificities and taking into account that any decision needs to be based on consensus. At the same time, any possible list of legitimate objectives should have such characteristics that would allow it to cover or be applicable to as many services sectors as possible. In addition, if Members agree on the necessity of a list, they should primarily concentrate on the development of additional legitimate policy objectives unrelated

134 WTO, WPDR (n 57 above) para 5.

135 See, for instance, the WPDR discussions in WTO, WPDR (n 20 above) paras 25ff.

to Article XIV GATS.[136] An alternative proposal advocated the listing of *non*-legitimate objectives. This latter approach has been promptly rejected by the majority of Members, as it would be too limiting. Finally, another approach would advance the idea of a non-exhaustive list coupled with a horizontal necessity test. In this case, Members would be free to add new sector-specific policy objectives when they deal with the development of sector-specific disciplines. Such an approach would have the advantage of avoiding any duplication.

As things stand now, Members appear to be focusing on the development of disciplines, leaving for a subsequent time the decision on whether to list legitimate objectives and if so, the form of this list.[137] Quite oddly, an issue that does not appear to have drawn Members' attention so far—at least during the formal discussions—is to what extent the policy objectives that are to be listed (if, in the end, Members decide to create such a list of legitimate objectives) have to be related to the objective of ensuring the *quality* of the service and, in the affirmative, how unequivocal this relation should be. The fact that measures relating to qualification, licensing, or standards usually aim to ensure a high level of quality of the service supplied does not suffice, since such measures may also serve other national policy objectives as well, which may, or not, be related to the broader objective of ensuring the quality of a given service.

For example, objectives such as consumer protection or ensuring professional competence would surely qualify as policy objectives related to the quality of the service supplier. But would the result be the same, assuming *arguendo* that a service supplier bears the obligation to supply a service in a bottleneck service sector in the underserved regions of the country at lower prices than in urban areas? Or an obligation that education services are provided by universities, be they public or private, on a non-profit basis? What about an obligation to provide telecommunications services at reasonable prices or to become member of a professional association and take an oath? Would 'quality' also encompass a regulation that aims at minimizing the environmental impact of a given service? Such objectives, while unambiguously being part of important social policies, do not seem at first sight to belong in the broad objective of ensuring the quality of a service by any means and therefore their treatment by the WTO adjudicating bodies cannot be anticipated in advance. This is another reason why Members ought to seek clarification, and probably expansion, of the objective of 'ensuring the quality of the service'.

2. Criteria for the necessity test

The main criteria for the necessity test in the form of a negotiating mandate are to be found in subparagraphs (a), (b), and (c) of Article VI:4. The key challenge

[136] WTO, WPDR (n 59 above) paras 11ff; also WPDR, 'Application of the Necessity Test: Issues for Consideration', Job No. 5929, 8 October 1999, p 2.

[137] WTO, WPDR, 'Report on the Meeting Held on 2 October 2001', S/WPDR/M/13, 21 November 2001, para 21.

for the negotiators is to define and make effective these criteria. Members have been holding discussions within the WPDR with a view to defining such terms as 'least trade-restrictive', 'not more trade-restrictive than necessary', 'proportionality', and 'not more burdensome than necessary' and to explore their respective legal and trade implications.

Members conducted discussions on the criteria for a necessity test mainly in informal mode and have been encouraged to bear in mind the necessity test developed for the accountancy disciplines when reflecting on the form and the content that a possible horizontally applicable necessity test may have, as the necessity test in the accountancy disciplines can be a good basis in the WPDR for the development of a necessity test applicable across the board (or at least to all professional services) owing to the fact that it appears to be comprised of many elements that could be applied in a broader context than the sectoral one of accountancy services.[138]

Members seem to be aware of the fact that, while any possible horizontally applicable rules with respect to necessity can by definition be fairly abstract to cover as many sector specificities as possible, they should also ensure coherence across sectors. Remaining sector specificities that cannot be covered in a horizontal legal framework of regulatory disciplines could be addressed at a later stage by possibly adding further provisions to cover such specificities.

a) *Not more* burdensome *than necessary versus not more* trade-restrictive *than necessary*

An important issue that has been explored, albeit not to the extent that it deserved, is the difference, if there is any, between the terms 'not more burdensome than necessary' and 'not more trade-restrictive than necessary'. As stated, Article VI:4 makes reference, inter alia, to the criterion of burdensomeness against which measures with respect to qualifications, licensing, and technical standards will be juxtaposed in the future to determine whether they violate the prospective horizontal disciplines. In other words, one of the objectives of the future horizontal disciplines should be to ensure that such measures are burdensome only to the extent that they ensure the quality of the service (and/or, arguably, of the service supplier), no matter how broad or how narrow 'quality' would be defined.

Furthermore, pursuant to the *chapeau* of Article VI:4, the Members' primary objective should be to ensure that the aforementioned types of measures do not impede trade in services in an unnecessary manner. This has been confirmed in both the *Decision on Professional Services* and the *Decision on Domestic Regulation*. Comparing the wording of Article VI:4 with paragraph 2 of the accountancy disciplines, one can observe that the latter added an important element to

[138] Ibid para 20 (Chairman's statement).

this objective, ie that regulatory measures should not be prepared, adopted or applied *with a view to, or with the effect of*, impeding trade in services more than is necessary.

Thus, the existence or creation of an unnecessary barrier to trade in services with respect to measures relating to qualifications, licensing, and standards should be neither the *intent* of the regulatory measure at issue nor the *result* of its application by the domestic competent authorities. Importantly, the accountancy disciplines seem to have replaced the rather 'problematic' phrase 'not more *burdensome* than necessary to ensure the quality of the service' endorsed in Article VI:4(b) with the phrase 'not more *trade-restrictive* than necessary to fulfil a legitimate objective', adopting that way a TBT-similar language as echoed in Article 2.2 TBT.

On the other hand, the accountancy disciplines do encompass the term 'burdensome', but only in the specific context of licensing *procedures* (para 15) and require that application procedures and the related documentation be not more burdensome than necessary to ensure that applicants fulfil qualification and licensing requirements and that the establishment of the authenticity of documents be sought through the least burdensome procedure. Since the WPPS was the first body to be requested by the CTS to pursue the Article VI:4 mandate, do the accountancy disciplines *a fortiori* confirm that burdensomeness and trade-restrictiveness have the same meaning for Members and hence are to be used interchangeably in the GATS, or alternatively that the latter is an evolution of the former, which initially was coupled with the quality of the service supplied? Or, rather, based on the above, would it be plausible to argue that the burdensomeness is a subset of trade-restrictiveness?

It has been argued, notably by the European Union, that these two terms mean essentially the same.[139] This is only one of the instances where these two concepts are confounded. In the course of the WPDR discussions, for instance, the same impression is created. Of course, the literature cannot remain unaffected.[140] The answer to the questions just posed is not as straightforward as one would think at first blush. An *advocatus diaboli* would suggest that nothing in the GATS text supports the view that the two concepts are to be considered as having the same meaning. The GATS text and particularly Article VI does not even entail the term 'not more trade-restrictive than necessary' at all, but merely requires that domestic regulation measures regarding qualifications, licensing, and technical standards do not constitute unnecessary barriers to trade in services.

In a summary of the discussions, which recapitulates the most important points made during informal discussions between Members in the WPDR, it was pointed out:[141]

[139] WTO, WPDR, 'Domestic Regulation: Necessity and Transparency', Communication from the European Communities and their Member States, S/WPDR/W/14, 1 May 2001, para 17.

[140] cf Leebron (n 32 above) 52.

[141] WTO, WPDR (n 52 above) p 10.

A question was raised concerning whether there was a difference between restrictiveness and burdensomeness in the context of Article VI:4. The Secretariat replied that *there was a difference, and that a measure could be more burdensome than necessary, but not to the point of being trade restrictive and vice-versa.* (emphasis added)

This would imply that these two terms should not be used as if they were synonymous. Among the many questions that can be mooted due to this approach brought forth by the Secretariat, the most critical ones appear to be the following: would a Member that creates or maintains a measure that is more burdensome than necessary but not to the point of being trade-restrictive be violating its obligations deriving from the GATS? Most importantly: *should* it be considered to have violated the GATS? In other words, a domestic regulation measure that is far from equivalent to a 'full-fledged' trade restriction—as one conceives such a restriction in GATT law—can still be considered by the WTO adjudicating bodies as unduly burdensome for market participants or potential entrants and hence be outlawed?[142]

In a communication submitted to the WPDR, Korea attempted to analyse the abovementioned differences in the wording and their legal implications, if any.[143] Korea emphasized that the two terms focus on different aspects of trade: the term 'not more trade-restrictive' refers to cross-border trade, whereas the term 'not more burdensome' focuses on domestic procedures.[144] According to Korea, the GATS founding fathers intentionally used this different wording in order to encompass all the four modes of supply that the GATS identifies. In contrast, according to Korea, trade-restrictiveness is a concept that is used with respect to cross-border trade, in particular trade in goods, as it demonstrates its use in both the TBT and SPS Agreements (Articles 2.2 and 5.6 thereof, respectively) as well as in cases where the exception of Article XX GATT has been invoked.

Apart from the clear reference on burdensomeness in Article VI:4(b), Korea finds support in the accountancy disciplines where the burdensomeness is mentioned with respect to licensing procedures (para 15). It further refers to the Import Licensing Agreement which provides in Article 3.2 in the relevant part that 'non-automatic licensing procedures... shall be no more administratively burdensome than absolutely necessary to administer the measure'. In addition, in Article VI:4(c), reference is made to the licensing procedures and the requirement not to be 'in themselves a restriction on the supply of the service'. Korea suggests that all these provisions, by including the concept of burdensomeness, acknowledge the specificity of services to be supplied in four different modes of supply instead of

[142] J Neumann and E Türk, 'Necessity Revisited: Proportionality in World Trade Organization Law After *Korea—Beef*, *EC—Asbestos* and *EC—Sardines*' (2003) 37(1) JWT 233.

[143] WTO, WPDR, 'The Necessity Test', Communication from the Republic of Korea, S/WPDR/W/9, 28 September 2000.

[144] Also WTO, WPDR (n 54 above) para 5.

only through cross-border trade and focus on avoiding any unreasonable burden to be imposed by a domestic procedure on the supply of a service.[145]

At first sight, Korea's view appears to concur with the aforementioned view expressed by the Secretariat based on the argument that a more-burdensome-than-necessary measure can still not be trade-restrictive. However, Korea falls short of going that far. Instead, it contends that, in the end, 'trade-restrictive' or 'burdensome' have the same implications by stating in relevant part that in spite of their differences in wording and nuance, the two terms

> . . . focus on preventing any unreasonable 'burden' or 'restriction' from being imposed on the import of foreign goods or the supply of services. And regardless of the wording that is being used, both phrases—'not more burdensome than necessary' and 'not more trade-restrictive than necessary'—appear to imply a need to determine whether there are less burdensome or less restrictive alternatives available.[146]

Then, according to this approach, which in its substance is no different than the view expressed by the European Union, all the questions that were posed above would be answered in the negative, as there is no important distinction between the notion of 'not more burdensome than necessary' and 'not more trade-restrictive than necessary'.[147] The opposite would allow the WTO adjudicating bodies to pronounce on the legality of unduly burdensome domestic regulation measures even in the absence of an international trade restriction, something that would be hardly accepted by the WTO Membership, at least for the moment. To be sure, an approach similar to the latter would undermine the right of Members to regulate, one of the important GATS principles cited in the Preamble of the Agreement as well as on several occasions, and would allow international trade dispute settlement organs to second-guess domestic choices about complex trade-offs between various regulatory objectives, risks, and regulatory instruments and hence would empower their judgment to supersede the judgment of domestic accountable legislature.

A possible approach to solve the problem that arises from the use of these two concepts is to take into account that, even though Article VI:4 does not mention at all the concept of trade-restrictiveness, this is implied in the *chapeau* of this Article. Indeed, the ultimate objective of Article VI:4, and hence the objective of a prospective necessity test, is to discipline 'unnecessary barriers to trade'.[148] Then, for a Panel or the Appellate Body to deal with a domestic regulation measure, this measure should in some way create a barrier to trade which is deemed unnecessary. Solely arguing that a regulation is inefficient or burdensome should not

145 WTO, WPDR (n 143 above) p 2.

146 Ibid.

147 Leebron (n 32 above) 52.

148 Ibid. Nevertheless, Leebron goes on to say that there needs to be somehow a discriminatory, in effect or purpose, element. In his view, if anything, the term 'unnecessary barriers to trade' in the *chapeau* of Art VI:4 provides evidence that this provision cannot cover only non-discriminatory measures.

suffice for challenging a measure on the basis of Article VI:4 and the disciplines developed thereunder.

Another approach that could be reasonably proposed would be anchored in the text of Article VI:4. This textual approach would advocate that, as a matter of fact, the necessity test consists of two subsets, ie an external and an internal aspect. For the sake of the analysis of this approach, let's take the elements identified in Article VI:4 in turn.

First, according to the *chapeau* of this provision, the disciplines that will be developed should ensure that domestic regulatory measures relating to qualifications, licensing, and technical standards are not unnecessary barriers to trade in services. In other words, these disciplines need to make sure that such measures do not hamper trade in an unnecessary manner, hence are no more trade-restrictive than necessary. This is what I call the external or cross-border trade aspect.

Second, the disciplines to be developed should further ensure (*inter alia*) that, again, such domestic regulatory measures are not more burdensome than necessary to ensure the quality of the service, or more broadly, to fulfil a legitimate objective. This is what I call the internal or domestic aspect.

Consequently, in an attempt to make a purely textual interpretation, the necessity test envisaged under Article VI:4 in its form in the aftermath of the Uruguay Round appears to be a twofold test with two different levels where the domestic regulatory measure at issue will be scrutinized: the first part of the test would entail an examination of whether the measure at issue unnecessarily impedes trade in services (external or cross-border trade test), while the second part would involve an examination of the burdensomeness of the measure vis-à-vis the legitimate objective that it seeks to pursue.

Hence, under such a methodological approach, the WTO adjudicating bodies would first examine if the measure at stake is more trade-restrictive than necessary. If they find out that this is the case, this is the end of the story and the measure is considered as violating its GATS obligations. If, however, their conclusion is rather that the measure does not restrict trade in services in an unnecessary manner, then they would proceed to evaluate whether the measure is more *burdensome* than necessary when juxtaposed against the regulatory (social or other) objective that led to its adoption. If the adjudicating bodies believe that the measure does not satisfy the internal necessity criterion,[149] the responding party would have no other option than to resort to the exceptions provision of Article XIV GATS.

While this approach may at first sight appear too intrusive an approach for the proponents of keeping the regulatory autonomy of Members unaffected, recall that it does not differ that much from the approach that has been followed with respect to the accountancy disciplines and paragraphs 2 and 15 therein. More specifically, whereas the former seeks to ensure that measures relating to

[149] This would be, for instance, the case of excessive licensing fees.

licensing, qualifications, or technical standards are not prepared, adopted, or applied with a view to, or with the effect of, creating *unnecessary* barriers to trade in accountancy services, paragraph 15 additionally requires that application procedures and the related documentation be not more *burdensome* than necessary to ensure that applicants satisfy qualification and licensing requirements.

A related interpretation of the two terms, ie burdensomeness *vs* trade-restrictiveness, would suggest that burdensomeness only refers to *procedural* obligations. Thus, when a procedure is at stake, the WTO judiciary would examine whether this procedure is more burdensome than necessary. On the other hand, trade-restrictiveness relates to *substantive* obligations. In the case where the legality of a qualification requirement is scrutinized, the benchmark would be whether this measure is more trade-restrictive than necessary.[150]

b) *'Third aspect' of the necessity test*[151]

It was stated earlier that domestic regulation measures with respect to qualification requirements and procedures, licensing requirements and procedures, and technical standards should not impede trade in services more than is necessary. But what is 'necessary'?

The 'third aspect' of the necessity test encompasses the idea that a measure that has the effect of restricting trade can be considered necessary only if there is no alternative measure less disruptive of trade which a Member may reasonably be expected to employ to achieve the same policy objective.[152] The other two aspects of the necessity test, as identified by the Secretariat in an informal Note on necessity provisions,[153] are, first, the general requirement that domestic regulatory measures not be more trade-restrictive than necessary, and, secondly, the examination as to whether a specific measure is actually necessary to achieve the legitimate objective that it seeks to pursue.

During the informal WPDR discussions, it has been argued that the 'third aspect' can be excessively burdensome taking into account the vast scale of service sectors. Other Members, however, felt that the 'third aspect' provides a means for examining alternatives to particular domestic regulatory measures.[154]

As one can infer, many of the concepts mentioned, and notably the 'third aspect', alias the definition of when a trade-restrictive measure can be deemed necessary, while fairly new for the domain of trade in services, have made a

[150] M Krajewski, 'Article VI GATS' in R Wolfrum, P-T Stoll, and C Feinäugle (eds), *Max-Planck Commentaries on World Trade Law, Volume 6: WTO—Trade in Services*, 2008.

[151] In the *Checklist of Issues*, the so-called 'third aspect' was deemed a third subcategory of the issues associated with the concept of necessity. Nevertheless, I prefer to examine it now, as the reader will realize that the question on the criteria for the necessity test includes the idea of the 'third aspect'.

[152] WTO, WPDR, 'Report on the Meeting Held on 19 October 1999', S/WPDR/M/3, 18 January 2000, para 5.

[153] WPDR (n 136 above) para 14 and fn 7.

[154] WTO, WPDR (n 54 above) p 5.

long—and sometimes winding—road throughout the years of GATT/WTO with respect to trade in goods. Inevitably, then, and probably also for the sake of consistency, the WPDR sought to find assistance to the jurisprudence relating to the interpretation of necessity in other WTO Agreements.

3. The conceptual issue of necessity as it has been endorsed, applied, and interpreted in other WTO agreements—Possible models for the necessity test envisaged in Article VI:4?

The non-discrimination rules notwithstanding, the necessity requirement is probably the most significant general discipline on domestic regulation in WTO law. In several WTO Agreements, there are provisions which encompass the concept of necessity in the form of a test. Such a test may be part of a WTO provision that envisages either an *obligation* or an *exception*. WTO provisions that fall in the first category are: Articles VI:4 and XII:2(d) GATS; Articles 2.2 and 2.5 TBT; Articles 2.2 and 5.6 SPS; and Article 8.1 TRIPs. Provisions, on the other hand, that provide for an exception and encompass a necessity test are: Article XI:2(b) and (c) and Article XX GATT; Article XIV GATS and paragraph 5(e) of the Annex on Telecommunications; Articles 3.2 and 27.2 TRIPs; and Article 23.2 GPA. With respect to the latter category of provisions, one could distinguish between necessity requirements that are part of a particular exception to the provision in which they appear (eg Article XI:2(b) GATT and (c) or paragraph 5(e) of the GATS Annex on Telecommunications) and necessity requirements that are part of a general exception, ie that apply to all measures falling under the scope of the respective agreement (as is the case in Article XX GATT or Article XIV GATS).

In this subheading, I will limit myself to the examination of the most important necessity tests as identified and interpreted in other covered Agreements. The analysis undertaken will cover only the necessity tests which the WTO adjudicating bodies have pronounced on, as these appear to be of particular relevance when it comes to the interpretation of the concept of necessity in Article VI:4. These rulings concern only necessity tests in the GATT, the SPS, and TBT Agreements, and the GATS.

At the outset, it is important to underscore that the necessity tests in provisions that provide for an exception (be it particular or general) are for the most part associated with an exhaustive set of policy objectives that are of a more limited and fundamental nature,[155] whereas the provisions that provide for an obligation

[155] The WTO case law is not consistent as to whether the provisions entailing an exception should be interpreted narrowly (according to the principle *exceptio est strictissimae interpretationis*). In *EC—Hormones*, the Appellate Body answered the question in the negative by stating that 'merely characterizing a treaty provision as an "exception" does not by itself justify a "stricter" or "narrower" interpretation of that provision than would be warranted by examination of the ordinary meaning of the actual treaty words, viewed in context and in the light of the treaty's object and purpose, or, in other words by applying the normal rules of treaty interpretation'. Appellate

are usually coupled with an open-ended list of objectives. More fundamentally, whether the necessity test is part of an exception provision or rather an obligation provision plays an important role for the allocation of the burden of proof. While in an exception provision the burden of proof lies on the party that has invoked that provision, by virtue of the maxim *quicunque exceptio invocat, ejusdem probare debet* (as in Art XX GATT), in an obligation provision it is the complaining party that bears the burden of proof (as is the case in Art 2.2 TBT).[156]

a) Article XX GATT[157]

Article XX GATT entails an exhaustive list of general exceptions to substantive obligations ensuring market access established in the GATT otherwise respected by Members, and not a positive rule establishing obligations in itself.[158] The domestic policies that such exceptions are embodied in, while incompatible with other GATT provisions, are deemed important and legitimate in character and therefore are justifiable.[159] Article XX GATT provides in the relevant part:[160]

> Subject to the requirement that such measures are not *applied* in a manner which would constitute a means of arbitrary or unjustifiable discrimination between countries where the same conditions prevail, or a disguised restriction on international trade, *nothing in this agreement shall be construed to prevent the adoption or enforcement by any* [Member] *of measures:*
>
> (a) *necessary to* protect public morals;
> (b) *necessary to* protect human, animal or plant life or health;
> ...
> (d) *necessary to* secure compliance with laws or regulations which are not inconsistent with the provisions of this Agreement... (emphasis added)

This provision encompasses a two-tier analysis of a measure that a Member seeks to justify.[161] First, it should be determined whether the impugned measure falls under one of the paragraphs (a) to (j) of Article XX. In this determination, it is required to demonstrate that the measure at issue addresses (or is designed

Body Report, *EC—Hormones*, para 104. Nevertheless, there are hints that, in certain instances, the opposite approach may still be valid. cf Appellate Body Report, *US—Gambling*, para 308; and Appellate Body Report, *US—Gasoline*, p 22.

[156] WTO, WPDR, '"Necessity Tests" in the WTO', S/WPDR/W/27, 2 December 2003, para 7.

[157] Also PC Mavroidis, *The General Agreement on Tariffs and Trade: A Commentary*, 2005, pp 184ff; for the Art XX jurisprudence, see Appellate Body Secretariat, *WTO Appellate Body Repertory of Reports and Awards 1995–2004*, May 2005.

[158] Appellate Body Report, *US—Wool Shirts and Blouses*, pp 15–16.

[159] Appellate Body Report, *US—Shrimp*, para121.

[160] From these three paras, only paras (b) and (d) have been the object of judicial review by a Panel or the Appellate Body with respect to their necessity requirement. Therefore, my analysis is confined to these two provisions, and does not cover the other paras of Art XX or its introductory clause (*chapeau*). I will address the public morals exception in the discussion of the necessity test contained in Art XIV GATS, as it was construed in the *US—Gambling* case.

[161] Appellate Body Report, *US—Gasoline*, p 22; also Appellate Body Report, *US—Shrimp*, paras 119–120, 147; and Appellate Body Report, *US—Gambling*, para 292.

to address)[162] the particular interest specified in the relevant paragraph and that there is a sufficient nexus between the measure and the interest protected.[163] After having determined that the measure at issue satisfies the first prong of the test, it needs *further* to be appraised against, and thus satisfy, the requirements of the *chapeau* of Article XX.[164] The *ratio legis* of these latter requirements, ie the prohibition on *applying* a measure in a manner which would constitute a means of 'arbitrary' or 'unjustifiable' discrimination[165] between countries where the same conditions prevail or a 'disguised restriction on international trade', is to ensure that Member's rights to avail themselves of exceptions are exercised reasonably, so as not to frustrate the rights of other Members deriving from the GATT substantive rules.[166] These requirements are necessarily broad in scope and reach, and their interpretation will vary.[167]

Article XX being an affirmative defence, the party invoking the exception bears the burden of demonstrating that a measure: (a) falls under one of the exceptions envisaged in Article XX and thus it is provisionally justified; and (b) when applied, is not an abuse of such exception under the *chapeau*.[168] The latter, according to the Appellate Body, 'is, of necessity, a heavier task than that involved in showing that an exception . . . encompasses the measure at issue'.[169]

With respect to the objectives of the measure at issue, the WTO adjudicating bodies have ruled in a consistent manner that their work is not to put in question the very legitimacy of the ends sought and their necessity.[170] Instead, their task is to examine whether the measure at issue is necessary to achieve one of the objectives laid down in Article XX; in other words, 'ends are not justiciable, means are'.[171] In *US—Gasoline*, the Appellate Body clarified the function of Article XX (here with respect to national measures intended to protect the environment):

> It is of some importance that the Appellate Body point out what this does *not* mean. It does not mean, or imply, that the ability of any WTO Member to take measures to control air pollution or, more generally, to protect the environment, is at issue. That would be to ignore the fact that Article XX of the *General Agreement* contains provisions designed to permit important state interests—including the protection of human health, as well as the conservation of exhaustible natural resources—to find expression. The provisions of Article XX were not changed as a result of the Uruguay Round of Multilateral Trade Negotiations. Indeed, in the preamble to the *WTO Agreement*

[162] Appellate Body Report, *Mexico—Taxes on Soft Drinks*, para 72.
[163] Appellate Body Report, *US—Gambling*, para 292.
[164] Appellate Body Report, *US—Shrimp*, paras 119, 157.
[165] Ibid para 150.
[166] Appellate Body Report, *US—Gasoline*, p 22.
[167] Appellate Body Report, *US—Shrimp*, para 120.
[168] Appellate Body Report, *US—Gasoline*, pp 22–23.
[169] Ibid p 23.
[170] That was made clear already during the GATT years. cf GATT Panel Report, *Japan—Alcoholic Beverages I*, para 5.13; also GATT Panel Report, *Thailand—Cigarettes*, para 73.
[171] Mavroidis (n 157 above) 191.

and in the *Decision on Trade and Environment*, there is specific acknowledgement to be found about the importance of coordinating policies on trade and the environment. WTO Members have a large measure of autonomy to determine their own policies on the environment (including its relationship with trade), their environmental objectives and the environmental legislation they enact and implement. So far as concerns the WTO, that autonomy is circumscribed only by the need to respect the requirements of the *General Agreement* and the other covered agreements.[172] (emphasis in the original; footnote omitted)

As to the level of attainment (or 'level of protection' as referred to in the SPS Agreement), the WTO adjudicating bodies recognized in several instances the absolute right of each Member to determine unilaterally the level of attainment that it considers appropriate.[173]

In *US—Shrimp*, the Appellate Body clarified that:

... conditioning access to a Member's domestic market on whether exporting Members comply with, or adopt, a policy or policies *unilaterally* prescribed by the importing Member may, to some degree, be a common aspect of measures falling within the scope of one or another of the exceptions (a) to (j) of Article XX.[174] (emphasis added)

With respect to Article XX(d) and the enforcement measures covered by this provision, the Appellate Body confirmed in *Korea—Beef* that

[I]t is not open to doubt that Members of the WTO have the right to determine for themselves the level of enforcement of their WTO-consistent laws and regulations.[175]

In addition, the Appellate Body reached the same conclusion with respect to Article XX(b) and measures relating to the protection of human health that aimed to attain a zero risk level:

it is undisputed that WTO Members have the right to determine the level of protection of health that they consider appropriate in a given situation.[176]

In GATT case law, the concept of necessity within the terms of Article XX was first tied to an examination of whether a satisfactory and effective alternative existed.[177] Later on, the *United States—Section 337* Panel, in reviewing whether

[172] Appellate Body Report, *US—Gasoline*, pp 30–31.

[173] Also G Marceau and JP Trachtman, 'The Technical Barriers to Trade Agreement, the Sanitary and Phytosanitary Measures Agreement, and The General Agreement on Tariffs and Trade: A Map of the World Trade Organization Law of Domestic Regulation of Goods' (2002) 36(5) JWT 837.

[174] Appellate Body Report, *US—Shrimp*, para 121.

[175] Appellate Body Report, *Korea—Various Measures on Beef*, para 176. By so ruling, the Appellate Body reversed the notorious *Tuna-Dolphin* case law established during the GATT years. See the unadopted Gatt Panel Report, *US—Tuna (Mexico)*, para 5.27.

[176] Appellate Body Report, *EC—Asbestos*, para 168. Hence, under Art XX, even an import ban, which, in the Appellate Body's words 'is, ordinarily the heaviest "weapon" in a Member's armoury of trade measures', can be justified. Appellate Body Report, *US—Shrimp*, para 171.

[177] GATT Panel Report, *US—Spring Assemblies*, para 58.

a US measure fell under Article XX(d), formulated the necessity test in the following terms:

> It was clear to the Panel that a contracting party cannot justify a measure inconsistent with another GATT provision as 'necessary' in terms of Article XX(d) *if an alternative measure which it could reasonably be expected to employ and which is not inconsistent with other GATT provisions is available to it.* By the same token, in cases where a measure consistent with other GATT provisions *is not reasonably available,* a contracting party is bound to use, among the measures reasonably available to it, that which entails the *least degree of inconsistency with other GATT provisions.*[178] (emphasis added)

Some years later, the tendency has been revealed to construe the term 'necessary' in a uniform way, although it denotes factually different situations.[179] In *Thailand—Cigarettes* during the GATT era, the Panel, applying a teleological interpretation, concluded that the term 'necessary' had the same meaning under paragraphs (b) and (d) and hence affirmed the approach of the Panel in *US—Section 337* regarding the meaning of the term 'necessary':

> In both paragraphs the same term was used and the same objective intended: to allow contracting parties to impose trade restrictive measures inconsistent with the General Agreement to pursue overriding public policy goals to the extent that such inconsistencies were unavoidable.[180]

In *Thailand—Cigarettes* and in *US—Section 337,* it was clarified that, in order for a measure to satisfy the necessity test of Article XX(b) and (d), it had to satisfy the 'least-trade-restrictiveness' requirement. From this jurisprudence it is also made clear that a Member is obliged to use a GATT-consistent measure rather than an inconsistent one only on condition that the objective that it seeks can be attained through either of the measures. This proposition remains valid in the WTO context, as will be explained in the following lines.

Passing to the post-Uruguay Round era, the Appellate Body, while endorsing the *US—Section 337* case law, elaborated further on the definition of the term 'necessary' in *Korea—Beef.*[181] In light of the interpretative rule of Article 31:1 of the *Vienna Convention*[182] and after reviewing dictionary definitions, the

[178] GATT Panel Report, *US—Section 337,* para 5.26.

[179] A Mattoo and PC Mavroidis, 'Trade, Environment and the WTO: The Dispute Settlement Practice Relating to Article XX of GATT' in E-U Petersmann (ed), *International Trade Law and the GATT/WTO Dispute Settlement System,* 1997, 336; also WTO, Committee on Trade and Environment, 'GATT/WTO Dispute Settlement Practice Relating to GATT Article XX, Paragraphs (b), (d), and (g)', WT/CTE/W/203, 8 March 2002, p 14.

[180] GATT Panel Report, *Thailand—Cigarettes,* para 74.

[181] Appellate Body Report, *Korea—Various Measures on Beef,* paras 160ff.

[182] In the Appellate Body's words, '... we look first to the ordinary meaning of the word "necessary", in its context and in the light of the object and purpose of Article XX...'. Appellate Body Report, *Korea—Various Measures on Beef,* para 159. Recently, the Appellate Body underscored that '[i]nterpretation pursuant to the customary rules codified in Article 31 of the *Vienna Convention* is ultimately a holistic exercise that should not be mechanically subdivided into rigid components. Considering particular surrounding circumstances under the rubric of "ordinary meaning" or

Appellate Body deduced that, with respect to Article XX(d), the term 'necessary' is not to be limited to that which is 'indispensable' or 'of absolute necessity' or 'inevitable'. Rather, the term 'necessary' refers to a 'range of degrees of necessity'. According to the Appellate Body:

> At one end of this continuum lies 'necessary' understood as 'indispensable'; at the other end, is 'necessary' taken to mean as 'making a contribution to'. We consider that a 'necessary' measure is, in this continuum, located *significantly closer* to the pole of 'indispensable' than to the opposite pole of simply 'making a contribution to'.[183] (emphasis added)

Hence, when a measure is indispensable, ie it is the only one available, its necessity cannot be challenged. When, on the other hand, other measures are also available and hence the measure is close to being deemed, but is not, indispensable, the Appellate Body suggested in the *Korea—Beef* case that the necessity test would involve a process of 'weighing and balancing a series of factors', which may be both *legal* (eg the context in which 'necessary' is located within a provision giving effect to its object and purpose) and *factual* (eg the reasonability, value and effect of the measure at issue).[184] This approach, then, takes for granted that a concrete alternative measure exists, which the responding Member could implement, and with which the WTO adjudicating bodies should compare the measure at issue. Hence, the Appellate Body explained that the determination as to whether a measure is 'necessary' within the meaning of Article XX(d):

> ... involves in every case a process of weighing and balancing a series of factors which *prominently include* the contribution made by the compliance measure to the enforcement of the law or regulation at issue [The greater the contribution, the more easily a measure might be considered to be 'necessary'], the importance of the common interests or values protected by that law or regulation [The more vital or important those common interests or values are, the easier it would be to accept as 'necessary' a measure designed as an enforcement instrument],[185] and the accompanying impact of the law or regulation on imports or exports. [A measure with a relatively slight impact upon imported products might more easily be considered as 'necessary' than a measure with intense or broader restrictive effects][186] (emphasis and footnote added)

"in the light of its context" would not, in our view, change the outcome of treaty interpretation'. Appellate Body Report, *EC—Chicken Cuts*, para 176.

[183] Appellate Body Report, *Korea—Various Measures on Beef*, para 161.

[184] Also Marceau and Trachtman (n 173 above) 850ff.

[185] To be sure, this phrase appears to 'suggest that there might be differing levels of scrutiny applicable to the analysis of the necessity test, depending on the importance of the "interests or values" it served'. WTO, Committee on Trade and Environment (n 179 above) p 16. In the same direction, AO Sykes, 'The Least Restrictive Means' (2003) 70(1) University of Chicago Law Review 416. For instance, when it comes to public health it is argued that '"necessary" carries a very flexible meaning that is relatively easy to meet'. M Matsushita, TJ Schoenbaum, and PC Mavroidis, *The World Trade Organization: Law, Practice and Policy*, 2003, 494. Indeed, the interests or values at stake appear to weigh more in the eyes of the Appellate Body, cf *US—Gambling*, para 307.

[186] Appellate Body Report, *Korea—Various Measures on Beef*, paras 162–164.

Then, according to this case-law, the necessity of a measure cannot be determined in the abstract, but for this determination, a comparison of the challenged measure to the alternative one that can achieve the same objective should occur. Consequently, a comparison of alternatives is crucial to a necessity test. The Appellate Body attempted to make operational the criteria dated back to the GATT era for evaluating the 'reasonable availability' of an alternative measure and identify some more precise factors that could assist in the comparison of the alternative measure with the impugned measure. The Appellate Body described this process of weighing and balancing of *at least* the three criteria identified in *Korea—Beef* (ie the relative importance of the interests or values furthered by the measure at issue, the contribution of the measure to the realization of the ends pursued by it, and the restrictive impact of the measure on international commerce) as one

> ...comprehended in the determination of whether a WTO-consistent alternative measure which the Member concerned could 'reasonably be expected to employ' is available, or whether a less WTO-inconsistent measure is 'reasonably available'.[187]

In addition, in *Korea—Beef*, the Appellate Body, while dismissing the argument that a 'consistency test' is introduced under Article XX, emphasized that the application of a WTO-compatible measure in a like, or at least similar, situation but not in the situation at stake can contravene the argument raised by the regulating Member that the measure at issue that is WTO-incompatible is nonetheless necessary, and may reveal that a *reasonably available* alternative WTO-consistent domestic regulatory instrument actually exists.[188] According to the Appellate Body:

> The application by a Member of WTO-*compatible* enforcement measures to the same kind of illegal behaviour... for like or at least similar products, provides a suggestive indication that an alternative measure which could 'reasonably be expected' to be employed may well be available. The application of such measures for the control of the same illegal behaviour for like, or at least similar, products raises doubts with respect to the objective *necessity* of a different, much stricter, and WTO-inconsistent enforcement measure.[189] (emphasis in the original)

A careful reader would notice that the Appellate Body adopted an evolutionary interpretation of the necessity requirement under Article XX(b) and (d). The evolutionary element hinges on the fact that the test that equated necessity with *least*-trade-restrictiveness as it was endorsed in *US—Section 337* was altered, notably after the *Korea—Beef* case law, to endorse a *less* trade-restrictive approach,

[187] Appellate Body Report, *Korea—Various Measures on Beef*, para 166.

[188] Ibid paras 170–172.

[189] Ibid para 172. Marceau and Trachtman correctly identified a 'soft consistency' requirement in this interpretation endorsed by the Appellate Body. Marceau and Trachtman (n 173 above) 847.

complemented with a sort of proportionality, means-ends test[190] (or 'a process of weighing and balancing a series of factors', in the Appellate Body's words). Even so, it is not certain whether one could talk about a shift of the position that the WTO adjudicating bodies previously adopted in the GATT years.[191] Arguably, there is indeed a shift that favours regulatory diversity and unilaterally-defined policy choice to a greater extent than in the pre-Uruguay Round years. This is so because, with the least-trade-restrictive test a second-best measure would probably be considered as non-justifiable,[192] whereas the less restrictive test allows for the adoption of a second-best measure, which, depending on the circumstances, could be deemed to satisfy the necessity requirement of Article XX(b) and (d).[193]

The abovementioned reasoning was also applied by the Appellate Body in *EC—Asbestos* with regard to Article XX(b). The Appellate Body reminded that one of the factors to determine whether a WTO-consistent alternative measure is reasonably available is the extent to which the measure at issue contributes to the realization of the objective of protecting human health, and the importance of the common values or interests pursued. The Appellate Body emphasized that the preservation of human life and health was both 'vital and important to the highest degree'.[194] The Appellate Body, then, sought to examine whether there was an alternative measure that would achieve the *same end* (ie the level of protection chosen by the EC) in an equally effective manner and that was less restrictive of trade than a total ban and answered the question in the negative.

Regarding the assessment of whether an alternative measure is *reasonably* available, the *US—Gasoline* Panel, in a finding not reviewed by the Appellate Body, stated, in essence, that an alternative measure can still be considered as reasonably available even in the existence of administrative difficulties.[195] The Appellate Body seized the opportunity to tackle this issue in *EC—Asbestos*. In this case, the Appellate Body somehow enriched the *US—Gasoline* Panel ruling and highlighted that the difficulty of implementation, as well as other factors

[190] The Appellate Body, in its interpretation of Art XX, appears to be open to the idea of using elements found in a proportionality test. cf Appellate Body Report, *US—Shrimp*, para 141. In fact, notably after the *Korea—Beef* ruling, the Appellate Body's interpretation of necessity has come closer to the proportionality test as it is applied by the ECJ. Compared to this latter test, the test that the WTO judiciary applies contains two out of the three conditions that the ECJ examines to decide whether a given measure is proportionate, that is, the suitability requirement and the necessity requirement. See Delimatsis (n 1 above); for the proportionality test in the EC legal order, see below under Section D.5 c) of this Chapter.

[191] In the negative, Neumann and Türk (n 142 above) 214.

[192] Mattoo and Subramanian suggested that there should be a presumption in favour of the economically first-best instrument accompanied by the widening of the objectives deemed legitimate under the body of Art XX. A Mattoo and A Subramanian, 'Regulatory Autonomy and Multilateral Disciplines: The Dilemma and a Possible Solution' (1998) 1 JIEL 317ff.

[193] In the WPDR discussions, for instance, the EC argued that the concept of 'least-trade-restrictiveness' would 'unduly restrict the choice of the regulatory tools available'. WTO, WPDR (n 139 above) para 17.

[194] Appellate Body Report, *EC—Asbestos*, para 172.

[195] Panel Report, *US—Gasoline*, paras 6.26, 6.28.

associated with administrative burden, such as cost, technical difficulties, and lack of expertise can be pertinent in determining that a measure does not qualify as reasonably available.[196]

Furthermore, in *Dominican Republic—Import and Sale of Cigarettes*, in the context of an examination of the necessity of a measure under Article XX(d), the Appellate Body supplemented the list of factors that can render an alternative measure reasonably *unavailable*. In this regard, the Appellate Body found relevant for the GATT context an earlier conclusion that it reached with respect to the factors that cause an alternative measure to be considered as not reasonably available in the services context under Article XIV GATS. Thus, the Appellate Body agreed that, in the goods realm (as in the case of services), an alternative measure can be deemed not to be reasonably available

> ...where it is merely theoretical in nature, for instance, where the responding Member is not capable of taking it, or where the measure imposes an undue burden on that Member, such as prohibitive costs or substantial technical difficulties. Moreover, a 'reasonably available' alternative measure must be a measure that would preserve for the responding Member its right to achieve its desired level of protection with respect to the objective pursued...[197]

I would only add that, as may be apparent from the preceding analysis, the mere fact that an alternative measure is more difficult or more expensive to implement does not automatically prevent this measure from being deemed reasonably available. Again, measures that call for an important administrative burden would more often than not be considered as not reasonably available. In any case, there are also other factors that need to be taken into consideration (eg the level of development of the responding Member) the ultimate standard of review being whether the alternative measure is as effective in achieving the objective pursued as the one adopted. Hence, the decision on the reasonable availability of a measure is a complex one and has to take into account various elements.

b) Article XIV GATS and paragraph 5(e) of the Annex on Telecommunications

Article XIV GATS[198] reads in relevant part:

> Subject to the requirement that such measures are not applied in a manner which would constitute a means of arbitrary or unjustifiable discrimination between countries

[196] cf Panel Report, *EC—Asbestos*, para 8.207. The Appellate Body endorsed the reasoning of the Panel regarding the application of the term 'reasonably available' *in concreto*. Appellate Body Report, *EC—Asbestos*, para 174; and Panel Report, *EC—Asbestos*, paras 8.208–8.216.

[197] Appellate Body Report, *Dominican Republic—Import and Sale of Cigarettes*, para 70; also Appellate Body Report, *US—Gambling*, para 308.

[198] For an exhaustive analysis of Art XIV GATS, see T Cottier, P Delimatsis, and N Diebold, 'Article XIV GATS' in R Wolfrum, P-T Stoll, and C Feinäugle (eds), *Max-Planck Commentaries on World Trade Law, Volume 6: WTO—Trade in Services*, 2008.

where like conditions prevail, or a disguised restriction on trade in services, *nothing in this Agreement shall be construed to prevent the adoption or enforcement by any Member of measures:*

(a) *necessary to* protect public morals or to maintain public order;[199]
(b) *necessary to* protect human, animal or plant life or health;
(c) *necessary to* secure compliance with laws or regulations which are not inconsistent with the provisions of this Agreement... (emphasis added)

The similarity of Article XIV GATS with Article XX GATT is striking. Importantly, however, Article XIV adds, next to the protection of public morals, the maintenance of public order as a legitimate policy objective. Arguably, this departure from the text of Article XX GATT allows for greater regulatory autonomy than in the goods context. Therefore, Article XIV GATS can hardly operate as a provision imposing some kind of deregulation. Rather, the terms used in the GATS context are wider, more inclusive and imply a higher degree of regulatory flexibility.[200] Nonetheless, footnote 5 to Article XIV attempts to limit the invocation of the public order exception only in cases of *genuine* and *sufficiently serious* threat to one of the *fundamental* societal interests.

What is more, Article XIV, just as Article XX GATT, aims to allow Members to adopt GATS-inconsistent measures for pre-defined purposes and subject to the specific requirements laid down therein. For this reason, the Article XX jurisprudence is instructive for any analysis under Article XIV GATS.[201] Nevertheless, Article XIV contains only five objectives that a Member can purport to pursue in order to justify the measure at issue, which is otherwise inconsistent with the Members' substantive obligations laid down in the GATS. Again, like Article XX GATT, it establishes three necessity tests with respect to objectives that are identical to those defined in Article XX GATT.[202]

In *US—Gambling*, the WTO adjudicating bodies had the opportunity to pronounce on the general exceptions provision of the GATS for the first time. In its analysis, the Appellate Body drew from its case-law under Article XX GATT and applied it accordingly to the measure at issue.[203] It started by underscoring that

[199] (original footnote) The public order exception may be invoked only where a genuine and sufficiently serious threat is posed to one of the fundamental interests of society.

[200] cf Panel Report, *US—Gambling*, para 6.467; and Appellate Body Report, *US—Gambling*, para 323.

[201] Also Appellate Body Report, *EC—Bananas III*, para 231 (encouraging Panels that tackle GATS claims to refer to the GATT only where the obligations are essentially of the same type). This was confirmed in the Appellate Body Report, *US—Gambling*, para 291. cf also Appellate Body Report, *EC—Sardines*, para 275 (where the Appellate Body criticizes the Panel because it failed to deploy a principle articulated under the SPS Agreement on the burden of proof in the TBT context, although there were conceptual similarities between the provisions in the two Agreements).

[202] cf with paras (a), (b), and (d) of Art XX GATT.

[203] To avoid repetition, I will focus only on the elements that are new *vis-à-vis* the jurisprudence with respect to goods, which, according to the Appellate Body, applies to the services realm *mutatis mutandis* (n 201 above).

the necessity standard contained in Article XIV is an *objective* standard[204] and therefore the task of the Panel is, based on the evidence submitted before it, to 'independently and objectively assess the "necessity" of the measure before it'.[205]

Based on *Korea—Beef* and *EC—Asbestos* jurisprudence, the Appellate Body reiterated that 'a comparison between the challenged measure and possible alternatives should be undertaken, and the results of such comparison should be considered in the light of the importance of the interests at issue'.[206] According to the Appellate Body, the necessity analysis entails a strict scrutiny of the measure at issue and this is so because the substantive obligations under the GATS should not be deviated from 'lightly'.

Furthermore, the Appellate Body elaborated more on the issue of the burden of proof in the context of a general exceptions provision, which is fairly important in the presence of information asymmetries. As already pointed out, the *responding* party bears the burden of adducing evidence to show that its measure falls under the scope of an affirmative defence and hence that it satisfies the requirements laid down therein. Nevertheless, the Appellate Body ruled for the first time in the *US—Gambling* case that the WTO dispute settlement organs cannot expect that the respondent identifies the 'universe of less trade-restrictive alternative measures' and subsequently establishes that only the measure at issue achieves the desired objective in the way that the Member initially wanted it and thus is the most reasonably available measure. This would be, according to the Appellate Body, an '*impracticable and often impossible burden*'.[207]

To be sure, one should expect that the respondent will first proffer evidence sufficient to raise a presumption that the measure at issue is necessary taking into account, inter alia, the three factors identified in *Korea—Beef*. Then, it is up to the *complainant* to effectively counter or refute the claimed necessity of the measure by raising alternatives and thus putting forward a *concrete*, reasonably available, WTO-consistent (or less WTO-inconsistent) alternative measure, if there is any.[208] In that case, the respondent will be called upon to demonstrate why the measure at issue, compared to the alternative proposed by the complainant, is still necessary, or why the purported alternative measure is not, in fact, reasonably available, always bearing in mind the interests and values pursued and the Member's desired level of protection.[209]

In *US—Gambling*, the Appellate Body reversed the Panel's ruling that engaging in consultations with Antigua with a view to settling their differences was an alternative measure that was reasonably available to the United States in

[204] cf Appellate Body Report, *Korea—Various Measures on Beef*, para 172.

[205] Appellate Body Report, *US—Gambling*, para 304.

[206] Ibid para 307.

[207] Appellate Body Report, *Japan—Agricultural Products II*, para 137.

[208] Also Appellate Body Report, *Japan—Agricultural Products II*, para 126. See also the discussion on Art 5.6 SPS below.

[209] Appellate Body Report, *US—Gambling*, paras 309–311.

order for the latter to achieve its legitimate objectives.[210] The Appellate Body was led to this conclusion by the fact that 'consultations are by definition a process, the results of which are uncertain and therefore not capable of comparison with the measure at issue'.[211] As the complainant, *in casu* Antigua, failed to identify any alternative measure, the Appellate Body agreed that the United States made a prima facie case that the measure at issue satisfied the necessity requirement laid down in Article XIV(a) GATS.[212]

The Panel in the *Mexico—Taxes on Soft Drinks* dispute, when interpreting Article XX(d) GATT, relied on this Appellate Body's ruling, made under Article XIV(a) GATS, and ruled it cannot be considered as a reasonably available alternative any measure which is of uncertain outcome; instead '. . . it would seem that there should be a degree of certainty in the results that may be achieved through the measure'.[213] The Appellate Body, however, reversed this finding by emphasizing that, first, it was improper to apply an interpretation made in another context to the case at stake, and, second, the measure at issue needed *not* be designed to guarantee the achievement of its result (in this case, securing compliance with domestic laws and regulations)[214] 'with *absolute* certainty'.[215] This latter reference, however, is difficult to reconcile with the Appellate Body's previous ruling in *Korea—Beef* that the term 'necessary' should be deemed to have a meaning that is significantly closer to the 'pole of indispensable'. Arguably, the Appellate Body's approach of the necessity standard became more lenient and flexible when compared with the *Korea—Beef* jurisprudence.

As to paragraph 5(e) of the GATS Annex on Telecommunications[216] and the necessity test set out therein, the Panel in *Mexico—Telecoms* interpreted it in a

[210] Panel Report, *US—Gambling*, paras 6.528–6.534.

[211] Appellate Body Report, *US—Gambling*, para 317.

[212] Ibid para 325. However, the Appellate Body ultimately found that the United States did not satisfy the requirements of the *chapeau*, as it had not demonstrated that the three federal laws at issue were not repealed from the Interstate Horseracing Act (IHA). Ibid para 371. This ambiguity as to the scope of the IHA led the DSU 21:5 Panel, which was recently established at the request of Antigua, to conclude that the United States did not comply with the DSB recommendations after the expiration of the reasonable period of time that it sought. The enactment of the Unlawful Internet Gambling Enforcement Act (UIGEA) did not alter this conclusion. See Panel Report, *US—Gambling (Article 21.5—Antigua)*, para 6.135.

[213] Panel Report, *Mexico—Taxes on Soft Drinks*, para 8.188.

[214] Under 'laws and regulations' one should understand 'rules that form part of the domestic legal system of a WTO Member, including rules deriving from international agreements that have been incorporated into the domestic legal system of a WTO Member or have direct effect according to that WTO Member's legal system'. Appellate Body Report, *Mexico—Taxes on Soft Drinks*, para 79.

[215] Appellate Body Report, *Mexico—Taxes on Soft Drinks*, para 74.

[216] Paragraph 5(e) of the GATS Annex on Telecommunications reads in the relevant part:

Each Member shall ensure that no condition is imposed on access to and use of public telecommunications transport networks and services other than as necessary:

(i) to safeguard the public service responsibilities of suppliers of public telecommunications transport networks and services, in particular their ability to make their networks or services available to the public generally;

manner that deviated from the WTO case-law. More specifically, this provision requires that Members ensure that the only conditions imposed on access and use of public telecommunications transport networks and services are those necessary to attain the policy objectives mentioned in paragraph 5(e).[217] The Panel, in a clear deviation from the *Korea—Beef* jurisprudence, favoured an interpretation that would consider 'necessary' as meaning 'making a contribution to' rather than 'indispensable' to achieve a policy objective and thus ruled that, for the purposes of this case, the necessity standard should not be considered as being closer to the 'pole of indispensable'.[218] Obviously, the Panel misinterpreted previous case-law as well as the very wording of paragraph 5(e) and read in the provision words that were simply not there and imported a concept that apparently was not intended, ie that 'necessary' equals to 'making a contribution to'.[219]

c) *Article 2.2 of the TBT Agreement*

The disciplines of the TBT Agreement seek to strike a balance between Members' freedom to adopt and implement technical regulations[220] which are considered as being necessary to attain *legitimate* policy objectives and the promotion of trade expansion through the elimination of unnecessary barriers to trade. Unlike Article XX GATT and XIV GATS, which become relevant after a violation of another provision in the GATT or GATS, respectively, Article 2.2 TBT entails a necessity requirement that applies *independently* and is expressed in the following terms:

> Members shall ensure that technical regulations are not prepared, adopted or applied *with a view to* or *with the effect of* creating unnecessary obstacles to international trade. For this purpose, *technical regulations shall not be more trade-restrictive than necessary to fulfil a legitimate objective, taking account of the risks non-fulfilment would create.* Such legitimate objectives are, *inter alia:* national security requirements; the prevention of deceptive practices; protection of human health or safety, animal or plant life or health, or the environment. In assessing such risks, relevant elements of consideration are, *inter alia:* available scientific and technical information, related processing technology or intended end-uses of products. (emphasis added)

Hence, in order for a technical regulation to comply with Article 2.2, it has to be deemed 'necessary' to pursue a legitimate objective. As the list of objectives is illustrative, Members can pursue an objective that is either explicitly mentioned

(ii) to protect the technical integrity of public telecommunications transport networks or services; or
(iii) to ensure that service suppliers of any other Member do not supply services unless permitted pursuant to commitments in the Member's Schedule.

217 Panel Report, *Mexico—Telecoms*, para 7.306.
218 Ibid paras 7.337–7.343.
219 cf Appellate Body Report, *India—Patents (US)*, para 45.
220 For a definition, see Annex 1.1 TBT; also Appellate Body Report, *EC—Sardines*, para 176.

in Article 2.2, or one that could fall under this category of objectives and further its achievement. This provision aims to ensure various elements governing all stages of the regulatory process, ie preparation, adoption, and application of technical regulations. As Article 2.2 is a substantive obligation, where there is a concern whether a Member's measure is the least trade-restrictive available for achieving a certain permissible objective, it is the *complaining* Member who should adduce evidence showing that the regulating Member has failed to ensure in its regulatory process that its measure is the least trade-restrictive.[221] In this respect, the WTO judiciary is called upon to consider the risks that the non-fulfilment of the intended legitimate objective would create. Hence, contrary to the previous necessity tests, Article 2.2 TBT implies a cost–benefit analysis and appears to give a considerable margin of appreciation to the domestic regulatory authorities when they exercise their functions.[222]

The WTO judiciary has not yet pronounced on the necessity test of Article 2.2. In *EC—Sardines*, however, where the interpretation of Article 2.4 TBT was at stake,[223] there were some indirect[224] references to Article 2.2, notably with respect to the term 'legitimate objectives'.[225] First, it has been confirmed that Article 2.2 includes an illustrative list of objectives that Members *explicitly* considered as legitimate. Second, both the Panel and the Appellate Body contended that the meaning of the term 'legitimate objective' is the same under Articles 2.2 and 2.4 TBT.

Moreover, the Panel, after having recalled the sixth recital of the TBT Preamble, confirmed that the TBT is no exception in the general philosophy of the GATT/WTO law by stating that 'it is up to the Members to decide which policy objectives they wish to pursue and the levels at which they wish to pursue them'.[226] Immediately afterwards, however, the Panel reiterated the qualification, well-known from the GATT years, that the *means*, alias the instruments, that a

[221] Also R Howse and E Türk, 'The WTO Impact on Internal Regulations—A Case Study of the Canada-EC Asbestos Dispute' in G de Búrca and J Scott (eds), *The EU and the WTO: Legal and Constitutional Issues*, 2001, 310.

[222] Marceau and Trachtman (n 173 above) 831. For a different approach, that nonetheless leads to a similar conclusion, see A Desmedt, 'Proportionality in WTO Law' (2001) 4 JIEL 459–460; also F Ortino, 'From "non-discrimination" to "reasonableness": a paradigm shift in international economic law?', Jean Monnet Working Paper 01/05, 2005, 44–45.

[223] Article 2.4 TBT provides :

Where technical regulations are required and relevant international standards *exist* or their completion is *imminent*, Members shall use them, or the relevant parts of them, *as a basis for* their technical regulations except when such international standards or *relevant parts* would be an *ineffective* or *inappropriate* means for the fulfilment of the legitimate objectives pursued, for instance because of fundamental climatic or geographical factors or fundamental technological problems. (emphasis added)

[224] The Appellate Body did not deal further with Article 2.2 because, in its view, 'the question whether a domestic regulatory measure is trade-restrictive is not relevant for the purpose of making a finding under Article 2.4'. Appellate Body Report, *EC—Sardines*, para 310.

[225] Panel Report, *EC—Sardines*, para 7.118; also Appellate Body Report, *EC—Sardines*, para 286.

[226] Panel Report, *EC—Sardines*, para 7.120.

Member chooses to employ in order to attain its domestic policy objectives will be exposed to the scrutiny of the WTO dispute settlement organs.[227]

Importantly, as to the burden of proof, the Panel underscored that, in the context of Article 2.4, the responding Member is expected to advance the objectives of its technical regulation at issue that it regards as legitimate. According to the Panel in *EC—Sardines*, only the responding Member can elaborate the objective that it pursues.[228] Nevertheless, the Panel's task is to objectively verify the legitimacy of this objective.

The Appellate Body reversed the Panel's ruling relative to the burden of proof and made clear that, Article 2.4 being a substantive obligation, the burden of proof lies with the *complaining* party to establish that an international standard has not been used 'as a basis for' the domestic regulatory measure, in case the responding Member does not use this relevant international standard, as well as establish that the international standard is effective and appropriate to fulfil the legitimate objectives pursued by the regulating Member.[229]

Hence, the complainant should make a prima facie case that the objectives pursued by the regulatory Member are not legitimate or that relevant international standards would not be ineffective or inappropriate for attaining the objectives. Nevertheless, inexplicably enough, the Appellate Body upheld the Panel's finding 'that the second part of Article 2.4 implies that there must be an examination and a determination on the legitimacy of the objectives of the measure'.[230]

In this case, the Appellate Body appears to endorse a different approach from the one discussed earlier with respect to the affirmative defence of Article XX GATT. In *EC—Sardines*, both parties agreed that the ends pursued by the European Communities (ie market transparency, consumer protection, and fair competition) should be deemed legitimate;[231] consequently, the Panel did not have a reason to insist on that. What is more, a Panel would not try to examine or determine the legitimacy of an objective that is explicitly mentioned in Article 2.2. This list, being illustrative, can of course encompass many other legitimate objectives. If one follows the Panel's and Appellate Body's approach, the latter objectives could be considered as legitimate only after a Panel or the Appellate Body has said so.

Arguably, then, in a case where the responding party disagrees that the objective that the responding party seeks to pursue is indeed legitimate, the WTO adjudicating bodies will have the authority to second-guess a Member's regulatory choices. If so, would this shift be a clear interference with an area that is considered to date as a prerogative of Members? And would not such an approach create two categories of legitimate policy objectives, that is, those that are explicitly

[227] Ibid.

[228] Ibid paras 7.50–7.52, 7.121.

[229] Appellate Body Report, *EC—Sardines*, paras 275, 282, 287.

[230] Panel Report, *EC—Sardines*, para 7.121 and Appellate Body Report, *EC—Sardines*, para 286.

[231] Panel Report, *EC—Sardines*, para 7.122.

mentioned in Article 2.2 and hence are 'sealed' and escape the legitimacy determination test, but will undergo only a means-ends test examining the 'degree of connection' between the measure and the objective, and those (let us call them, for obvious reasons 'the disadvantaged ones') that are only implied in Article 2.2[232] and therefore the WTO adjudicating bodies, in the case of disagreement between the parties, should first and foremost *determine* that the objective sought is legitimate?[233] If anything, this would be a far-reaching, precarious approach, at least in the present stage of integration in the WTO. Such an interpretation also purports to contradict the Appellate Body's earlier statement that '[t]he TBT acknowledges the right of every WTO Member to establish for itself the objectives of its technical regulations ...'.[234]

Moreover, Article 2.5 in its second sentence, by recognizing the important role that international standards play in promoting harmonization and facilitating trade,[235] provides that whenever a technical regulation is prepared, adopted or applied for one of the legitimate objectives of Article 2.2 and is in accordance with international standards, it is to be rebuttably presumed not to create an unnecessary obstacle to trade, that is, it will be considered as being 'necessary'.[236] Interestingly, in *EC—Sardines*, the Panel found that, since the EC measure did not conform to the relevant international standard of the *Codex Alimentarius*, it should be considered as being an *unnecessary* obstacle to trade, that is, '*more* trade-restrictive than necessary'.[237] This would suggest that the burden of proof shifts to the responding party. The Appellate Body emphasized that this was an *obiter dictum* and thus declared the Panel's statements moot and without legal effect.[238]

It is clear, however, that the Panel's statement takes issue with the spirit of Article 2.5 TBT to create a *reverse* presumption. Indeed, it 'extracts a reverse inference that if a measure does not conform to international standards, the Member imposing such a measure must bear the burden of proof in any complaint of

[232] Potential additional legitimate objectives and rationales for domestic regulation measures mentioned in TBT notifications in 2004 include: consumer information and labelling; quality requirements; harmonization; lowering or removal of trade barriers and trade facilitation; and cost saving and increasing productivity. WTO, Committee on Technical Barriers to Trade, 'Tenth Annual Review of the Implementation and Operation of the TBT Agreement', G/TBT/15, 4 March 2005, para 10.

[233] That the WTO judiciary will, in certain instances, examine the legitimacy of the declared objective of a measure is arguably confirmed in *US—Shrimp*. Appellate Body Report, *US—Shrimp*, para 149.

[234] Appellate Body Report, *EC—Sardines*, para 276.

[235] Ibid paras 214–215.

[236] Also Panel Report, *EC—Sardines*, para 7.75, and Appellate Body Report, *EC—Sardines*, paras 211–212, 214. The presumption of necessity suggests that the *complaining* party will bear the burden of proof as to the inconsistency of the measure at hand with the necessity requirement. See, with respect to Art 3.2 SPS, which also provides for a rebuttable presumption, Appellate Body Report, *EC—Hormones*, paras 102, 104.

[237] Panel Report, *EC—Sardines*, para 6.11 and fn 35.

[238] Appellate Body Report, *EC—Sardines*, para 311.

inconsistency with the provision of the [TBT] Agreement'.[239] The *EC—Hormones* Panel reached an identical finding with respect to Article 3.2 SPS,[240] which, like Article 2.5 TBT, creates a rebuttable presumption that a domestic regulation measure is necessary if it conforms to international standards.

The Appellate Body in the *EC—Hormones* case was given the opportunity to pronounce on this issue. In the Appellate Body's view, while Article 3.2 SPS (and, by possible implication, Article 2.5 TBT) may well be an incentive for Members to use international standards when designing their domestic regulatory measures,[241] a decision by a Member *not* to take a relevant international standard into account when promulgating a domestic regulatory measure should not result in the imposition of a special or generalized burden of proof on that Member. To be sure, this would be an unfair burden that would indeed amount to a 'penalty'.[242] Thus, the Appellate Body rejected the 'converse' or '*a contrario*' presumption created by the Panel.[243] One would expect that, *mutatis mutandis*, the Appellate Body will seize the first chance that it will have to pronounce on the issue with respect, this time, to the TBT Agreement in order to extend this jurisprudence also to the area of technical barriers to trade, and in particular, Article 2.5 TBT and consequently reject for good the Panel's statement in *EC—Sardines* relative to the reverse presumption or implication that the Panel read in Article 2.5. This should be considered as merely a matter of time, taking into account that the Appellate Body already pronounced on the similar issue of the burden of proof under Art. 2.4 TBT by underscoring that it is for the *complaining* party to bear the burden of proving the effectiveness and appropriateness of an international standard for fulfilling the legitimate objective pursued by the defending party.

d) Article 5.6 of the SPS Agreement

The most important necessity test envisaged in the SPS Agreement is to be found in Article 5.6, which provides in the relevant part:

> ...when *establishing or maintaining* sanitary or phytosanitary measures to achieve the *appropriate level of sanitary or phytosanitary protection*, Members shall ensure that such measures are not more trade-restrictive than *required* to achieve *their* appropriate level of sanitary or phytosanitary protection, *taking into account technical and economic feasibility*. (emphasis added)

[239] Appellate Body Report, *EC—Hormones*, para 101.

[240] Panel Report, *EC—Hormones (US)*, paras 8.86–8.87.

[241] When interpreting Art 3.2 SPS, which also creates a rebuttable presumption of consistency in the context of SPS measures, the Appellate Body made clear that a measure would benefit from this presumption provided that it 'embod[ies] the international standard completely and, for practical purposes, convert[s] it into a municipal standard'. Appellate Body Report, *EC–Hormones*, para 170. Such a finding can be applicable *mutatis mutandis* for the purposes of Art 2.5 TBT.

[242] Appellate Body Report, *EC—Hormones*, para 102.

[243] Ibid. Also para 105.

This necessity test is subject to a 'reasonable availability' qualification[244] which provides:[245]

For purposes of paragraph 6 of Article 5, a measure is not more trade-restrictive than required unless there is another measure, *reasonably* available *taking into account technical and economic feasibility*, that achieves the appropriate level of sanitary or phytosanitary protection and is *significantly* less restrictive to trade. (emphasis added)

Hence, the SPS Agreement is the only WTO agreement that provides, in its very text, a definition that can be considered as a guidance regarding the elements that make a measure 'more trade-restrictive than required'. Indeed, footnote 3 to Article 5.6 appears to encapsulate the long-established jurisprudence with respect to Article XX GATT, but, at the same time, adds new elements to it. Being one of the fairly new features of the multilateral trading system, the drafters of the SPS Agreement benefited from earlier jurisprudence and the Members' determination to abolish any ambiguities in the text of the Agreement to the greatest extent possible by using definitions that reflect a consistent jurisprudence. To be sure, in this footnote one can see a crystallization of the GATT *acquis*,[246] accompanied by the *de minimis* requirement that the alternative SPS measure be *significantly* less trade-restrictive.

With respect to the application of the necessity test in the SPS Agreement, *Australia —Salmon* is the first case to tackle the concepts associated with Article 5.6 SPS. Under Article 5.6, the issue at hand was whether the import prohibition on fresh, chilled or frozen salmon that Australia implemented was more trade-restrictive than required to achieve Australia's appropriate level of protection. The Appellate Body started its analysis by endorsing the Panel's view that this provision entails a three-pronged test for establishing a violation of Article 5.6, which consists of three separate elements that apply *cumulatively*:

We agree with the Panel that Article 5.6 and, in particular, the footnote to this provision clearly provides a three-pronged test to establish a violation of Article 5.6. As already noted, the three elements of this test under Article 5.6 are that there is an [alternative] SPS measure which:

(1) is reasonably available taking into account technical and economic feasibility;
(2) achieves the Member's appropriate level of sanitary or phytosanitary protection; and
(3) is significantly less restrictive to trade than the SPS measure contested.

These three elements are cumulative in the sense that, to establish inconsistency with Article 5.6, all of them have to be met. If any of these elements is not fulfilled, the measure in dispute would be consistent with Article 5.6. Thus, if there is no alternative measure available, taking into account technical and economic feasibility, *or* if the alternative measure does not achieve the Member's appropriate level of sanitary or phytosanitary

[244] cf JP Trachtman, 'Lessons for the GATS from Existing WTO Rules on Domestic Regulation' in A Mattoo and P Sauvé (eds), *Domestic Regulation and Service Trade Liberalization*, 2003, 65.

[245] Art 5.6 SPS, fn 3.

[246] cf for instance Art XVII:2, 3 GATS.

protection, *or* if it is not significantly less trade-restrictive, the measure in dispute would be consistent with Article 5.6.[247] (emphasis in the original)

The Appellate Body took issue with the Panel's findings regarding the appropriate level of protection[248] and criticized it for confounding the SPS measure with the appropriate level of protection sought by the regulating Member, *in casu* Australia. At the outset, the Appellate Body reiterated that it is an irrefutable prerogative of each Member, and not of a Panel or of the Appellate Body, to determine its appropriate level of protection.[249] Earlier, the Appellate Body confirmed that a Member is not precluded from choosing a 'zero risk' level of protection.[250]

Furthermore, the appropriate level of protection is an *objective* whose determination will be part of the domestic decisionmaking process and needs to be clearly distinguished from the SPS measure at hand, the latter being an *instrument* chosen to achieve the objective sought. In addition, the Member's determination of the level of protection that it considers appropriate will usually precede, and be separate from, the adoption or the decision to maintain an SPS measure.[251]

In the Appellate Body's view, 'it is the appropriate level of protection which determines the SPS measure to be introduced or maintained' and not the other way around.[252] The Appellate Body summarized by stating that Article 5.6 SPS requires that an examination be conducted as to whether an alternative SPS measure exists that meets the appropriate level of protection *as determined by the regulating Member*.[253] According to the Appellate Body, it is important that Members determine clearly the appropriate level of protection that they seek and the SPS Agreement contains an implicit obligation to this effect.[254] Nevertheless, one would be compelled to follow the Panel's methodology and hence second-guess the appropriate level of protection by examining the SPS measure *actually applied*, only in the absence of a determination of the appropriate level of protection, or because it was determined with insufficient precision.[255]

[247] Appellate Body Report, *Australia—Salmon*, para 194. Also Appellate Body Report, *Japan—Agricultural Products II*, para 95.

[248] Also Marceau and Trachtman (n 173 above) 834.

[249] Also Annex A.5 to the SPS Agreement.

[250] Appellate Body Report, *Australia—Salmon*, para 125. Of course, the right of a Member to determine its appropriate level of protection, while being 'an autonomous right and not an "exception" from a "general obligation" under Article 3.1 [SPS]', is not 'an absolute or unqualified right'. Appellate Body Report, *EC—Hormones*, paras 172–173. Additionally, this right is somehow restrained due to Art 5.4 SPS which encourages Members, when determining the appropriate level of protection, to take into account the objective of *minimizing negative trade effects*. The *EC—Hormones* Panel, while acknowledging that this provision does not entail an obligation, emphasized that this objective will be taken into account in the interpretation of other SPS provisions. Panel Report, *EC—Hormones (US)*, para 8.166.

[251] Appellate Body Report, *Australia—Salmon*, paras 199–201.

[252] Ibid para 203.

[253] Ibid para 204.

[254] Ibid para 206.

[255] Ibid para 207. For example, in *Korea—Various Measures on Beef*, the Appellate Body presumed the appropriate level of protection. Appellate Body Report, *Korea—Various Measures on Beef*, para 178.

An important issue with respect to the necessity tests in the SPS Agreement (with possible legal implications for the respective necessity tests in other obligation provisions, such as those in the TBT Agreement and Article VI:4 GATS) is the allocation of the burden of proof. First in the *EC—Hormones* case it was clarified that:

> The initial burden lies on the complaining party, which must establish a *prima facie* case of inconsistency with a particular provision of the *SPS Agreement* on the part of the defending party, or more precisely, of its SPS measure or measures complained about. When that *prima facie* case is made, the burden of proof moves to the defending party, which must in turn counter or refute the claimed inconsistency.[256]

In *Japan—Agricultural Products*, the Appellate Body tackled the issue of the allocation of the burden of proof with respect to Article 5.6 SPS and confirmed that the *complaining* party bears the burden of proof and hence should make a prima facie case that, first, a violation of Article 5.6 has occurred and, second, that there are alternative, less restrictive, technically and economically feasible measures reasonably available.[257] Absent a *prima facie* establishment of inconsistency based on specific legal claims asserted by the complaining party, the Panel is not allowed to make the case for it.[258]

As mentioned earlier with respect to Article 2.5 TBT, in the *EC—Hormones* case, the WTO adjudicating bodies interpreted Article 3.2 SPS,[259] which embodies a rebuttable presumption that an SPS measure is SPS-consistent, and is to be considered as 'necessary' to protect human, animal or plant life and health, provided that this measure conforms to an international standard.[260] The Appellate Body clarified the content and function of Article 3.2 SPS vis-à-vis Articles 3.1 and 3.3 SPS, and shed some light on the critical issue of the allocation of the burden of proof, reversing in both cases the Panel's findings.

For an SPS domestic regulatory measure to benefit from this presumption, it should 'embody the international standard completely and, for practical purposes, convert[s] it into a municipal standard'.[261] This provision constitutes an *incentive* for Members to introduce international standards in their entirety in their domestic legal orders, but in no way obliges a Member to act in this manner. Nevertheless, it is a Member's sovereign right not to adopt international standards and therefore imposing a 'special or generalized' burden of proof on this Member would result in penalizing them. Equally, in a case where a Member adopts an

[256] Appellate Body Report, *EC—Hormones*, para 98.

[257] Appellate Body Report, *Japan—Agricultural Products II*, para 126.

[258] Ibid para 129.

[259] Art 3.2 SPS reads:

> Sanitary or phytosanitary measures which conform to international standards, guidelines or recommendations shall be deemed to be necessary to protect human, animal or plant life or health, and presumed to be consistent with the relevant provisions of this Agreement and of GATT 1994.

[260] Also Appellate Body Report, *EC—Hormones*, para 170.

[261] Ibid.

SPS measure that is *based on* the existing international standard, this Member, while not benefiting, as in the previous case, from the presumption of consistency laid down in Article 3.2 SPS, should not be 'penalised by exemption of a complaining Member from the normal burden of showing a prima facie case of inconsistency with Article 3.1 or any other relevant article of the SPS Agreement or of the GATT 1994'.[262]

Article 2.2 SPS also envisages a necessity test expressed in the following terms:

> Members shall ensure that any sanitary or phytosanitary measure is *applied* only to the extent *necessary* to protect human, animal or plant life or health, is based on scientific principles and is not maintained without sufficient scientific evidence, except as provided for in paragraph 7 of Article 5. (emphasis added)

This necessity test focuses on the unnecessary *application* of regulatory measures, whereas Article 5.6 outlaws the *adoption* of unnecessary measures. However, a violation of Article 5.6 would also lead to a violation of Article 2.2 when the measure in question has been applied by the regulatory state, unless there is a challenge of a measure *as such*.[263] Importantly, the Appellate Body emphasized that:

> the establishment or maintenance of an SPS measure which implies or reflects a *higher* level of protection than the appropriate level of protection *determined by an importing Member*, could constitute a violation of the necessity requirement of Article 2.2.[264] (emphasis added)

This finding begs the question of whether the Appellate Body would invalidate a measure that reflects a change in a Member's beliefs regarding its appropriate level of protection. In other words, once the appropriate level of protection for a Member is determined, does this Member have the right to adopt a new measure that would reflect a higher level of protection or would it thereby violate its obligations under Article 2.2 TBT? The Appellate Body's statement appears to suggest, quite astonishingly, that such a change would, in all likelihood, violate Article 2.2 TBT.

e) A tentative conclusion

While it is true that it should not be automatically assumed that an interpretation of a necessity test in one agreement might be transferable to another agreement,[265] useful elements for a possible, horizontally applicable necessity test with respect to trade in services are to be traced in every necessity test analysed above. Of course, one should not lose sight of the fact that the Article VI:4 necessity test

[262] Ibid para 171.

[263] Also Appellate Body Report, *Australia—Salmon*, para 213.

[264] Ibid para 213, fn 166.

[265] See the Secretariat's intervention in WTO, WPDR, 'Report on the Meeting Held on 3 December 2003', S/WPDR/M/24, 22 January 2004, para 41.

belongs to Part II of the GATS (General Obligations and Disciplines) and hence falls under the category of the necessity tests scrutinized earlier establishing an *obligation* rather than an *exception*.

Hence important issues that need to be clarified during the development of a prospective horizontal necessity test based on Article VI:4, such as the allocation of the burden of proof, the permissible range of legitimate objectives and the determination of the level of attainment, the definition of terms like 'necessary', 'reasonably available', 'least or less trade-restrictiveness', etc, could be elucidated by the aforementioned discussion on similar concepts set out in *obligations* provisions of other WTO Agreements, such as Article 2.2 TBT or 5.6 SPS.[266]

Furthermore, the whole discussion will be inevitably informed and enriched *mutatis mutandis* by the rich jurisprudence on Article XX GATT. Despite the fact that the latter provision falls under the category of *exceptions* provisions, one should bear in mind that under this provision the GATT Panels brought forward decisive interpretations of the concept of 'necessity'; these interpretations have been very influential even with respect to the fairly new Agreements of the TBT and the SPS, which entail necessity as part of *obligations* provisions. Hence, Article XX GATT can still play a significant role relating to the interpretation of the central concept of necessity, particularly due to the fact that this concept overall comprises common characteristics which seem to surpass the narrow confines of any covered Agreement. Thus, one could refer to this concept of being a universal concept the very core of which, ie the less trade-restrictiveness, the balancing or means-ends test along with a reasonableness prong, and the comparison between alternatives, remains essentially the same regardless of the Agreement where one locates it.

4. The necessity requirement with respect to services trade in regional integration agreements

In principle, the distinguishing feature of RIAs[267] vis-à-vis the multilateral trading system is that the former typically strive for deeper integration.[268] This integration is considered to be more easily achieved due to similarities in preferences between the participating countries but also because consensus is more easily

[266] *But* see the United States' intervention, in WTO, WPDR, 'Report on the Meeting Held on 31 March 2004', S/WPDR/M/25, 18 May 2004, para 63; also the comment of Mexico that 'the parameters in Article VI:4 were somewhat loose compared to other instruments, while those in TBT and SPS agreements were much more specific and tangible'. Ibid para 65.

[267] The discussion in this sub-section focuses on regional agreements that have a component that liberalizes trade in services at a bilateral or plurilateral level. In the WTO parlance, these agreements are known as 'Economic Integration Agreements'.

[268] Whether this is to the detriment of global welfare is open to question. P Krugman, 'Is Bilateralism Bad?' in E Helpman and A Razin (eds), *International Trade and Trade Policy*, 1991, 9.

reached at a regional level with few countries on the negotiating table.[269] In the aftermath of the Uruguay Round, RIAs on services have flourished. This proliferation is to be justified by economic as well as political considerations. In addition, the time-consuming request–offer process of services negotiations and the overall sluggish progress of the multilateral trade negotiations lead Members to the detection of alternatives.[270] Nonetheless, research to date suggests that, apart from the EU's far-reaching integration model, there has been no substantial progress in any RIA as to the demarcation of possible elements with a view to developing a strong necessity test aiming to tackle unnecessary barriers to regional services trade.[271]

Especially with respect to trade in services, RIAs are not considered to distort trade as is the case with RIAs in goods because trade diversion in the former case is minimal. But while preferential liberalization in services is welfare enhancing, the gains from multilateral liberalization can be even higher at a domestic and global level compared to those created by the emergence of a RIA.[272] Again, regional and multilateral efforts of liberalizing trade in services, while concurrent, have proven, and will continue, to be advancing in parallel and benefiting from each other.[273]

Several RIAs have already benefited from the wording and the structure of the GATS. Notably Article VI GATS is one of the provisions that, with few changes, are to be found in various RIAs. Hence, manifold RIAs have a certain degree of standardization. On the other hand, the GATS will be benefiting from the RIAs, as Members participating in such agreements will acquire enhanced negotiating capacity for the multilateral negotiations and, due to their regional experience, they will enrich and hopefully expedite the negotiations in the GATS. Furthermore, several RIAs can be considered as useful 'laboratories' where rules are tested and significant lessons can be drawn.[274]

The most illustrative examples of the latter are the necessity tests to be found in the MERCOSUR and the Trans-Pacific Strategic Economic Partnership. Both of these agreements incorporate a GATS-type approach with respect to services. This is notably the case of MERCOSUR, which also uses a positive list approach

[269] G Marceau and C Reiman, 'When and How Is a Regional Trade Agreement Compatible with the WTO?' (2001) 28(3) Legal Issues of Economic Integration 299.

[270] Also J-A Crawford and RV Fiorentino, 'The Changing Landscape of Regional Trade Agreements', WTO Discussion Paper No 8, 2005.

[271] OECD, 'The Relationship between Regional Trade Agreements and the Multilateral Trading System—Services', TD/TC/WP(2002)27/FINAL, 2002, 12.

[272] A Mattoo and C Fink, 'Regional Agreements and Trade in Services—Policy Issues', PRWP No 2852, 2002, 10.

[273] P Sauvé, 'Adding Value at the Periphery: Aiming for GATS+ Advances in Regional Agreements on Services', 2006.

[274] cf GP Sampson, 'Compatibility of Regional and Multilateral Trading Agreements: Reforming the WTO Process' (1996) 86(2) AER 89.

regarding the sectoral coverage.[275] One of the most comprehensive regional provisions on domestic regulation is to be found in MERCOSUR's Protocol of Montevideo, which was signed in December 1997 and entered into force on 7 December 2005. Article X:4 of the Protocol echoes Article VI:4 GATS in its entirety. Importantly, then, Article X:4 does not envisage the establishment of a work programme, but it rather enjoins *directly* that measures relating to licensing, qualifications and technical standards do not create unnecessary barriers to trade in services. Likewise, paragraph 2 of Article 12.10 of the Trans-Pacific Strategic Economic Partnership (Brunei, Chile, New Zealand, and Singapore), which entered into effect on 28 May 2006, duplicates Article VI:4 GATS, but, contrary to the latter, foresees a straightforward horizontal necessity test.[276] Given that the Trans-Pacific adopts a negative list approach, this agreement is even more ambitious than MERCOSUR with respect to services trade liberalization. As to the role of these two necessity tests, it would be too early to suggest that they will be determining for any regulatory reform domestically in the near future, as these tests have just become binding obligations that the participating countries should adhere to. *Arguendo*, such tests will affect not only the respective regional markets, but also the negotiations at the multilateral level, as Members will be interested to see how a horizontal necessity test can work in practice.

There are also agreements that embody a VI:4-type horizontal necessity test, but the language that they use is hortatory. This is the case, for instance, in the bilateral agreements that the United States concluded with Chile, Singapore, and Australia. Notwithstanding the fact that Members are requested to 'endeavour to ensure' the objectivity, transparency, and necessity of the measures relating to licensing, qualifications, and technical standards, Members are also bound to accept the results of the WPDR negotiations on Article VI:4 when they enter into force.[277]

Article 64:5 of the Japan-Singapore FTA equally incorporates a necessity test, but it includes qualifications of the type found under Article VI:5 GATS, notably that it is applicable only to committed sectors and that the complainant should prove that the application of a given measure coming under this provision resulted in a nullification or impairment of commitments that could not have been reasonably anticipated.[278] A variant of this type of RIAs includes a provision requiring that Members 'jointly review' the results of the WPDR negotiations and, in the meantime, Members shall respect an Article VI:5-type obligation. The latter is a feature that is included in the RIAs that Singapore separately concluded with EFTA, Australia, and New Zealand.

[275] Also SM Stephenson, '"Deeper" Integration in Services Trade in the Western Hemisphere: Domestic Regulation and Mutual Recognition in OECD', *Trade and Regulatory Reform: Insights from Country Experience*, 2001, 84.

[276] This test, just as the entire chapter on services, will apply to Brunei two years after its entry into force.

[277] Arts 11.8 US–Chile FTA, 8.8 US–Singapore FTA, and 10.7 US–Australia FTA.

[278] Similar wording adopts the EFTA–Singapore FTA. See Art 28 thereof.

In the Western Hemisphere, neither NAFTA nor NAFTA-type agreements include a provision on domestic regulation per se in their respective chapters on trade in services.[279] Instead, such arrangements encompass more narrowly-drawn disciplines relating to licensing and certification of professionals.[280] The equivalent of Article VI of GATS in NAFTA is to be found in Article 1210 with respect to measures relating to the licensing and certification of professionals.[281] While this provision requires that licensing or certification measures be based on objective and transparent criteria, not more burdensome than necessary to ensure the quality of the service, and not be a disguised restriction on the cross-border supply of the service, it uses a rather weak, 'best-endeavour' language.[282] On the other hand, those arrangements call for comprehensive mutual recognition of foreign education credentials and professional qualifications in several professions based on explicit timetables. Furthermore, Parties to NAFTA and NAFTA-type agreements are bound to eliminate citizenship or permanent residency requirements in respect to the licensing or certification of professional service suppliers of another Party. Progress, however, appears to be rather sluggish in those areas even in sub-regional agreements with few signatories.

It stems from the above that the overwhelming majority of RIAs have nothing to add to the concept of necessity of domestic regulations and to the interpretation that should be advanced by the WTO judicature. Rather, these RIAs borrow the wording of Article VI:4/5 GATS and merely adjust it conditional on their needs, preferences, and the level of homogeneity among the participating countries. Indeed, the aforementioned evidence demonstrates that countries participating in those RIAs are reluctant to elaborate on Article VI:4 criteria or include more categories of measures than the *chapeau* of Article VI:4 currently covers; and this even in the lowest regional setting.

More generally, the experience to date with respect to regional agreements disciplining trade in services exemplifies the difficulties that countries have in order to promote deeper integration than the one that Article VI GATS offers in the form of a work programme. These difficulties are apparent even in cases where one would acknowledge that cultural, educational or social differences are not so important in comparison with the diversity that a multilateral forum such as the WTO demonstrates. Then the argument that has been advanced that the

[279] Also Stephenson (n 275 above) 82.

[280] cf Art H-10 Canada-Chile FTA or Arts 10–12 Chile-Mexico FTA.

[281] It is worth noting that the provisions regulating trade in services in NAFTA are dispersed. The NAFTA chapter on services, for instance, covers only the cross-border supply of services. The NAFTA includes rules regarding services in several chapters, eg technical standards for both goods and services are treated in Chapter 9 (cf Art 904), while commercial presence issues are tackled in Chapter 11, which applies equally to both goods and services. As to mode 4, it is covered in a separate chapter of the Agreement dedicated to the temporary entry for business persons.

[282] cf M Krajewski, 'Services Liberalization in Regional Trade Agreements: Lessons for GATS "Unfinished Business"?' in L Bartels and F Ortino (eds), *Regional Trade Agreements and the WTO Legal System*, 2006, 187.

creation of optimum harmonization areas may be an optimal first step of further liberalization on trade in services is denied by the reality.[283] Nevertheless, one should recognize the important contributions that several RIAs have made in the elaboration and betterment of the transparency provisions that are a necessary complement of any effort to liberalize domestic regulations relating to licensing, qualifications or standards. In this case, one could indeed speak of GATS+ outcomes at a regional level.

Despite the slow progress in other RIAs, admittedly, the EU experience[284] appears to work in a fairly satisfactory way. In the EU case, however, there are two distinguishing elements that cannot be traced, at least not yet, in other regional agreements: first, the political will was clear and Members were aware that they have conferred sovereignty on the Community; and second, there has been an integration-promoting supranational judiciary and Member States have silently accepted its interpretations, even those that have been very far-reaching in the sense that they do not arise directly from a textual interpretation of the relevant Treaty provisions.

5. Proposals submitted to the WPDR with respect to the creation of a horizontal necessity test

Article VI:4 GATS has a powerful positive-integration potential. For this reason, the completion of the Article VI:4 work programme under the auspices of the WPDR will in all likelihood contribute to higher levels of regulatory cooperation and convergence, while pressures towards harmonization and mutual recognition of domestic regulations dealing with licensing, qualifications and technical standards are expected to emerge and, in the longer term, multiply. Such tendencies are also to be traced in the proposals submitted to the WPDR that tackle horizontal issues and, inter alia, propose a horizontal necessity test when it comes to domestic regulation measures relating to qualifications, licensing and technical standards.

To date there have been seven communications to the WPDR referring to several elements to be considered in a prospective development of the concept of necessity. Those proposals were submitted by (in chronological order): Australia, Korea, the European Union, Japan, Switzerland, Brazil *et al*, and Australia *et al.* The last proposal is probably the most comprehensive one. It bears noting that there have also been proposals that suggest the inclusion of a necessity test with respect to a specific category of the measures coming under the scope of Article VI:4 GATS, eg on licensing procedures (EC),[285] on qualification requirements

[283] See also the discussion above on optimum harmonization areas under Chapter II.D.

[284] EU is taken to mean here not only the EU Member States, but also the countries which have been attributed a pre-accession status (usually through a bilateral agreement with the EC, the so-called 'Europe Agreement').

[285] WTO, WPDR (n 110 above).

and procedures (Chile *et al*),[286] or even on technical standards (Switzerland).[287] These proposals will not be analysed here.

a) The proposal submitted by Australia[288]

In Australia's view, the success of the work on necessity will determine the success of the work on the other three policy areas, namely transparency, equivalence and international standards. Australia believes that a prospective necessity test should of course draw on the criteria established in Article VI(a), (b), and (c), but, most importantly, it should be 'tighter' and take into account the general consistency with other WTO Agreements.[289] Australia's paper puts forward a necessity test, based on Article 5.6 SPS. In fact, the proposed necessity test reflects fully the footnote 3 to Article 5.6 SPS, the only difference being that it replaces the phrase 'appropriate level of sanitary and phytosanitary protection' with the more adequate for the services context 'legitimate policy objective'.[290] Australia had explained in an earlier communication that Article 5.6 SPS is preferable *vis-à-vis* Article 2.2 TBT, as the SPS language is more clear-cut and the concepts appear to be 'more relevant to services'.[291] Thus, according to Australia, the following test could provide a basis for the disciplines to be developed under Article VI:4:

> A measure is not more trade-restrictive than required unless there is another measure, reasonably available taking into account technical and economic feasibility, that achieves a legitimate policy objective and is significantly less restrictive to trade.

With respect to legitimate objectives, Australia favours a short, illustrative list of legitimate objectives, building on those listed in the accountancy disciplines. Australia suggests as possible objectives the protection of consumers, the quality of the service, professional competence, the integrity of the profession at hand, and administrative efficiency and fairness.[292]

b) The proposal submitted by Korea[293]

As to Korea's proposal, it subscribed to other Members' view that there are certain elements which are indispensable for the creation of a mechanism for regulating domestic measures relating to qualifications, licensing, and technical standards. In this regard, Korea stressed that a measure should be qualified as necessary if it satisfies the following three requirements: first, it has to strive for the achievement

[286] WPDR (n 95 above).

[287] WTO, WPDR (n 123 above).

[288] WTO, WPDR, 'Necessity and Transparency', Communication from Australia, S/WPDR/W/8, 15 September 2000.

[289] WTO, WPDR (n 32 above) paras 4–5.

[290] Arguably, Australia suggests that the jurisprudence on Art 5.6 SPS, as it has been developed above under Chapter IV.D.3.d), is also applicable to the proposed necessity test *mutatis mutandis*.

[291] WTO, WPDR (n 32 above) para 5.

[292] WTO, WPDR (n 288 above) para 5.

[293] WTO, WPDR (n 143 above).

of a legitimate policy objective, ie there needs to be a sort of balance between the means (regulatory measure) and the ends (policy objective). Second, this regulatory measure should be the least restrictive measure available. Third, Korea emphasized that, as a minimum, economic and technological feasibility (as mentioned in Art 5.6 SPS) and administrative burden in general should be part of the scrutiny of the reasonable availability of an alternative regulatory measure. Then, Korea proposed the following wording for a horizontal necessity test:

> Members shall ensure that such measures are not more restrictive to trade in service than necessary to achieve a legitimate policy objective [as specified herein]. [For this purpose,] a measure is deemed not more restrictive to trade in services than necessary, unless there is another less restrictive measure reasonably available taking into account technical and economic feasibility.

This language incorporates the so-called 'third aspect' that was analysed above as well as the GATT/WTO case-law with respect to necessity.

c) The proposal submitted by the European Union[294] *and the concept of proportionality as applied in EC law*

In contrast, the communication submitted by the European Union does not denote a precise wording for a prospective horizontally applicable necessity test for all service sectors, but it underlines the need for a consensus-based definition regarding the concept of necessity. In this respect, it makes reference to several elements that the European Union considers as essential for defining what is 'necessary'. Hence, in the European Union's view, those elements are to be included in the necessity test that will be designed according to the Article VI:4 mandate. The European Union drew the Members' attention to the importance of having clear obligations and avoiding the creation of an 'unpredictable mandate for dispute settlement procedures'.[295]

The European Union favoured an approach seeking a definition of necessity that would be coherent across all sectors, but would still permit sectoral interpretation. Such an approach, according to the European Union, would be the most appropriate one for assessing the trade-restrictiveness of a measure. Technical and economic feasibility, as well as the development level of a Member and sectoral specificities would be important factors to be considered in this assessment.

In this regard, the European Union proposed the introduction of the proportionality standard when assessing the trade impact of a domestic regulatory measure that falls under the scope of Article VI:4. According to this standard, after having taken into account the level of development of a Member, a measure that is disproportionate to the intended policy objective should be considered as more trade-restrictive than necessary. Hence it is the specific objective pursued that the

[294] WTO, WPDR (n 139 above).
[295] Ibid para 6.

degree of trade-restrictiveness meeting the necessity requirement will depend on and be assessed against.[296] Consequently, in the European Union's view, the validity, rationale or appropriateness of any policy objective should not be an issue to be examined by the WTO dispute settlement organs.[297]

The principle of proportionality is recognized as an overarching principle of EC law.[298] Whereas Article 5:3 ECT incorporates one part of the three-pronged proportionality test, that is, the necessity requirement, and there is also a Protocol expanding on proportionality, the ECJ rarely seeks to base its reasoning on any ECT provision.[299] In the case of free movement of goods, the ECJ uses as a legal basis for its reasoning Article 30 ECT which provides that prohibitions or restrictions on imports, exports or goods in transit shall not constitute 'a means of arbitrary discrimination or a disguised restriction on trade between Member States'.[300] According to settled ECJ case law,[301] a measure is considered to pass the test of proportionality if it cumulatively satisfies the following requirements:

(i) it is *suitable* or appropriate to protect the interest calling for protection. This means that a causal link is to be demonstrated between the measure and the aim pursued;

[296] Ibid para 17.

[297] WTO, WPDR, 'Report on the Meeting Held on 12 March 2002' (n 56 above) para 57.

[298] For the origins of proportionality, see M Hilf and S Puth, 'The Principle of Proportionality on its Way into WTO/GATT Law' in A von Bogdandy, PC Mavroidis, and Y Mény (eds), *European Integration and International Coordination—Studies in Transnational Economic Law in Honour of Claus-Dieter Ehlermann*, 2002, 200–201. The proportionality principle can also be traced in other ECT Arts providing for an exception, such as Arts 39:3, 39:4, 45, and 46 ECT. Even so, it is clear by now that the ECJ has never looked for a legal basis to support the use of the proportionality standard, since, in its view, proportionality is a general principle of Community law.

[299] Of course, it should be clarified that Art 5:3 ECT, just as the Protocol (No 30) on proportionality and subsidiarity, only covers action taken by Community organs. Thus, it does not establish a proportionality test for Member States' measures.

[300] Case 174/82 *Criminal Proceedings against Sandoz BV* [1983] ECR 2445, para 18. The proportionality principle can also be traced in other ECT Articles providing for an exception, such as Arts 39:3, 39:4, 45, and 46 ECT. Even so, it is clear by now that the ECJ has never looked for a legal basis to support the use of the proportionality standard, since, in its view, proportionality is a general principle of Community law.

[301] See, among numerous cases, Case 331/88 *The Queen v Minister of Agriculture, Fisheries and Food and Secretary of State for Health, ex parte Fedesa and Others* [1990] ECR I-4023, para 13, and Case C-180/96 *United Kingdom v Commission (BSE)* [1998] ECR I-2265, para 96. The by now 'traditional' wording that the ECJ uses goes as follows:

> The Court has consistently held that the principle of proportionality is one of the general principles of Community law. By virtue of that principle, the lawfulness of the prohibition of an economic activity is subject to the condition that the prohibitory measures are appropriate and necessary in order to achieve the objectives legitimately pursued by the legislation in question; when there is a choice between several appropriate measures recourse must be had to the least onerous, and the disadvantages caused must not be disproportionate to the aims pursued.

Also JH Jans, 'Proportionality Revisited' (2000) 27(3) Legal Issues of Economic Integration 243ff; and N Emiliou, *The Principle of Proportionality in European Law: A Comparative Study*, 1996; also P Craig and G De Búrca, *EU Law: Text, Cases and Materials*, 2003, 371ff.

(ii) it is necessary, ie the measure must be the least onerous when there is a choice between several appropriate measures. In other words, there must be no other measure less restrictive, but still adequate, available to achieve the intended objective, so that it does not infringe on intra-Community trade and thus jeopardize the European market integration; and
(iii) it should be *stricto sensu* proportionate. Hence, the disadvantages caused should not be disproportionate to the aims pursued. This part of the test entails a weighing of the disadvantages (eg the damages to individual interests) against the benefits (eg the benefits accruing to the general interest). In other words, the ECJ applies a cost–benefit analysis, the only difference being vis-à-vis the traditional cost–benefit analysis that was explored in Chapter III the fact that, depending on the nature of the benefits, it is not always necessary that the benefits exceed the costs.[302]

While the first element of the test does not differ much from a usual judicial activity, the second element, ie seeking the least restrictive alternative, requires a complex appreciation of the national measure at issue. The most problematic element, however, is the third one which calls for an examination of the true proportionality of the measure at hand that includes a balancing of often-conflicting interests, notably domestic policy objectives against the EC interest in free intra-Community trade.[303] This latter element, which contains a weighing process that resembles the traditional cost–benefit analysis, would have far-reaching implications as regards the relationship between the supranational judiciary and the national legislatures, and with respect to the separation of powers between the EC and its Member States.[304] Indeed, 'the more intensive the Court of Justice's scrutiny of national restrictions in the light of the proportionality principle, the greater the shift in powers from the national legislatures to the European judiciary'.[305]

In reality, however, the ECJ, depending on the circumstances of the case that it had to adjudicate on, exercised its judicial review duty in a manner that varied considerably in its intensity, ranging from a very deferential approach to a rigorous scrutiny of the justification of the measure at issue.[306] Hence, the application

[302] Also J Trachtman, 'Trade and… Problems, Cost-Benefit Analysis and Subsidiarity', (1998) 9(1) EJIL 35. For a clear application of all stages of the proportionality test in a concrete case, see Joined Cases T-125/96 and 152/96, *Boehringer Ingelheim Vetmedica GmbH and C.H. Boehringer Sohn v Council of the European Union* (T-125/96)H and *Commission* (T-152/96) [1999] ECR II-3427, paras 73ff. For an illustrative application of this 'weighing of interests' process, see paras 102–103.

[303] cf Case C-169/91 *Council of the City of Stoke-on-Trent and Norwich City Council v B & Q plc* [1992] ECR I-6635, para 15; also F Ortino, *Basic Legal Instruments for the Liberalisation of Trade—A Comparative Analysis of EC and WTO Law*, 2004, 413ff.

[304] Desmedt argues that such a balancing could be considered not to be too far-reaching, if such a process is limited to a balancing of interests that are *effectively* protected by the measure at issue. Desmedt (n 222 above) 446.

[305] Jans (n 301 above) 242.

[306] G De Búrca, 'The Principle of Proportionality and its Application in EC Law' (1993) 13 Yearbook of European Law 111. The US Supreme Court appears to endorse a similar approach

of the principle of proportionality has been very flexible; depending on the context, proportionality has been applied in a different manner to protect different interests, something that is further demonstrated by the varying degrees of judicial review.[307]

For instance, the ECJ undertakes an intensive judicial review when it comes to the exercise of the four fundamental freedoms and national measures that restrict this exercise.[308] Furthermore, the ECJ has exercised some self-restraint in cases where the ECJ was called to examine the legality and proportionality of a measure after having identified the complexity of the assessments that the Community organ or the Member State (or a delegated authority) had to undertake in order to adopt that measure. In such cases, the ECJ noted that the legality of that measure cannot be challenged unless the measure is 'manifestly inappropriate having regard to the objective which the competent institutions are seeking to pursue'[309] or the Community legislative choice 'appeared manifestly incorrect or if the resultant disadvantages for certain economic operators were wholly disproportionate to the advantages otherwise offered'.[310] In other cases, the ECJ put an emphasis on the necessity test without considering *stricto sensu* proportionality.[311]

In sum, in the majority of the cases where the principle of proportionality has been applied, it was correctly noted that the ECJ, *au lieu* of explicitly examining the proportionality *stricto sensu*, it has preferred engaging in a marginal review of costs and benefits of the measure at hand under the guise of the second element of the proportionality standard, ie the necessity requirement.[312] Viewed under this lens, the necessity requirement lies at the heart of the test of proportionality. It should be noted, however, that the proportionality test does not necessarily focus on the existence of alternatives, but its quintessence appears to be a balancing test weighing the objective of a given measure against its deleterious effects.

when adjudicating on regulatory measures under the Dormant Commerce Clause. Hence, a 'strict scrutiny' standard or a rather deferential approach will characterize the judicial review, depending on the case. Leebron (n 32 above) 45–48; also Hilf and Puth (n 298 above) 208.

[307] FG Jacobs, 'Recent Developments in the Principle of Proportionality in European Community Law' in E Ellis (ed), *The Principle of Proportionality in the Laws of Europe*, 1999, 20. The ECJ indeed appears to adjust its reasoning to the importance of the national policy objective pursued. See Case C-124/97 *Markku Juhani Läärä Cotswold Microsystems Ltd and Oy Transatlantic Software Ltd v Kihlakunnansyyttäjä (Jyväskylä) and Suomen valtio (Finnish State)* [1999] ECR I-6067, para 36; also Case C-384/93 *Alpine Investments BV v Minister van Financiën* [1995] ECR I-1141, para 51.

[308] Case C-55/94 *Reinhard Gebhard v Consiglio dell'Ordine degli Avvocati e Procuratori di Milano* [1995] ECR I-4165, para 37; also Emiliou (n 301 above) 173.

[309] See, among others, Case C-210/03 *Swedish Match v Secretary of State for Health* [2004] ECR I-11893, para 48.

[310] Case C-233/94 *Germany v Parliament and Council* [1997] ECR I-2405, para 56.

[311] cf Case C-368/95 *Vereinigte Familiapress Zeitungsverlags- und vertriebs GmbH v Heinrich Bauer Verlag* [1997] ECR I-3689, paras 19ff.

[312] J Snell, 'True Proportionality and Free Movement of Goods and Services' (2000) European Business Law Review 52ff.

This implies that no general criteria with respect to the test of necessity and proportionality can be identified, but rather, the ECJ will decide depending on the circumstances of each case before it.[313]

During the WPDR discussions, Members appeared to be reluctant to introduce an EC law concept when assessing the necessity of a domestic regulation measure. Nevertheless, the European Union itself clarified that, when suggesting the usefulness of the concept of proportionality for the purposes of the Article VI:4 necessity test, it did not seek an EC-type of proportionality test for the GATS.[314] In this respect, it is revealing that the European Union in its proposal rejects the use of the term 'least trade-restrictive' as being unduly restrictive with respect to the choice of the regulatory tools available,[315] while the ECJ in its numerous judgments regarding the proportionality principle clearly emphasized that the measure at issue should be the least onerous or restrictive. The European Union's stance is not surprising given the objectives of the EC internal market and the process of widening and deepening integration among Member States as opposed to the rather 'immature' WTO legal order when it comes to the introduction of integrationist concepts.[316] A far-reaching concept of proportionality as it is endorsed in the EU legal order would not be appropriate for a Member-driven organization such as the WTO, at least at this stage of development.[317]

d) The proposal submitted by Japan[318]

Japan's proposal was the first to contain generic regulatory disciplines for horizontal application covering all the five items identified in the *chapeau* of Article VI:4.[319] In Japan's view, the most appropriate form that the future disciplines could be contained in would be an Annex to the GATS relative to domestic regulation. This Annex would be an integral part of the GATS by virtue of Article XXIX GATS. The disciplines proposed by Japan draw heavily from several provisions already included in the accountancy disciplines. The core of the proposed disciplines, like the accountancy disciplines, would apply only to sectors

[313] It is worth noting that, according to the new EU Services Directive, Member States are required to adhere to the principles of necessity and proportionality when they make access to or exercise of a service activity conditional on compliance with any requirements. Dir (EC) 2006/123 (n 33 above) Art 16.

[314] WTO, WPDR, 'Report on the Meeting Held on 3 July 2001', S/WPDR/M/12, 16 August 2001, para 52. The EU representative noted during the same meeting that a sort of proportionality test was already implied in Art VI:4 by the term 'not more burdensome than necessary'.

[315] WTO, WPDR (n 139 above) para 17.

[316] Nevertheless, proportionality and its components do not leave indifferent the WTO adjudicating bodies. cf Appellate Body Report, *US—Shrimp*, para 141.

[317] Desmedt (n 222 above) 443.

[318] WPDR, 'Draft Annex on Domestic Regulation', JOB(03)/45, 3 March 2003 (and JOB(03)/45/Rev.1, 2 May 2003).

[319] For the WPDR discussions on the proposal, see WTO, WPDR (n 69 above) paras 8ff.

where each Member undertook specific commitments.[320] Japan's proposal is also influenced by the TBT Agreement in several instances.

The proposal does not restrain itself to the five categories of regulatory measures identified in Article VI:4, but it also puts forward provisions that would cover the need for transparency and predictability and thus supplement Article III GATS, as well as provisions that relate to other paragraphs of Article VI, notably paragraph 1 with respect to the administration of regulatory measures and paragraph 2 relating to judicial review. Provisions within the proposal that build on Articles III and VI:2 apply to all service sectors, ie they are not conditional on the existence of specific commitments, in accordance with the GATS text.

The proposal also includes new elements.[321] The first relates to the adverse administrative dispositions relating to licences and qualifications and covers measures that are taken after granting a licence of qualification. It aims to establish clear standards and procedures for adverse administrative dispositions (eg arbitrary withdrawal of licences) and thus enhance transparency and predictability for potential or already established service suppliers. The second new element refers to the administrative guidance relating to licences and qualifications. Under 'administrative guidance' Japan understands guidance, recommendations, and advice by administrative bodies to service suppliers requiring that these services suppliers do or refrain from doing anything without at the same time imposing obligations or limiting the rights of these service suppliers. The rationale behind this element is the prevention of abuse of administrative discretionary power so that the domestic administrative practice is characterized by consistency and transparency.

The Japanese version of a necessity test applicable to all sectors is to be found in Part III of the proposal (Preparation, Adoption and Application of Measures). Paragraph 6 thereof provides:

> Each Member shall ensure, in sectors where specific commitments are undertaken, that measures *of general application* relating to licensing requirements and procedures, qualification requirements and procedures as well as technical standards are not prepared, adopted or applied *with a view to or with the effect of* creating *unnecessary* barriers to trade in services. For this purpose, each Member shall ensure that such measures are *not more burdensome than necessary* in order to fulfil *its national policy objectives.* (emphasis added)

Hence, Japan proposes a horizontal necessity test that, for its most part, mirrors the sector-specific necessity test that has been agreed on with respect to accountancy services. Japan suggested that there was no particular reason that would prevent the latter test from being applied horizontally to other service sectors.[322] There are, however, some noteworthy differences between the wording used in

[320] Although Japan's initial position was in favour of an unconditional application of the prospective regulatory disciplines. See Japan's statement in WTO, WPDR (n 266 above) para 38.

[321] WTO, WPDR (n 69 above) para 8.

[322] Ibid para 50.

paragraph 2 of the accountancy disciplines and the wording that Japan uses to formulate its necessity test which may alter the legal implications of the horizontally applicable necessity test advanced by Japan.

First, while the necessity test of the accountancy disciplines applies to measures not subject to scheduling under Articles XVI and XVII GATS, Japan's necessity test applies to measures of *general application*. From the WPDR discussions one cannot infer whether Japan considers that the terms 'measures of general application' and 'measures not subject to scheduling under Articles XVI and XVII GATS' mean one and the same thing. In the absence of some clarification on this, one could plausibly argue that the wording that Japan proposes also aims to cover those measures that have been scheduled under market access or national treatment and which 'relate to' licensing, qualifications, or technical standards.[323] In this case, its scope of application would be broader than the accountancy disciplines 'bite' for the following reason: if such measures, when prepared, adopted or applied, create on their face or *de facto* unnecessary barriers to trade in services, they will be automatically outlawed. In other words, the regulatory aspects as well as the administration of the measures falling under Articles XVI and XVII GATS will be juxtaposed with Article VI:4 prospective disciplines. Hence, if the wording advanced by Japan is interpreted in this manner, it would be considered as a considerable 'liberalization vector' taking into account that it would cover important behind-the-border measures in respect to licensing, qualifications, and standards for all service sectors.

Second, whilst the accountancy disciplines refer to 'legitimate objectives', Japan favours the term 'national policy objectives' as mentioned in the GATS Preamble. In Japan's view, the latter wording duly protects the regulatory freedom of each Member. Otherwise, it would be possible for a Panel or the Appellate Body to *de facto* assess the legitimacy of a policy objective. Nevertheless, by choosing the term 'national policy objectives', the Japanese argument goes, it is ascertained that the objective of a measure cannot be scrutinized by the dispute settlement organs, which will be confined to merely examine the appropriateness of the means employed to pursue an objective.[324] In this respect, national policy objectives remain undefined and it is for Members to determine them as they deem appropriate.[325] Consequently, a list of objectives would not be necessary.[326]

[323] This interpretation of the term 'measures of general application' appears to be the correct one taking into account the fact that the same term is interpreted broadly under Art VI:1 GATS.

[324] WTO, WPDR (n 266 above) para 66. In the same direction, see the intervention by Hong Kong, China, in WTO, WPDR (n 265 above) para 46.

[325] The last draft submitted by the WPDR Chairman adopts this terminology. WPDR (n 74 above). Even so, the WTO judiciary will be obliged to juxtapose any national policy objective that a Member seeks to pursue against the multilateral interest of expanding further trade in services. A protectionist or unreasonable objective would most likely be outlawed. Hence, the fact that Members do not use the term 'legitimate' does not mean that the WTO judiciary will not examine whether the objective is one that justifies a derogation from the virtues of trade liberalization.

[326] This approach seems to gain ground within the WPDR (n 74 above) para 3.

e) *The proposal submitted by Switzerland*[327]

The Swiss proposal identifies several elements for modalities that would facilitate WPDR negotiations on disciplines on domestic regulation. Necessity comes into play in two instances: First, as part of the overall objective of the disciplines. In this regard, the proposal embodies the entirety of Article VI:4, but in the form of an obligation of preambular nature whose overarching rationale is to inform the rest of the proposed disciplines. Second, the proposal entails a horizontal necessity test with respect to the preparation, adoption and application of measures relating to licensing, qualifications, and technical standards which reads:

> Members agree to ensure that measures *of general application* relating to licensing requirements and procedures, qualification requirements and procedures as well as technical standards are not more *trade-restrictive* than necessary to fulfil a *national policy objective, taking account of the risks non-fulfilment would create.* Bearing in mind that nothing shall prevent a Member from availing of the rights granted under XIV, XIV*bis*, such national policy objectives are, *inter alia*: the access to essential services; the quality of the service; professional competence; or the integrity of the profession. Requirements shall be based on objective and transparent criteria. (emphasis added)

Let us unravel this provision. To start with, Switzerland subscribed to the (well-established within the WPDR by now) view that the proposed necessity test should also cover measures which are subject to scheduling as regards their regulatory aspects. This is not the only similarity that this proposal has with the Japanese proposal; on the contrary, Switzerland agrees with Japan that the term 'national policy objective' is more appropriate than the term 'legitimate objective'. In fact, the former term is to be found in the GATS Preamble and, therefore, can be considered as more 'GATS-specific'. Hence, contrary to Japan, Switzerland does not adopt this term because it considers that all national policy objectives are *de facto* legitimate. This is corroborated by the fact that, contrary to the Japanese proposal, Switzerland puts forward a list of objectives that it regards as national policy objectives, such as access to essential services or professional competence.

The proposal also takes issue with the Australian proposal, as it considers that the TBT-type language is better suited for the purposes of the GATS. Hence, the risks of non-fulfilment of a given objective should, according to this proposal, be taken into account by the WTO judiciary when it exercises its judicial review. Another TBT element in the Swiss proposed necessity test is the term 'trade-restrictive' instead of the term 'burdensome' that appears in Article VI:4 in its current form. However, and quite importantly, this proposal does not incorporate a purpose and effect test, contrary to the Japanese proposal, paragraph 2 of the accountancy disciplines, and Article 2.2 TBT. Again, as a general comment, a careful reader can detect the Swiss eagerness to apply TBT concepts of good

[327] WPDR, 'Initial Elements for Modalities for Negotiations on Disciplines on Domestic Regulation', Communication from Switzerland, JOB(05)/68, 2 May 2005.

regulation and due process to the context of the Article VI:4 negotiations. That was also exemplified in the Swiss proposals dealing with technical standards.

f) The proposal submitted by Brazil et al [328]

Initially, Brazil *et al* submitted a proposal that incorporated a horizontally applicable necessity test. This test echoed Article VI:4 language, as it provided:

> Each Member shall ensure that measures relating to licensing requirements and procedures, qualification requirements and procedures and technical standards are: (i) based on objective and transparent criteria, such as competence and the ability to supply the service; (ii) not more *burdensome* than necessary to meet *national policy objectives*; and (iii) in the case of *qualification and licensing procedures*, not in themselves a restriction on the supply of the service. (emphasis added)

Hence, there are two instances where this proposal deviates from Article VI:4: first, it expands the list of objectives that domestic regulation measures can seek. Brazil *et al*, just as Japan and Switzerland, also use the term 'national policy objectives'. *Arguendo*, ensuring the quality of the service at stake does fall under this category of objectives. Second, not only licensing, but also qualification procedures are not permitted to function in themselves as a restriction on the supply of a given service. This modification appears to reflect a broad consensus within the WPDR by now. Since unduly burdensome qualification procedures usually interfere with the attempts of natural persons to gain access to a given market, adding this element can be a significant additional step towards further liberalization of mode 4.

Nevertheless, the proponents came back with a revised proposal from which the aforementioned necessity test was withdrawn.[329] The proponents argued that there is no actual requirement in Article VI:4 nor any legal obligation for Members to translate the necessity test laid down therein into any regulatory disciplines. This viewpoint clearly deviates from the explicit wording, but also the spirit of Article VI:4. The mandate embodied in Article VI:4 assigned to Members the work of drawing the line between the right to regulate and the undue burdensomeness of domestic regulations relating to qualifications, licensing and technical standards. In the absence of a necessity test, it is unclear in the revised proposal which element will help Members and the WTO judiciary to draw the dividing line between these two poles. To be sure, the recent approach advanced by Brazil finds no support either in the text of the GATS or the negotiating history that led to the creation of the WPPS and the WPDR.

[328] WPDR, 'Elements for Draft Disciplines on Domestic Regulation', Communication from Brazil, Colombia, Dominican Republic, Indonesia, Peru and the Philippines, JOB(06)/34, 24 February 2006.

[329] WPDR, 'Communication from Brazil, Indonesia and the Philippines', JOB(06)/133, 2 May 2006.

In a proposal that coincided chronologically, the ACP Group[330] asserted that the adoption of a necessity test would curtail the regulatory flexibility that developing countries notably need and therefore any similar test, if ultimately adopted, should not be applied to developing countries.

g) *The proposal submitted by Australia* et al [331]

This is the most recent and probably most comprehensive proposal to date. The sponsors of this proposal purport to have employed three sources when drafting it: other Members' proposals, WPDR discussions thereon, and the relevant provisions of the accountancy disciplines. As the recent trend within the WPDR also implies, the disciplines embodied in this proposal are to be applied only in sectors where commitments have been made. Significantly, these disciplines are applicable to measures *administering* any limitations subject to scheduling under Articles XVI and XVII that relate to licensing, qualifications, or technical standards. The necessity test that the proponents advance essentially transforms the wording of Article VI:4 into a legal obligation by providing:

> The purpose of these disciplines is to facilitate trade in services by ensuring that measures relating to licensing requirements and procedures, qualification requirements and procedures, and technical standards do not constitute *unnecessary* barriers to trade in services. In applying these disciplines, Members shall have regard to the objectives of Article VI:4 of the GATS. In this regard, these disciplines aim to ensure that such measures are (a) based on objective and transparent criteria, such as competence and the ability to supply the service; (b) not more *burdensome* than necessary to meet *specific national policy objectives including* to ensure the quality of the service; and (c) in the case of licensing and *qualification* procedures, not in themselves a restriction on the supply of the service. (emphasis added)

Furthermore, Members are required, when they prepare or adopt Article VI:4 measures, to ascertain that they 'are not formulated, introduced, implemented, administered or applied with a view to creating unnecessary barriers to trade in services'. Hence, this proposal, by outlawing only the *intent* and not the effect of creating unnecessary barriers to services trade, deviates from the accountancy disciplines as well as the Japanese proposal.

The necessity test advanced by this proposal includes an open-ended list of specific national policy objectives. Arguably, then, and the objective of ensuring the quality of the service notwithstanding, the *raison d'être* of a measure falling under Article VI:4 should be easily identifiable. The proposal also highlights the potential undue burdensomeness that qualification procedures may entail.

[330] WPDR, 'Pro-Development Principles for GATS Article VI:4 Negotiations', Communication from the ACP Group, JOB(06)/136, 2 May 2006.

[331] WPDR, 'Article VI:4 Disciplines—Proposal for a Draft Text', Communication from Australia; Chile; Colombia; Hong Kong, China; Korea; New Zealand, and the Separate Customs Territory of Taiwan, Penghu, Kinmen and Matsu, JOB(06)/193, 19 June 2006.

The originality of this paper is that, aside from the general necessity test at the beginning of the proposal, it foresees specific necessity tests with respect to licensing and qualification procedures, and technical standards. In this case, then, the general necessity test constitutes a yardstick or a guideline to national regulators and the WTO judiciary as regards a concept that they should always take account of in their work.

E. The prospects of, and some essential elements for, a horizontal necessity test

Discussions to date within the WPDR have progressed more slowly than expected. For this lack of progress is also to blame the unsatisfactory involvement of domestic regulators to date in the negotiations. This fact can put into jeopardy the overall success of any prospective disciplines on domestic regulation in services. Unless domestic regulators become more active and address the unnecessary barriers with respect to licensing, qualifications, or technical standards that their nationals face when they attempt to gain access to a market, the final outcome will be unbalanced and of poor quality.

The discussions within the WPDR revealed many areas where a consensus appears to emerge. These areas of convergence can be viewed as confirming the following statements:[332] the scope of Article VI:4 covers exclusively the five sub-categories of measures identified under the *chapeau* of this provision; the aim of the prospective disciplines was not to interfere with the substance of any domestic regulation, nor to promote any harmonization of Members' domestic regulations or impose any particular regulatory approach; the prospective disciplines would still allow Members to justify their domestic policies under the GATS exceptions provisions; the development of horizontal disciplines does not exclude the creation of sector-specific disciplines; enhancing transparency in a horizontal manner can be likely, as many similar provisions can be identified across horizontal or sector-specific proposals submitted to the WPDR.

On the other hand, several issues remain unresolved. In this regard, mode 4 is at the heart of the WPDR discussions. It is a challenge for the WTO Membership to address mode 4 issues through Article VI:4 prospective disciplines, especially in the light of a negotiating round that has been characterized as a 'development round'. It is indubitable that the endorsement of fully-fledged disciplines also depends greatly on the proposals that potential *demandeurs* for all-four-mode coverage of the disciplines may bring forth. A relevant issue is the possibility of including special and differential treatment provisions related to mode 4 in favour of developing and LDCs such as reduced administrative fees.

[332] cf Switzerland's intervention in WTO, WPDR (n 28 above) paras 151ff.

Another key issue that needs further clarification is the relationship between measures falling under Articles XVI and XVII and the measures with respect to licensing, qualifications, and standards. As implied earlier, the connection of these two categories of measures can have important legal implications towards achieving a higher level of liberalization of trade in services. In addition, the question regarding the necessity of an agreement on a list of national policy objectives remains open, although several Members appear to feel all the more comfortable with the idea of not having such a list, as this may leave more leeway to regulatory authorities. Taking into account the interpretation that the WTO judiciary has advanced to date with respect to an illustrative list of legitimate objectives in TBT, it may be preferable that Members do not opt for such a list, as this would create two categories of objectives which would be treated by the WTO judiciary in a different manner.

The introduction of a necessity test in the prospective disciplines on domestic regulation would allow striking a balance between permitting a country to pursue its objectives and to determine the level at which these objectives should be achieved, and disciplining the choice of instruments that can pursue such objectives. Importantly, Members should seek to give specific guidance to domestic regulatory authorities in order to assist them in the identification and elimination of disguised trade restrictions. In this respect, Members are expected to benefit not only from the existing settled case-law with respect to the interpretation of the necessity standard in other WTO provisions, but also from the sector-specific work that took place regarding accountancy services.[333] The necessity test, as articulated in the accountancy disciplines, could provide a good basis for developing a necessity requirement horizontally, keeping, however, in mind that such a requirement would need to be of fairly general nature in order to be applicable across as many sectors as possible. Sector specificities can always be addressed whenever the circumstances are expedient.

As noted earlier, a prospective necessity test would seek to minimize the scope of a given regulatory measure to what is necessary to achieve the intended policy objective. Minimizing the scope of regulatory measures in this manner could also be conducive to minimizing the economic costs of such measures and probably removing economic distortions of international trade and competition. This is especially germane to the regulation of infrastructure services.

As to the movement of natural persons, the existence of a necessity test would at a minimum allow the attenuation of the most egregious qualification and licensing requirements entrenched in several domestic regulatory regimes. More importantly, a necessity test would bring about in the medium and long run

[333] Also D Honeck, 'Developing Regulatory Disciplines in Professional Services: The Role of the World Trade Organization' in Y Aharoni and L Nachum (eds), *Globalization of Services: Some Implications for Theory and Practice*, 2000, 68.

extensive recognition of foreign qualifications, licensing, or standards.[334] This is so because, for instance, once a measure relating to a qualification requirement is considered as unnecessary, domestic authorities will be forced to recognize the qualifications of the supplier that have been obtained abroad, perhaps by requesting that the supplier undertakes an additional examination to verify her competence. This is one of the reasons why it is argued here that, contrary to common belief notably in developing and least-developed countries, the introduction of a necessity test in the future disciplines on domestic regulation can be a development-friendly element.

Regarding recognition issues, Members have held extensive discussions. While it is not clear whether Article VII GATS is part of the mandate that WPDR has to accomplish,[335] recognition issues surely fall under Article VI:4[336] to the extent that they concern the five sub-categories identified therein, ie licensing requirements and procedures, qualifications requirements and procedures, and technical standards.[337] In this respect, several delegations submitted papers containing proposals for future disciplines[338] or clarifying the domestic regulatory framework that they have in place with regard to recognition of professional qualifications.[339] Such issues may be—and indeed have been—discussed either under the WPDR item relative to professional services (sectoral-based approach), or under the rubric concerning equivalence (horizontal-based approach).[340]

The Article VI:4 work programme, if implemented, would allow the creation of positive-integration-type obligations and would contribute to greater regulatory cooperation and convergence. In all likelihood, harmonization and recognition of domestic regulations coping with measures relating to licensing, qualifications, or technical standards would follow. Therefore, it is expected that Members would probably reject an unconditional, far-reaching necessity test that could be regarded as being too intrusive in the short run. Such political concerns could be considered as legitimate if one takes into account the different levels of

[334] See Aaditya Mattoo's comment in Productivity Commission/Australian National University, *Achieving Better Regulation of Services*, 2000, 56.

[335] Whereas Art VII provides legal coverage for recognition agreements with respect to their deviation from the MFN requirement under Art II, there seems to be a link between Arts VI:4, VI:6, and VII notably with respect to qualification requirements.

[336] Also Nicolaidis and Trachtman (n 38 above) 260, 263.

[337] WTO, WPDR (n 111 above) paras 77–99.

[338] cf WPDR, 'Recognition Issues—Agenda Item: Development of Disciplines for Professional Services', Communication from India, JOB(03)/192, 30 September 2003.

[339] cf WTO, WPDR, 'Professional Recognition in Australia', Communication from Australia, S/WPDR/W/28, 22 June 2004; also WPDR, 'Implementation of Article VI:6 Obligations in Engineering Services', Communication from New Zealand, JOB(03)/219, 3 December 2003.

[340] In this respect, it would be useful to expand the Guidelines for MRAs in the accountancy sector, perhaps first at a plurilateral level and for all professional services, or specific categories thereof. Honeck (n 333 above) 68; also AB Zampetti, 'Market Access through Mutual Recognition: The Promise and Limits of GATS Article VII' in P Sauvé and RM Stern (eds), *GATS 2000: New Directions in Services Trade Liberalization*, 2000, 283; and OECD, 'Service Suppliers on the Move: Mutual Recognition Agreements', TD/TC/WP(2002)48/FINAL, 2003, 27–28.

development within the WTO Membership, the difficulties of ensuring homogeneous application of multilateral obligations at sub-regional levels of government in federal Members, as well as the principle of progressive liberalization. It is not surprising that so many extensive discussions were dedicated to the issue of adopting a necessity test. As explained earlier, non-discriminatory measures that affect trade in services constitute the majority of domestic regulations in services and the differentiation of measures seeking legitimate regulatory objectives from those that are intentionally or unintentionally trade-inhibitory is not an easy task to perform.

In the present stage of GATS negotiations, as a minimum, it needs to be ensured that by the end of the current negotiating round, Members would agree on the need to ensure that protectionist or needlessly burdensome regulation does not emasculate market access commitments. Particularly with regard to the existence of alternatives, a less intrusive attitude would suggest that if there is a doubt concerning the availability or effectiveness of a less-trade-restrictive-alternative measure, this doubt should benefit the Member implementing the measure under scrutiny.[341] The necessity test proposed by many Members that limits the scope of application of the horizontal necessity test only to the sectors where specific commitments have been undertaken can provide a good basis for negotiations in this respect. Such an approach would not, in all probability, influence in a negative manner Members' willingness to undertake new or improved commitments.[342] This is so, because Members would be aware of the services sectors that they opened and where a necessity test applies. While such a qualification is not in accordance with the letter of Article VI:4, limiting the application of a prospective necessity test only to committed sectors can be an indispensable element for its political acceptance. In fact, the most recent proposals adopt this approach.

As is clear from the analysis above, the discussions in the WPDR on the development of a horizontally applicable necessity test could be informed by the wordings that have been chosen and the interpretations that the dispute settlement organs have advanced with respect to the concept of necessity throughout the GATT/WTO years of existence. Sub-concepts of necessity such as the less trade-restrictiveness or the minimal trade impact, the balancing or means-ends test, and, most importantly, the comparison between alternatives and their reasonable availability,[343] appear to be essential elements that surpass the strict boundaries of a particular WTO agreement. Hence, forms and rulings already present in other Agreements, such as the TBT, the SPS, or the GATT, can be instructive

[341] This would be the outcome of a correct application of the *in dubio mitius* maxim in this context. This maxim holds that, in a doubtful case, that solution is to be preferred which is less onerous to the party assuming an obligation, or which interferes less with the territorial and personal supremacy of a party, or involves less general restrictions upon the parties. cf Appellate Body Report, *EC—Hormones*, para 165 and fn 154.

[342] Also A Mattoo, 'Services in a Development Round: Three Goals and Three Proposals' (2005) 39(6) JWT 1231.

[343] See the intervention of Hong Kong, China, in WTO, WPDR (n 265 above) para 47.

as to the crucial elements for a necessity test to be developed pursuant to Article VI:4 GATS. The concept of proportionality as it has been applied and interpreted in EC law can also be useful in this regard, although a direct transfer of this concept to WTO law would not be feasible at this stage of WTO integration.

It has also been proposed that a necessity test creating a presumption in favour of economic efficiency should be developed. In that case, a Member not choosing the economically superior, first-best measure for pursuing an objective would be required to justify this choice or demonstrate the non-feasibility of economically superior instruments.[344] Such an approach would have the advantage of offering a sound and consistent methodology for choosing interventions to remedy market failure or to implement social objectives.[345] This approach, however, can be criticized on two grounds: first, it would call for complex measurements based on meticulous economic analysis;[346] and, secondly, it would require capacities that many Members, notably developing countries, do not have, at least for the time being. Moreover, it would require that the WTO adjudicating bodies have the necessary expertise to perform successfully the task of evaluating domestic measures and their efficiency based on economics.

It is for Members to use all the elements of these models that they consider useful to develop a concise necessity test which would be applicable horizontally to all sectors. There are voices in the WPDR that favour a clear wording that would not allow the WTO adjudicating bodies to construe the prospective wording in a manner that would be broader than originally desired or anticipated. Indeed, Members should not only strive for the creation of a horizontally applicable necessity test, but they should also fit into it terms and concepts that could allow them to tailor this test in a less intrusive and more valuable manner for all Members. While constructive ambiguity has many times been Members' favourite behaviour when drafting WTO legal texts, in this case, it is argued that more intensive endeavours to specify what the concept of necessity in services encompasses can be worthwhile for the long-term viability of the disciplines on domestic regulation.

On the other hand, a test that would simply echo the wording of Article VI:4 could have the advantage that it can be easily accepted, all the more because Members are familiar with it since GATS came into force. Negotiating reality and the theory of incomplete contracts would suggest that a detailed wording is more often than not fairly difficult to achieve, especially in this case of Article VI:4, as a

[344] Mattoo and Subramanian (n 192 above) 315, 317ff; also C Gamberale and A Mattoo, 'Domestic Regulations and Liberalization of Trade in Services' in B Hoekman, A Mattoo, and P English (eds), *Development, Trade, and the WTO: A Handbook*, 2002, 296–297. Something similar was suggested some years earlier in G Feketekuty, *International Trade in Services: An Overview and Blueprint for Negotiations*, 1988, 219.

[345] Low and Mattoo (n 78 above) 464.

[346] Indeed, policy ranking that would lead to the identification of the first-best solution can prove to be a very difficult task. J Bhagwati and VK Ramaswami, 'Domestic Distortions, Tariffs and the Theory of Optimum Subsidy', (1963) 71(1) The Journal of Political Economy 44.

prospective necessity test should be build on general terms to cover a wide range of services sectors and an ever-growing number of Members.[347] Therefore, at the end of the day, a test that would elaborate on the necessity test entailed in the accountancy disciplines (probably without a listing of legitimate objectives) appears to be the lowest common denominator. In the case of horizontal disciplines, however, there will be a need to introduce derogations, transitional periods, sunset provisions, or best-endeavour language for LDCs[348] and perhaps for developing countries as well, depending on the level of development of their service sector. This would be the least that Members could agree on to accommodate concerns expressed by LDCs and developing countries.[349]

While civil society groups, domestic lobbies, or NGOs voice their opposition against the development of horizontally applicable disciplines on domestic regulation *overall*, the introduction of a necessity test draws the attention of these constituents the most. This is because, as explained in this chapter, it is under Article VI and the proposed necessity test that the dichotomy between liberalization of trade in services and preservation of policy space and regulatory flexibility becomes apparent. These polemics form part of the broader rhetoric about the WTO and its deleterious effects on sovereignty. In this chapter, it was attempted to demonstrate the opposite, at least as far as Article VI GATS is concerned. A well-structured necessity test applicable across sectors could aid in distinguishing between protectionist regulations and regulations that serve essential societal objectives.

Surely, opposition against a horizontal necessity test can also stem from developed countries. The WPDR discussions revealed the reluctance by the United States, and of its powerful domestic regulatory authorities, to agree on a necessity test that would attempt to harness their non-discriminatory regulatory conduct.[350] This is a paradox for a country that has a long tradition of applying cost–benefit analysis when regulating domestically. In fact, a necessity test would go in a similar direction. What is more, the United States' producers of goods are already subject to a necessity test under the TBT and SPS. One would rather expect the opposite stance by a country that has such an internationalized services industry, which usually suffers from unnecessarily burdensome regulations abroad. A careful reading of the WPDR discussions seems to suggest that the

[347] In fact, it was argued that 'all feasible contracts are necessarily incomplete'. A Dixit, *The Making of Economic Policy—A Transaction-Cost Politics Perspective,* 1996, 53.

[348] The LDC Modalities also imply such flexibilities for LDCs. WTO, CTS (Special Session), 'Modalities for the Special Treatment for Least-Developed Country Members in the Negotiations on Trade in Services', TN/S/13, 5 September 2003, para 11.

[349] In fact, the prospective disciplines will have a section addressing development concerns. See WPDR (n 74 above) Section X.

[350] WTO, WPDR (n 265 above) para 49. Also WPDR, 'Outline of US Position on a Draft Consolidated Text in the WPDR', Communication from the United States, JOB(06)/223, 11 July 2006, para 3. The United States instead propose the inclusion, in the preamble of the disciplines, of a commitment that Members will undertake to respect necessity when they develop any new disciplines. Thus, the proposed clause would have a grandfathering effect.

United States would be ready to accept the adoption of a horizontal necessity test if the negotiations' final outcome also incorporates its proposal for horizontal transparency disciplines. From a public-interest viewpoint, a trade-off between necessity and transparency would overall improve the GATS framework tackling unduly trade-inhibitory domestic regulations. A combination of multilateral necessity and transparency disciplines would be a highly desirable outcome, as it would assist in the betterment of domestic rulemaking in both substantive and procedural terms and would increase national welfare.

This chapter has aimed to demonstrate that the adoption of a necessity test is not only required by the Article VI:4 legal mandate in order to be completed, but is also indispensable for the enforcement of the prospective disciplines to be developed under Article VI:4. Necessity tests are embodied in almost all WTO agreements simply because they serve as a benchmark to draw the dividing line between legitimate regulatory intervention and protectionist abuse. Prospective disciplines under Article VI:4 cannot but include a sort of necessity test so that measures falling under these disciplines are judged against this test to confirm the essentiality of their adoption at the domestic level. Recent tendencies show Members' readiness not to incorporate a necessity test in the future disciplines under Article VI:4. This would of course go against the letter and spirit of Members' legal mandate. More importantly, however, it could generate a fairly unpredictable outcome: when the WTO judiciary is called upon to rule over the consistency of a domestic regulation measure with the disciplines, it could use its own benchmarks or a sort of a test based on necessity, since the latter principle will be creeping into the disciplines anyway.[351] This, nonetheless, would mean that Members will miss the opportunity to design themselves a necessity test that would encompass concepts and elements on which Members could reach a consensus.[352]

[351] For instance, it has been suggested that the preamble of the prospective disciplines should reiterate the principle laid down in the *chapeau* of Art VI:4, ie that measures relating to licensing, qualifications and standards should not constitute *unnecessary* barriers to trade in services.

[352] For instance, Dixit argued that *ex post* institutions such as dispute-settlement mechanisms are important for completing contracts such as the WTO agreements. However, he did warn that these mechanisms are not perfect, as the state of the world may not be observable *ex post*, or, in case members observe the contract, may not be verifiable to the person that is entitled to enforce it. Dixit (n 347 above) 53.

V

Transparency and Domestic Regulations in Services

A. Introductory remarks

Transparency is part of the regulatory policymaking process and is deemed as one of the most important principles for regulatory reform and a fundamental requirement for good governance.[1] Indeed, transparency in regulation contributes to the openness of decisionmaking in all of its forms, from the preparation to the enforcement of new or amended regulations. It adds to impartial, more fair and effective governance (through the betterment of public, both domestic and foreign, confidence in governmental and regulatory performance) and ultimately to economic efficiency, as transparent domestic laws and regulations would allow the affected economic actors or supranational bodies to point to distortions that may otherwise negatively affect domestic policy objectives.[2]

The principle of transparency usually requires that information be provided regarding laws and regulations, as well as procedures for their administration. To all intents and purposes, transparency increases the information available to interested parties and allows for their surveillance and possibly their participation in regulatory policymaking, usually through prior comment or prior consultation mechanisms, which both are considered to be essential parts of an advanced transparent regulatory framework and important aspects of good governance.[3] Transparent laws and regulations foster fair competition in trade in services, as they make important information accessible and equally available to domestic and foreign competitors. This provides an even-handed starting point

[1] G Feketekuty, 'Regulatory Reform and Trade Liberalization in Services' in P Sauvé and RM Stern (eds), *GATS 2000: New Directions in Services Trade Liberalization,* 2000, 228. The issue of transparency has also been the focal point of many studies within the OECD. See, among others, OECD, 'Integrating Market Openness into the Regulatory Process: Emerging Patterns in OECD Countries', TD/TC/WP(2002)25/FINAL, 17 February 2003, 9; also OECD, 'Transparency in Domestic Regulation: Practices and Possibilities', TD/TC/WP(2001)31/FINAL, 15 February 2002.

[2] K Iida and J Nielson, 'Transparency in Domestic Regulation: Practices and Possibilities' in A Mattoo and P Sauvé (eds), *Domestic Regulation and Service Trade Liberalization*, 2003, 8.

[3] DC Esty, 'Good Governance at the Supranational Scale: Globalizing Administrative Law' (2006) 115 Yale Law Journal 1528.

for like economic actors, be they domestic or foreign, and eulogizes economic performance rather than privileged access to vital information,[4] usually available to vested interests representing domestic special interest groups.

Furthermore, giving the opportunity to foreign constituents to be equally informed or participate in some, even marginal, way could be valuable in terms of disseminating international best practices for achieving national policy objectives. A transparent regulatory framework can also contribute significantly to the reduction of international trade disputes, since purported WTO law violations with respect to new or modified regulations could be dealt with already at an early stage due to the easily accessible regulatory framework. In addition, transparency can induce Members to behave in a WTO-consistent manner, as their activities can be better monitored by other Members or WTO mechanisms, such as the TPRM. Regarded from another viewpoint, enhanced transparency could favour recognition, since similarities among procedures relating to certification, licensing, qualifications, etc would be identified more easily if the national regulatory systems were transparent.

Transparency in terms of dissemination of more extensive and accurate information can mobilize countervailing forces against domestic interests that favour protectionism and facilitate the development of coalitions for regulatory change within the society. Consequently, enhanced transparency can increase the number of voices calling for regulatory reform and liberalization of regulatory impediments to the benefit of trade and investment. This is especially important for small countries against which other Members have no incentive to bring a dispute because of their relatively small market size. In this case, the WTO has a role to play as a monitoring device, eg through its TPRM. Thereby, information can be generated so that domestic groups make the case for implementation of existing GATS commitments or for further liberalization of services trade, along with appropriate regulatory reforms.[5]

It can be expected that enhanced regulatory transparency can bring forth long-established systemic deficiencies usually entrenched in administrative rules and procedures that entail unduly discretionary or discriminatory elements. Covert discrimination stemming from discretionary or arbitrary decisions made by regulatory authorities, administrative guidance, 'privileged' exemptions from competition laws, and denial of access to crucial networks, important resources or professional bodies, and associations limited to foreign suppliers can be identified more easily due to regulatory transparency.

It goes without saying that transparency would also induce regulatory authorities and administrative bodies and officials not to deviate from their legislative mandate. A transparent system would also protect regulators from 'tempting

[4] Feketekuty (n 1 above) 229.

[5] F Eschenbach and B Hoekman, 'Services Policies in Transition Economies: On the EU and WTO as Commitment Mechanisms', PRWP No 3951, June 2006.

sirens' alias special interest groups, which traditionally try to capture the regulatory authorities and impinge on their independence and autonomy. This change in regulators' attitude would also improve public confidence in government and enhance its political legitimacy and its credibility.[6]

Transparency in trade-related domestic regulations creates predictable conditions for doing business in foreign markets. Investors and possible newcomers can be easily and accurately informed about the conditions and constraints they will face in a market, the regulatory requirements that they need to comply with, the time limits that they have at their disposal to adjust to potential regulatory changes, as well as the approximate benefits and costs of their presence based on the clear domestic regulatory framework.[7] Such information could facilitate the business of small and medium enterprises (SMEs), which otherwise would not have the financial means to gain information about regulations that affect their ability to effectively enter foreign markets.[8] Only on condition that service suppliers have access to full and transparent information concerning the circumstances and potential constraints that may affect their access to foreign markets, together with the requirements, the necessary competence, and the regulatory instances in charge of deciding their case (if applicable), can they in fact engage in trade in goods and services.[9] Hence, transparency contributes to the diminution of transaction costs.

Not only does transparency enhance predictability and legal certainty, but it also improves the accountability and legitimacy of regulatory authorities at all stages of regulatory policymaking.[10] Transparency elements that enrich notably the *application* and *administration* of domestic regulations would assist in decreasing arbitrariness of regulatory practices and reducing unnecessary barriers to trade in services and unduly burdensome administrative practices related to licensing, qualifications, or standards.

This is true particularly in the case of services. Transparency is indispensable to the facilitation of trade in services. Due to the regulatory intensity that characterizes many services sectors and frequently the inherent opaqueness of

[6] C Findlay and J-D Kim, 'Issues in Domestic Regulation of Services', 2001, 14.

[7] Research demonstrates that countries with transparent trade and investment regimes attract more FDI than those that endorse non-transparent practices. Z Drabek and W Payne, 'The Impact of Transparency on Foreign Direct Investment', World Trade Organization, Economic Research and Analysis Division, Staff Working Paper ERAD-99–02, 2001, 7ff.

[8] WTO, WPDR, 'Report on the Meeting Held on 24 September 2004', S/WPDR/M/27, 15 November 2004, paras 4, 6, 9, 21, 27.

[9] R Blackhurst, N Marian, and J Tumlir, 'Trade Liberalization, Protectionism and Interdependence', GATT Studies in International Trade No 5, 1977, 9.

[10] See, for instance, at the European Union level, the *Interporc* case where the ECJ implicitly confirmed that the principle of transparency is intended to enable citizens to participate more closely in the decisionmaking process, to guarantee that the administration enjoys greater legitimacy and is more effective and more accountable to the citizen, and to contribute to strengthening the principles of democracy and respect for fundamental rights. See Case C-41/00 P *Interporc Im- und Export GmbH v Commission* [2003] ECR I-2125, para 39. It bears mention that the principle of transparency has not yet been recognized by the ECJ as a general principle of Community law.

domestic regulatory measures that affect services supply when prepared, adopted, or applied, effective multilateral disciplines dealing with transparency are of paramount importance, as the lack of regulatory transparency increases the complexity and the costs of supplying services in a cross-border manner or through commercial presence. In fact, opaque regulatory practices can bring about a shift in patterns of supplying services.[11] In the absence of border measures, transparency in domestic regulation is the only tool that can make several domestic laws, regulations and practices publicly available. Potential service suppliers can make use of this tool in order to have effective access to third markets.

Thus, improving transparency of regulatory processes can be an essential part of regulatory reforms. It includes not only the endorsement of procedures that characterize more open systems of government, such as the public availability of existing and prospective regulations, the opportunity to comment and to be heard in administrative proceedings, but it also encompasses the adoption of higher standards for the operation of firms dealing with issues such as solvency, transparency in intra-firm transactions and reliable financial reporting.

It bears mention that the OECD, in its ongoing work on regulatory reform, deployed six 'efficient regulation principles' to facilitate the assessment of whether domestic regulations are economically efficient and trade- and investment-friendly. The principle of transparency is the first of these principles[12] (the other five being: ensuring non-discrimination; avoidance of unnecessary trade-restrictiveness; use of internationally harmonized measures; recognition of the equivalence of other countries' regulatory measures; and application of competition policy from an international perspective). These principles are relevant with respect to all WTO Agreements, and particularly the GATS, TBT, and SPS which have provisions with strong implications on domestic regulations.[13]

With respect to transparency and openness of decisionmaking, the OECD identified five areas that appear to be important in a government's effort to enhance regulatory transparency: (a) systematic availability of information using various channels; (b) clear, open and simple procedures to ensure predictability in the making and implementing of rules; (c) systematic and rigorous reliance on public consultations; (d) clear, open and effective appeals procedures; and (e) ensuring transparency in particular areas such as government procurement, self-regulation, or development of standards.[14]

Conscious of the potential problems that the lack of transparency can bring about, the GATS drafters included several provisions guaranteeing an enhanced

[11] cf Chapter II above.

[12] P Czaga, 'Regulatory Reform and Market Openness: Understanding the Links to Enhance Economic Performance', OECD Trade Policy Working Paper No 9, TD/TC/WP(2004)10/FINAL, 15 December 2004, 8.

[13] For an analysis of these principles from an OECD viewpoint, see A Kleitz, 'Integrating Market Openness into Regulatory Systems: Some Experience and Emerging Best Practices', 2002, 67ff.

[14] OECD, 'Integrating Market Openness into the Regulatory Process' (n 1 above), 9ff.

degree of transparency in the realm of services. The main transparency provision laid down in the GATS, Article III, will be analysed only marginally in this study,[15] since the core objective of this chapter is to tackle the issue of transparency as part of the mandate originated in Article VI:4 GATS.

B. The transparency as a general principle of WTO law [16]

Transparency, along with MFN and national treatment, is one of the fundamental GATT/WTO principles and is already conceived in a broader manner than the one expressed in Article X GATT[17] (which is entitled 'Publication and Administration of Trade Regulations' instead of using the mere term 'Transparency').[18] Here, reference is made to the bottom-up transparency, to be found in several WTO provisions, such as Articles X GATT or III GATS. A top-down approach with respect to transparency is reflected in the TPRM. Under the bottom-up approach, it is up to Members to send all the necessary information to the WTO, whereas in the top-down transparency it is the WTO that surveys Members' policies. The latter kind of transparency falls out of the purview of this study.

As a general rule, bottom-up transparency should be conceived to include three main components, which refer not only to discriminatory, but also to *non*-discriminatory domestic regulatory measures:

(i) The obligation to publish, or make publicly available, all relevant regulations and subordinate measures, including judicial decisions, administrative guidelines and rulings, of *general application* that affect trade.[19] Such publication should in most cases take place *before* the application or enforcement of these regulations and measures;

[15] For a detailed analysis of Art III GATS, see P Delimatsis, 'Article III GATS' in R Wolfrum, P-T Stoll, and C Feinäugle (eds), *Max-Planck Commentaries on World Trade Law, Volume 6: WTO-Trade in Services*, 2008.

[16] Also WTO, Working Group on the Interaction between Trade and Competition Policy, *The Fundamental WTO Principles of National Treatment, Most-Favoured-Nation Treatment and Transparency*, WT/WGTCP/W/114, 14 April 1999, p 14.

[17] Also WTO, Working Group on the Relationship between Trade and Investment, 'Transparency', WT/WGTI/W/109, 27 March 2002, p 3.

[18] Art X GATT requires that 'laws, regulations, judicial decisions and administrative rulings of general application' affecting goods in several ways 'shall be published promptly in such a manner as to enable governments and traders to become acquainted with them'. 'Agreements affecting international trade policy...shall also be published'. Moreover, the enforcement of new or more burdensome, restrictive rules, or prohibition, on imports and payments therefor shall not be made before any measure has been 'officially published'. Hence, any retroactive application is excluded. The term 'transparency' appeared for the first time in GATT history in the *Decision on Notification Procedures* which set out the general obligation to notify and established a Central Registry of Notifications. According to the Decision's preamble, that Decision aims to 'contribute to the transparency of Members' trade policies'.

[19] For the interpretation of the term 'of general application', see the analysis in Chapter III.C.2.

(ii) The obligation to notify various forms of governmental action and their possible changes to the WTO and other Members; and
(iii) The obligation for consistent, impartial, uniform and reasonable administration of such regulations and measures as well as the right of review of decisions taken in conformity with them.

The obligation to publish will usually concern a governmental authority or a non-governmental one with delegated power.[20] It is fairly broad and covers 'laws, regulations, judicial decisions and administrative rulings of general application'. In each WTO agreement where a transparency obligation is identified, one could note that such an obligation extends to the full range of issues covered by the agreement at hand.

Furthermore, this obligation for publication of relevant laws should be adhered to before any application or enforcement of these laws. Nonetheless, whereas GATT panels have ruled in support of the notion that a trade regulation cannot be applied unless it has been published,[21] Article X GATT has *not* been interpreted to require publication of trade regulations *in advance* of their entry into force or to require that domestic and foreign suppliers have access to the information at stake *at the same time*.[22]

The requirement of 'prompt publication' has been interpreted very narrowly during the GATT years in that it was satisfied if publication and entry into force of a domestic measure coincided. This has admittedly been a very sovereignty-friendly approach, but it provided no legal certainty or predictability. However, the rising demand for transparency in the WTO years would not seem to have a place for such an approach that renders inutile the phrase that follows—'as to enable governments and traders to become acquainted with them'. One would rather expect that the WTO adjudicating bodies will be sceptical of endorsing any proposition of this type that does not seem to reflect the growing demand for enhanced transparency.

The Appellate Body, when interpreting Article X:2 GATT, had the opportunity to denote the importance of this expression of the transparency principle:

> Article X:2, *General Agreement*, may be seen to embody a principle of fundamental importance—that of promoting full disclosure of governmental acts affecting Members and private persons and enterprises, whether of domestic or foreign nationality. The relevant policy principle is widely known as the principle of transparency and has obviously due process dimensions. The essential implication is that Members and other persons affected, or likely to be affected, by governmental measures imposing restraints, requirements and other burdens, should have a reasonable opportunity to acquire authentic

[20] *But* see para 2.3 of the Reference Paper on Basic Telecommunications which provides that the major supplier, obviously a non-governmental entity, is obliged to 'make publicly available either its interconnection agreements or a reference interconnection offer'.

[21] GATT Panel Report, *EEC—Dessert Apples*, paras 12.1, 12.29; and GATT Panel Report, *EEC—Apples (US)*, paras 5.20–5.23 (regarding the prohibition of the use of back-dated quotas).

[22] GATT Panel Report, *Canada—Provincial Liquor Boards (US)*, para 5.34.

information about such measures and accordingly to protect and adjust their activities or alternatively to seek modification of such measures.[23]

Nevertheless, the obligation to publish is subject to an exception allowing Members not to disclose confidential information which would impede law enforcement or otherwise be contrary to the public interest, or which would prejudice legitimate commercial interests of particular companies, public or private.

Transparency is considered to be a significant principle of the multilateral trading system nowadays and a means for:

- Promoting a rules-based approach to trade policy at the national level. The rule of law requires that all legal requirements be published and more generally made publicly available and, wherever possible, enforced after having given the chance to affected economic actors to become familiar with them. In this respect, various provisions relating to the impartial administration of such legal requirements and the scope for review by an independent judicial or administrative body when it comes to their application are essential;
- Providing information so that service suppliers can take full advantage of the opportunities generated by WTO rules and market access commitments;
- Facilitating the surveillance of compliance with WTO obligations and consequently the avoidance of disputes; and
- Facilitating future multilateral trade negotiations in order to promote further liberalization of international trade.[24]

Notably with respect to the function of transparency as a means for providing information to economic actors, the obligations stemming from the principle of transparency do not only refer to the horizontal relationship among Members, but they are also pertinent to the *vertical* relationship between a given Member and the affected economic actors. In *Argentina—Hides and Leather*, the Panel, in interpreting Article X GATT and notably paragraph 3(a) thereof relating to the uniform, impartial and reasonable administration of trade-related regulations, confirmed that 'the focus [when dealing with Article X] is on the treatment accorded by government authorities to the traders in question'.[25] To reach this conclusion, the Panel focused on the wording of Article X:1 which calls for a prompt publication of trade-related measures 'in such a manner as to enable governments and traders to become acquainted with them'. The Panel concluded by noting that '[w]hile it is normal that the GATT 1994 should require this sort of transparency between Members, it is significant that Article X:1 goes

[23] Appellate Body Report, *US—Underwear*, p 21.

[24] For instance, in several regional trade agreements, such as the CARICOM, Members agreed to establish inventories of trade-restrictive measures that affect trade in services and which do not conform to the obligations agreed. In a second stage, participating Members will gradually abolish these measures through negotiations.

[25] Panel Report, *Argentina—Hides and Leather*, para 11.76.

further and specifically references the importance of transparency to individual traders'.

Somehow paradoxically at first sight, the existence of the principle of transparency is all the more important in those areas where WTO obligations fall short of providing a straightforward satisfactory solution.[26] For instance, one such case is non-automatic licensing. More generally, in cases where there is a large scope for discretionary regulatory measures, due to their actual or potential direct control over specific economic transactions affecting trade, such as in state trading, or because national measures of general application bestow a large margin of executive discretion in the establishment of trade measures, such as in the area of licensing, enhanced transparency can provide the solutions and improve the legitimacy and accountability of regulatory authorities.

A second area where transparency serves a similar function is the one associated with internal measures that seek to promote legitimate policy objectives. As discussed in the previous chapters, such measures, usually non-discriminatory (at least, on their face), may have a significant impact on trade. Hence, the freedom that the WTO legal order allows to Members to pursue their policy objectives may, in fact, be abused. In attempting to draw the line between legitimate domestic regulation measures and covert restrictions on trade, several provisions call for the adoption and application of domestic laws on a non-discriminatory basis and the application of a necessity test, as explored in the previous chapter, as well as several other transparency obligations, notably in case of deviating from international standards, as is the case in the TBT and SPS Agreements.[27] In similar situations, other Members will usually have the opportunity to express their views beforehand.

C. The principle of transparency in the GATS

It is commonplace that the GATS borrows several GATT concepts and the concept of transparency is one of the most significant ones. In fact, while the GATT, as noted earlier, falls short of referring to the term 'transparency' not only within its Article X, ie the principal transparency provision of this Agreement, but also within the text of the whole Agreement, the GATS denotes the concept of transparency already in the second recital of its Preamble.[28]

[26] WTO, Working Group on the interaction between Trade and Competition Policy (n 16 above) para 58.

[27] For the TBT and SPS transparency provisions, see OECD, 'Strengthening Regulatory Transparency: Insights for the GATS from the Regulatory Reform Country Reviews', TD/TC/WP(99)43/FINAL, 2000, 7.

[28] As the Panel noted in *US—Gambling*, 'this requirement of transparency [laid down in the Preamble] is undoubtedly an object and purpose of the GATS—and the WTO in general . . .'. Panel Report, *US—Gambling*, para 6.107.

Nonetheless, promoting regulatory transparency in the GATS is not an unqualified objective, but it should be viewed through the lens of various elements, the most crucial of them being:

- the overall balance of rights and obligations, while giving due respect to national policy objectives (third recital of the GATS Preamble);
- the right of Members to regulate, and to adopt new regulations, on the supply of services within their territories in order to meet national policy objectives (fourth recital of the GATS Preamble);
- most importantly, the less advanced situation that developing and least-developed countries encounter, which does not allow them to implement at the same pace several GATS provisions aiming at building a more transparent multilateral framework for services, typically due to the administrative burden associated with the enforcement of provisions seeking more transparent national regulatory systems (fifth and sixth recital of the GATS Preamble, Article IV GATS).

In comparison with the GATT, the GATS theoretically contains a weaker obligation when it comes to the stage prior to the entry into force of a regulatory measure. This is so because the GATS does not specifically require that measures be published in a manner that enables other Members as well as private economic actors to become acquainted with them, as the GATT does. This omission should, however, not be regarded as deliberate, taking into account the nature and the general function of the principle of transparency.

Service suppliers are the first to be affected by the opaqueness of domestic laws and regulations when doing business. An additional element which also proves that the GATS takes account of the service suppliers' interests is to be found in Article VI:2. This provision requires that Members maintain or establish review procedures through which service suppliers can challenge administrative decisions that affect them negatively. These procedures are there in order to protect the rights of individual service suppliers damaged by administrative decisions.[29]

In practice, however, this divergence in wording between GATT and GATS does not make any real difference in the adjudicators' view. As highlighted earlier, GATT panels have interpreted the requirement of 'prompt publication . . . to enable governments and traders to become acquainted with them' as if the publication of a domestic measure and its entry into force could occur the same day. This is an interpretation that disregards the explicit wording of Article X GATT and deprives it of its *effet utile*. If the WTO adjudicating bodies ultimately endorse this unfortunate interpretation established in the GATT era, then there is no difference in substance between Article X:1 GATT and Article III:1 GATS regarding their 'bite'.

[29] cf Panel Report, *Argentina—Hides and Leather*, para 11.68.

Nevertheless, taking into account the Appellate Body's interpretation of Article X:2 GATT in *US—Underwear*,[30] it could be reasonably argued that the Appellate Body will seize the first opportunity that it has to give full effect to the phrase 'as to enable governments and traders to become acquainted with them' in that it will establish that prompt publication cannot mean coincident publication and entry into force of a domestic regulation. Unfortunately, Article III GATS allows for such a coincident publication and entry into force of a regulation affecting trade in services. Remarkably, this Article even allows the publication of a measure *after* its entry into force, but only in emergency situations. Hence, everyday service suppliers may suffer from this lack of predictability which goes against any contemporary notion of transparency in policymaking.

As to the TBT and SPS Agreements, both of them (Arts 2.9, 2.11, 2.12, 5.9 TBT, and Annex B, paras 1 and 2 SPS) already provide for a strong transparency obligation by explicitly calling for a 'reasonable interval' between the publication of a measure and its entry into force 'in order to allow time for producers in exporting Members, and particularly in developing country Members, to adapt their products and methods of production to the requirements of the importing Member'.

Theoretically, then, service suppliers are more vulnerable to sudden regulatory changes than their counterparts trading goods are.[31] The requirement of 'prompt' publication endorsed in Article III GATS should be considered too abstract to read in it an obligation of a Member putting in place a new law to allow, for the sake of transparency, for a reasonable interval between the publication of these laws and their entry into force. Rather, an interpretation in the opposite direction would seem more plausible. Therefore, envisaging the introduction of such a provision in the services realm as well, in accordance with the TBT and SPS Agreements, would greatly enhance the current level of required transparency in the GATS.

Unlike the GATT, wherein Article X alone, entitled 'Publication and Administration of Trade Regulations', depicts the framework dealing with the issue of transparency relating to trade in goods, the requirements on publication and administration of domestic regulations affecting trade in services that the GATS foresees are for the most part enclosed in two separate Articles: Article III contains the requirement to publish regulations, along with various requirements for WTO notifications; Article VI, on the other hand, determines the requirements on *administration* of domestic regulations and includes several due process requirements that enhance transparency in everyday trade in services. Article VI:4 also calls upon Members to develop disciplines that will ensure that measures relating to licensing, qualifications, and technical standards are based on transparent and objective criteria.

[30] Appellate Body Report, *US—Underwear*, p 21.

[31] As explained above, this is not the case in the GATT.

Furthermore, Article IV:2 GATS foresees the establishment by developed countries (and, if possible, other Members) of 'contact points' where service suppliers stemming from developing countries can be informed about (a) the commercial and technical aspects of the supply of services, (b) the registration, recognition and obtaining of professional qualifications, and (c) the availability of services technology. This provision can facilitate market access of developing country Members' service suppliers, notably in developed country markets. In addition, specific requirements on notifications to the WTO and bilateral consultations with other Members are to be traced throughout the GATS. These are Articles VII, VIII, and IX GATS.[32]

1. Article III GATS

Transparency constitutes, for the time being, the second most important general obligation (after MFN) under GATS that Members should abide by. Taking into account that the main transparency provision with respect to services to be found in Article III GATS is unconditional and does not allow for exceptions, it could even be argued that Article III is at present probably the most powerful provision establishing an important general obligation for Members regarding trade in services. Of course, the main transparency provision under GATS could be further enhanced, especially when compared with the corresponding provisions dealing with the issue of transparency laid down in the TBT and SPS Agreements.

Article III GATS contains the general obligation with regard to transparency of domestic regulation measures of general application affecting trade in services. According to this provision, Members are required to publish, or make otherwise publicly available, eg via an internet website, all relevant domestic measures, within the meaning of Article XXVIII(a) GATS, of general application which pertain to or affect the operation of the GATS (Art III:1, III:2 GATS).

Moreover, Members are obliged to inform the CTS of the introduction of any new, or any changes in existing, *laws, regulations* or *administrative guidelines* which *significantly* affect trade in services covered by its specific commitments under the GATS (Art III:3 GATS). Just as in paragraph 1 of Article III relating to 'measures of general application which pertain to or affect the operation of the GATS' that a Member has to publish, paragraph 3 allows, too, each regulating state to decide which 'laws, regulations, or administrative guidelines' *significantly* affect trade in services. This exercise of discretion in both paragraphs is justiciable.

The notification requirement of Article III:3 is the only one that can be found in Article III GATS and covers only laws, regulations or administrative guidelines (as opposed to measures of general application that pertain to or affect the

[32] OECD (n 27 above) 10.

operation of the GATS). A similar, but more detailed obligation also exists in the TBT and SPS Agreements. These two agreements foresee a special notification procedure in a case where a Member adopts a domestic measure for which no equivalent international standard exists or, even if it exists, the proposed domestic measure at hand has not substantially the same content. Provided that this domestic measure *significantly* affects trade of other Members,[33] the Member that regulates is required to notify prospective standards to other Members through the WTO Secretariat at a sufficiently early stage in their drafting (as a general rule, at least 60 days before their formal adoption)[34] in order to allow reasonable time for other Members to make comments.[35] Arguably, such strict notification requirements aim to diminish any protectionist intent through enhanced transparency disciplines.

In addition, Members are required to respond promptly to all requests made by other Members for specific information on measures of general application or international agreements within the meaning of Article III:1 and III:3 and establish enquiry points to do so, again upon request (Art III:4 GATS).[36] Once more, the TBT and SPS Agreements include more comprehensive provisions, notably the TBT, with respect to the function of such enquiry points at the national level.[37]

Furthermore, under Article III.5, any Member is entitled to notify measures adopted by any other Member which it believes may pertain to the GATS, when those measures purportedly creating barriers to trade in services have not been notified by the government putting them into place. This possibility for reverse notification can enhance transparency regarding barriers to trade in services, but it definitely requires a well-established system that would collect complaints by suppliers that provide their services in foreign markets.

Article III does not envisage any obligation for conducting prior consultations. Such an obligation would probably entail a 'notice and comment' procedure, ie first, a public announcement of the consultation procedures that will be subsequently followed by the proposed regulation and the potential comments. Intuitively, allowing foreign interest parties to participate likewise in this procedure may to a great extent inform the work of a benevolent regulatory authority seeking to set up efficient and least-trade-restrictive regulatory measures, which

[33] Art 2.9 TBT and Annex B.5 to SPS.

[34] According to the *Code of Good Practice for the Preparation, Adoption and Application of Standards*, Annex 3 to the TBT Agreement, para L. Art 4.1 TBT provides that compliance with the Code is obligatory for the central government standardizing bodies.

[35] WTO, WPPS, 'Background Information on the Agreement on Technical Barriers to Trade and the Agreement on Import Licensing Procedures', S/WPPS/W/6, 29 February 1996, p 4.

[36] For the (rather poor) efficiency of the GATS enquiry points, see OECD (n 27 above) 15; also SM Stephenson, 'Deepening Disciplines for Trade in Services', 2001, 8. For instance, as of September 2004, the European Union's contact point received only one enquiry. WTO, WPDR (n 8 above) para 16. For some proposals in order to improve the efficiency of the enquiry and contact points (eg through sector-specific or mode-4-only enquiry points), see Iida and Nielson (n 2 above) 22–23.

[37] Art 10 TBT and Annex B.3 to SPS.

could benefit from the collection of the views of all economic stakeholders, be they domestic or foreign.

Such an obligation already exists in paragraph 6 of the draft accountancy disciplines, but it is limited to cases where the new measures *significantly* affect trade in accountancy services, as mentioned in the previous chapter. Additionally, this stipulation is weakened by the best-endeavour language that it uses. Again, it can be argued that this provision, because of the way that is formulated, strikes the right balance between reasonable administrative burden and the need for enhanced transparency.[38] In contrast, in both the TBT and SPS Agreements, Members are required, in cases where the measure at issue significantly affects trade, to 'allow reasonable time for other Members to make comments in writing, discuss these comments upon request, and take these written comments and the results of these discussions into account'; and this even in urgent situations where Members are otherwise allowed not to follow the entirety of the notification procedure.[39]

The accountancy disciplines entail another pertinent 'good practice' provision established in paragraph 5 by requiring that all Members should, upon request, provide information with respect to the rationale behind domestic regulation measures and its connection with a legitimate objective within the meaning of paragraph 2 of the accountancy disciplines. When the accountancy disciplines become binding, this provision should be expected to enhance transparency in the accountancy sector, even more so because its wording does not include any best-endeavour language, but, instead, foresees a strong, straightforward obligation. According to G Feketekuty, 'a requirement to disclose the objective of a regulation is implicit in any provision that requires that a domestic regulation be the least trade-restrictive means necessary to achieve a regulatory purpose'.[40] Consequently, enhanced transparency should be expected to facilitate the hard task of distinguishing between necessary and unnecessary domestic regulatory measures by revealing, at least theoretically, the protectionist intent. In other words, any necessity test would be strengthened by such a provision, as the latter would require Members to explain the link between domestic regulation measures and the public policy objectives, which may be expressly listed in the necessity provision, as is the case with paragraph 2 of the accountancy disciplines.

A similar provision is to be found in the TBT Agreement. Article 2.5 thereof provides that a Member shall upon request explain the reasons that justify the preparation, adoption or application of a technical regulation as regards Articles 2.2 and 2.4. Nevertheless, Article 2.5 is fairly weak because, unlike the aforementioned obligation foreseen under paragraph 5 of the accountancy disciplines,

[38] See Korea's comment, WTO, WPDR, 'Report on the Meeting Held on 11 May 2001', S/WPDR/M/11, 7 June 2001, para 16.

[39] Arts 2.9.4 and 2.10.3 TBT and Annex B.5(d) and 6(c) to SPS.

[40] G Feketekuty, 'Deepening Sectoral Disciplines for Services Regulation: How to Move Forward in the GATS', 2002, 17.

it concerns only technical regulations that *significantly* affect trade of other Members.

The remaining transparency provisions contained in the accountancy disciplines (paragraphs 3, 4, 7) do nothing more than to clarify the application of Article III GATS to the accountancy sector. These paragraphs require that Members make publicly available specific information. More particularly, paragraph 3 calls for public availability of the names and addresses of competent authorities, paragraph 4 requires the diffusion of information concerning technical standards, professional titles, licensing, etc, while paragraph 7 elaborates on Article VI:2 GATS by requiring the publication of details relating to the review of administrative decisions, including the prescribed time-limits, if any, for requesting such a review.

Finally, the GATS includes two exceptions from the general obligation requiring transparency. First, Article III *bis*, like Article X:1 GATT, allows Members to deny providing confidential information, provided that its disclosure would impede law enforcement, or otherwise be contrary to the public interest, or would prejudice the legitimate commercial interests of public or private enterprises.[41] Second, Article XIV *bis*, paragraph 1(a), exempts Members from providing information that they consider would be contrary to essential security interests.[42]

2. Article VI GATS

With the exception of Article VI:4(a), there is no reference to the concept of transparency in Article VI. Just as in various agreements pertaining to goods, the GATS contains disciplines that require consistent, uniform, impartial and reasonable administration of measures of general application affecting trade in services, but only with respect to sectors where specific commitments have been undertaken. Article III:1 GATS, which also refers to measures of general application, is not dependent on specific commitments undertaken.

It follows that, while 'all relevant measures of general application which pertain to, or affect, the operation' of the GATS only have to be published promptly, the measures of general application affecting trade in services in sectors where specific commitments are undertaken should, *in addition to their prompt publication*, be administered in a reasonable, objective, and impartial manner. *A contrario*, then, a Member is not required to administer in a reasonable, objective, and impartial manner the measures of general application affecting trade in services which do *not* relate to sectors where specific commitments are made.

[41] For a succinct analysis of this provision, see P Delimatsis, 'Article III *bis* GATS' in R Wolfrum, P-T Stoll, and C Feinäugle (eds), *Max-Planck Commentaries on World Trade Law, Volume 6: WTO-Trade in Services*, 2008.

[42] For a detailed commentary of this provision, see T Cottier and P Delimatsis, 'Article XIV *bis* GATS' in R Wolfrum, P-T Stoll, and C Feinäugle (eds), *Max-Planck Commentaries on World Trade Law, Volume 6: WTO-Trade in Services*, 2008.

This approach deviates from Article X:3(a) GATT where the reasonable, objective, and impartial administration covers all measures specified in Article X:1 GATT and creates gratuitous confusion and uncertainty to service suppliers. First, because it creates two distinct categories of suppliers; depending on the committed services sectors, some service suppliers can benefit from the due administration of their operations, whereas others, in uncommitted sectors, cannot. Secondly, because this obligation covers, in committed sectors, those measures of general application that *affect* trade in services. Consequently, and depending on the interpretations that the WTO judiciary will advance, this obligation can have an unpredictably broad scope of application, which may be advantageous for some service suppliers but not for others. This provision, as it is formulated, provides no legal certainty either vis-à-vis the service suppliers or as regards the domestic regulatory authorities, since entire categories of measures adopted by the latter can unintentionally become subject to this obligation, depending, again, on the interpretations put forward by the WTO adjudicating bodies.

The chief intention of various Article VI requirements is to create more transparent domestic regulatory decisionmaking, adoption, administration, and enforcement through the introduction of obligations of reasonable, objective, and impartial *administration*. Hence, the GATS, like other WTO Agreements, recognizes that 'the way rules are applied can be as significant as the substance of the rules themselves'.[43]

Contrary to Article III, which addresses transparency at a multilateral, intergovernmental level, Article VI contains provisions that mainly seek to enhance transparency as regards the *vertical* relationship between the domestic regulatory authority and a private person, ie the affected service supplier, in order to ensure effective market access by service suppliers.[44] This Article does not require any kind of notification to the WTO (as does Art III) or the organization of bilateral consultations held with other Members (as does Art IX with respect to restrictive business practices, which obliges Members to enter into bilateral consultations when another Member requests it to do so with a view to eliminating 'those practices that may restrain competition and restrict trade in services').

It does, however, contain obligations that seek to enhance procedural or administrative transparency in accordance with due process, notably by including provisions that explicitly recognize the right of a (foreign or domestic) service supplier to independent judicial and administrative review and appeals processes, and the right to be informed on regulatory and administrative decisions (Arts VI:2 and VI:3).[45] More specifically, the obligation endorsed in Article VI:2 to establish or maintain mechanisms allowing, upon request of the affected service

[43] WTO, Working Group on the Relationship between Trade and Investment (n 17 above) p 1.

[44] cf Canada's intervention in WTO, CTS (Special Session), 'Report of the Meeting Held on 5, 8 and 12 October 2001', S/CSS/M/12, 28 November 2001, para 99.

[45] See the more detailed analysis of these provisions in Chapter III, Sections C.3 and C.4 above.

suppliers, the prompt review of, and where justified, appropriate remedies for, administrative decisions affecting trade in services is not dependent on the existence of specific commitments undertaken. The influence of its GATT counterpart, Article X:3(b), on the wording of this important due process obligation of general application in the services context is clear.

The GATS incorporates even higher standards than the GATT, as Article VI:3 GATS requires, albeit only in sectors where specific commitments were made, that in case of an authorization requirement as a prerequisite for supplying a service, the competent authorities shall, within a reasonable period of time, inform the applicant of the decision regarding its application. What is more, any information with respect to the status of the application shall be provided without any undue delay at the request of the applicant.

D. The issue of transparency as discussed in the WPDR

1. Organizing the WPDR work with respect to transparency

The issue of transparency has been a crucial element of the WPDR discussions. Recall that the Article VI:4 mandate calls for the development of horizontal or sector-specific disciplines that will ensure that the five subcategories of measures identified in the *chapeau* of Article VI:4 (qualification requirements and procedures, licensing requirements and procedures, and technical standards) are, *inter alia*, based on *objective* and *transparent* criteria, such as competence and the ability to supply the service (Article VI:4(a)).[46]

In addition, as will be seen, discussions in the WPDR also delved into the possibility of enhancing disciplines located elsewhere in Article VI. More particularly, Members reflected on the possibility of improving the disciplines foreseen under paragraph 2 relating to domestic prompt review and appeal procedures against administrative decisions affecting trade in services; Members also discussed provisions that would elaborate on paragraph 3 with respect to the necessary information provided by the domestic competent authorities to an applicant seeking an authorization to provide services domestically and the timeliness of the decisions on similar applications.

As noted in the previous Chapter relating to necessity, the WPDR decided to organize their discussions based on a *Checklist of Issues*[47] which identified four issues for the WPDR discussions, ie necessity, transparency, equivalence, and international standards. According to the Secretariat's view these are the areas where the development of domestic regulation disciplines is the most likely to

[46] The criteria of competence and the ability to supply a service relate more to the element of objectivity than transparency.

[47] See Chapter IV.C.2 above.

emerge.[48] Members considered that the first two areas, ie necessity and transparency, would be the most appropriate to focus on, on a priority basis, while also considering at a later stage issues of relevance for equivalence and international standards.

Transparency and necessity are considered to be equally important in respect of the work of the WPDR. This is all the more so, because transparency, just as necessity, can be an area where the development of horizontal[49] rules on domestic regulation applicable to all five types of measures listed in Article VI:4 is possible.[50] Of course, such rules should not duplicate the requirements foreseen under Article III GATS, but should nonetheless take account and build on this provision. Any new horizontally applicable disciplines specifically referring to licensing, qualifications, and standards would be useful only on condition that they add value to the requirements already established under Article III, as these requirements are also meant to address measures under Article VI:4.[51]

Finally, it is worth noting that Members feel the need to elaborate on Article III as well as on the other paragraphs of Article VI because, presumably, they recognize the importance of measures relating to the categories of Article VI:4, ie licensing, qualifications, and technical standards. Indeed, these categories of measures encompass a vast pool of measures affecting trade in services that Members have every interest to harness in order to ensure that such measures will not gratuitously hinder trade in services. The great advantage of this mandate is that Members have the opportunity to ameliorate the obligations of transparency and objectivity under GATS *horizontally*, ie for all services sectors in the specific categories of licensing, qualifications, and technical standards.

2. Relevant issues touching upon transparency

Apart from the general issues that it contains, which are also germane to the concept of transparency,[52] the *Checklist of Issues* identified five issues that can be

[48] WTO, CTS, 'Article VI:4 of the GATS: Disciplines on Domestic Regulation Applicable to All Services', S/C/W/96, 1 March 1999, para 16.

[49] cf the discussions in WTO, WPDR (n 8 above) paras 6ff.

[50] WTO, CTS (n 48 above) para 16.

[51] WTO, WPDR, 'Domestic Regulation: Necessity and Transparency', Communication from the European Communities and their Member States, S/WPDR/W/14, 1 May 2001, para 25.

[52] Those general issues are: (1) examples of actual regulatory issues; (2) the linkage between transparency and necessity; (3) the relationship between Art VI:4 and Arts XVI/XVII; (4) the scope of Art VI:4; (5) the possible administrative burden of the regulatory disciplines under development; (6) definition of regulations; and (7) application of the disciplines to be developed at a federal *vs* sub-federal level (ie whether the disciplines will also be applicable at a sub-federal or sub-national level).

deemed pertinent to the development of any disciplines relating to transparency, be they horizontal or sector-specific. These are the following:

(i) Transparency objectives (objectives of further transparency provisions; addressees of transparency provisions; potential applicability of the TBT and SPS transparency provisions);
(ii) Prior comment provisions (constitutional impediments that prohibit such provisions; regulations, if any, that such provisions should not apply; applicability of such provisions not only to national, but also to a sub-national level);
(iii) Notifications related to prior comment provisions (necessity of having notifications made to the WTO);
(iv) Compliance with existing notification requirements (necessity of further disciplines to ensure adherence to the existing GATS notification requirements); and
(v) Appropriate levels of transparency (appropriate extent and limits of transparency requirements; role of cost–benefit analysis regarding notifications).

Another issue, which is of particular relevance for developing countries and surely speaks against the development of any additional transparency disciplines, is the administrative burden associated with the obligation to implement new, enhanced, and probably costly domestic regulation measures with regard to transparency. From a developing-country perspective, the costs will mostly fall on developing countries, since future transparency disciplines will generally reflect current regulatory standards in developed countries.[53] The costs for developing countries would be even higher if any additional transparency disciplines should also be implemented at a sub-national or regional level (eg the mandatory establishment of prior consultations mechanisms at that level). Nevertheless, the regulatory authorities of developed countries could also be concerned by unnecessarily burdensome disciplines that are, by their nature, resource-intensive. This is to demonstrate that diminishing the administrative burden can be a concern for all Members.

While the issue of eschewing administrative burden to the extent possible is particularly relevant to any transparency obligations that are enunciated during negotiations, it was finally classified in the *Checklist* under the 'general issues' rubric. This was decided because a possible development of disciplines under the Article VI:4 mandate could generate a considerable burden on national

[53] B Hoekman, 'Operationalizing the Concept of Policy Space in the WTO: Beyond Special and Differential Treatment' in E-U Petersmann (ed), *Reforming the World Trading System—Legitimacy, Efficiency, and Democratic Governance*, 2005, 229.

administrations and regulators overall. Of course, prospective transparency disciplines would only be one component of this burden.

Accordingly, Members focused their discussions within the WPDR on the aforementioned issues. Following the Chairman's advice,[54] Members used as a basis the transparency provisions that the WPPS agreed on with respect to the accountancy disciplines. These provisions appear to be the only available that relate to trade in services[55] and which Members could employ as a starting point with a view to developing transparency disciplines applicable across sectors at the end of the current negotiations.

In a Note addressed to Members,[56] the Secretariat identified at least two elements which Members could agree to consider during the work within the WPDR when exploring the possibility of creating horizontal transparency disciplines on domestic regulation. The first element echoes the obligation already established in paragraph 5 of the accountancy disciplines and Article 2.5 TBT to provide, upon request, the rationale behind domestic regulatory measures with reference to the pursued policy objective. Such an element would (among the other advantages that it has, as noted earlier) enhance administrative transparency to a considerable extent.

The second element would allow interested or affected parties, notably service suppliers, to make comments before the adoption of measures which impinge on trade in services in a significant manner. Such a prior consultation obligation would usually be respected through a public notice of the consultation procedures taking place, followed by a proposed regulation that takes into account any potential comments submitted by affected stakeholders or trading partners.

As noted above, paragraph 6 of the accountancy disciplines foresees an identical 'best-endeavour' provision, limited to cases where the new measures significantly affect trade in accountancy services. Additionally, similar provisions in both the TBT and SPS Agreements contain mandatory disciplines which require that, when domestic regulatory measures significantly affect trade, Members set meaningful prior consultation periods. This would provide affected parties with a reasonable assurance that they would be aware of the announcement and have adequate time to respond. They would also count on the fact that the competent authorities will consider the input provided through the consultation procedure in the final version of the regulatory measures at hand.

[54] WTO, WPDR, 'Report on the Meeting Held on 3 July 2001', S/WPDR/M/12, 16 August 2001, para 56.

[55] From the area of goods trade, TBT and SPS are the most relevant in these discussions.

[56] WTO, CTS (n 48 above) para 31.

3. The most controversial issues identified in the proposals that have been submitted—Notifications, prior consultations, and application processes

It bears mention that there has been only one comprehensive proposal, submitted by the United States, addressing exclusively the issue of transparency across all service sectors and modes of supply and all levels of government, including sub-central jurisdictions.[57] This proposal initially took the form of a room document that has been regularly revised in order to reflect the comments made by Members during the WPDR meetings.[58] There have been several other, equally or sometimes less comprehensive proposals that tackled the issue of transparency, either horizontally or as part of disciplines relating to one of the categories of measures referred to in the *chapeau* of Article VI:4 GATS, that is, licensing, qualifications, or standards.

Most proposals require the pre-establishment and public availability of VI:4 measures. In addition, information relating to licensing, qualification, or standards should be easily accessible, by printed or, preferably, through electronic means and/or domestic enquiry or contact points, and make public crucial elements, such as criteria for obtaining a licence or the equivalence of a qualification, names and addresses of the authorities in charge, etc. It was also proposed that Members designate an official journal/gazette for this purpose.[59] Suggestions for prior comment procedures have also been put on the negotiating table. The latter are usually coupled with a requirement that new measures are published well in advance to enable affected suppliers or other Members to comment.[60]

[57] WTO, WPDR, 'Report on the Meeting Held on 22 June 2005', S/WPDR/M/30, 6 September 2005, para 41. The United States confirmed that the adoption by the WPDR of horizontal transparency disciplines is the highest priority for the US in the current WPDR negotiations. WPDR, 'Outline of US Position on a Draft Consolidated Text in the WPDR', Communication from the United States, JOB(06)/223, 11 July 2006, para 15.

[58] Some of the elements that the United States based their proposal on can be found in WTO, WPDR, 'GATS Article VI:4: Possible Disciplines on Transparency in Domestic Regulation', Communication from the United States, S/WPDR/W/4, 3 May 2000; also WTO, CTS (Special Session), 'Transparency in Domestic Regulation', Communication from the United States, S/CSS/W/102, 13 July 2001. A summary of their initial proposal is contained in WPDR, 'U.S. Proposal for Transparency Disciplines in Domestic Regulation: Building on Existing International Disciplines and Proposals—Summary', Communication from the United States, JOB(04)/128, 15 September 2004. The most recent version of the United States' proposal is contained in WPDR, 'Horizontal Transparency Disciplines in Domestic Regulation', Communication from the United States, JOB(06)/182, 9 June 2006.

[59] WPDR, 'Proposed Disciplines on Domestic Regulation under Article VI:4 of the GATS', Communication from China and Pakistan, JOB(06)/158, 29 May 2006. Japan made a similar proposition in its 'Draft Annex on Domestic Regulation', JOB(03)/45, 3 March 2003 (and JOB(03)/45/Rev.1, 2 May 2003).

[60] cf the proposal by Australia *et al*, WPDR, 'Article VI:4 Disciplines—Proposal for a Draft Text', Communication from Australia; Chile; Colombia; Hong Kong, China; Korea; New Zealand, and the Separate Customs Territory of Taiwan, Penghu, Kinmen and Matsu, JOB(06)/193, 19 June

Two detailed proposals have been submitted by Japan, the first pointing to some elements that Japan considers essential for enhancing transparency under Article VI,[61] and the second proposing some transparency disciplines within a broader draft Annex on domestic regulation.[62] The European Union also included in its proposal on necessity various elements for consideration with respect to transparency,[63] as did Australia.[64] Both proposals draw on the transparency provisions included in the accountancy disciplines. Several important elements with respect to licensing procedures are also to be found in the European Union's proposal submitted on this score.[65] Australia *et al* also included various transparency provisions that mainly encapsulate similar provisions that had been submitted in previous proposals.[66]

Nevertheless, as the United States' proposal has been the most comprehensive one, it will guide the analysis that follows with regard to the most important, and, arguably, controversial, issues that may ultimately lead to the adoption of significant additional, horizontally applicable disciplines relating to transparency at the end of the services negotiations. These disciplines, according to the proposal, are to be applied by the LDCs only on a best-endeavour basis.

In line with the Article VI:4 mandate, the proposal addresses only the five subcategories of measures identified in the *chapeau* of Article VI:4 and consists of three parts: the first part refers to the establishment of mechanisms to respond to enquiries from interested persons (hence not only from other governments) and aims to build on Article III GATS with a view to extending the obligation that enquiry points provide information to the vertical relationship between governments and *interested* persons, ie individual service suppliers.

The second part of the proposal addresses the issues associated with publication of domestic regulation measures. In this part, again, the proposal elaborates on Article III and expands its scope by requiring publication of information relating to processing deadlines, rights of appeal, and notification concerning violations of the licence terms. According to the proposal, Members would be required to provide for advance notice and comment with respect to new regulatory measures or

2006, para 13. In this proposal, contrary to the Japanese proposal, the obligation would apply regardless of specific commitments made. Again, the language used in both proposals is hortatory.

61 These elements refer to six categories of measures: publication of measures; notifications to the WTO; responding to queries and complaints; establishing standards for applying measures; publicizing the standards for applying measures; and procedures for receiving public comments. WTO, WPDR, 'Elements for Consideration for Enhancing Transparency in the Context of Domestic Regulation under Article VI of the GATS', Communication from Japan, JOB(01)/77, 28 May 2001; also WTO, WPDR (n 38 above) para 12.

62 WPDR, 'Draft Annex on Domestic Regulation' (n 59 above) paras 8–13.

63 WTO, WPDR (n 51 above) paras 24–29.

64 WTO, WPDR, 'Necessity and Transparency', Communication from Australia, S/WPDR/W/8, 15 September 2000, para 8.

65 WTO, WPDR, 'Proposal for Disciplines on Licensing Procedures', Communication from the European Community and its Member States, S/WPDR/W/25, 10 July 2003, p 5.

66 WPDR (n 60 above).

changes therein. This requirement concerns only sectors where specific commitments have been undertaken and provides for appropriate flexibility in order to accommodate developing country concerns by using best-endeavour language ('to the extent practicable'). The same language is also used when it comes to the requirement endorsed in the proposal to respond to substantive public comments in writing. More importantly, the proposal allows interested persons to participate actively in the relevant procedures. Furthermore, the United States' proposal requires that regulations be published in 'plain language', be readily understandable, and allow a reasonable interval between their publication and their entry into force.

In a third part, the proposal refers to the issue of licensure and elaborates on Article VI. It calls for the establishment of clear, publicly available procedures with respect to all forms of licensing or authorization that fall under Article VI:3 GATS. More specifically, the United States emphasized the importance of having in place the procedures necessary to decide on an application within a reasonable period of time; provide all the information for complete applications; notify the applicants of the status of their applications; and inform them of the reasons for a denial, if applicable. Moreover, qualifying examinations are addressed in this part of the proposal with a view to ensuring that they are non-discriminatory and are offered at reasonable intervals and costs. Examinations relating to financial services are, however, exempted. Again, such disciplines are to be applied in sectors where commitments are made.

a) Additional notifications to the WTO

One of the issues that were discussed within the WPDR concerned the possibility of creating additional disciplines providing for better notifications to the WTO, for instance, through easier formats and fixed timeframes with respect to the submission of WTO notifications.[67] In its first proposal, Japan called for stricter notification obligations and more prompt publication of measures through the WTO so as to render operational the Article III obligations. Many Members took issue with this approach and underscored the excessive administrative burden. To them, Article III provisions were already far-reaching and needed no further clarification or enhancement.[68] Hence, the Japanese proposal did not gain any considerable support. Many Members suggested, instead, that the WPDR should rather reflect on ways to implement existing notification obligations,[69] as several Members, both developed and developing countries, appeared to have difficulties in implementing them.[70]

[67] WTO, WPDR, 'Report on the Meeting Held on 25 May 2000', S/WPDR/M/6, 29 June 2000, para 7.

[68] cf WTO, WPDR (n 51 above) para 29, and WTO, WPDR (n 54 above) paras 56ff.

[69] WTO, WPDR, 'Report on the Meeting Held on 12 March 2002', S/WPDR/M/15, 10 April 2002, para 50.

[70] Ibid paras 63ff, and WTO, WPDR, 'Report on the Meeting Held on 2 October 2000', S/WPDR/M/8, 17 November 2000, p 6; also WTO, WPDR (n 38 above) p 12.

b) Prior consultations (advance notice and comment procedure)

A considerable part of the WPDR discussions regarding transparency has focused on the desirability of prior comment and consultations procedures and the language that should be used in the drafting of disciplines foreseeing such procedures, considering that the level of detail cannot be too high in an effort to generate horizontally applicable transparency disciplines. This has indeed been one of the most controversial and extensively discussed issues within the WPDR.[71]

As highlighted earlier, the United States' proposal contains an advance notice and comment mechanism, open to all interested parties, be they government or private service suppliers, in sectors where specific commitments have been made which is fairly flexible as it requires Members to implement it 'to the extent practicable', echoing in essence the best-endeavour language of paragraph 6 of the accountancy disciplines. It bears noting that this requirement concerns all measures of general application and not only those that significantly affect trade in services, as is the case in the accountancy disciplines.

According to the United States, giving the right to private service suppliers and firms to comment on domestic regulation measures before their adoption would increase efficiency and credibility of the measures at issue.[72] Furthermore, a prior comment mechanism allows all interested parties to be better-informed thereby reducing uncertainty and discriminatory treatment in a given market. In the United States' view, the countries worrying about the burdensome costs of implementing a prior consultations mechanism should take into account the benefits associated with such a mechanism, all the more so because the cost of it can be fairly low, eg through the use of the internet, after the initial start-up costs.[73]

In its proposal for an Annex on domestic regulation, Japan also referred to the introduction of 'public comment procedures' to address similar issues.[74] Again, the proposed disciplines with respect to such procedures would be applicable only to sectors where specific commitments are undertaken, unless the domestic regulation measures are of purely minor nature or their adoption is urgent. Drawing from the accountancy disciplines as well as the TBT and SPS Agreements, these procedures would provide to the public (hence, not only other Members) an

[71] This issue is not new. During the Uruguay Round, Switzerland suggested that Members allow 'for advance commentary by interested parties, to be taken into account on the basis of reciprocity'. Switzerland considered this provision as one that would help to avoid disputes. GATT, 'General Agreement on Trade in Services—A Draft Blueprint', Communication from Switzerland, MTN.GNS/W/69, 15 September 1989, p 9; also GATT, 'Agreement on Trade in Services', Communication from the United States, MTN.GNS/W/75, 17 October 1989, Art 12.3.2.

[72] cf K Iida and J Nielson, 'Transparency in Domestic Regulation: Prior Consultation' in OECD, *Trade in Services: Negotiating Issues and Approaches*, 2001, 115.

[73] WTO, WPDR, 'Report on the Meeting Held on 3 December 2003', S/WPDR/M/24, 22 January 2004, paras 37–38.

[74] WPDR, 'Draft Annex on Domestic Regulation' (n 59 above) para 13.

opportunity for comments, while the domestic regulator would be compelled to take into account these comments before adoption, publish them and answer to them by making public the government's views on such comments.

With respect to licensing procedures,[75] the European Union proposed likewise a provision that would allow affected parties to comment on the introduction or change of licensing procedures when trade in services is significantly affected, while the authorities would be obliged to give consideration to such comments before the entry into force of these new or changed procedures. Like the accountancy disciplines, the proposed provision used best-efforts language.

Many Members challenged the necessity of introducing a prior consultations mechanism by arguing that the possibility of its introduction is not provided for in their constitution or that it is not allowed to be part of the domestic lawmaking process.[76] Others based their opposition on the additional administrative burden that such a mechanism would bring about, notably for the lower levels of government[77] that lack the sufficient financial means or the technical capacity (or both) in order to establish a prior comment mechanism. Surely, several Members would not be in a position to set up this type of mechanism unless substantial technical assistance flows into their administrations to strengthen the regulatory capacities of these Members.[78]

The purported incompatibility with several domestic regulatory and legislative systems and the implied unwillingness of a considerable part of the WTO Membership to internationalize their decisionmaking processes through a prior consultations mechanism equally strong to the one foreseen under the TBT and SPS Agreements has led Members to contemplate the relevance of the respective prior comment provision laid down in paragraph 6 of the accountancy disciplines.[79] The latter, because of the best-endeavour language that it uses, provides some flexibility that, for some Members, appears to be an attractive and balanced starting point for discussions.

A relevant issue concerns the addressees of the advance notice and the parties eligible to make comments. The United States, drawing from the corresponding TBT disciplines, opts for an all-inclusive, participatory approach allowing all interested parties to participate fully in the prior consultations and *a fortiori* to have the ability to make comments regarding new regulations or proposed

[75] WTO, WPDR (n 65 above) para 19.14.

[76] WTO, WPDR, 'Report on the Meeting Held on 20 March 2001', S/WPDR/M/10, 10 May 2001, para 21.

[77] WTO, WPDR (n 70 above) 5.

[78] The last draft relating to the domestic regulation disciplines includes a fairly detailed provision on technical assistance supplied by developed country Members to developing countries and LDCs upon the request of the latter Members and 'on *mutually* agreed terms and conditions'. The latter qualification could be construed as weakening the 'bite' of this obligation. WPDR, 'Disciplines on Domestic Regulation Pursuant to GATS Article VI:4', Informal Note by the Chairman, Room Document, 18 April 2007, para 45.

[79] cf WTO, WPDR (n 51 above) paras 27–28; also WTO, WPDR (n 64 above) para 8.

amendments thereof. Under 'interested parties', one could visualize other Members or private persons, and affected service suppliers or service suppliers that would like to enter the market in the future. As to the issue of advance notice, the United States would not call for notifications made individually to each interested party, but rather timely[80] notifications in the official government gazette.[81]

Nonetheless, with respect to notifications related to prior comment procedures, other Members were persuaded that the Member-to-Member notifications as foreseen under Article III:3 GATS were sufficient and there was no need to change.[82] Japan's proposal, for instance, relating to elements for adding to the transparency disciplines reserved the use of enquiry points exclusively to other Members. What is more, only Members, according to Japan's proposal, should be entitled to ask for the rationale behind domestic regulatory measures. The United States took issue with both of these elements by not challenging the substance of these two proposed disciplines, but rather the restrictions to the use of such rights, as the latter should be available to all interested parties, and not only to Members.[83] *A propos*, this appears to be a correct expansion of such rights, since private service suppliers are the active players in the everyday commercial activities. Notably allowing individuals to address questions to the contact and enquiry points would benefit greatly their use (and, indeed, usefulness). The poor use of the contact points at the intergovernmental level to date should not be considered coincidental.[84]

Furthermore, an issue that has also been mooted with respect to the holders of rights of prior comment and, more generally, of participation in prior consultations procedures, is whether these rights also cover regulatory procedures at a sub-national level. This is of relevance for all four concepts discussed under the Article VI:4 work programme (necessity, transparency, equivalence, international standards) and all five sub-categories of measures identified in Article VI:4. The United States' proposal advocates a far-reaching application of these rights to cover all levels of government, including sub-central jurisdictions. Some Members, on the other hand, referred to the additional burden that a conferral of such rights would bring about to sub-national entities, which by definition, have a more limited financial capacity than a central government to establish and carry out a prior consultations framework.

However, the United States' proposal is consistent with a correct interpretation of the GATS coverage in light of Articles I:3(a) and XXVIII(a) GATS.[85]

[80] In the United States' view, this equates to 'reasonable advance notice [meaning that] final laws should be published with a lag before actual introduction'. WTO, WPDR (n 76 above) para 17.

[81] WTO, WPDR, 'Report on the Meeting Held on 12 July 2000', S/WPDR/M/7, 19 September 2000, para 12.

[82] cf Japan's and European Union's comments in WTO, WPDR (n 54 above) paras 60–61.

[83] Ibid para 58.

[84] See also the relevant comments made by Mexico in WTO, WPDR (n 8 above) para 21.

[85] Also WTO, WPDR, 'Report on the Meeting Held on 29 November 2001', S/WPDR/M/14, 29 January 2002, paras 45–51.

Indeed, the GATS makes clear that 'measures taken by Members' also include those taken by regional or local governments and authorities. Furthermore, the GATS requires that Members take all reasonable steps available to them to ensure that regional and local governments and authorities observe the central government's obligations under GATS.[86]

Of course, this legal interpretation does not take into account the economic and administrative difficulties of several sub-national entities or regions, notably in developing countries, to operationalize a prior consultations mechanism in the near future.[87] Therefore, the best-endeavour language that the United States' proposal endorses ('to the extent practicable') constitutes a balancing act. Again, sub-federal regulations should be subject to any transparency and other disciplines to be developed under Article VI:4 (eg disciplines on necessity and unnecessary burdensomeness) in the long run, without jeopardizing the right of sub-federal entities to regulation nor seeking harmonization of sub-federal regulations, as it appears that several services barriers are sometimes higher at the sub-federal level,[88] while regulations may differ between sub-federal jurisdictions, notably in the areas of licensing and qualifications.

c) Application processes

Several proposals submitted to the WPDR touched upon the issue of application processing, particularly with respect to licensing and qualification procedures. The United States' proposal on horizontal transparency disciplines builds on Article VI:3. Contrary to the latter Article, however, the disciplines regarding licensure that the United States' proposal puts forward are not dependent on specific commitments undertaken. On the other hand, these obligations fall short of establishing strong, clear-cut obligations, as they use best-efforts language ('to the extent practicable'). In any case, according to these disciplines, Members are required, if feasible, to create clear, publicly available domestic procedures for a juridical or natural person to obtain or renew any qualification, licence, or other form of permission that fall under the definition of an authorization as foreseen in Article VI:3 GATS.

Compared with Article VI:3, there are two new elements in this proposal: first, the established procedures shall ensure that information concerning the requirements, including any documentation required, for completing applications is provided to the interested service suppliers. Secondly, Members and the competent authorities shall ensure that the applicant will be informed, upon request, of the reasons that led to the denial of its application. Notably with respect to the proposed obligation to give reasons for the rejection of an application, the existence of a procedure that informs of the reasons for such rejection is an important

[86] See also Chapter IV.C.3 above.
[87] Also K Iida and J Nielson (n 2 above) 14.
[88] WTO, WPDR (n 76 above) para 10.

due process and good governance element. The Appellate Body emphasized in *US—Shrimp* that the absence of similar procedures can, together with other elements such as the absence of prompt review of a denial of an application, lead to the conclusion that 'exporting Members applying for certification whose applications are rejected are denied basic fairness and due process, and are discriminated against, *vis-à-vis* those Members which are granted certification'.[89] This reasoning appears to be particularly relevant for the creation of appropriate licensing and qualification procedures, which will be in line with the contemporary due process and 'good' regulation advocacy.

Again, the content and scope of these procedures and their transparency elements need to be developed further, as the requirements that the United States' proposal endorses are mentioned in an illustrative manner, bearing always in mind that the disciplines need to be fairly general in their wording to be horizontally applicable. After all, the United States' proposal is the only comprehensive proposal to date that addresses the issue of transparency, hence for all sectors and modes of supply, and all five sub-categories of measures contained in the *chapeau* of Article VI:4.

A third new element that deserves to be mentioned separately, as it did not entail a best-endeavour clause, addresses the issue of qualifying examinations as part of the domestic application process for a licence or authorization.[90] Furthering the Article VI:4(c) objective that licensing procedures should not be in themselves a restriction on the supply of a service, the proposal suggested that such examinations should be first and foremost non-discriminatory and hence allow both domestic and foreign service suppliers to bid for a licence or authorization on an equal basis. Furthermore, the participation fees should not be prohibitive in order to discourage service suppliers from applying for a licence. Finally, competent authorities shall be bound to organize such examinations at reasonable intervals so that interested service suppliers have the opportunity to apply again for an authorization.[91]

With respect to the latter element, Japan's comprehensive proposal on an Annex on domestic regulation also contains similar provisions in its part relating to qualification procedures requiring the organizing of non-discriminatory examinations at reasonably frequent intervals and the reasonableness of fees to reflect only the administrative costs involved. Nonetheless, the proposed disciplines only concern sectors where specific commitments were undertaken.

[89] Appellate Body Report, *US—Shrimp*, para 181; also M Shapiro, 'The Giving Reasons Requirement' (1992) University of Chicago Legal Forum 179.

[90] For the mode 4 implications, see CTS (Special Session), 'Mode 4—Transparency Issues', Communication from Argentina, Brazil, Chile, China, Colombia, Dominican Republic, Egypt, Guatemala, India, Mexico, Pakistan, Peru, Philippines and Thailand, JOB(04)/142, 29 September 2004.

[91] Also WTO, CTS (Special Session) (n 58 above) paras 7–9.

E. Horizontally applicable transparency disciplines and the linkage with necessity

Members agree on the importance of regulatory transparency in building a predictable, impartial, fair and investment-friendly domestic regulatory framework. This is even more the case when it comes to the vertical relationship between regulators and service suppliers. Article III GATS addresses, for the most part, the need for transparency at the inter-governmental level in a sufficient manner. Where the WPDR needs to concentrate is on the development of transparency disciplines, be they horizontal or sector-specific,[92] that provide an assurance to private service suppliers that the domestic framework that regulates their activities will be non-discriminatory, consistent, predictable, and simple. It is actually this relationship between regulatory authorities and service suppliers that Article VI GATS refers to.

One could identify at this point the most important elements that seem to emerge from the discussions in the WPDR along the following lines:[93]

- The possibility of creating mechanisms, or strengthening existing ones, to respond to inquiries by interested persons (ie not only other Members, but also individual service suppliers) that pertain to Article VI:4 issues;
- Strengthening the Members' obligations with respect to the publication of domestic regulation measures. This would include, inter alia, the public availability to interested persons of domestic requirements (eg requirements for granting or renewing a licence or certificate) and mechanisms (eg application processing, related deadlines, review/appeal mechanisms, etc);
- Providing prior notice and the opportunity for comment. This would include prior publication or public availability of prospective regulations relating to Article VI:4 issues, prior comment mechanisms also foreseeing response mechanisms to substantive comments, and reasonable intervals between publication and entry into force of the measures at stake;
- Enhancing transparency of the procedures governing licensing application. This would require the establishment, if they do not already exist, of clear, publicly available procedures accessible by interested persons, including interested foreign service suppliers, with respect to licensing, covering information about requirements/documentation, reasonable timeframe for decisions, information on application status, and sufficient explanation of the reasons that led to a possible denial of the application;
- Of great importance is also the further amplification of transparency with respect to qualification requirements and procedures, including administrative

[92] For this discussion, see Iida and Nielson (n 2 above), 14–15.

[93] WTO, WPDR, 'Report of the Chairman of the Working Party on Domestic Regulation to the Special Session of the Council for Trade in Services', JOB(05)/280, 15 November 2005.

and procedural rules relating to the administration of qualification requirements and criteria thereof. Of relevance is also the organization of qualifying examinations on a non-discrimination basis, frequency of examinations and reasonable costs for participating therein, and the existence of review/appeal mechanisms.

- With respect to transparency elements in the domain of domestic technical standards, their pre-establishment, public availability, and objectivity are considered an essential part of the horizontal transparency disciplines to be developed. In addition, Members discuss the possibility of providing an opportunity for comments when preparing such standards and the need to review regularly their necessity.

Of course, transparency is only one of the elements that needs to be developed with a view to achieving the Article VI:4 objectives.[94] Transparency on its own would not assist in the accomplishment of the Article VI:4 mandate.[95] Members should also seek to bring forward the creation of disciplines under Article VI:4 in the other three areas of interest, ie necessity, equivalence, and international standards, in order to have a balanced outcome that would fulfil the legal mandate incorporated in Article VI:4. From the WPDR discussions it becomes clear that Members favour the development of horizontal disciplines in these four areas, notably with respect to necessity and transparency, without, however, excluding the possibility of creating more precise disciplines to address sectoral specificities at a later stage, if necessary. Of course, consensus varies, depending on the issue in question, and, therefore, each of these four areas is not discussed with the same pace nor benefits from the same degree of support.

More specifically, as to the need for developing horizontally applicable transparency disciplines, Members' views vary when it comes to their scope, content, or level of detail. Regarding the establishment of prior comment mechanisms, for example, it is clear that no strong obligation will emerge at least from this negotiations round, especially with regard to sub-national authorities and local governments, as the administrative burden seems to be, for many Members, unbearable.

If anything, the wording that was adopted in paragraph 6 of the accountancy disciplines could be accepted by the majority of Members, possibly with some changes of minor importance. Indeed, the best-endeavour language that paragraph 6 thereof adopts as well as the fact that it limits the obligation of prior comment only to measures that *significantly* affect trade in accountancy services would satisfy the sensitivities of many Members and their demand for appropriate flexibility. A similar formulation of an obligation for a prior comment mechanism (for example, only in sectors where specific commitments have been undertaken, perhaps accompanied by a sunset provision) would most likely gain a sufficient

[94] cf WTO, WPDR (n 57 above) paras 40ff.
[95] WTO, WPDR (n 51 above) paras 32–33.

acceptance in the WPDR. To be sure, even in this weak form, such a provision can bring the desired results progressively, as one can expect that Members that use such mechanisms will encourage their use by other Members, ideally by demonstrating how the benefits of the establishment of prior consultations mechanisms override the anticipated costs. On the other hand, it would not be wise to exempt sub-federal measures from the scope of the disciplines, as such measures can indeed restrict trade in an excessive manner.

From a policy perspective, Members favouring the endorsement of additional transparency disciplines must find ways to reassure Members that call upon administrative burden to prevent any agreement on additional transparency disciplines, mostly developing countries, that this is not the case. Administrative burden can be the least possible depending on the wording of the disciplines; and the latter, of course, is subject to negotiations. Moreover, a Member cannot avoid some kind of administrative burden as regards transparency obligations. But it is only these good practices and principles of good governance which, when implemented, allow Members to reap long-term benefits, while diminishing short-term costs that fade out quickly because of the experience that the respective officials have acquired. Indeed, Members should seek to use existing structures and practices for optimal results and low costs. In addition, LDCs and developing countries should also call for provisions that will ensure technical assistance by developed countries in the attempt of the former countries to implement their obligations with respect to transparency.

It is worth noting that transparency is a crucial element when it comes to the need for further enhancement of trade through mode 4, which is of great interest notably for the developing countries. Ameliorating the transparency obligations with respect to licensing and notably qualification procedures could improve the possibilities of temporary movement of service suppliers to a considerable extent. This presupposes a facilitated access of private persons to the relevant information made available by the host countries. What is more, licensing procedures sometimes entail ENTs, which may be used to *de facto* hinder the access to the domestic market. Hence, more transparency relating to ENTs can be beneficial for service suppliers seeking to enter a market, again if information is accessible to private persons as well.

Not only should the developing countries seek new transparency disciplines that respond favourably to their demand for low administrative burden, but—most importantly—they should also call for the implementation of existing transparency provisions under the GATS. For instance, more complete and timely notifications could be valuable in terms of prospective market access. In the host countries, enquiry and contact points could, and should, be further improved.[96] Strengthening their capacity to disseminate relevant information pertaining to effective market access and domestic regulations and practices, as well as allowing

[96] For a recent list of enquiry and contact points, see WTO, CTS, 'Contact and Enquiry Points Notified to the Council for Trade in Services', S/ENQ/8/Rev.8, 3 November 2005.

private service suppliers to refer to these points can be of assistance for many suppliers who lack the necessary information with respect to a given domestic regulatory system. In this respect, countries that have a comparative advantage in mode 4 could benefit from such mechanisms.

Furthermore, one of the general issues that were identified in the *Checklist of Issues* prepared by the Secretariat was the one dealing with the link between necessity and transparency, ie to what extent greater transparency can play a role in determining whether a measure is necessary. This question can only be answered in the positive. Indeed, since enhanced transparency equates to more information, other Members, service suppliers, and the WTO adjudicating bodies can have all the relevant information for a given domestic regulatory framework which is essential for an assessment of the necessity of a particular measure. Furthermore, transparent domestic regulations reduce the trade-restrictiveness of domestic measures by increasing predictability and legal certainty and by assisting in the identification of potential impediments to trade in services.[97] Enhanced transparency generates better accountability and contributes to making domestic measures less burdensome and less vulnerable to regulatory capture, thereby aiding such measures to meet the necessity standard.

In this regard, an important provision that highlights the interdependency and complementarity between necessity and transparency, and which would strengthen the necessity test if added in a text of horizontal transparency disciplines is the one that requires Members to make known, upon request, the rationale behind regulatory measures in relation to legitimate objectives.[98] This provision is already part of the accountancy disciplines and Japan also included it in its proposal for a draft Annex on domestic regulation, using the same strong language as that used in paragraph 5 of the accountancy disciplines.

As underscored earlier, a necessity standard implicitly contains the requirement to disclose the objective of a regulation. Therefore, requiring that a Member provides information about the rationale behind a given domestic regulation measure with respect to a public policy objective would more easily allow the distinction between necessary and unnecessary barriers to trade in services. It is commonplace now that transparency is most needed in areas where the scope for discretion is considerable and the area of necessary versus unnecessary domestic regulation is one of these latter areas. In those cases where trade is not the foremost reason for a government intervention, a strong necessity test, accompanied by far-reaching transparency disciplines that eliminate the confusion with regard to the intent of a given regulatory measure, can make the difference and 'protect' adjudicating bodies (and, *a fortiori*, the WTO Membership) from misleading decisions regarding the necessity, or not, of that measure.[99]

[97] Also WTO, WPDR (n 76 above) p 8.

[98] Also WTO, WPDR (n 85 above) para 64.

[99] G Feketekuty, 'Assessing and Improving the Architecture of the GATS' in P Sauvé and RM Stern (eds), *GATS 2000: New Directions in Service Trade Liberalization*, 2000, 102.

Concluding Remarks—Challenges for the Future

The negotiations on trade in services at a multilateral level have been a serious enterprise that generated tangible results, which, however, are regarded as scarce in some areas.[1] The obstacles, both conceptual and political, that have been a manifest feature of the services negotiations during the Uruguay Round display their effects in the Agreement's complex architecture as well as in the considerable amount of unfinished business, both in terms of substantive rulemaking and liberalization commitments, left for the next rounds of negotiations. Most importantly, Members agreed on a mechanism, laid down in Article XIX GATS, that warrants the initiation of negotiations every five years (at the latest) with a view to further liberalizing trade in services.[2] Recall that, according to the second recital of the GATS Preamble, progressive liberalization is one of the fundamental principles that underlies the new legal framework regulating the multilateral trade in services.

As noted in the introductory chapter, positive development and welfare prospects abound in the services sector. Nonetheless, services negotiations rely on a resource-intensive and time-consuming request–offer process[3] that may delay liberalization. To be sure, the well-known approach from the goods realm of reciprocal exchange of market access concessions may not yield results so easily and rapidly in the services domain as in trade in goods; instead, it may render any

[1] Indeed, the GATS cannot be regarded as 'a scourge of protection, but as a rather stodgy reaper of liberalization accomplished elsewhere'. A Mattoo, 'Shaping Future Rules for Trade in Services: Lessons from the GATS', 2001, 3.

[2] P Delimatsis, 'Article XIX GATS', in R Wolfrum, P-T Stoll, and C Feinäugle (eds), *Max-Planck Commentaries on World Trade Law, Volume 6: WTO—Trade in Services*, 2008.

[3] For the inadequacy of the request–offer method and some alternative negotiating approaches, see R Thompson, 'Cross-Cutting ('Formula') Approaches to Multilateral Services Negotiations' in OECD, *Trade in Services: Negotiating Issues and Approaches,* 2001, 51; also J Nielson, C Pellegrino, R Morris, and R Thompson, 'Using "Cluster" Approaches to Specific Commitments for Interdependent Services', in OECD, *Trade in Services: Negotiating Issues and Approaches,* 2001, 61; also A Mattoo and S Wunsch, 'Pre-empting Protectionism in Services: The WTO and Outsourcing', PRWP No 3237, 2004, 21. It is worth noting that Members agreed in Hong Kong to allow not only bilateral, but also plurilateral requests, ie groups of Members can coordinate themselves and prepare requests to another Member or Members regarding any sector or mode of supply. These plurilateral negotiations have started on 28 February 2006, in accordance with the timeline set by the Hong Kong Ministerial Declaration. Annex C to the *Hong Kong Ministerial Declaration,* adopted on 18 December 2005, WT/MIN(05)/DEC, paras 7 and 11(b).

efforts to liberalize trade in services more difficult to realize.[4] At any rate, these GATS-intrinsic setbacks cannot reverse the pace of services liberalization in the future. The GATS will continue to constitute the legal framework that regulates multilateral trade in services for the coming years and its scope is expected to expand, as Members increasingly recognize the value of this Agreement.

In the Uruguay Round, Members have for the most part bound modest liberalization levels, which sometimes did not even reflect the actual liberalization levels at that time, mostly due to the fact that trade in services was *terra incognita* for most Members. Therefore, in the current negotiating round, apart from codifying the sometimes fairly high level of *de facto* liberalization that has been reached in several services sectors in previous years, Members shall also strive, when feasible, for the expansion of 'lock-in' through their Schedules. This evidently requires, above all, clear political will, as the WTO remains in essence a Member-driven, consensus-based, international organization[5] with asymmetrically weak legislative and executive powers. Admittedly, then, meaningful liberalization may be accomplished progressively through more than one negotiating round, driven primarily by domestic priorities and forces that will gradually comprehend the extensive pay-offs associated with the pursuit of regulatory reforms in the service sector.[6] Indeed, any reform endeavour can be sustainable in political and economic terms only when it is implemented due to the recognition of national self-interest, rather than on the orders of trading partners or international organizations.

In this respect, the political context surrounding the current negotiating round on services is quite different from the one in 1986 when the Uruguay Round was launched. Members have diffidently started acknowledging the important gains that they can reap from the (unilateral and multilateral) liberalization of trade in services. The GATS can aid with neutralizing domestic competing interests and hence eliminating any possibility of backsliding, channelling protection to economically superior instruments (eg subsidies instead of quantitative restrictions), promoting deeper liberalization by pairing domestic regulatory reform and market access commitments with reforms and liberalization commitments of other countries on the basis of reciprocity, lending credibility to domestic policies through legally binding commitments which can be reviewed by a comprehensive compulsory third party adjudication system, and guaranteeing non-discrimination through the enforcement of the MFN principle.

Furthermore, the emergence of disciplines on domestic regulation can contribute to the promotion and consolidation of domestic regulatory reform and

[4] B Hoekman, 'The Next Round of Services Negotiations: Identifying Priorities and Options' (2000) 82(4) Federal Reserve Bank of St. Louis Review 31.

[5] Also JH Jackson, 'The WTO "Constitution" and Proposed Reforms: Seven "Mantras" Revisited' (2001) 1 JIEL 72.

[6] B Hoekman and A Mattoo, 'Services, Economic Development and the Next Round of Negotiations on Services' (2000) 12 Journal of International Development 295.

assist in addressing unduly burdensome regulatory barriers. Ensuring that liberalization gains are not undermined by inadequate regulation or domestic policy choice appears to be a daunting, but still essential task in order to make the GATS system a success. On the other side, allowing diversity in national regulatory systems is equally essential and, indeed, desirable if any trade gains are to materialize. The challenge that negotiators are facing is the shield of regulatory diversity, while attempting to devise principles and concepts that will allow international trade to grow under conditions of transparency and predictability.

It is commonplace that, probably also because of the negotiating fatigue identified in most countries following the completion of the Uruguay Round, the progress in the services negotiations has been poor up to date. Therefore, several voices expressed their growing concerns as to the desirability of accomplishing further services trade liberalization. As of November 2005, that is, more than five years after the inauguration of the negotiating round on services, 69 initial offers (representing 93 Members) and 30 revised offers (representing 54 Members) have been tabled, while 23 initial offers remain outstanding, excluding LDCs.[7] If anything, this situation demonstrates a dire lack of impetus. Members, however, agreed in Hong Kong to submit final draft Schedules by 31 October 2006.[8] Due to the negotiations' stalemate, however, this date was not observed.

Being more realistic as far as the Doha Round negotiations held in Geneva are concerned, meaningful specific commitments, binding of applied policies, and future 'lock in' in services are unlikely to emerge without a *quid pro quo*.[9] What is more, during the Doha Development Round, one could reasonably argue that services were many times considered not as an important area in its own right where substantial mutual gains can be achieved, but rather another area forming part of the negotiating chips at Members' disposal. In this sense, services negotiations have been held hostage, as their lack of progress is not to be attributed to factors that relate to trade in services. Radical reform with respect to trade in services will not take place in this round of negotiations—nor probably in the next. A glance at the negotiations in the Working Party on GATS rules is convincing in respect of this—rather pessimistic or conservative—assumption.

The degree to which the Agreement 'juridifies' the process of liberalization is yet to be determined. Several elements speak for an expansion of this 'juridification': the tentative attempts for the elaboration of standards within the GATS itself; the availability of prototypes from the experience with other agreements such as the European Community Treaty (ECT); the institution at the WTO of

[7] WTO, CTS (Special Session), 'Report of the Chairman to the Trade Negotiations Committee', TN/S/23, 28 November 2005, para 2. At the Hong Kong Ministerial Conference, Members acknowledged that LDCs should not be expected to make new liberalization commitments. *Hong Kong Ministerial Declaration* (n 3 above) para 26.

[8] Ibid, Annex C, para 11(d).

[9] For example, a possible trade-off in services can be a mode 3–mode 4 exchange. B Hoekman and M Kostecki, *The Political Economy of the World Trading System: The WTO and Beyond*, 2001, 272; also, in this respect, the *Hong Kong Ministerial Declaration* (n 3 above) para 27.

a more rigorous dispute settlement mechanism; and, of course, the automaticity of the initialization of successive GATS negotiating rounds, which have been foreshadowed in the GATS text.

For an area that was considered non-tradable only a few years ago, services have already covered a long way to winning an important percentage of trade flows. As noted in Chapter II, the gains from liberalizing trade in services may be substantially greater than those from liberalizing merchandise trade. This is so because, first, the current levels of protection are higher in services industries and, second, because services liberalization would also create additional positive spillovers from the associated movement of capital and labour.

In many service industries, FDI tends to be spread relatively widely, reflecting the importance of proximity to consumers. The growth of both trade and FDI flows echoes the well-established internationalization of services. Trade and FDI in services have benefited by the increased dependence of the manufacturing sector on information and knowledge-intensive services as well as by numerous innovations in information and communications technology that allowed a reduction of costs and an increased tradability of services, and induced a global rationalization of production, increasing geographic specialization, international fragmentation of the production (value added) chain (ie outsourcing), and product differentiation.[10]

Traditionally, service industries have been less exposed to international trade and so lacked this stimulus to control costs, develop products, and innovate. FDI is meant to offset this deficiency by enhancing the degree of competition in domestic service markets and by transferring best practices from abroad. Government policies entailing deregulation, liberalization and regulatory reform that improve competition have contributed to this rapid increase of FDI in services, particularly in sectors that have been—until recently—heavily 'protected', eg banking, communications, finance, transport, and media.[11] The fact that service sector FDI dominates FDI in manufacturing, although major regulatory barriers still remain in place, demonstrates the potential for a further development of FDI in services and the importance of an effective, investment-friendly regulatory regime.[12]

In this regard, binding commitments, even unilaterally undertaken, through GATS, can demonstrate consistency and irreversibility of reforms ('lock-in'). They can also send powerful signals to domestic and foreign service suppliers as well as potential investors. Given the importance of commercial presence as a means of competing in services markets, such a signalling effect is apt to yield considerable FDI inflows, other things being equal.

[10] The World Bank, *Global Economic Prospects and the Developing Countries 2003*, 2003, 53–54.

[11] B Hoekman and CAP Braga, 'Protection and Trade in Services: A Survey', PRWP No 1747, 1997, 1.

[12] The World Bank (n 10 above) 52.

Importantly, this can be achieved without compromising regulatory autonomy at any considerable rate. Throughout this study, it has been argued that relinquishing a part, even a small one, of policy discretion is seldom a walkover for a government usually due to powerful domestic lobbies or voices arguing for national sovereignty primacy. Nonetheless, Members traditionally sought to be more tolerant with respect to trade and the accompanying sacrifices in policy discretion in favour of the GATT and now of the WTO. Deferring to WTO rules and disciplines has been offset by the increasing stability and predictability that current and future multilateral trade rules ensure, and by the associated positive welfare effects that trade brings about.

The development of horizontally applicable disciplines on necessity and transparency is expected to have positive welfare effects for the entire WTO Membership and provide the necessary impetus for further liberalization of international trade in services. Dismantling regulatory barriers in the services domain would be definitely beneficial not only for the service industry or the supplier that has put up with them, but also for the government that gets rid of unnecessary and usually costly trade-restrictive domestic regulatory measures. Given that some of the most important impediments to trade in services are entrenched in domestic regulatory systems, the GATS needs to have a powerful provision entailing a straightforward horizontal necessity test sooner rather than later, which will allow striking a balance between, on the one side, a Member's prerogative to pursue national policy objectives and determine for itself the desired level of attainment, and, on the other side, the imposition of order on the choice of instruments for doing so.

The development of such a test is also inevitable if effective market access is to be ensured. In other words, the absence of a strong provision on domestic regulations can render Article XVI GATS without any real value. The major challenge that Members should confront when dealing with restoring the 'bite' of Article VI GATS is to pursue principles of 'good' regulation through the creation of meaningful and, above all, coherent horizontally applicable rules relating to licensing, qualifications, and technical standards that will take into account the existing considerable sectoral diversity. The latter element implies that detailed horizontal rules on domestic regulation may be not only difficult to apply, but also expensive to abide by and enforce.

Taking into account that some Members are wary of the introduction of a horizontal necessity test, as it may be too intrusive an obligation, consensus could still be achieved by exploring several alternatives, eg by limiting the scope of the prospective necessity test only to sectors where specific commitments have been undertaken, by transforming the most controversial elements in the proposed disciplines into best-efforts obligations, or by including sunset provisions and transitional periods as to the application of the necessity test by developing countries and LDCs. While not the best solution from an economic efficiency viewpoint, this balancing articulation could allow the overcoming of most objections regarding the purported necessity test's interference with the Members' right to regulate. There were proposals in the WPDR that moved towards this direction, for instance the one proposing an Annex on domestic regulation submitted by Japan or the more recent proposals submitted by the ACP Group.[13] To be sure, Members have now at their disposal plenty of elements and concepts included in several proposals submitted by Members in the WPDR or interpreted by the WTO adjudicating bodies in cases dealing with trade in goods.

In any case, a necessity test is indispensable provided that Members decide to create disciplines as regards licensing, qualifications, and technical standards because adjudicators need to have an instrument to judge these disciplines against. It was proposed to introduce a simple clause that measures relating to licensing, qualifications, or standards should not constitute unnecessary barriers to trade. To me, this appears to be a highly unpredictable necessity test so that Members cannot anticipate its interpretation by the WTO adjudicating bodies. Therefore, it would be preferable for Members to create a necessity test that would embody the crucial qualifications so that Members avoid any far-reaching interpretations by the WTO judiciary. By way of illustration, this is what Members decided to do in the case of Article 5.6 SPS and footnote 3 thereto.

Horizontally applicable disciplines on transparency appear to have considerable momentum, notably due to the United States' willingness to bring forward this item of the agenda. Of course, when this issue is on the negotiating table, Members' views vary as to their scope, content, or level of detail. At a minimum, Members should endeavour to enhance existing and create additional procedural transparency disciplines with respect to the vertical relationship between regulators and individual service suppliers. Many Members, ranging from LDCs to developed countries, have been wary of the administrative burden associated with any new disciplines relating to transparency.

While these Members are correct to point to the implementation shortcomings with respect to the transparency provisions that emerged in the aftermath of the Uruguay Round in order to demonstrate the inutility of additional transparency

[13] WPDR, 'Pro-Development Principles for GATS Article VI:4 Negotiations', Communication from the ACP Group, JOB(06)/136/Rev.1, 19 June 2006; Australia *et al* also proposed longer timeframes for implementation of the disciplines by developing countries and LDCs. WPDR, 'Article VI:4 Disciplines—Proposal for a Draft Text', Communication from Australia; Chile; Colombia; Hong Kong, China; Korea; New Zealand, and the Separate Customs Territory of Taiwan, Penghu, Kinmen and Matsu, JOB(06)/193, 19 June 2006. A similar 'phase-in' provision for the compliance of developing countries and LDCs with the new disciplines is also comprehended in the proposal advanced by China and Pakistan. WPDR, 'Proposed Disciplines on Domestic Regulation under Article VI:4 of the GATS', Communication from China and Pakistan, JOB(06)/158, 29 May 2006. In addition, the United States' proposal on horizontal transparency disciplines is to be applied by the LDCs on a best-endeavour basis. WPDR, 'Horizontal Transparency Disciplines in Domestic Regulation', Communication from the United States, JOB(06)/182, 9 June 2006. The last draft of the WPDR Chairman goes even further by exempting the LDCs from the application of the future disciplines. See WPDR, 'Disciplines on Domestic Regulation Pursuant to GATS Article VI:4', Informal Note by the Chairman, Room Document, 18 April 2007, para 46.

obligations vis-à-vis their implementation costs, they overestimate the burdens associated with new disciplines. The costs will possibly be temporary, while the domestic economy will reap the long-term returns of good regulation and good administrative practices. Furthermore, the involvement of private suppliers may also allow the correct implementation of the transparency obligations that were created during the last negotiating round, as they are expected to be more active in their enquiries than Members have been to date, and thus induce regulators to be more efficient. Additionally, creating new transparency disciplines across sectors does not imply in any way that the current transparency provisions and structures would be of no value. On the contrary, new disciplines should be considered as complementary obligations that strengthen the current ones.

In the end, a balanced text, along the lines proposed in Chapter V can alleviate any remaining concerns. As was the case with necessity, in the case of transparency the accountancy disciplines include provisions that attempt to synthesize different approaches, interests, and concerns. The result may not be optimal, but at least it enjoys a rather large political support, a fact that should not be underestimated, especially when it comes to 'sensitive' issues relating to regulatory autonomy.

In this regard, developing countries should exploit the opportunity that they have to discuss issues associated with licensing, qualifications, and standards, ie areas where some of the most important barriers that hinder market access to developed markets exist. One cannot but observe the incremental assertiveness with which developing countries are presented in services negotiations, as interesting proposals by developing countries have proliferated recently. Nonetheless, the margins of improvement are fairly significant. To the benefit of developing countries and global trade in services in general, mode 4 can be the net winner from the emergence of a necessity test with respect to licensing, qualifications, and standards, which would allow screening out some of the most significant barriers to trade in services[14]. This would definitely require that developing countries get seriously involved to achieve this target with an open and flexible spirit. In the short term, one could plausibly argue that developing countries should strive to submit requests demanding increased market access in sectors that are of interest them. It is indubitable that the progress on commitments relating to commercial presence could very well be linked to a progress *pari passu* on commitments pertaining to the movement of natural persons. The GATS is the most appropriate forum for negotiations and trade-offs of this kind leading to mutually advantageous outcomes and, *a fortiori*, services trade growth.

In effect, the omens have been propitious for developing country interests at the beginning of the Doha Round, the so-called 'development round'. The focus on developing countries came fairly naturally, as political momentum to overcome

[14] For the benefits and costs of liberalizing mode 4, see WTO, *World Trade Report 2004—Exploring the Linkage between the Domestic Policy Environment and International Trade*, 2004, 46ff.

the Uruguay Round fatigue and the political backlash created by efforts to deal with politically sensitive issues would not be generated otherwise. As a result, the new 'Doha Development Agenda' (DDA) extensively caters to the interests and concerns of developing countries. What is more, the 'Singapore issues',[15] which for many developing countries represented a threat to their regulatory autonomy, were dropped from the agenda—at least for this negotiating round.

Hence, the conditions appear to be fairly favourable for developing countries to promote their interests in a manner that would ensure their greater integration into the multilateral trading system and their reaping of the multiple benefits emanating from increased trade. Notably with respect to services negotiations, Members agreed during the Hong Kong Ministerial to pay particular attention to 'sectors and modes of supply of export interest to developing countries', ie sectors and modes of supply where developing-country Members have a comparative advantage.[16] In addition, negotiations should take into account the size of economies of individual Members, both overall and in individual sectors. Especially as far as the LDCs are concerned, Members are requested to develop those mechanisms that would allow the according of special priority, including to sectors and modes of supply of interest, to LDCs pursuant to Article IV:3 GATS and paragraph 7 of the LDC Modalities.[17] Such a development should take place before the second round of revised offers, which, according to the timelines, was due on 31 July 2006. In any event, these mechanisms should be agreed on before the end of the round.

Finally, a related challenge for the current GATS negotiating round is to respond credibly to the rising chorus of criticisms directed against the GATS. Much of the polemic is legitimate and aims at the betterment of the many shortcomings that the Agreement has, while other critiques are overtly exaggerated and belie the aims and operation of the GATS, a highly technical and complex trade agreement.[18] The ongoing negotiations provide a ready-made opportunity

[15] These include investment, competition, transparency in government procurement, and trade facilitation. Members agreed on 1 August 2004 to proceed only with the negotiations on trade facilitation.

[16] *Hong Kong Ministerial Declaration* (n 3 above) para 27.

[17] Ibid, Annex C, paras 9(a) and 11(e); and WTO, CTS (Special Session), 'Modalities for the Special Treatment for Least-Developed Country Members in the Negotiations on Trade in Services', TN/S/13, 5 September 2003.

[18] According to Adlung and Roy, there is a certain degree of ignorance that has led GATS to become 'a convenient rallying point for dyed-in-the-wool skeptics to express their general frustration with market access mechanisms, private ownership, globalization, and other perceived evils'. R Adlung and M Roy, 'Turning Hills into Mountains? Current Commitments under the GATS and Prospects for Change' (2005) 39(6) JWT 1163. For example, this is the case with the current trend of outsourcing key services to providers overseas. Contrary to public belief, a recent NBER study demonstrated that service offshoring can increase the productivity of a United States' firm that decides to outsource a part of its production chain, eg technical support. Service outsourcing, then, is expected to increase efficiency, as the firms that outsource services to locations abroad usually relocate the *less* efficient parts of their production chain. M Amiti and S-J Wei, 'Service Offshoring and Productivity: Evidence from the United States', NBER Working Paper No 11926, January 2006.

for governments to inform concerned constituencies about the GATS and how it affects national economic and social goals. In a world where globalization of information takes apace, the WTO, as a public institution, has no other solution than to 'go public' in order to allow the civil society to make informed judgements. In the future, public awareness could either stimulate further liberalization or put it in jeopardy, depending on the case. Politics is the art of convincing and hence one should expect informed government officials to disseminate information relating to the gains from trade vis-à-vis its costs and the role of the WTO in the creation of these benefits. The GATS definitely forms part of this framework which aims at the creation of welfare through progressive liberalization of trade in services, without impinging on Members' prerogative to regulate.

Bibliography

A. BOOKS

Y Aharoni and L Nachum (eds), *Globalization of Services: Some Implications for Theory and Practice*, Routledge, 2000;

K Anderson and B Hoekman (eds), *The Global Trading System*, Vols 1–4, IB Tauris Publishers, 2002;

KJ Arrow, RW Hahn, ML Cropper, GC Eads, LB Lave, RG Noll, PR Portney, M Russell, RL Schmalensee, KV Smith, and RN Stavins, *Benefit-Cost Analysis in Environmental, Health, and Safety Regulation—A Statement of Principles*, AEI Press, 1996;

C Arup, *The New World Trade Organization Agreements: Globalizing Law Through Services and Intellectual Property*, Cambridge University Press, 2000;

K Bagwell and RW Staiger, *The Economics of the World Trading System*, MIT Press, 2002;

VN Balasubramanyam (ed), *Writings on International Economics*, Oxford University Press, 1997;

RE Baldwin, *Non-Tariff Distortions in International Trade*, Brookings Institution, 1971;

——'The Political Economy of Trade Policy: Integrating the Perspectives of Economists and Political Scientists' in RC Feenstra, GM Grossman, and DA Irwin (eds), *The Political Economy of Trade Policy—Papers in Honor of Jagdish Bhagwati*, MIT Press, 1996;

——'Regulatory Protectionism, Developing Nations, and a Two-Tier World Trade System' in SM Collins and D Rodrik (eds), *Brookings Trade Forum: 2000*, Brookings Institution Press, 2001;

——and C McCrudden, *Regulation and Public Law*, Weidenfeld and Nicolson, 1987;

——and M Cave, *Understanding Regulation—Theory, Strategy, and Practice*, Oxford University Press, 1999;

CE Barfield (ed), *International Financial Markets: Harmonization versus Competition*, AEI Press, 1996;

——*Free Trade, Sovereignty, Democracy: The Future of the World Trade Organization*, AEI Press, 2001;

——*High-Tech Protectionism—The Irrationality of Antidumping Laws*, AEI Press, 2003;

L Bartels and F Ortino (eds), *Regional Trade Agreements and the WTO Legal System*, Oxford University Press, 2006;

D Barth, 'Liberalizing International Trade in Services: The European Perspective' in K Deutsch and B Speyer (eds), *The WTO Millennium Round—Free Trade in the 21st Century*, Routledge, 2001;

GJ Benston, *Regulating Financial Markets: A Critique and some Proposals*, Institute of Economic Affairs, 1998;

J Bhagwati (ed), *International Trade: Selected Readings*, MIT Press, 1981;

——*Protectionism*, The Ohlin Lectures 1, MIT Press, 1988;

J Bhagwati (ed), *The World Trading System at Risk*, Princeton University Press, 1991;

—— (ed), *Going Alone: The Case for Relaxed Reciprocity in Freeing Trade*, MIT Press, 2002;

—— 'The Generalized Theory of Domestic Distortions and Welfare' in J Bhagwati, RA Mundell, RW Jones, and J Vanek (eds), *Trade, Balance of Payments and Growth: Essays in Honor of Charles P. Kindleberger*, North-Holland Publishing Co, 1971;

—— 'International Trade in Services and its Relevance for Economic Development' in O Garini (ed), *The Emerging Service Economy*, Pergamon Press, 1987;

—— 'The Demands to Reduce Domestic Diversity among Trading Nations' in J Bhagwati and R Hudec (eds), *Fair Trade and Harmonization: Prerequisites for Free Trade?*, Vol 1: Economic Analysis, MIT Press, 1996;

—— 'Trade in Services and the Multilateral Trade Negotiations' in VN Balasubramanyam (ed), *Writings on International Economics*, Oxford University Press, 1997;

—— 'After Seattle: Free Trade and the WTO' in R Porter, P Sauvé, A Subramanian, and AB Zampetti (eds), *Equity, Efficiency and Legitimacy: the Multilateral System at the Millennium*, Brookings Institution, 2001;

—— 'Introduction: The Unilateral Freeing of Trade versus Reciprocity' in J Bhagwati (ed), *Going Alone: The Case for Relaxed Reciprocity in Freeing Trade*, MIT Press, 2002;

—— RA Mundell, RW Jones, and J Vanek (eds), *Trade, Balance of Payments and Growth: Essays in Honor of Charles P. Kindleberger*, North-Holland Publishing Co, 1971;

—— and R Hudec (eds), *Fair Trade and Harmonization: Prerequisites for Free Trade?*, Vol 1: Economic Analysis, MIT Press, 1996;

——and R Hudec (eds), *Fair Trade and Harmonization: Prerequisites for Free Trade?*, Vol 2: Legal Analysis, MIT Press, 1996;

——and M Hirsch (eds), *The Uruguay Round and Beyond—Essays in Honour of Arthur Dunkel*, Springer-Verlag, 1998;

A von Bogdandy, PC Mavroidis, and Y Mény (eds), *European Integration and International Coordination—Studies in Transnational Economic Law in Honour of Claus-Dieter Ehlermann*, Kluwer Law International, 2002;

DD Bradlow and A Escher (eds), *Legal Aspects of Foreign Direct Investment*, Kluwer Law International, 1999;

JA Brander, 'Rationales for Strategic Trade and Industrial Policy' in P Krugman (ed), *Strategic Trade Policy and the New International Economics*, MIT Press, 1986;

S Breyer, *Regulation and its Reform*, Harvard University Press, 1982;

M Bronckers and R Quick (eds), *New Directions in International Economic Law: Essays in Honour of John H. Jackson*, Kluwer Law International, 2000;

JM Buchanan and G Tullock, *The Calculus of Consent: Logical Foundations of Constitutional Democracy*, University of Michigan Press, 1974;

N Byron, L Gropp, and K Gusberti, 'Principles for Regulating the Professions' in Productivity Commission and Australian National University, *Achieving Better Regulation of Services*, Conference Proceedings, AusInfo, 2000;

RA Cass and JR Haring, 'Domestic Regulation and International Trade: Where's the Race? Lessons from Telecommunications and Export Controls' in DLM Kennedy and JD Southwick (eds), *The Political Economy of International Trade Law: Essays in Honor of Robert E. Hudec*, Cambridge University Press, 2002;

R Caves, HG Johnson, and PB Kenen (eds), *Trade, Growth, and the Balance of Payments: Essays in Honor of Gottfried Haberler*, North-Holland Publishing Co, 1965;

S Claessens, A Demirgüç-Kunt, and H Huizinga, 'The Role of Foreign Banks in Domestic Banking Systems' in S Claessens and M Jansen (eds), *The Internationalization of Financial Services: Issues and Lessons for Developing Countries*, WTO/The World Bank, Kluwer Law International, 2000;

RH Coase, *The Firm, the Market, and the Law*, Chicago University Press, 1988;

M Corden, *Trade Policy and Economic Welfare*, 1974;

T Cottier and PC Mavroidis (eds), *Regulatory Barriers and the Principle of Non-Discrimination in World Trade Law,* Michigan University Press, 2000;

——and——(eds), *Intellectual Property: Trade, Competition, and Sustainable Development,* Michigan University Press, 2003;

——and——(eds), *The Role of the Judge in International Trade Regulation: Experience and Lessons for the WTO*, Michigan University Press, 2003;

——P Delimatsis, and N Diebold, 'Article XIV GATS' in R Wolfrum, P-T Stoll, and C Feinäugle (eds), *Max-Planck Commentaries on World Trade Law, Volume 6: WTO—Trade in Services*, Brill Publishers, 2008 (forthcoming);

——and P Delimatsis, 'Article XIV *bis* GATS' in R Wolfrum, P-T Stoll, and C Feinäugle (eds), *Max-Planck Commentaries on World Trade Law, Volume 6: WTO—Trade in Services*, Brill Publishers, 2008 (forthcoming);

P Craig, *EU Administrative Law*, Oxford University Press, 2006;

——and G De Búrca, *EU Law: Text, Cases and Materials*, Oxford University Press, 2003;

SP Croley and JH Jackson, 'WTO Dispute Panel Deference to National Government Decisions: The Misplaced Analogy to the U.S. Chevron Standard-of-Review Doctrine' in E-U Petersmann (ed), *International Trade Law and the GATT/WTO Dispute Settlement System*, Kluwer Law International, 1997;

J Croome, *Reshaping the World Trading System: A History of the Uruguay Round*, Kluwer Law International/WTO, 2nd edition, 1999;

KW Dam, *The GATT: Law and International Economic Organization*, Chicago University Press, 1970;

WJ Davey and W Zdouc, 'The Triangle of TRIPs, GATT and GATS' in T Cottier and PC Mavroidis (eds), *Intellectual Property: Trade, Competition, and Sustainable Development,* Michigan University Press, 2003;

AV Deardorff 'The Economics of Government Market Intervention, and Its International Dimension' in M Bronckers and R Quick (eds), *New Directions in International Economic Law: Essays in Honour of J. H. Jackson*, Kluwer Law International, 2000;

——and RM Stern, *Measurement of Non-Tariff Barriers*, Studies in International Economics, Michigan University Press, 1998;

G De Búrca and J Scott (eds), *The EU and the WTO: Legal and Constitutional Issues*, Hart Publishing, 2001;

H Delany, *Judicial Review of Administrative Action—A Comparative Analysis*, Round Hall, Sweet & Maxwell, 2001;

P Delimatsis, 'Article III GATS' in R Wolfrum, P-T Stoll, and C Feinäugle (eds), *Max-Planck Commentaries on World Trade Law, Volume 6: WTO—Trade in Services*, Brill Publishers, 2008 (forthcoming);

P Delimatsis, 'Article III *bis* GATS' in R Wolfrum, P-T Stoll, and C Feinäugle (eds), *Max-Planck Commentaries on World Trade Law, Volume 6: WTO—Trade in Services*, Brill Publishers, 2008 (forthcoming);

—— and M Molinuevo, 'Article XVI GATS' in R Wolfrum, P-T Stoll, and C Feinäugle (eds), *Max-Planck Commentaries on World Trade Law, Volume 6: WTO—Trade in Services*, Brill Publishers, 2008 (forthcoming);

K Deutsch and B Speyer (eds), *The WTO Millennium Round—Free Trade in the 21st Century*, Routledge, 2001;

A Dixit, *The Making of Economic Policy—A Transaction-Cost Politics Perspective*, 1996;

—— and BJ Nalebuff, *Thinking Strategically—The Competitive Edge in Business, Politics, and Everyday Life*, WW Norton & Company, 1991;

A Downs, *An Economic Theory of Democracy*, Harper & Row, 1957;

G Dunkley, *The Free Trade Adventure: The Uruguay Round and Globalism—A Critique*, Melbourne University Press, 1997;

C-D Ehlermann and G Campogrande, 'Rules on Services in the EEC: A Model for Negotiating World-Wide Rules' in E-U Petersmann and M Hilf (eds), *The New GATT Round of Multilateral Trade Negotiations: Legal and Economic Problems*, Kluwer Law and Taxation Publishers, 1988;

E Ellis (ed), *The Principle of Proportionality in the Laws of Europe*, Hart Publishing, 1999;

N Emiliou, *The Principle of Proportionality in European Law: A Comparative Study*, Kluwer Academic Publishers, 1996;

European Commission, *GATS: The General Agreement on Trade in Services—A Guide for Business*, EU Publications, 1995;

—— *GATS 2000—L'Ouverture des Marchés de Services*, EU Publications, 1998;

—— IMF; OECD; UN; UNCTAD; and WTO, *Manual on Statistics of International Trade in Services*, 2002;

RC Feenstra, GM Grossman, and DA Irwin (eds), *The Political Economy of Trade Policy—Papers in Honor of Jagdish Bhagwati*, MIT Press, 1996;

G Feketekuty, *International Trade in Services: An Overview and Blueprint for Negotiations*, Ballinger, 1988;

—— 'Trade in Services—Bringing Services into the Multilateral Trading System' in J Bhagwati and M Hirsch (eds), *The Uruguay Round and Beyond—Essays in Honour of Arthur Dunkel*, Springer-Verlag, 1998;

—— 'Assessing and Improving the Architecture of GATS' in P Sauvé and RM Stern (eds), *GATS 2000: New Directions in Services Trade Liberalization*, Brookings Institution Press, 2000;

—— 'Regulatory Reform and Trade Liberalization in Services' in P Sauvé and RM Stern (eds), *GATS 2000: New Directions in Services Trade Liberalization*, Brookings Institution Press, 2000;

C Findlay and T Warren (eds), *Impediments to Trade in Services: Measurement and Policy Implications*, Routledge, 2000;

MJ Finger and A Olechowski, 'Trade Barriers: Who Does What to Whom' in H Giersch (ed), *Free Trade in the World Economy: Towards an Opening of Markets*, Mohr, 1987;

—— and AL Winters, 'Reciprocity in the WTO' in B Hoekman, A Mattoo, and P English (eds), *Development, Trade, and the WTO: A Handbook*, The World Bank, 2002;

C Forsyth (ed), *Judicial Review and the Constitution*, Hart Publishing, 2000;

C Gamberale and A Mattoo, 'Domestic Regulations and Liberalization of Trade in Services' in B Hoekman, A Mattoo, and P English (eds), *Development, Trade, and the WTO: A Handbook*, The World Bank, 2002;

H Giersch (ed), *Free Trade in the World Economy: Towards an Opening of Markets*, Mohr, 1987;

J Goldstein, 'International Institutions and Domestic Politics: GATT, WTO, and the Liberalization of International Trade' in AO Krueger (ed), *The WTO as an International Organization*, Chicago University Press, 1998;

W Goode, 'Services' in K Anderson (ed), *Strengthening the Global Trading System: From GATT to WTO*, University of Adelaide, 1996;

GM Grossman (ed), *Imperfect Competition and International Trade*, MIT Press, 1994;

——and E Helpman, *Special Interest Politics*, MIT Press, 2001;

RW Hahn, *Reviving Regulatory Reform: A Global Perspective*, AEI Press, 2000;

M Hart, *A Trading Nation: Canadian Trade Policy from Colonialism to Globalization*, British Columbia University Press, 2002;

E Helpman and A Razin (eds), *International Trade and Trade Policy*, MIT Press, Cambridge, Massachusetts, 1991;

M Hilf and S Puth, 'The Principle of Proportionality on its Way into WTO/GATT Law' in A von Bogdandy, PC Mavroidis, and Y Mény (eds), *European Integration and International Coordination—Studies in Transnational Economic Law in Honour of Claus-Dieter Ehlermann*, Kluwer Law International, 2002;

B Hindley, 'Services' in JJ Schott (ed), *Completing the Uruguay Round: A Results-Oriented Approach to the GATT Trade Negotiations*, IIE Press, 1990;

J Hodge, 'Liberalization of Trade in Services in Developing Countries' in B Hoekman, A Mattoo, and P English (eds), *Development, Trade, and the WTO: A Handbook*, The World Bank, 2002;

B Hoekman, *General Agreement on Trade in Services*, in OECD, *The New World Trading System: Readings*, OECD Publications, 1995;

——'Services-Related Production, Employment, Trade, and Factor Movements' in PA Messerlin and KP Sauvant (eds), *The Uruguay Round: Services in the world economy*, The World Bank/The United Nations Centre on Transnational Corporations, 1990;

——'Towards a More Balanced and Comprehensive Services Agreement' in JJ Schott (ed), *The WTO After Seattle*, IIE Press, 2000;

——'Operationalizing the Concept of Policy Space in the WTO: Beyond Special and Differential Treatment' in E-U Petersmann (ed), *Reforming the World Trading System—Legitimacy, Efficiency, and Democratic Governance*, Oxford University Press, 2005;

——and M Kostecki, *The Political Economy of the World Trading System: From GATT to WTO*, Oxford University Press, 1995;

——and——*The Political Economy of the World Trading System: The WTO and Beyond*, Oxford University Press, 2001;

——and W Martin (eds), *Developing Countries and the WTO: A Pro-active Agenda*, Blackwell Publishing, 2001;

B Hoekman, A Mattoo, and P English (eds), *Development, Trade, and the WTO: A Handbook*, The World Bank, 2002;

——and PA Messerlin, 'Liberalizing Trade in Services: Reciprocal Negotiations and Regulatory Reform' in P Sauvé and RM Stern (eds), *GATS 2000: New Directions in Services Trade Liberalization*, Brookings Institution Press, 2000;

D Honeck, 'Developing Regulatory Disciplines in Professional Services: The Role of the World Trade Organization' in Y Aharoni and L Nachum (eds), *Globalization of Services: Some Implications for Theory and Practice*, Routledge, 2000;

H Horn and PC Mavroidis (eds), *The WTO Case Law of 2001*, Cambridge University Press, 2003;

——and——(eds), *The WTO Case Law of 2003*, Cambridge University Press, 2006;

——and——'US—Lamb: United States—Safeguard Measures on Imports of Fresh, Chilled or Frozen Lamb Meat from New Zealand and Australia: What Should be Required of a Safeguard Investigation?' in H Horn and PC Mavroidis (eds), *The WTO Case Law of 2001*, Cambridge University Press, 2003;

R Howse (ed), *The World Trading System: Critical Perspectives on the World Economy*, Routledge, 1998;

——'The Most Dangerous Branch? WTO Appellate Body Jurisprudence on the Nature and Limits of the Judicial Power' in T Cottier and PC Mavroidis (eds), *The Role of the Judge in International Trade Regulation: Experience and Lessons for the WTO*, Michigan University Press, 2003;

——and E Türk, 'The WTO Impact on Internal Regulations—A Case Study of the Canada-EC Asbestos Dispute' in G De Búrca and J Scott (eds), *The EU and the WTO: Legal and Constitutional Issues*, Hart Publishing, 2001;

RE Hudec, *Enforcing International Trade Law: The Evolution of the Modern GATT Legal System*, 1993;

——(ed), *Essays on the Nature of International Trade Law*, Cameron May, 1999;

——'"Circumventing Democracy": The Political Morality of Trade Negotiations' in RE Hudec (ed), *Essays on the Nature of International Trade Law*, Cameron May, 1999;

——'Mirror, Mirror on the Wall: The Concept of Fairness in U.S. Foreign Trade Policy' in RE Hudec (ed), *Essays on the Nature of International Trade Law*, Cameron May, 1999;

K Iida and J Nielson, 'Transparency in Domestic Regulation: Practices and Possibilities' in A Mattoo and P Sauvé (eds), *Domestic Regulation and Service Trade Liberalization*, World Bank/Oxford University Press, 2003;

U Immenga, W Möschel, and D Reuter (eds), *Festschrift für Ernst-Joachim Mestmäcker*, Nomos Verlagsgesellschaft, 1996;

MD Ingco (ed), *Agriculture, Trade, and the WTO: Creating a Trading Environment for Development*, World Bank, 2002;

D Irwin, *Against the Tide: An Intellectual History of Free Trade*, Princeton University Press, 1996;

——*Free Trade Under Fire*, Princeton University Press, 2002;

T Ito and AO Krueger (eds), *Deregulation and Interdependence in the Asia-Pacific Region*, Chicago University Press, 2000;

JH Jackson, *World Trade and the Law of the GATT: A Legal Analysis of the General Agreement on Tariffs and Trade*, Bobbs-Merrill Company, Inc, 1969;

—— *The World Trade Organization: Constitution and Jurisprudence*, Chatham House Papers, The Royal Institute of International Affairs, 1998;

—— *The World Trading System: Law and Policy of International Economic Relations*, 2nd edition, MIT Press, 1999;

—— *The Jurisprudence of GATT and the WTO: Insights on Treaty Law and Economic Relations*, Cambridge University Press, 2000;

—— *Sovereignty, the WTO, and Changing Fundamentals of International Law*, Cambridge University Press, 2006;

—— 'Regulating International Economic Behavior—The WTO and the Challenge of Constructing Institutions to Manage Global Interdependence' in U Immenga, W Möschel, and D Reuter (eds), *Festschrift für Ernst-Joachim Mestmäcker*, Nomos Verlagsgesellschaft, 1996;

—— 'The Uruguay Round Results and National Sovereignty' in J Bhagwati and M Hirsch (eds), *The Uruguay Round and Beyond—Essays in Honour of Arthur Dunkel*, Springer-Verlag, 1998;

—— 'The Evolution of the WTO Dispute Settlement Mechanism and the Prospects for the Millennium Round' in P Ruttley, I MacVay, and A Masa'deh (eds), *Liberalization and Protectionism in the World Trading System*, World Trade Law Association, 1999;

—— 'Sovereignty, Subsidiarity, and Separation of Powers: The High-Wire Balancing Act of Globalization' in DLM Kennedy and JD Southwick (eds), *The Political Economy of International Trade Law: Essays in Honor of Robert E. Hudec*, Cambridge University Press, 2002;

FG Jacobs, 'Recent Developments in the Principle of Proportionality in European Community Law' in E Ellis (ed), *The Principle of Proportionality in the Laws of Europe*, Hart Publishing, 1999;

R Janda, 'GATS Regulatory Disciplines Meet Global Public Goods: The Case of Transportation Services' in A Mattoo and P Sauvé (eds), *Domestic Regulation and Services Trade Liberalization*, World Bank/Oxford University Press, 2003;

HG Johnson, 'Optimal Trade Intervention in the Presence of Domestic Distortions' in R Caves, HG Johnson, and PB Kenen (eds), *Trade, Growth, and the Balance of Payments: Essays in Honor of Gottfried Haberler*, North-Holland Publishing Co, 1965;

G Karsenty, 'Assessing Trade in Services by Mode of Supply' in P Sauvé and RM Stern (eds), *GATS 2000: New Directions in Service Trade Liberalization*, Brookings Institution Press, 2000;

DLM Kennedy and JD Southwick (eds), *The Political Economy of International Trade Law: Essays in Honor of Robert E. Hudec*, Cambridge University Press, 2002;

NK Komesar, *Imperfect Alternatives—Choosing Institutions in Law, Economics, and Public Policy*, Chicago University Press, 1994;

M Krajewski, *National Regulation and Trade Liberalization in Services—The Legal Impact of the General Agreement on Trade in Services (GATS) on National Regulatory Autonomy*, Kluwer Law International, 2003;

—— 'Services Liberalization in Regional Trade Agreements: Lessons for GATS "Unfinished Business"?' in L Bartels and F Ortino (eds), *Regional Trade Agreements and the WTO Legal System*, Oxford University Press, 2006;

RJ Krommenacker, *World-Traded Services: The Challenge for the Eighties*, Artech House, Inc, 1984;

AO Krueger (ed), *The WTO as an International Organization*, Chicago University Press, 1998;

P Krugman (ed), *Strategic Trade Policy and the New International Economics*, MIT Press, 1986;

——'Is Bilateralism Bad?' in E Helpman and A Razin (eds), *International Trade and Trade Policy*, MIT Press, 1991;

——'Import Protection as Export Promotion: International Competition in the Presence of Oligopoly and Economies of Scale' in G Grossman (ed), *Imperfect Competition and International Trade*, MIT Press, 1994;

——and M Obstfeld, *International Economics: Theory and Policy*, 7th edition, Pearson Addison Wesley, 2006;

DW Leebron, 'Lying Down with Procrustes: An Analysis of Harmonization Claims' in J Bhagwati and RE Hudec (eds), *Fair Trade and Harmonization: Prerequisites for Free Trade?*, Vol 1: Economic Analysis, MIT Press, 1996;

——'Regulatory Discrimination in Domestic United States Law: A Model for the GATS?' in A Mattoo and P Sauvé (eds), *Domestic Regulation and Service Trade Liberalization*, World Bank/Oxford University Press, 2003;

P Low and A Mattoo, 'Is There a Better Way? Alternative Approaches to Liberalization under the GATS' in P Sauvé and RM Stern (eds), *GATS 2000: New Directions in Services Trade Liberalization*, Brookings Institution Press, 2000;

D Luff, 'Regulation of Health Services and International Trade Law' in A Mattoo and P Sauvé (eds), *Domestic Regulation and Service Trade Liberalization*, World Bank/Oxford University Press, 2003;

G McGuire, 'Methodologies for Measuring Restrictions on Trade in Services' in PA Messerlin and KP Sauvant (eds), *The Uruguay Round: Services in the World Economy*, The World Bank/The United Nations Centre on Transnational Corporations, 1990;

M Marconini, 'The Uruguay Round Negotiations on Services: An Overview' in PA Messerlin and KP Sauvant (eds), *The Uruguay Round: Services in the World Economy*, The World Bank/The United Nations Centre on Transnational Corporations, 1990;

J Mashaw, *Due Process in the Administrative State*, Yale University Press, 1985;

M Matsushita, TJ Schoenbaum, and PC Mavroidis, *The World Trade Organization: Law, Practice and Policy*, Oxford University Press, 2003;

——, ——and—— *The World Trade Organization: Law, Practice and Policy*, 2nd edition, Oxford University Press, 2006;

A Mattoo, 'MFN and the GATS' in T Cottier and PC Mavroidis (eds), *Most-Favoured Nation Treatment: Past and Present*, Michigan University Press, 2000;

——'Developing Countries in the New Round of GATS Negotiations: Towards a Pro-Active Role' in B Hoekman and W Martin (eds), *Developing Countries and the WTO: A Pro-active Agenda*, Blackwell Publishing, 2001;

——'Negotiating Improved Market Access Commitments' in B Hoekman, A Mattoo, and P English (eds), *Development, Trade, and the WTO: A Handbook*, The World Bank, 2002;

——and PC Mavroidis, 'Trade, Environment and the WTO: The Dispute Settlement Practice Relating to Article XX of GATT' in E-U Petersmann (ed), *International Trade Law and the GATT/WTO Dispute Settlement System*, Kluwer Law International, 1997;

——and P Sauvé (eds), *Domestic Regulation and Service Trade Liberalization*, World Bank/Oxford University Press, 2003;

——and A Carzaniga (eds), *Moving People to Deliver Services*, World Bank/Oxford University Press, 2003;

A Maurer and P Chauvet, 'The Magnitude of Flows of Global Trade in Services' in B Hoekman, A Mattoo, and P English (eds), *Development, Trade, and the WTO: A Handbook*, The World Bank, 2002;

PC Mavroidis, 'Come Together? Producer Welfare, Consumer Welfare, and WTO Rules' in E-U Petersmann (ed), *Reforming the World Trading System—Legitimacy, Efficiency, and Democratic Governance*, Oxford University Press, 2005;

—— *The General Agreement on Tariffs and Trade: A Commentary*, Oxford University Press, 2005;

PA Messerlin, *La Nouvelle Organization Mondiale du Commerce*, Ifri, 1995;

——*Measuring the Cost of Protection in Europe: European Commercial Policy in the 2000s*, IIE, September 2001;

——'Non-Discrimination, Welfare Balances, and WTO Rules: An Historical Perspective' in E-U Petersmann (ed), *Reforming the World Trading System—Legitimacy, Efficiency, and Democratic Governance*, Oxford University Press, 2005;

JS Mill, *Principles of Political Economy*, [1848], Ashley, W. J., ed London: Longmans, Green, 1909;

PK Morrison, 'WTO Dispute Settlement in Services: Procedural and Substantive Aspects' in E-U Petersmann (ed), *International Trade Law and the GATT/WTO Dispute Settlement System*, Kluwer Law International, 1997;

D Neven and PC Mavroidis, 'Mexico—Measures Affecting Telecommunications Services (WT/DS204/R) A Comment on "El Mess in TELMEX"' in H Horn and PC Mavroidis (eds), *The WTO Case Law of 2003*, Cambridge University Press, 2006;

K Nicolaidis and PJ Trachtman, 'From Policed Regulation to Managed Recognition in GATS' in P Sauvé and RM Stern (eds), *GATS 2000: New Directions in Services Trade Liberalization*, Brookings Institution Press, 2000;

RG Noll, *The Economics and Politics of the Slowdown in Regulatory Reform*, AEI-Brookings Joint Center for Regulatory Studies, 1999;

——'Regulatory Reform and International Trade Policy' in T Ito and AO Krueger (eds), *Deregulation and Interdependence in the Asia-Pacific Region*, Chicago University Press, 2000;

J Nusbaumer, *Services in the Global Market*, Kluwer Academic Press, 1987;

A Ogus, *Regulation: Legal Form and Economic Theory*, Oxford University Press, 1994;

D O'Keeffe and A Bavasso (eds), *Judicial Review in European Union Law, Liber Amicorum in Honour of Lord Slynn of Hadley*, Kluwer Law International, 2000;

M Olson, *The Logic of Collective Action: Public Goods and the Theory of Groups*, Harvard University Press, 1965;

T Oppermann and J Molsberger (eds), *A New GATT for the Nineties and Europe '92*, Nomos Verlagsgesellschaft, 1991;

F Ortino, *Basic Legal Instruments for the Liberalisation of Trade—A Comparative Analysis of EC and WTO Law*, Hart Publishing, 2004;

D Palmeter, 'National Sovereignty and the World Trade Organization' in K Anderson and B Hoekman (eds), *The Global Trading System*, Vol 4: 'New' Issues for the WTO, IB Tauris Publishers, 2002;

L Papi and D Revoltella, 'Foreign Direct Investment in the Banking Sector: A Transitional Economy Perspective' in S Claessens and M Jansen (eds), *The Internationalization of Financial Services: Issues and Lessons for Developing Countries*, WTO/The World Bank, Kluwer Law International, 2000;

V Pareto, *Manual of Political Economy*, AM Kelley, 1971;

J Pauwelyn, *Conflict of Norms in Public International Law—How WTO Law Relates to Other Rules of International Law*, Cambridge University Press, 2003;

E-U Petersmann (ed), *International Trade Law and the GATT/WTO Dispute Settlement System*, Kluwer Law International, 1997;

—— (ed), *Reforming the World Trading System—Legitimacy, Efficiency, and Democratic Governance*, Oxford University Press, 2005;

—— 'From Negative to Positive Integration in the WTO: The TRIPs Agreement and the WTO Constitution' in T Cottier and PC Mavroidis (eds), *Intellectual Property: Trade, Competition, and Sustainable Development*, Michigan University Press, 2003;

AC Pigou, *The Economics of Welfare*, 4th edition (reprinted), London: Macmillan; New York: St Martin's Press, 1962;

R Porter, P Sauvé, A Subramanian, and AB Zampetti (eds), *Equity, Efficiency and Legitimacy: the Multilateral System at the Millennium*, Brookings Institution, 2001;

P Raworth, *International Regulation of Trade in Services*, Vols 1–5, Oceana Publications, 2003;

VJ Reyna, 'Services' in TP Stewart (ed), *The GATT Uruguay Round: A Negotiating History (1986–1992)*, Vol II: Commentary, Kluwer Law and Taxation Publishers, 1993;

F Roessler, 'Diverging Domestic Policies and Multilateral Trade Integration' in J Bhagwati and RE Hudec (eds), *Fair Trade and Harmonization: Prerequisites for Free Trade?*, Vol 2: Legal Analysis, MIT Press, 1996;

—— 'The Concept of Nullification and Impairment in the Legal System of the World Trade Organization' in E-U Petersmann (ed), *International Trade Law and the GATT/WTO Dispute Settlement System*, Kluwer Law International, 1997;

P Ruttley, 'Financial services and The General Agreement on Trade in Services' in P Ruttley, I MacVay, and A Masa'deh (eds), *Liberalization and Protectionism in the World Trading System*, World Trade Law Association, 1999;

—— I MacVay, and A Masa'deh (eds), *Liberalization and Protectionism in the World Trading System*, World Trade Law Association, Cameron May—International Law and Policy, 1999;

P Sauvé, 'Assessing the General Agreement on Trade in Services—Half-Full or Half-Empty?' in R Howse (ed), *The World Trading System—Critical Perspectives on the World Economy*, Vol IV of the series The Uruguay Round and Beyond, Routledge, 1998;

——, 'Completing the GATS Framework: Safeguards, Subsidies, and Government Procurement' in B Hoekman, A Mattoo, and P English (eds), *Development, Trade, and the WTO: A Handbook*, The World Bank, 2002;

—— and RM Stern (eds), *GATS 2000: New Directions in Services Trade Liberalization*, Brookings Institution Press, 2000;

JJ Schott (ed), *Completing the Uruguay Round: A Results-Oriented Approach to the GATT Trade Negotiations*, IIE Press, 1990;

—— *The Uruguay Round: An Assessment*, IIE Press, November 1994;

J Schwarze, 'The Role of the European Court of Justice in Shaping Legal Standards for Administrative Action in the Member States: A Comparative Perspective' in D O'Keeffe and A Bavasso (eds), *Judicial Review in European Union Law, Liber Amicorum in Honour of Lord Slynn of Hadley*, Kluwer Law International, 2000;

R Senti, *WTO—System und Funktionsweise der Welthandelsordnung*, Verlag Österreich, 2000;

H Siebert, *The World Economy*, Routledge, 1999;

H-D Smeets, G Hofner, and A Knorr, 'A Multilateral Framework of Principles and Rules for Trade in Services' in T Oppermann and J Molsberger (eds), *A New GATT for the Nineties and Europe '92*, Nomos Verlagsgesellschaft, 1991;

RH Snape, 'Principles in Trade in Services' in PA Messerlin and KP Sauvant (eds), *The Uruguay Round: Services in the World Economy*, The World Bank/The United Nations Centre on Transnational Corporations, 1990;

—— 'Reaching Effective Agreements Covering Services' in AO Krueger (ed), *The WTO as an International Organization*, Chicago University Press, 1998;

—— 'The WTO Agenda: Next Steps' in C Findlay and T Warren (eds), *Impediments to Trade in Services: Measurement and Policy Implications*, Routledge, 2000;

J Snell, *Goods and Services in EC Law*, Oxford University Press, 2002;

DP Steger, 'The World Trade Organization: A New Constitution for the Trading System' in M Bronckers and R Quick (eds), *New Directions in International Economic Law: Essays in Honour of John H. Jackson*, Kluwer Law International, 2000;

FH Stephen, *The Economics of the Law*, Iowa State University Press / Ames, 1988;

AO Sykes, *The WTO Agreement on Safeguards: A Commentary*, Oxford University Press, 2006.

—— '"Efficient Protection" through WTO Rulemaking' in R Porter, P Sauvé, A Subramanian, and AB Zampetti (eds), *Equity, Efficiency and Legitimacy: the Multilateral System at the Millennium*, Brookings Institution, 2001;

—— 'Regulatory Protectionism and the Law of International Trade' in K Anderson and B Hoekman (eds), *The Global Trading System*, Vol 4: 'New' Issues for the WTO, IB Tauris Publishers, 2002;

DG Tarr, 'Arguments For and Against Uniform Tariffs' in B Hoekman, A Mattoo, and P English (eds), *Development, Trade, and the WTO: A Handbook*, The World Bank, 2002;

JP Trachtman, 'Lessons for the GATS from Existing WTO Rules on Domestic Regulation' in A Mattoo and P Sauvé (eds), *Domestic Regulation and Service Trade Liberalization*, World Bank/Oxford University Press, 2003;

MJ Trebilcock and R Howse, *The Regulation of International Trade*, 3rd edition, Routledge, 2005;

C Trolliet and J Hegarty, 'Regulatory Reform and Trade Liberalization in Accountancy Services' in A Mattoo and P Sauvé (eds), *Domestic Regulation and Service Trade Liberalization*, World Bank/Oxford University Press, 2003;

United Nations Conference on Trade and Development (UNCTAD) and The World Bank, *Liberalizing International Transactions in Services: A Handbook*, United Nations, 1994;

D Vogel, *Trading Up—Consumer and Environmental Regulation in a Global Economy*, Harvard University Press, 1995;

T Warren and C Findlay, '"Sins of Commission and Omission": Measuring Regulatory Impediments to Trade in Services' in Productivity Commission and Australian National University, *Achieving Better Regulation of Services*, Conference Proceedings, AusInfo, November 2000;

LJ White, *Reducing the Barriers to International Trade in Accounting Services*, AEI Studies on Services Negotiations, AEI Press, 2001;

—— 'Competition versus Harmonization—An Overview of International Regulation of Financial Services' in CE Barfield (ed), *International Financial Markets: Harmonization versus Competition*, AEI Press, 1996;

—— 'Unilateral International Openness: The Experience of the U.S. Financial Services Sector' in J Bhagwati (ed), *Going Alone: The Case for Relaxed Reciprocity in Freeing Trade*, MIT Press, 2002;

WHO and WTO, *WTO Agreements and Public Health*, Geneva, 2002;

JS Wilson, 'Standards, Regulation, and Trade: WTO Rules and Developing Country Concerns' in B Hoekman, A Mattoo, and P English (eds), *Development, Trade, and the WTO: A Handbook*, The World Bank, 2002;

AL Winters, 'The Economic Implications of Liberalizing Mode 4 Trade' in A Mattoo and A Carzaniga (eds), *Moving People to Deliver Services*, World Bank/Oxford University Press, 2003;

C Wolf, Jr, *Markets or Governments—Choosing between Imperfect Alternatives*, 2nd edition, MIT Press, 1994;

R Wolfrum, P-T Stoll, and C Feinäugle (eds), *Max-Planck Commentaries on World Trade Law, Volume 6: WTO—Trade in Services*, Brill Publishers, 2008 (forthcoming);

The World Bank, *Doing Business in 2004—Understanding Regulation*, The World Bank/Oxford University Press, 2004;

WTO, *The Legal Texts: The Results of the Uruguay Round of Multilateral Trade Negotiations*, Cambridge University Press, 2000;

—— *The Future of the WTO—Addressing Institutional Challenges in the New Millennium* ('The Sutherland Report'), 2004;

D Wyss, *Bankdienstleistungen im Allgemeinen Dienstleistungsabkommen der WTO: Auswirkungen auf das Schweizerische Bankenrecht*, Studien zum globalen Wirtschaftsrecht, Vol 2, Peter Lang, 1999;

K Yamamura, 'Caveat Emptor: The Industrial Policy of Japan' in P Krugman (ed), *Strategic Trade Policy and the New International Economics*, MIT Press, 1986;

AM Young, 'Where Next for Labor Mobility under GATS?' in P Sauvé and RM Stern (eds), *GATS 2000: New Directions in Service Trade Liberalization*, Brookings Institution, 2000;

AB Zampetti, 'Market Access through Mutual Recognition: The Promise and Limits of GATS Article VII' in P Sauvé and RM Stern (eds), *GATS 2000: New Directions in Service Trade Liberalization*, Brookings Institution, 2000;

W Zdouc, *Legal Problems Arising under the General Agreement on Trade in Services—Comparative Analysis of GATS and GATT*, Difo-Druck GmbH, 2002.

B. JOURNALS

AK Abu-Akeel, 'Definition of Trade in Services Under the GATS: Legal Implications' (1999) 32(1) George Washington Journal of International Law and Economics 189;

R Adlung, 'Services Negotiations in the Doha Round: Lost in Flexibility?' (2006) 4 JIEL 865;
——'Negotiations on Safeguards and Subsidies in Services: A Never-Ending Story?' (2007) 2 JIEL 235;
——and M Roy, 'Turning Hills into Mountains? Current Commitments under the GATS and Prospects for Change' (2005) 39(6) JWT 1161;
GA Akerlof, 'The Market for "Lemons": Quality Uncertainty and the Market Mechanism' (1970) 84(3) The Quarterly Journal of Economics 488;
J Bacchus, 'The Bicycle Club: Affirming the American Interest in the Future of the WTO' (2003) 37(3) JWT 429;
K Bagwell and RW Staiger, 'A Theory of Managed Trade' (1990) 80(4) AER 779;
——PC Mavroidis, and RW Staiger, 'It's a Question of Market Access' (2002) 96(1) AJIL 56;
RE Baldwin, 'The Political Economy of Trade Policy' (1989) 3(4) The Journal of Economic Perspectives 119;
GS Becker, 'A Theory of Competition Among Pressure Groups for Political Influence' (1983) 98(3) The Quarterly Journal of Economics 371;
JH Bello, 'The WTO Dispute Settlement Understanding: Less is More' (1996) 90(3) AJIL 415;
TG Berg, 'Trade in Services: Toward a "Development Round" of GATT Negotiations Benefiting Both Developing and Industrialized States' (1987) 28(1) Harvard International Law Journal 1;
FC Bergsten, 'A Renaissance for United States Trade Policy?' (2002) Foreign Affairs 86;
J Bhagwati, 'The Pure Theory of International Trade: A Survey' (1964) 74(293) The Economic Journal 1;
——'Directly Unproductive, Profit-Seeking (DUP) Activities' (1982) 90(5) The Journal of Political Economy 988;
——'Splintering and Disembodiment of Services and Developing Nations' (1984) 7(2) The World Economy 133;
——'Free Trade: Old and New Challenges' (1994) 104(423) Economic Journal 231;
——and VK Ramaswami, 'Domestic Distortions, Tariffs and the Theory of Optimum Subsidy' (1963) 71(1) The Journal of Political Economy 44;
——and TN Srinivasan, 'Optimal Intervention to Achieve Non-Economic Objectives' (1969) 36(1) The Review of Economic Studies 27;
——VK Ramaswami, and TN Srinivasan, 'Domestic Distortions, Tariffs and the Theory of Optimum Subsidy: Some Further Results' (1969) 77(6) Journal of Political Economy 1005;
——A Panagariya, and TN Srinivasan, 'The Muddles Over Outsourcing' (2004) 18(4) Journal of Economic Perspectives 93;
LS Brainard and D Martimort, 'Strategic Trade Policy with Incompletely Informed Policymakers' (1997) 42 Journal of International Economics 33;
JA Brander and BJ Spencer, 'Tariffs and the Extraction of Foreign Monopoly Rents under Potential Entry' (1981) 14(3) The Canadian Journal of Economics 371;
——and——'Export Subsidies and International Market Share Rivalry' (1985) 18 Journal of International Economics 83;
TL Brewer and S Young, 'Investment Issues at the WTO: The Architecture of Rules and the Settlement of Disputes' (1998) 3 JIEL 457;

S Breyer, 'Analyzing Regulatory Failure: Mismatches, Less Restrictive Alternatives, and Reform' (1979) 92(3) Harvard Law Review 547;
WE Brock, 'A Simple Plan for Negotiating on Trade in Services' (1982) 5(3) The World Economy 229;
JM Buchanan and WC Stubblebine, 'Externality' (1962) 29(116) Economica 371;
DZ Cass, 'The "Constitutionalization" of the International Trade Law: Judicial Norm-Generation as the Engine of Constitutional Development in International Trade' (2001) 12(1) EJIL 39;
S Cassese, 'Global Standards for National Administrative Procedure' (2005) 68 Law and Contemporary Problems 109;
P Chang, G Karsenty, A Mattoo, and J Richtering, 'GATS, the Modes of Supply and Statistics on Trade in Services' (1999) 33(3) JWT 93;
RH Coase, 'The Problem of Social Cost' (1960) 3 Journal of Law and Economics 1;
——'The Lighthouse in Economics' (1974) 17(2) Journal of Law and Economics 357;
——'The New Institutional Economics' (1998) 88(2) AER 72;
E Colombatto, 'An Explanation of the Dynamics of Protectionism' (2000) 11 Open Economies Review 279;
SP Croley, 'Theories of Regulation: Incorporating the Administrative Process' (1998) 98(1) Columbia Law Review 1;
MR Darby and E Karni, 'Free Competition and the Optimal Amount of Fraud' (1973) 16(1) Journal of Law and Economics 67;
G De Búrca, 'The Principle of Proportionality and its Application in EC Law' (1993) 13 Yearbook of European Law 105;
P Delimatsis, 'Don't Gamble with GATS—The Interaction between Articles VI, XVI, XVII and XVIII GATS in the Light of the *US—Gambling* Case' (2006) 40(6) JWT 1059;
——'Due Process and "Good" Regulation Embedded in the GATS—Disciplining Regulatory Behaviour in Services Through Article VI of the GATS' (2007) 10 JIEL 13;
——'Determining the Necessity of Domestic Regulations in Services—The Best is Yet to Come' (2008) EJIL (forthcoming);
JV DeLong, 'New Wine for a New Bottle: Judicial Review in the Regulatory State' (1986) 72(2) Virginia Law Review 399;
A Desmedt, 'Proportionality in WTO Law' (2001) 4 JIEL 441;
A Downs, 'An Economic Theory of Political Action in a Democracy' (1957) 65(2) Journal of Political Economy 135;
WJ Drake, and K Nicolaidis, 'Ideas, Interests, and Institutionalization: "Trade in Services" and the Uruguay Round' (1992) 46(1) International Organization 37;
DC Esty, 'Good Governance at the Supranational Scale: Globalizing Administrative Law' (2006) 115 Yale Law Journal 1490;
——and D Geradin, 'Regulatory Co-opetition' (2000) 2 JIEL 235;
DA Farber and RE Hudec, 'Free Trade and the Regulatory State: a GATT's-Eye View of the Dormant Commerce Clause' (1994) 47 Vanderbilt Law Review 1401;
MJ Finger, KH Hall, and DR Nelson, 'The Political Economy of Administered Protection' (1982) 72(3) AER 452;

JA Finlayson and MW Zacher, 'The GATT and the Regulation of Trade Barriers: Regime Dynamics and Functions' (1981) 35(4) International Organization 561;

J Francois, 'Producer Services, Scale and the Division of Labor' (1990) 42 Oxford Economic Papers 715;

——and I Wooton, 'Market Structure, Trade Liberalization, and the GATS' (2001) 17 European Journal of Political Economy 389;

JP Gaffney, 'Due Process in the World Trade Organization: The Need for Procedural Justice in the Dispute Settlement System' (1999) 14 American University International Law Review 1173;

——'The GATT and the GATS: Should they be Mutually Exclusive Agreements?' (1999) 12 Leiden Journal of International Law 135;

J Goldstein, 'The Political Economy of Trade: Institutions of Protection' (1986) 80(1) The American Political Science Review 161;

GM Grossman and H Horn, 'Infant-Industry Protection Reconsidered: The Case of Informational Barriers to Entry' (1988) 103(4) The Quarterly Journal of Economics 767;

——and E Helpman, 'Protection for Sale' (1994) 84(4) AER 833;

——and——'Trade Wars and Trade Talks' (1995) 103(4) The Journal of Political Economy 675;

——and——, 'Electoral Competition and Special Interest Politics' (1996) 63(2) The Review of Economic Studies 265;

A Guzman and BA Simmons, 'To Settle or Empanel? An Empirical Analysis of Litigation and Settlement at the World Trade Organization' (2002) 31 Journal of Legal Studies 205;

RW Hahn and RE Litan, 'Counting Regulatory Benefits and Costs: Lessons for the US and Europe' (2005) 8 JIEL 473;

G Hardin, 'The Tragedy of the Commons' (1968) 162 Science 1243;

C Harlow, 'Global Administrative Law: The Quest for Principles and Values' (2006) 17(1) EJIL 187;

TP Hill, 'On Goods and Services' (1977) 23(4) The Review of Income and Wealth 315;

B Hindley and A Smith, 'Comparative Advantage and Trade in Services' (1984) 7(1) The World Economy 369;

B Hoekman, 'The Next Round of Services Negotiations: Identifying Priorities and Options' (2000) 82(4) Federal Reserve Bank of St. Louis Review 31;

——and A Mattoo, 'Services, Economic Development and the Next Round of Negotiations on Services' (2000) 12 Journal of International Development 283;

R Howse, 'From Politics to Technocracy—and Back Again: The Fate of the Multilateral Trading Regime' (2002) 96(1) AJIL 94;

RE Hudec, 'International Economic Law: The Political Theatre Dimension' (1996) 17(9) University of Pennsylvania Journal of International Economic Law 9;

——'GATT/WTO Constraints on National Regulation: Requiem for an "Aim and Effects" Test' (1998) 32(3) The International Lawyer 619;

DA Irwin, 'The GATT in Historical Perspective' (1995) 85(2) AER 323;

JH Jackson, 'The Crumbling Institutions of the Liberal Trade System' (1979) 12(2) JWT 93;

——'The WTO Dispute Settlement Understanding—Misunderstandings on the Nature of Legal Obligation' (1997) 91(1) AJIL 60;

JH Jackson, 'Global Economics and International Economic Law' (1998) 1 JIEL 1;
—— 'International Economic Law in Times that Are Interesting' (2000) 1 JIEL 3;
—— 'The WTO "Constitution" and Proposed Reforms: Seven "Mantras" Revisited' (2001) 1 JIEL 68;
—— 'Sovereignty-Modern: A New Approach to an Outdated Concept' (2003) 97(4) AJIL 792.
JH Jans, 'Proportionality Revisited' (2000) 27(3) Legal Issues of Economic Integration 239;
HG Johnson, 'Optimum Tariffs and Retaliation' (1953–1954) 21(2) The Review of Economic Studies 142;
—— 'The Economic Approach to Social Questions' (1968) 35(137) Economica 1;
ML Katz and C Shapiro, 'Network Externalities, Competition, and Compatibility' (1985) 75(3) AER 424;
MC Kemp and T Nagishi, 'Domestic Distortions, Tariffs, and the Theory of Optimum Subsidy' (1969) 77(6) The Journal of Political Economy 1011;
B Kingsbury, N Krisch, and RB Stewart, 'The Emergence of Global Administrative Law' (2005) 68 Law and Contemporary Problems 15;
M Krajewski, 'Public Services and Trade Liberalization: Mapping the Legal Framework' (2003) 2 JIEL 341;
—— 'Playing by the Rules of the Game? Specific Commitments after *US—Gambling and Betting* and the Current GATS Negotiations' (2005) 32(4) Legal Issues of Economic Integration 417;
R Krommenacker, 'Trade Related Services and GATT' (1979) 13(6) JWT 510;
AO Krueger, 'Government Failures in Development' (1990) 4(3) The Journal of Economic Perspectives 9;
—— 'Government, Trade, and Economic Integration' (1992) 82(2) AER 109;
P Krugman, 'Is Free Trade Passé?' (1987) 1(2) The Journal of Economic Perspectives 131;
—— 'Free Trade: A Loss of (Theoretical) Nerve?—The Narrow and Broad Arguments for Free Trade' (1993) 83(2) AER 365;
—— 'What Should Trade Negotiators Negotiate About?' (1997) 35(1) Journal of Economic Literature 113;
WM Landes and RA Posner, 'The Independent Judiciary in an Interest-Group Perspective' (1975) 18(3) Journal of Law and Economics 875;
J Le Grand, 'The Theory of Government Failure' (1991) 21(4) British Journal of Political Science 423;
K Leitner and S Lester, 'WTO Dispute Settlement 1995–2002: A Statistical Analysis' (2003) 1 JIEL 251;
K Lenaerts, '"In the Union We Trust": Trust-Enhancing Principles of Community Law' (2004) 41 CML Rev 317;
M Lennard, 'Navigating by the Stars: Interpreting the WTO Agreements' (2002) 5 JIEL 17;
AP Lerner, 'The Concept of Monopoly and the Measurement of Monopoly Power' (1934) 1(3) The Review of Economic Studies 157;
EH Leroux, 'What is a "Service Supplied in the Exercise of Governmental Authority" Under Article I:3(b) and (c) of the General Agreement on Trade in Services?' (2006) 40(3) JWT 345;

SJ Liebowitz and SE Margolis, 'Network Externality: An Uncommon Tragedy' (1994) 8(2) The Journal of Economic Perspectives 133;

G Maggi and A Rodriguez-Clare, 'The Value of Trade Agreements in the Presence of Political Pressures' (1998) 106(3) The Journal of Political Economy 574;

HB Malmgren, 'Negotiating International Rules for Trade in Services' (1985) 8(1) The World Economy 11;

G Marceau and JP Trachtman, 'The Technical Barriers to Trade Agreement, the Sanitary and Phytosanitary Measures Agreement, and The General Agreement on Tariffs and Trade: A Map of the World Trade Organization Law of Domestic Regulation of Goods' (2002) 36(5) JWT 811;

——and C Reiman, 'When and How Is a Regional Trade Agreement Compatible with the WTO?' (2001) 28(3) Legal Issues of Economic Integration 297;

HP Marvel and JE Ray, 'Countervailing Duties' (1995) 105(433) The Economic Journal 1576;

M Matsushita, 'Governance of International Trade Under World Trade Organization Agreements—Relationships between World Trade Organization Agreements and Other Trade Agreements' (2004) 38(2) JWT 185;

A Mattoo, 'National Treatment in the GATS: Corner Stone or Pandora's Box?' (1997) 31(1) JWT 107;

——'Services in a Development Round: Three Goals and Three Proposals' (2005) 39(6) JWT 1223;

——and A Subramanian, 'Regulatory Autonomy and Multilateral Disciplines: The Dilemma and a Possible Solution' (1998) 1 JIEL 303;

——R Rathindran, and A Subramanian, 'Measuring Services Trade Liberalization and its Impact on Economic Growth: An Illustration', (2006) 21 Journal of Economic Integration 64;

PC Mavroidis, 'Highway XVI Re-Visited—The Road from Non-Discrimination to Market Access in GATS' (2007) 6(1) World Trade Review 1;

PA Messerlin and G Reed, 'Antidumping Policies in the United States and the European Community' (1995) 105(433) The Economic Journal 1565;

——and PKM Tharakan, 'The Question of Contingent Protection' (1999) 22(9) The World Economy 1251;

HV Milner and PB Rosendorff, 'Democratic Politics and International Trade Negotiations: Elections and Divided Government as Constraints on Trade Liberalization' (1997) 41(1) The Journal of Conflict Resolution 117;

D Mitra, 'Endogenous Lobby Formation and Endogenous Protection: A Long-Run Model of Trade Policy Determination' (1999) 89(5) AER 1116;

E Montaguti and M Lugard, 'The GATT 1994 and other Annex 1A Agreements: Four Different Relationships?' (2000) 3 JIEL 473;

DA Motaal, 'The "Multilateral Scientific Consensus" and the World Trade Organization' (2005) 38(5) JWT (2005) 855;

N Mukherjee, 'GATS and the Millennium Round of Multilateral Negotiations: Selected Issues from the Perspective of the Developing Countries' (1999) 33(4) JWT 87;

P Nelson, 'Information and Consumer Behavior' (1970) 78(2) Journal of Political Economy 311;

J Neumann and E Türk, 'Necessity Revisited: Proportionality in World Trade Organization Law After *Korea—Beef, EC—Asbestos* and *EC–Sardines*' (2003) 37(1) JWT 199;

F Ortino, 'Treaty Interpretation and the WTO Appellate Body Report in *US—Gambling*: A Critique' (2006) 1 JIEL 117;

J Pauwelyn, 'Enforcement and Countermeasures in the WTO: Rules are Rules—Toward a More Collective Approach' (2000) 94(2) AJIL 335;

——'Rien ne Va Plus? Distinguishing Domestic Regulation from Market Access in GATT and GATS' (2005) 4(2) World Trade Review 131;

E-U Petersmann, 'How to Promote the International Rule of Law? Contributions by the World Trade Organization Appellate Review System' (1998) 1 JIEL 25;

——'How to Reform the United Nations? Lessons from the "International Economic Law Revolution"' (1998) 53(2) Aussenwirtschaft 193;

—— 'Dispute Settlement in International Economic Law—Lessons for Strengthening International Dispute Settlement in Non-Economic Areas' (1999) 2 JIEL 189;

RH Pildes and CR Sunstein, 'Reinventing the Regulatory State' (1995) 62(1) University of Chicago Law Review 1;

RA Posner, 'Theories of Economic Regulation' (1974) 5(2) The Bell Journal of Economics and Management Science 335;

DH Regan, 'The Supreme Court and State Protectionism: Making Sense of the Dormant Commerce Clause' (1986) 84 Michigan Law Review 1091;

—— 'Judicial Review of Member-State Regulation of Trade within a Federal or Quasi-Federal System: Protectionism and Balancing, Da Capo' (2001) 99(8) Michigan Law Review 1853;

D Rodrik, 'Policy Targeting with Endogenous Distortions: Theory of Optimum Subsidy Revisited' (1987) 102(4) The Quarterly Journal of Economics 903;

JG Ruggie, 'International Regimes, Transactions, and Change: Embedded Liberalism in the Postwar Economic Order' (1982) 36(2) International Organization 379;

GP Sampson, 'Compatibility of Regional and Multilateral Trading Agreements: Reforming the WTO Process' (1996) 86(2) AER 88;

——'The World Trade Organization after Seattle' (2000) 23(9) The World Economy 1097;

——and RH Snape, 'Identifying the Issues on Trade in Services' (1985) 8(2) The World Economy 171;

PA Samuelson, 'The Gains from International Trade' (1939) 5(2) The Canadian Journal of Economics and Political Science 195;

——'The Gains from International Trade Once Again' (1962) 72(4) Economic Journal 820;

A Sapir, 'North-South Issues in Trade in Services' (1985) 8(1) The World Economy 27;

——'The General Agreement on Trade in Services: From 1994 to the Year 2000' (1999) 33(1) JWT 51;

C Schede, 'The Strengthening of the Multilateral System—Article 23 of the WTO Dispute Settlement Understanding: Dismantling Unilateral Retaliation under Section 301 of the 1974 Trade Act?' (1996) 20(1) World Competition 109;

Y Shany, 'Toward a General Margin of Appreciation Doctrine in International Law?' (2005) 16(5) EJIL 907;

M Shapiro, 'The Giving Reasons Requirement' (1992) University of Chicago Legal Forum 179;
DE Siegel, 'Legal Aspects of the IMF/WTO Relationship: The Fund's Articles of Agreement and the WTO Agreements' (2002) 96(3) AJIL 561;
J Snell, 'True Proportionality and Free Movement of Goods and Services' (2000) European Business Law Review 50;
B Speyer, 'The WTO Dispute Settlement Mechanism—A New Era for the World Economy?' (1998) 53(1) Aussenwirtschaft 129;
RW Staiger and G Tabellini, 'Discretionary Trade Policy and Excessive Protection' (1987) 77(5) AER 823;
E Stein, 'International Integration and Democracy: No Love at First Sight' (2001) 95(3) AJIL 489;
GJ Stigler, 'The Economics of Information' (1961) 69(3) The Journal of Political Economy 213;
—— 'The Theory of Economic Regulation' (1971) 2(1) The Bell Journal of Economics and Management Science 11;
WF Stolper and PA Samuelson, 'Protection and Real Wages' (1941) 9(1) The Review of Economic Studies 58;
AO Sykes, 'Comparative Advantage and the Normative Economics of International Trade Policy' (1998) 1 JIEL 49;
—— 'The (Limited) Role of Regulatory Harmonization in International Goods and Services Markets' (1999) 1 JIEL 49;
—— 'Regulatory Competition or Regulatory Harmonization? A Silly Question?' (2000) 2 JIEL 257;
—— 'The Least Restrictive Means' (2003) 70(1) University of Chicago Law Review 403;
PKM Tharakan, 'Political Economy and Contingent Protection' (1995) 105(433) The Economic Journal 1550;
JC Thomas and D Palmeter, 'The Need for Due Process in WTO Proceedings' (1997) 31(1) JWT 45;
RD Tollison, 'Public Choice and Legislation' (1988) 74(2) Virginia Law Review 339;
JP Trachtman, 'Reflections on the Nature of the State: Sovereignty, Power and Responsibility' (1994) 20 Canada-United States Law Journal 399;
—— 'The Theory of the Firm and the Theory of the International Economic Organization: Toward Comparative Institutional Analysis' (1996/7) 17(2/3) Northwestern Journal of International Law & Business 470;
—— 'Accounting Standards and Trade Disciplines—Irreconcilable Differences?' (1997) 31(6) JWT 63;
—— 'Trade and... Problems, Cost-Benefit Analysis and Subsidiarity' (1998) 9(1) EJIL 32;
—— 'Regulatory Competition and Regulatory Jurisdiction' (2000) 3 JIEL 331;
M Trebilcock and R Howse, 'Trade Liberalization and Regulatory Diversity: Reconciling Competitive Markets with Competitive Politics' (1998) 6 European Journal of Law and Economics 6;
I Van Damme, 'The Interpretation of Schedules of Commitments' (2007) 41(1) Journal of World Trade 1;

KW Viscusi, 'Regulating the Regulators' (1996) 63(4) University of Chicago Law Review 1423;

M Wallerstein, 'Unemployment, Collective Bargaining, and the Demand for Protection' (1987) 31(4) American Journal of Political Science 729;

A Watts, 'The International Rule of Law' (1995) German Yearbook of International Law 14;

JHH Weiler, 'The Rule of Lawyers and the Ethos of Diplomats: Reflections on the Internal and External Legitimacy of WTO Dispute Settlement' (2001) 35(2) JWT 191;

F Weiss, 'The General Agreement on Trade in Services 1994' (1995) CML Rev 1177;

B Wilson, 'Compliance by WTO Members with Adverse WTO Dispute Settlement Rulings: The Record to Date' (2007) 2 JIEL 397;

W Zdouc, 'WTO Dispute Settlement Practice relating to the GATS' (1999) 2 JIEL 295;

RJ Zedalis, 'When Do the Activities of Private Parties Trigger WTO Rules?' (2007) 2 JIEL 335;

C. OECD PUBLICATIONS

All available on the OECD official website at <http://www.oecd.org>

P Czaga, 'Regulatory Reform and Market Openness: Understanding the Links to Enhance Economic Performance', OECD Trade Policy Working Paper No 9, TD/TC/WP(2004)10/FINAL, 15 December 2004;

N Dihel, 'Quantifying Costs to National Welfare from Barriers to Services Trade: A Review of the Literature' in OECD, *Quantifying the Benefits of Liberalizing Trade in Services*, 2003;

F Fortanier and M Maher, *Foreign Direct Investment and Sustainable Development*, Financial Market Trends, No 79, June 2001, p 107;

K Iida, 'Trade and Regulatory Reform: Insights from the OECD Country Reviews and Other Analyses' in OECD, *Trade and Regulatory Reform: Insights from Country Experience*, 2001;

——and J Nielson, 'Transparency in Domestic Regulation: Prior Consultation' in OECD, *Trade in Services: Negotiating Issues and Approaches*, 2001;

A Kleitz, 'Integrating Market Openness into Regulatory Systems: Some Experience and Emerging Best Practices', Second Workshop of the APEC–OECD Co-Operative Initiative on Regulatory Reform, Merida, Mexico, April 2002;

K Nicolaidis, 'Harmonization and Recognition: What Have We Learned? Some Preliminary Reflections' in OECD, *Trade and Regulatory Reform: Insights from Country Experience*, 2001;

J Nielson, C Pellegrino; R Morris, and R Thompson, 'Using "Cluster" Approaches to Specific Commitments for Interdependent Services' in OECD, *Trade in Services: Negotiating Issues and Approaches*, 2001;

——and D Taglioni, 'Services Trade Liberalization: Identifying Opportunities and Gains', OECD Trade Policy Working Paper No 1, TD/TC/WP(2003)23/FINAL, 6 February 2004;

C Oman, 'Policy Competition for Foreign Direct Investment: A Study of Competition among Governments to Attract FDI', Development Centre Studies, OECD, 2000;

OECD, 'The New World Trading System: Readings', OECD documents, Paris, 1995;
OECD, 'The OECD Report on Regulatory Reform—Synthesis', 1997;
OECD, Directorate for financial, fiscal and enterprise affairs (Insurance Committee), 'Convergence in the Financial Services Industry', DAFFE/AS/WD(99)12, September 1999;
OECD, Working Party of the Trade Committee, 'Assessing Barriers to Trade in Services: Cross-cutting ("Formula") Approaches to Multilateral Services Negotiations', TD/TC/WP(99)42/FINAL, 1999;
OECD, Committee on Competition Law and Policy, 'Competition in Professional Services', DAFFE/CLP(2000)2, 22 February 2000;
OECD, Working Party of the Trade Committee, 'Strengthening Regulatory Transparency: Insights for the GATS from the Regulatory Reform Country Reviews', TD/TC/WP(99)43/FINAL, 11 April 2000;
OECD, Working Party of the Trade Committee, 'Strengthening Regulatory Transparency: Insights for the GATS from the Regulatory Reform Country Reviews', TD/TC/WP(99)43/FINAL, April 2000;
OECD, 'The Implementation and the Effects of Regulatory Reform: Past Experience and Current Issues', Economics Department Working Papers No 251, 29 June 2000;
OECD, Working Party of the Trade Committee, 'Assessing Barriers to Trade in Services—The Scheduling of Economic Needs Tests in the GATS: An Overview', TD/TC/WP(2000)11/FINAL, 10 November 2000;
OECD, *Trade in Services: Negotiating Issues and Approaches*, 2001;
OECD, *Trade and Regulatory Reform: Insights from Country Experience*, 2001;
OECD, Working Party of the Trade Committee, 'Assessing Barriers to Trade in Services: Revised Consolidated List of Cross-Sectoral Barriers', TD/TC/WP(99)58/FINAL, 28 February 2001;
OECD, Working Party of the Trade Committee, 'Trade in Services: A Roadmap to GATS MFN Exemptions', TD/TC/WP(2001)/25/FINAL, 29 October 2001;
OECD, 'Open Services Markets Matter', Policy Brief, October 2001;
OECD, Working Party of the Trade Committee, 'Quantification of Costs to National Welfare from Barriers to Services Trade: A Literature Review', TD/TC/WP(2000)24/FINAL, 14 November 2001;
OECD, 'Trade in Services: Negotiating Issues and Approaches', 2001;
OECD, Trade Directorate for financial, fiscal and enterprise affairs, Joint Group on Trade and Competition, 'The Role of "Special and Differential Treatment" at the Trade, Competition and Development Interface', COM/TD/DAFFEE/CLP(2001)21/FINAL, 4 December 2001;
OECD, Working Party of the Trade Committee, 'Transparency in Domestic Regulation: Practices and Possibilities', TD/TC/WP(2001)31/FINAL, 15 February 2002;
OECD, Working Party of the Trade Committee, 'The Relationship between Regional Trade Agreements and the Multilateral Trading System—Services', TD/TC/WP(2002)27/FINAL, 9 October 2002;
OECD, *GATS: The Case for Open Services Markets*, 2002;
OECD, *Agricultural Policies in OECD Countries: Monitoring and Evaluation 2002—Highlights*, 2002;
OECD, *Quantifying the Benefits of Liberalizing Trade in Services*, 2003;

OECD, *Regionalism and the Multilateral Trading System*, 2003;

OECD, Working Party of the Trade Committee, 'Service Providers on the Move: Mutual Recognition Agreements', TD/TC/WP(2002)48/FINAL, 6 February 2003;

OECD, Working Party of the Trade Committee, 'Integrating Market Openness into the Regulatory Process: Emerging Patterns in OECD Countries', TD/TC/WP(2002)25/FINAL, 17 February 2003;

OECD, Working Party of the Trade Committee, 'Overview of Non-Tariff Barriers: Findings from Existing Business Surveys', TD/TC/WP(2002)38/FINAL, 6 March 2003;

OECD, Directorate for Financial and Enterprise Affairs, 'Trends and Recent Developments in Foreign Direct Investment', June 2004;

OECD, *International Investment Perspectives*, 2005;

D Rodrigo, 'Regulatory Impact Analysis in OECD Countries—Challenges for Developing Countries', South Asian–Third High Level Investment Roundtable, Dhaka, Bangladesh, June 2005;

P Sauvé, 'Services' in OECD, *Regionalism and the Multilateral Trading System*, 2003;

SM Stephenson, '"Deeper" Integration in Services Trade in the Western Hemisphere: Domestic Regulation and Mutual Recognition' in OECD, *Trade and Regulatory Reform: Insights from Country Experience*, 2001;

R Thompson, 'Cross-Cutting ("Formula") Approaches to Multilateral Services Negotiations' in OECD, *Trade in Services: Negotiating Issues and Approaches*, 2001;

D. UNCTAD DOCUMENTS

All available on the UNCTAD official website at <http://www.unctad.org>

C Findlay, 'Services Sector Reform and Development Strategies: Issues and Research Priorities', UNCTAD: Policy Issues in International Trade and Commodities, Study Series No 8, 2001;

G McGuire, 'Trade in Services—Market Access Opportunities and the Benefits of Liberalization for Developing Economies', UNCTAD, Policy Issues in International Trade and Commodities Study Series No 19, 2002;

M Marconini, 'Emergency Safeguard Measures in the GATS: Beyond Feasible and Desirable', UNCTAD/DITC/TNCD/2005/4, 9 March 2005;

UNCTAD, 'Assessment of Trade in Services of Developing Countries: Summary of Findings', UNCTAD/ITCD/TSB/7, 16 August 1999;

UNCTAD, 'List of Economic Needs Tests in the GATS Schedules of Specific Commitments', UNCTAD/ITCD/TSB/8, 6 September 1999;

UNCTAD, *World Investment Report 2004: The Shift Towards Services*, United Nations, 2004;

UNCTAD, 'Exports of Services and Economic Growth in Developing Countries', UNCTAD/DITC/TNCD/MISC/2003/6, 3 June 2004;

UNCTAD, 'Report of the Expert Meeting on Universal Access to Services', TD/B/COM.1/EM.30/3, 26 December 2006;

UNCTAD, 'Report of the Commission on Trade in Goods and Services, and Commodities on its Eleventh Session', TD/B/COM.1/88, 5 April 2007;

Wyplosz, Charles, 'How Risky is Financial Liberalization in the Developing Countries?', G-24 Discussion Paper No. 14, UNCTAD, September 2001;

E. PAPERS OF THE WORLD BANK

All available on the World Bank official website at: <http://www.worldbank.org>

M Amin and A Mattoo, 'Do Institutions Matter More for Services?', PRWP No 4032, October 2006;

J Bhagwati, AO Krueger, and RH Snape, 'Introduction' (1987) 1(4) The World Bank Economic Review 539;

S Chaudhuri, A Mattoo, and R Self, 'Moving People to Deliver Services: How Can the WTO Help?', PRWP No 3238, March 2004;

R Chrishna, 'Antidumping in Law and Practice', PRWP No 1823, September 1997;

F Eschenbach and B Hoekman, 'Services Policy Reform and Economic Growth in Transition Economies, 1990–2004', PRWP No 3663, July 2005;

——and—— 'Services Policies in Transition Economies: On the EU and WTO as Commitment Mechanisms', PRWP No 3951, June 2006;

MJ Finger and L Schuknecht, 'Market Access Advances and Retreats: The Uruguay Round and Beyond', PRWP No 2232, November 1999;

——and JJ Nogués, 'The Unbalanced Uruguay Round Outcome: The New Areas in Future WTO Negotiations', PRWP No 2732, December 2001;

LJ Guasch and RW Hahn, 'The Costs and Benefits of Regulation—Implications for Developing Countries', PRWP No 1773, June 1997;

P Harms, A Mattoo, and L Schuknecht, 'Explaining Liberalization Commitments in Financial Services Trade', PRWP No 2999, March 2003;

B Hindley, 'Service Sector Protection: Considerations for Developing Countries' (1988) 2(2) World Bank Economic Review 205;

B Hoekman, 'Developing Countries and the Uruguay Round: Negotiations on Services', PRWP No 1220, November 1993;

——'Trade Laws and Institutions—Good Practices and the World Trade Organization', Discussion Paper No 282, April 1995;

——'Tentative First Steps: An Assessment of the Uruguay Round Agreement on Services', PRWP No 1455, May 1995;

——'Assessing the General Agreement on Trade in Services' in W Martin and AL Winters (eds), *The Uruguay Round and the Developing Economies*, World Bank Discussion Paper No 307, 1995;

——'Liberalizing Trade in Services: A Survey', PRWP No 4030, October 2006;

——and P Sauvé, 'Liberalizing Trade in Services', Discussion Paper No. 243, 1994;

——and CAP Braga, 'Protection and Trade in Services: A Survey', PRWP No 1747, April 1997;

——and PC Mavroidis, 'WTO Dispute Settlement, Transparency and Surveillance', November 1999;

——and K Saggi, 'Multilateral Disciplines for Investment-Related Policies?', PRWP No 2138, 1999;

B Hoekman, C Michalopoulos, and AL Winters, 'More Favorable and Differential Treatment of Developing Countries: Toward a New Approach in the World Trade Organization', PRWP No 3107, August 2003;

AO Krueger, 'The Developing Countries and the Next Round of Multilateral Trade Negotiations', PRWP No 2118, May 1999;

K Kubota, 'Trade Negotiations in the Presence of Network Externalities', PRWP No 2317, April 2000;

P Low and A Yeats, 'Nontariff Measures and Developing Countries: Has the Uruguay Round Leveled the Playing Field?', PRWP No 1353, August 1994;

—— and A Subramanian, 'TRIMs in the Uruguay Round: An Unfinished Business?' in W Martin and AL Winters, (eds), *The Uruguay Round and the Developing Economies*, World Bank Discussion Paper No 307, 1995;

J Markusen, TF Rutherford, and D Tarr, 'Foreign Direct Investment in Services and the Domestic Market for Expertise', PRWP No 2413, August 2000;

W Martin and AL Winters, (eds), *The Uruguay Round and the Developing Economies*, World Bank Discussion Paper No 307, 1995;

A Mattoo, 'Financial Services and the WTO: Liberalization in the Developing and Transition Economies', 16 March 1998;

—— 'Shaping Future Rules for Trade in Services: Lessons from the GATS', July 2001;

—— 'Services in a Development Round', Trade Note 11, 10 September 2003;

—— and M Olarreaga, 'Should Credit be Given for Autonomous Liberalization in Multilateral Trade Negotiations?', PRWP No 2374, June 2000;

—— and L Schuknecht, 'Trade Policies for Electronic Commerce', 2000;

—— and C Fink, 'Regional Agreements and Trade in Services—Policy Issues', PRWP No 2852, June 2002;

P Messerlin, 'Agriculture in the Doha Agenda', PRWP No 3009, April 2003;

C Michalopoulos, 'Trade Policy and Market Access Issues for Developing Countries: Implications for the Millennium Round', PRWP No 2214, 1999;

—— 'The Role of Special and Differential treatment for Developing Countries in GATT and the World Trade Organization', PRWP No 2388, July 2000;

SM Stephenson, 'Approaches to Liberalizing Services', PRWP No 2107, May 1999;

J Whalley, 'Developing Countries and System Strengthening in the Uruguay Round' in W Martin and AL Winters, (eds), *The Uruguay Round and the Developing Economies*, World Bank Discussion Paper No 307, 1995;

The World Bank, *Global Economic Prospects and the Developing Countries 1997*, September 1997;

The World Bank, *Entering the 21st Century: World Development Report 1999/2000*, Washington DC, 1999;

The World Bank, *World Development Report 2002: Building Institutions for Markets*, September 2001;

The World Bank and IMF, 'Market Access for Developing Country Exports—Selected Issues', 26 September 2002;

The World Bank, *Global Economic Prospects and the Developing Countries 2002: Making Trade Work for the World's Poor*, 2002;

The World Bank, *Global Economic Prospects and the Developing Countries 2003—Investing to Unlock Global Opportunities*, 2003;

The World Bank, *World Development Report 2004: Making Services Work for Poor People*, World Bank/Oxford University Press, 2003;

The World Bank, *Global Economic Prospects 2006—Economic Implications of Remittances and Migration*, 2006;

F. GATT/WTO DOCUMENTS AND PUBLICATIONS

All available on the WTO official website at: <http://www.wto.org>

R Adlung, 'The GATS Turns Ten: A Preliminary Stocktaking', WTO, Economic Research and Statistics Division, Staff Working Paper ERSD-2004–05, August 2004;

—— 'Public Services and the GATS', WTO, Economic Research and Statistics Division, Staff Working Paper ERSD-2005–03, July 2005;

Appellate Body Secretariat, *WTO Appellate Body Repertory of Reports and Awards 1995–2004*, Cambridge University Press, May 2005;

M Bacchetta and B Bora, 'Industrial Tariff Liberalization and the Doha Development Agenda', WTO Discussion Paper No 1, 2003;

—— and M Jansen, 'Adjusting to Trade Liberalization: The Role of Policy, Institutions, and WTO Policies', WTO Special Studies No 7, April 2003;

R Blackhurst, N Marian, and J Tumlir, *Trade Liberalization, Protectionism and Interdependence*, GATT Studies in International Trade No 5 (November 1977);

Committee on Specific Commitments, 'Consideration of Issues Relating to Article XX:2 of the GATS', JOB(03)/213, 20 November 2003;

Committee on Specific Commitments, 'Consideration of Issues Relating to Article XX:2 of the GATS', Communication from Switzerland, JOB(03)/214, 27 November 2003;

Committee on Specific Commitments, 'Discussion of Residency Requirements in the Context of the Development of the Accountancy Disciplines and Scheduling Guidelines', JOB(06)/159, 30 May 2006

M Cossy, 'Determining "Likeness" under the GATS: Squaring the Circle', WTO Staff Working Paper ERSD-2006–08, September 2006;

J-A Crawford and RV Fiorentino, 'The Changing Landscape of Regional Trade Agreements', WTO Discussion Paper No 8, 2005;

CTS (Special Session), 'Mode 4—Transparency Issues', Communication from Argentina, Brazil, Chile, China, Colombia, Dominican Republic, Egypt, Guatemala, India, Mexico, Pakistan, Peru, Philippines and Thailand, JOB(04)/142, 29 September 2004;

Z Drabek and W Payne, 'The Impact of Transparency on Foreign Direct Investment', Economic Research and Analysis Division, Staff Working Paper ERAD-99–02, November 2001;

GATT, 'Communication from Brazil', MTN.GNS/W/3, 11 March 1987;

GATT, 'General Agreement on Trade in Services—A Draft Blueprint', Communication from Switzerland, MTN.GNS/W/69, 15 September 1989;

GATT, 'Agreement on Trade in Services', Communication from the United States, MTN.GNS/W/75, 17 October 1989;

GATT, 'Draft Multilateral Framework for Trade in Services', MTN.GNS/35, 23 July 1990;

GATT, Note on the Meeting of 27 May to 6 June 1991, MTN.GNS/42, 24 June 1991;

GATT, 'Services Sectoral Classification List', MTN.GNS/W/120, 10 July 1991;

GATT, Note on the Meeting of 24–28 June 1991, MTN.GNS/43, 15 July 1991;

GATT, 'Note of the Meeting of 10–25 July 1991', MTN. GNS/44, 28 August 1991;

GATT, 'Note of the Meeting of 17–27 September 1991', MTN.GNS/45, 18 October 1991;

GATT, 'Draft Final Act Embodying the Results of the Uruguay Round of Multilateral Trade Negotiations', MTN.TNC/W/FA, 20 December 1991;

GATT, 'Scheduling of Initial Commitments in Trade in Services: Explanatory Note', MTN.GNS/W/164 and MTN.GNS/W/164/Add.1, 3 September 1993;

GATT, *The Results of the Uruguay Round of Multilateral Negotiations—Market Access for Goods and Services: Overview of the Results*, November 1994;

M Kono, P Low, M Luanga, A Mattoo, M Oshikawa, and L Schuknecht, 'Opening Markets in Financial Services and the Role of the GATS', WTO Special Studies No 1, August 1997;

WPDR, 'Application of the Necessity Test: Issues for Consideration', Informal Note by the Secretariat, JOB No 5929, 8 October 1999;

WPDR, 'Synthesis of Results to Date of the Domestic Consultations in Professional Services', Informal Note by the Secretariat, JOB No 7667, 29 November 2000;

WPDR, 'Chairman's Note', JOB(01)/59, 27 April 2001;

WPDR, 'Examples of Measures to be Addressed by Disciplines Under GATS Article VI:4', JOB(01)/62, 10 May 2001;

WPDR, 'Checklist of Issues for WPDR', Informal Note by the Secretariat, JOB(01)/92 (5067/Rev.1), 19 June 2001;

WPDR, 'Report on the Meeting Held on 3 July 2001', S/WPDR/M/12, 16 August 2001;

WPDR, 'Chairman's Note', JOB(01)/159, 22 November 2001;

WPDR, 'Results of Secretariat Consultations with International Professional Services Associations', Informal Note by the Secretariat, JOB(03)/126, 25 June 2003;

WPDR, 'Recognition Issues—Agenda Item: Development of Disciplines for Professional Services', Communication from India, JOB(03)/192, 30 September 2003;

WPDR, 'Implementation of Article VI:6 Obligations in Engineering Services', Communication from New Zealand, JOB(03)/219, 3 December 2003;

WPDR, 'U.S. Proposal for Transparency Disciplines in Domestic Regulation: Building on Existing International Disciplines and Proposals—Summary', Communication from the United States, JOB(04)/128, 15 September 2004;

WPDR, 'Examples of Measures to be Addressed by Disciplines under GATS Article VI:4', JOB(02)/20/Rev.10, 31 January 2005;

WPDR, 'Initial Elements for Modalities for Negotiations on Disciplines on Domestic Regulation', Communication from Switzerland, JOB(05)/68, 2 May 2005;

WPDR, 'Elements for Draft Disciplines on Domestic Regulation', Communication from Brazil, Colombia, Dominican Republic, Indonesia, Peru and the Philippines, JOB(06)/34, 24 February 2006;

WPDR, 'State-of-Play in the Negotiations on Regulatory Disciplines under GATS Article VI:4', JOB(06)/37, 3 March 2006;

WPDR, 'Communication from Brazil, Indonesia and the Philippines', JOB(06)/133, 2 May 2006;

WPDR, 'Pro-Development Principles for GATS Article VI:4 Negotiations', Communication from the ACP Group, JOB(06)/136, 2 May 2006;

WPDR, 'Proposed Disciplines on Domestic Regulation under Article VI:4 of the GATS', Communication from China and Pakistan, JOB(06)/158, 29 May 2006;

WPDR, 'Horizontal Transparency Disciplines in Domestic Regulation', Communication from the United States, JOB(06)/182, 9 June 2006;

WPDR, 'Pro-Development Principles for GATS Article VI:4 Negotiations', Communication from the ACP Group, JOB(06)/136/Rev.1, 19 June 2006;

WPDR, 'Article VI:4 Disciplines—Proposal for a Draft Text', Communication from Australia; Chile; Colombia; Hong Kong, China; Korea; New Zealand, and the Separate Customs Territory of Taiwan, Penghu, Kinmen and Matsu, JOB(06)/193, 19 June 2006;

WPDR, 'Outline of US Position on a Draft Consolidated Text in the WPDR', Communication from the United States, JOB(06)/223, 11 July 2006;

WPDR, 'Disciplines on Domestic Regulation Pursuant to GATS Article VI:4—Consolidated Working Paper', Note by the Chairman, JOB(06)/225, July 2006;

WPDR, 'Disciplines on Domestic Regulation Pursuant to GATS Article VI:4', Informal Note by the Chairman, Room Document, 18 April 2007;

WPPS, 'Discussion of Matters Relating to Articles XVI and XVII of the GATS in Connection with the Disciplines on Domestic Regulation in the Accountancy Sector', Informal Note by the Chairman, JOB No 6496, 25 November 1998;

WTO, Trade in Services, 'Decision on Professional Services', S/L/3, 4 April 1995;

WTO, WPPS, 'Functions of the Working Party on Professional Services in Relation to Accountancy', Note by the Secretariat, S/WPPS/W/1, 27 June 1995;

WTO, WPPS, 'Work in the Area of Professional Services', Communication from the OECD, S/WPPS/W/4, 14 November 1995, and Addenda 1 and 2 (S/WPPS/W/4/Add.1, and S/WPPS/W/4/Add.2, both dated 5 January 1996);

WTO, *Annual Report 1996, Volume 1* (Special topic: Trade and Foreign Direct Investment), 1996;

WTO, WPPS, 'Report of the Meeting of 16 January 1996', S/WPPS/M/3, 30 January 1996;

WTO, WPPS, 'Background Information on the Agreement on Technical Barriers to Trade and the Agreement on Import Licensing Procedures', S/WPPS/W/6, 29 February 1996;

WTO, WPPS, 'The Relevance of the Disciplines of the Agreements on Technical Barriers to Trade (TBT) and on Import Licensing Procedures to Article VI.4 of the General Agreement on Trade in Services', S/WPPS/W/9, 11 September 1996;

WTO, WPPS, 'Note on the Meeting Held on 2 October 1996', S/WPPS/M/6, 12 November 1996;

WTO, WPPS, 'Note on the Meeting Held on 24 March 1997', S/WPPS/M/8, 5 May 1997;

WTO, WPPS, 'Synthesis of the Responses to the Questionnaire on the Accountancy Sector', S/WPPS/W/11, 5 May 1997;

WTO, WPPS, 'Recommendation of the Working Party on Professional Services to the Council for Trade in Services', S/WPPS/W/14/Rev.1, 15 May 1997;

WTO, WPPS, 'Guidelines for Mutual Recognition Agreements or Arrangements in the Accountancy Sector', S/WPPS/W/12/Rev.1, 20 May 1997;

WTO, 'Economic Effects on Services Liberalization', S/C/W/26, Background Note by the Secretariat, 7 October 1997;

WTO, 'Economic Effects of Services Liberalization: Overview of eEpirical Studies', Background Note by the Secretariat, S/C/W/26/Add.1, 29 May 1998;

WTO, CTS, 'Construction and Related Engineering Services', Background Note by the Secretariat, S/C/W/38, 8 June 1998;

WTO, WPPS, 'Note on the Meeting Held on 29 July 1998', S/WPPS/M/21, 29 September 1998;

WTO, Trade in Services, 'Decision on Disciplines Relating to the Accountancy Sector', S/L/63, 15 October 1998;

WTO, CTS, 'Report of the Meeting Held on 14 October 1998', S/C/M/30, 12 November 1998;

WTO, CTS, 'Financial Services', Background Note by the Secretariat, S/C/W/72, 2 December 1998;

WTO, CTS, 'Accountancy Services', Background Note by the Secretariat, S/C/W/73, 4 December 1998;

WTO, WPPS, 'Report to the Council for Trade in Services on the Development of Disciplines on Domestic Regulation in the Accountancy Sector', S/WPPS/4, 10 December 1998;

WTO, Trade in Services, 'Disciplines on Domestic Regulation in the Accountancy Sector', S/L/64, 17 December 1998;

WTO, WPPS, 'Note on the Meeting Held on 4 December 1998', S/WPPS/M/24, 18 December 1998;

WTO, 'Developing Countries and the Multilateral Trading System: Past and Present', Background Note by the Secretariat (Background Document for the High Level Symposium on Trade and Development), March 1999;

WTO, CTS, 'Article VI:4 of the GATS: Disciplines on Domestic Regulation Applicable to All Services', Note by the Secretariat, S/C/W/96, 1 March 1999;

WTO, CTS, 'International Regulatory Initiatives in Services', S/C/W/97, 1 March 1999;

WTO, WPPS, 'Note on the Meeting Held on 9 February 1999', S/WPPS/M/25, 5 March 1999;

WTO, Committee on Specific Commitments, 'Revision of Scheduling Guidelines', S/CSC/W/19, 5 March 1999;

WTO, Working Group on the Interaction between Trade and Competition Policy, 'The Fundamental WTO Principles of National Treatment, Most-Favoured-Nation Treatment and Transparency', WT/WGTCP/W/114, 14 April 1999;

WTO, CTS, 'Report of the Meeting Held on 22 and 23 March 1999', S/C/M/34, 16 April 1999;

WTO, Trade in Services, 'Decision on Domestic Regulation', S/L/70, 28 April 1999;

WTO, CTS, 'Report of the Meeting Held on 26 April 1999', S/C/M/35, 17 May 1999;

WTO, 'The Developmental Impact of Trade Liberalization under GATS', Informal Note by the Secretariat, JOB No 2748/Rev.1, 7 June 1999;

WTO, WPDR, 'Report on the Meeting Held on 17 May 1999', S/WPDR/M/1, 14 June 1999;

WTO, WPDR, 'Communication from Australia', S/WPDR/W/1, 19 July 1999;

WTO, WPDR, 'Report on the Meeting Held on 14 July 1999', S/WPDR/M/2, 2 September 1999;

WTO, 'An Introduction to the GATS', October 1999;

WTO, 'Procedures for the Implementation of Article XXI of the General Agreement on Trade in Services (GATS) (Modification of Schedules)', S/L/80, 29 October 1999;

WTO, WPDR, 'Report on the Meeting Held on 19 October 1999', S/WPDR/M/3, 18 January 2000;

WTO, CTS, 'Procedures for the Certification of Rectifications or Improvements to Schedules of Specific Commitments', S/L/84, 18 April 2000;

WTO, WPDR, 'GATS Article VI:4: Possible Disciplines on Transparency in Domestic Regulation', Communication from the United States, S/WPDR/W/4, 3 May 2000;

WTO, CTS (Special Session), 'The Cluster Approach', Communication from the European Communities and their Member States, S/CSS/W/3, 22 May 2000;

WTO, CTS (Special Session), 'Report of the Meeting Held on 26 May 2000', S/CSS/M/3, 26 June 2000;

WTO, WPDR, 'Report on the Meeting Held on 25 May 2000', S/WPDR/M/6, 29 June 2000;

WTO, WPDR, 'Necessity and Transparency', Communication from Australia, S/WPDR/W/8, 15 September 2000;

WTO, WPDR, 'Report on the Meeting Held on 12 July 2000', S/WPDR/M/7, 19 September 2000;

WTO, WPDR, 'The Necessity Test', Communication from the Republic of Korea, S/WPDR/W/9, 28 September 2000;

WTO, WPDR, 'Report on the Meeting Held on 2 October 2000', S/WPDR/M/8, 17 November 2000;

WTO, 'Market Access: Unfinished Business—Post-Uruguay Round Inventory and Issues', WTO Special studies No 6, 2001;

WTO, WPDR, 'Report on the Meeting Held on 29 November 2000', S/WPDR/M/9, 12 March 2001;

WTO, 'Guidelines for the Scheduling of Specific Commitments under the General Agreement on Trade in Services (GATS)', S/L/92, 28 March 2001;

WTO, 'Guidelines and Procedures for the Negotiations on Trade in Services', S/L/93, 29 March 2001;

WTO, WPDR, 'Domestic Regulation: Necessity and Transparency', Communication from the European Communities and their Member States, S/WPDR/W/14, 1 May 2001;

WTO, WPDR, 'Report on the Meeting Held on 20 March 2001', S/WPDR/M/10, 10 May 2001;

WTO, WPDR, 'Report on the Meeting Held on 11 May 2001', S/WPDR/M/11, 7 June 2001;

WTO, CTS, 'Transparency in Domestic Regulation', Communication from the United States, S/CSS/W/102, 13 July 2001;

WTO, WPDR, 'Report on the Meeting Held on 3 July 2001', S/WPDR/M/12, 16 August 2001;
WTO, WPDR, 'Report on the Meeting Held on 2 October 2001', S/WPDR/M/13, 21 November 2001;
WTO, *Annual Report 2002*, 2002;
WTO, WPDR, 'Report on the Meeting Held on 29 November 2001', S/WPDR/M/14, 29 January 2002;
WTO, CTS (Special Session), 'Report of the Meeting Held on 3–6 December 2001', S/CSS/M/13, 26 February 2002;
WTO, Committee on Trade and Environment, 'GATT/WTO Dispute Settlement Practice Relating to GATT Article XX, Paragraphs (b), (d) and (g)', WT/CTE/W/203, 8 March 2002;
WTO, Working Group on the Relationship between Trade and Investment, 'Transparency', WT/WGTI/W/109, 27 March 2002;
WTO, WPDR, 'Report on the Meeting Held on 12 March 2002', S/WPDR/M/15, 10 April 2002;
WTO, WPDR, 'Report on the Meeting Held on 4 and 7 June 2002', S/WPDR/M/16, 8 July 2002;
WTO, Committee on Specific Commitments, 'Additional Commitments under Article XVIII of the GATS', Note by the Secretariat, S/CSC/W/34, 16 July 2002;
WTO, CTS, 'Report of the Meeting Held on 17 July 2002', S/C/M/61, 23 September 2002;
WTO, WPDR, 'Report on the Meeting Held on 16 July 2002', S/WPDR/M/17, 1 October 2002;
WTO, WPDR, 'Report on the Meeting Held on 22 October 2002', S/WPDR/M/18, 3 December 2002;
WTO, 'Report of the Working Party on Domestic Regulation to the Council for Trade in Services (2002)', S/WPDR/4, 6 December 2002;
WTO, *World Trade Report 2003*, 2003;
WTO, *WTO Analytical Index—Guide to WTO Law and Practice*, Vols 1 and 2, 2003;
WTO, WPDR, 'Report on the Meeting Held on 4 December 2002', S/WPDR/M/19, 29 January 2003;
WPDR, 'Draft Annex on Domestic Regulation', JOB(03)/45, 3 March 2003 (and JOB(03)/45/Rev.1 of 2 May 2003);
WTO, CTS (Special Session), 'Modalities for the Treatment of Autonomous Liberalization', T/N/S/6, 10 March 2003;
WTO, CTS (Special Session), 'An Assessment of Services Trade and Liberalization in the United States and Developing Economies', Communication from the United States, TN/S/W/12, 31 March 2003;
WTO, CTS (Special Session), 'Draft Modalities for the Special Treatment for Least-Developed Country Members in the Negotiations on Trade in Services', Communication from the LDC Group, TN/S/W/13, 7 May 2003;
WTO, Negotiating Group on Rules, 'Korea's View on the Improvement of the Sunset System', Submission of the Republic of Korea, TN/RL/W/111, 27 May 2003;
WTO, WPDR, 'Report on the Meeting Held on 15 May 2003', S/WPDR/M/21/Rev.1, 25 June 2003;

WTO, CTS (Special Session), 'Proposed Liberalization of Mode 4 under GATS Negotiations', Communication from Argentina, Bolivia, Chile, the People's Republic of China, Colombia, Dominican Republic, Egypt, Guatemala, India, Mexico, Pakistan, Peru, Philippines and Thailand, TN/S/W/14, 3 July 2003;

WTO, WPDR, 'Proposal for Disciplines on Licensing Procedures', Communication from the European Community and its Member States, S/WPDR/W/25, 10 July 2003;

WTO, CTS (Special Session), 'Modalities for the Special Treatment for Least-Developed Country Members in the Negotiations on Trade in Services', TN/S/13, 5 September 2003;

WTO, WPDR, 'Report on the Meeting Held on 1 July 2003', S/WPDR/M/22, 22 September 2003;

WTO, WPDR, 'Report on the Meeting Held on 30 September 2003', S/WPDR/M/23, 27 November 2003;

WTO, WPDR, '"Necessity Tests" in the WTO', S/WPDR/W/27, 2 December 2003;

WTO, *World Trade Report 2004—Exploring the Linkage between the Domestic Policy Environment and International Trade*, 2004;

WTO, Committee on Specific Commitments, 'Report of the Meeting Held on 4 December 2003', S/CSC/M/31, 14 January 2004;

WTO, WPDR, 'Report on the Meeting Held on 3 December 2003', S/WPDR/M/24, 22 January 2004;

WTO, CTS, 'Fifth Decision on Negotiations on Emergency Safeguard Measures', S/L/159, 17 March 2004 (adopted by the CTS on 15 March 2004);

WTO, CTS, 'Consideration of Issues Relating to Article XX:2 of the GATS', Report by the Chairman of the Committee on Specific Commitments, S/C/W/237, 24 March 2004;

WTO, WPDR, 'Report on the Meeting Held on 31 March 2004', S/WPDR/M/25, 18 May 2004;

WTO, WPDR, 'Professional Recognition in Australia', Communication from Australia, S/WPDR/W/28, 22 June 2004;

WTO, WPDR, 'Examples of Measures Relating to Administrative Procedures for Obtaining Visas or Entry Permits', Communication from Colombia, S/WPDR/W/29, 7 July 2004;

WTO, WPDR, 'Report on the Meeting Held on 24 June 2004', S/WPDR/M/26, 8 September 2004;

WTO, WPDR, 'Mexico's Experience of Disciplines on Technical Standards and Regulations in Services', Communication from Mexico, S/WPDR/W/30, 24 September 2004;

WTO, WPDR, 'Report on the Meeting Held on 24 September 2004', S/WPDR/M/27, 15 November 2004;

WTO, *Annual Report 2005*, 2005;

WTO, CTS (Special Session), 'Postal/Courier: Proposal for a Reference Paper', Communication from the European Communities and their Member States, TN/S/W/26, 17 January 2005;

WTO, WPDR, 'Report on the Meeting Held on 22 November 2004', S/WPDR/M/28, 25 January 2005;

WTO, WPDR, 'Proposal for Disciplines on Technical Standards in Services', Communication from Switzerland, S/WPDR/W/32, 1 February 2005;

WTO, Committee on Technical Barriers to Trade, 'Tenth Annual Review of the Implementation and Operation of the TBT Agreement', G/TBT/15, 4 March 2005;

WTO, WPDR, 'Proposed Elements for Disciplines on Qualification Requirements and Procedures', Communication from Chile, India, Mexico, Pakistan and Thailand, JOB(05)/50, 30 March 2005;

WTO, WPDR, 'Report on the Meeting Held on 7 and 18 February 2005', S/WPDR/M/29, 11 July 2005;

WTO, WPDR, 'Report on the Meeting Held on 22 June 2005', S/WPDR/M/30, 6 September 2005;

WTO, WPDR, 'Definitions of Qualification Requirements, Qualification Procedures, Licensing Requirements, Licensing Procedures and Technical Standards', Communication from the Separate Customs Territory of Taiwan, Penghu, Kinmen and Matsu, S/WPDR/W/37, 6 October 2005;

WTO, WPDR, 'Proposal for Disciplines on Technical Standards in Services', Communication from Switzerland and Mexico, S/WPDR/W/32/Rev.1, 28 October 2005;

WTO, CTS, 'Contact and Enquiry Points Notified to the Council for Trade in Services', S/ENQ/8/Rev.8, 3 November 2005;

WTO, WPDR, 'Report of the Chairman of the Working Party on Domestic Regulation to the Special Session of the Council for Trade in Services', JOB(05)/280, 15 November 2005;

WTO, CTS (Special Session), 'Report of the Chairman to the Trade Negotiations Committee', TN/S/23, 28 November 2005;

WTO, WPDR, 'Proposed Disciplines on Qualification Requirements and Procedures', Communication from Chile, India, Mexico, Pakistan, Peru and Thailand, JOB(06)/160, 30 May 2006;

G. OTHER SOURCES

MD Adler and EA Posner, 'Rethinking Cost-Benefit Analysis', University of Chicago, John M. Olin Law and Economics Working Paper No 72 (2nd series), April 1999;

M Amiti and S-J Wei, 'Service Offshoring and Productivity: Evidence from the United States', NBER Working Paper No 11926, January 2006;

SP Anderson and N Schmitt, 'Non-Tariff Barriers and Trade Liberalization', January 2000, available at: <http://ftp.virginia.edu/pub/bk5x/RePEc/vir/virpap/papers/virpap340.pdf> (visited 30 May 2007);

K Bagwell and RW Staiger, 'GATT-Think', NBER Working Paper No. 8005, November 2000;

K Bhattarai and J Whalley, 'The Division and Size of Gains from Liberalization in Service Networks', NBER Working Paper No 6712, August 1998;

CAP Braga, C Fink, and B Hoekman, 'Telecommunications-Related Services: Market Access, Deeper Integration and the WTO', Hamburgisches Welt-Wirtschafts-Archiv, Institut für Wirtschaftsforschung Discussion Paper No 158, Hamburg, 2002;

JA Brander, 'Strategic Trade Policy', NBER Working Paper No 5020, February 1995;

S Claessens, E Feijen, and L Laeven, 'Political Connections and Preferential Access to Finance: The Role of Campaign Contributions', 22 September 2006, available at: http://ssrn.com/abstract=935488 (visited 1 November 2006);

P Coghlan, 'The Principles of Good Regulation' in Productivity Commission/Australian National University, *Achieving Better Regulation of Services,* Conference Proceedings, AusInfo, November 2000;

C Coglianese, R Zeckhauser, and E Parson, 'Securing Truth for Power: Informational Strategy and Regulatory Policy Making', Regulatory Policy Program Working Paper RPP-2004–07, Center for Business and Government, John F Kennedy School of Government, Harvard University, Cambridge, MA, 2004;

Council of Europe, *Convention for the Protection of Human Rights and Fundamental Freedoms.* The text of the Convention is available at: <http://www.echr.coe.int/NR/rdonlyres/D5CC24A7-DC13–4318-B457–5C9014916D7A/0/EnglishAnglais.pdf>;

A Crosby and TJ Vielma, 'Trade in Services, the GATS and Sustainable Development' (2000) 4 BRIDGES 11;

AV Deardorff, 'International Provision of Trade Services, Trade and Fragmentation', Research Seminar in International Economics, Discussion Paper No 463, 30 August 2000. The paper is available at: <http://www.spp.umich.edu/rsie/workingpapers/wp.html> (visited 30 May 2007);

——'Tariffication in Services', Research Seminar in International Economics, Discussion Paper No 473, 2 August 2001;

P Dee and K Hanslow, 'Multilateral Liberalization of Services Trade', Productivity Commission Staff Research Paper, AusInfo, March 2000, available at: <http://www.pc.gov.au/research/staffres/multilatlib/multilatlib.pdf> (visited 30 May 2007);

Deloitte & Touche, *Report Relating to the Industry Consultation in the Context of Preparatory Work for GATS 2000 via the 'SIS'*, December 1999;

European Commission, 'Communication of the Commission on Impact Assessment', COM(2002) 276 final, 5 June 2002;

European Commission, 'Impact Assessment: Next Steps—In Support of Competitiveness and Sustainable Development', Commission Staff Working Paper, SEC(2004)1377, 21 October 2004;

European Commission, 'Impact Assessment Guidelines', SEC(2005) 791, 15 June 2005;

G Feketekuty, 'Deepening Sectoral Disciplines for Services Regulation: How to Move Forward in the GATS' Paper prepared for the Workshop on 'Towards Improving Regulation in the Services Sector' of the Menu of Options, Phase III, APEC Group on Services (GOS), 18 May 2002;

C Findlay, 'Introduction to the Regulation of Services' in Productivity Commission and Australian National University, *Achieving Better Regulation of Services,* Conference Proceedings, AusInfo, November 2000;

—— and J-D Kim, 'Issues in Domestic Regulation of Services', Paper prepared for the meeting of APEC Group on Services (GOS) in Beijing, China, January 2001;

J Francois, HH Glissman, and D Spinanger, 'The Cost of EU Trade Protection in Textiles and Clothing', Kiel Institute of World Economics, Working Paper No 997, August 2000;

G Grossman and G Maggi, 'Free Trade vs. Strategic Trade: A Peek into Pandora's Box', Discussion Paper No 190, Discussion Papers in Economics: Woodrow Wilson School of Public and International Affairs, Princeton University, September 1997;

RW Hahn and CR Sunstein, 'A New Executive Order for Improving Federal Regulation? Deeper and Wider Cost-Benefit Analysis', University of Chicago, John M. Olin Law and Economics Working Paper No. 150 (2nd series), April 2002;

H Horn, G Maggi, and RW Staiger, 'The GATT/WTO as an Incomplete Contract', September 2005, mimeo;

——, —— and —— 'Trade Agreements as Endogenously Incomplete Contracts', NBER Working Paper No 12745, 2006;

R Howse and E Türk, 'The WTO Negotiations on Services: The Regulatory State Up for Grabs' (2002) 9(1/2) Canada Watch;

GC Hufbauer and B Goodrich, 'Steel Policy: The Good, the Bad, and the Ugly', International Economics Policy Briefs, Institute of International Economics, Number PB03–1, January 2003. The article is available at: <http://www.iie.com/publications/pb/pb03–1.pdf> (visited 30 May 2007);

Institute for Agriculture and Trade Policy and Polaris Institute, 'Five Danger Signs—The GATS Assault on Sovereignty and Democracy', 2006, available at: <http://www.tradeobservatory.org> (visited 30 May 2007);

DA Irwin, 'Ohlin versus Stolper-Samuelson?', NBER Working Paper No 7641, April 2000;

JH Jackson, 'Dispute Settlement in the WTO: Policy and Jurisprudential Considerations', Research Seminar in International Economics, Discussion Paper No 419, 9 February 1998, available at: <http://www.spp.umich.edu/rsie/workingpapers/wp.html> (visited 30 May 2007);

RJ Kopp, AJ Krupnick, and M Toman, 'Cost–Benefit Analysis and Regulatory Reform: An Assessment of the Science and the Art', Resources for the Future Discussion Paper 97–19, January 1997, available at: <http://www.rff.org/Documents/RFF-DP-97–19.pdf> (visited 30 May 2007);

A Lehmann, NT Tamirisa, and J Wieczorek, 'International Trade in Services: Implications for the IMF', IMF Policy Discussion Paper, PDP/03/6, December 2003;

F Ortino, 'From "non-discrimination" to "reasonableness": a paradigm shift in international economic law?', Jean Monnet Working Paper 01/05, April 2005 available at: <http://www.jeanmonnetprogram.org> (visited 30 May 2007);

S Ostry, 'The Uruguay Round North–South Grand Bargain: Implications for Future Negotiations', prepared for a Conference on 'The Political Economy of International Trade Law', University of Minnesota, 2000;

—— 'Doha and After' (2002) 9(1/2) Canada Watch;

Productivity Commission and Australian National University, *Achieving Better Regulation of Services,* Conference Proceedings, AusInfo, November 2000;

D Rodrik, 'What Does the Political Economy Literature on Trade Policy (Not) Tell Us What We Ought to Know?', NBER Working Paper No 4870, September 1994;

P Sauvé, 'Adding Value at the Periphery: Aiming for GATS+ Advances in Regional Agreements on Services', NCCR Working Paper, available at: <http://www.nccr-trade.org>;

WF Schwartz and AO Sykes, 'The Economic Structure of Renegotiation and Dispute Resolution in the WTO/GATT System', Chicago John M. Olin Law and Economics Working Paper No 143 (2nd series), March 2002. The paper is available at: <http://www.law.uchicago.edu/Lawecon/wp101–150.html> (visited 30 May 2007);

A Sidorenko and C Findlay, 'Issues in Domestic Regulations of Services: Horizontal versus Sectoral Disciplines', Asia Pacific School of Economics and Management—The Australian National University, February 2002;

S Sinclair, 'The GATS, Democratic Governance, and Public Interest Regulation' (2002) 9(1/2) Canada Watch;

RH Snape, 'Regulating Services Trade: Matching Policies to Objectives', 2000, available at: <http://www.pc.gov.au/research/confpaper/rstmpto/index.html> (visited 30 May 2007);

SM Stephenson, 'Deepening Disciplines for Trade in Services', Organization of American States, Trade Unit Studies, March 2001;

RM Stern, 'Quantifying Barriers to Trade in Services', Research Seminar in International Economics, Discussion Paper No 470, University of Michigan, 8 November 2000, available at: <http:www.spp.umich.edu/rsie/workingpapers/wp.html> (visited 30 May 2007);

CR Sunstein, 'The Cost–Benefit State', University of Chicago, John M. Olin Law and Economics Working Paper No 39, May 1996, available at: <http://www.law.uchicago.edu/Lawecon/wp1–50.html> (visited 30 May 2007);

JP Trachtman, 'The "Necessity Test" in Domestic Services Regulation: How to Move Forward in the GATS?', APEC Group on Services, Workshop II: Towards Improving Regulation in the Services Sector, 15 May 2002;

United Nations, *Report of the International Law Commission—Fifty-third Session (23 April–1 June and 2 July–10 August 2001)*, Official Records of the General Assembly, Fifty-sixth Session, Supplement No. 10 (A/56/10), 2001;

USTR, 'US National Study on Trade in Services: A Submission by the United States Government to the General Agreement on Tariffs and Trade', 25 January 1984;

USTR, '2004 Annual Report of the President of the United States on the Trade Agreements Program', 2005, available at: <http://www.ustr.gov>;

AL Winters, 'Regionalism versus Multilateralism', 23 August 1996, available at: <http://www.cid.harvard.edu/cidtrade/issues/regionalismpaper.html> (visited 30 May 2007);

AL Winters, TL Walmsley, Z Kun Wang, and R Grynberg, 'Negotiating the Liberalization of the Temporary Movement of Natural Persons', Discussion Paper in Economics No 87, University of Sussex at Brighton, October 2002;

J Wouters and D Coppens, 'Domestic Regulation within the Framework of GATS', Working Paper 93, Institute for International Law, K.U.Leuven, May 2006, available at: <http://www.law.kleuven.ac.be/iir/nl/wp/WP/WP93e.pdf> (visited 30 May 2007);

Index

The manufacturer's authorised representative in the EU for product safety is Oxford University Press España S.A. of el Parque Empresarial San Fernando de Henares, Avenida de Castilla, 2 – 28830 Madrid (www.oup.es/en or product.safety@oup.com). OUP España S.A. also acts as importer into Spain of products made by the manufacturer.

www.ingramcontent.com/pod-product-compliance
Lightning Source LLC
LaVergne TN
LVHW011908200926
848484LV00002B/569
9780199533152